# MASTERING

modern German history

## Palgrave Master Series

Accounting
Accounting Skills
Advanced English Language
Advanced Pure Mathematics
Arabic
Basic Management
Biology
British Politics
Business Communication
Business Environment
C Programming
C++ Programming
Chemistry
COBOL Programming
Communication
Computing
Counselling Skills
Counselling Theory
Customer Relations
Database Design
Delphi Programming
Desktop Publishing
e-Business
Economic and Social History
Economics
Electrical Engineering
Electronics
Employee Development
English Grammar
English Language
English Literature
Fashion Buying and Merchandising
 Management
Fashion Marketing
Fashion Styling
Financial Management
Geography
Global Information Systems
Globalization of Business
Human Resource Management

Information Technology
International Trade
Internet
Java
Language of Literature
Management Skills
Marketing Management
Mathematics
Microsoft Office
Microsoft Windows, Novell
 NetWare and UNIX
Modern British History
Modern European History
Modern German History
Modern United States History
Modern World History
Networks
Novels of Jane Austen
Organisational Behaviour
Pascal and Delphi Programming
Personal Finance
Philosophy
Physics
Poetry
Practical Criticism
Psychology
Public Relations
Shakespeare
Social Welfare
Sociology
Spanish
Statistics
Strategic Management
Systems Analysis and Design
Team Leadership
Theology
Twentieth-Century Russian History
Visual Basic
World Religions

www.palgravemasterseries.com

**Palgrave Master Series**
Series Standing Order ISBN 0-333-69343-4
(outside North America only)

You can receive future titles in this series as they are published by
placing a standing order. Please contact your bookseller or, in case
of difficulty, write to us at the address below with your name and
address, the title of the series and the ISBN quoted above.

Customer Services Department, Macmillan Distribution Ltd
Houndmills, Basingstoke, Hampshire RG21 6XS, England

# MASTERING
## modern German history

John Traynor

palgrave
macmillan

First published 2008 by
PALGRAVE MACMILLAN
Houndmills, Basingstoke, Hampshire RG21 6XS and
175 Fifth Avenue, New York, N.Y. 10010
Companies and representatives throughout the world

PALGRAVE MACMILLAN is the global academic imprint of the Palgrave Macmillan division of St. Martin's Press, LLC and of Palgrave Publishers Ltd. Macmillan® is a registered trademark in the United States, United Kingdom and other countries. Palgrave is a registered trademark in the European Union and other countries.

ISBN-13: 978-0-333-98710-0
ISBN-10: 0-333-98710-1

The book is printed on paper suitable for recycling and made from fully managed and sustained forest sources. Logging, pulping and manufacturing processes are expected to conform to the environmental regulations of the country of origin.

A catalogue record for this book is available from the British Library.

10   9   8   7   6   5   4   3   2   1
17   16   15   14   13   12   11   10   09   08

Printed and bound in Great Britain by
Creative Print & Design (Wales), Ebbw Vale

For Harry, Michael, Kevin and Sue

# Contents

list of maps

list of tables

# acknowledgements

The number of people I would like to thank in helping me in the preparation of this book have increased in proportion to the length of time it has taken me to complete. My interest in German history was instilled by the late Emeritus Professor of History at the University of Sheffield, William Carr. For the sense that I could go further with my history I am grateful to Richard Carwardine, now Rhodes Professor of American History at the University of Oxford. More recently, I have been helped in my thinking by Professor Brent Davies and Professor John West-Burnham at the International Centre for Educational Leadership at the University of Hull.

I owe a huge debt to the Leadership Team and the rest of my colleagues at Ormskirk School, and in particular I would like to thank John Doyle for his constant support and encouragement. In addition, I would also like to thank Robert Furlong, Andrew Sharples, David Kereszteny Lewis, Adrian Moulding, Lee Hopkins and Greg Ivory for their friendship, and at Palgrave, I would like to acknowledge the patience and support offered by Suzannah Burywood and Karen Griffiths. Successive generations of sixth-form students at Hinchingbrooke School in Cambridgeshire, Lymm High School and Christleton High School in Cheshire and Ormskirk School in Lancashire have been a source of interest and enthusiasm. I also owe a great deal, in different ways, to Martin Griggs, Paul Wainwright, Roger Lounds, Alan Hall, Patrick Adamson, Graham Clark, Jamie Goodfellow, Eric Wilmot, Chris Steer, Peter Hodkinson and John Jones.

Finally, and most of all, I must thank Linda, Hannah and Patrick for their patience with this project and for all the practical help they have given me over the years that this book has taken, from typing up the sources to searching for two days for the lost pen-drive! Without them, the book would literally never have been completed, and I am very grateful.

# the creation of the German nation

## 1.1 Bismarck and the unification of Germany

### introduction

Since medieval times a complex, patchwork mosaic of several hundred states, great and small, occupied the space we now know as Germany, to form the Holy Roman Empire of the German nation. However, as the Empire entered the nineteenth century, the turbulence of the Napoleonic Wars underlined a need for national security which was difficult to provide for the smaller states in such a tangled geographical area and also aroused a common sense of Germanic antipathy towards the French, creating, in a sense some of the first modern stirrings of what could be called German nationalism. Under the Vienna peace settlement of 1815 a process of rationalisation saw 350 states ranging from the powerful, deeply conservative and absolutist kingdoms of Austria and Prussia to the tiny principalities of the imperial knights, welded into 39 states brought loosely together as the German Confederation. Despite its name, the German Confederation was no more a national, united state than its predecessor had been. Those who created the German Confederation did not imagine that barriers of religious differences between Protestants and Catholics, a strong sense of regional identity, customs and independence or the distinctive nature of the two most powerful member states, Prussia and Austria, could be overcome to create a single German state. In any case, Austria and Prussia showed no interest at this stage in bringing the German states together in a process of unification. Both were initially content to preserve their general influence over the other states and in broad terms respected the other's position in a period of 'peaceful dualism'. However, Prussia's growing economic strength meant that the permanence of this stance of mutual respect could not be guaranteed for ever. Prussia's position was bolstered by the creation of the German Customs Union (Zollverein) in 1834, a single economic unit consisting of 18 states, although recent research has highlighted the self-interest of the member states at the expense of loyalty to a common entity. While the prestigious Habsburg

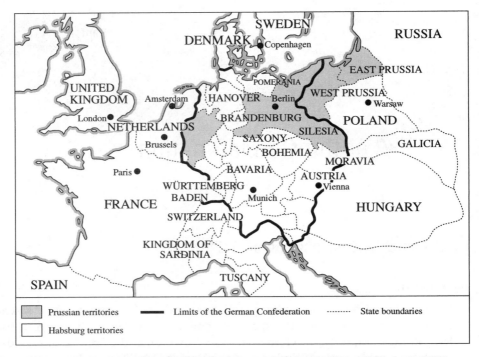

map **1** – **the 39 states of the German Confederation established by the Vienna Settlement of 1815**

map **2** – **the impact of Prussian expansion following the war with Austria of 1866 and the creation of the North German confederation**

map **3 – the German Empire in 1871**

monarchy of Austria may have retained political sway within the Confederation, the burgeoning commercial prowess of Prussia cannot have escaped the attention of those who imagined that Prussia's economic ascendancy amongst the German states could one day be matched by her political leadership. Austria's relatively weak economic position meant that the Habsburgs faced a degree of isolation from the increasingly cohesive economic coalition of the German states that were operating within the gravitational pull of Prussia. By the mid-nineteenth century a gradually emerging struggle for dominance was emerging within the Confederation between the 'Little German' solution led by Prussia and the 'Greater German' solution offered by Austria. Both concepts reflected the gradual emergence of a nationalist vision over a regional one, although independent sentiments remained particularly powerful amongst some of the states in the south. The most passionate advocates of German nationalism believed that a strong Germany would bring stability, culture and progressive, humanistic values to their subjects and fulfil the general desire for security. It was the forces of nationalism, economic liberalism, industrial and technological growth, military prowess and political will that coalesced to lead Prussia towards a position of leadership amongst the German states that was to be sealed in 1871.

## The unification of Germany

At moments of high importance every public gesture, every utterance, every detail was carefully calculated. On this occasion, 18 January 1871, with the moment of German unification at hand and with the armies of France, his most bitter enemy, defeated, the 'founder of the Empire' or 'Reichsgrunder' chose, as was his habit, to wear a uniform that carefully cultivated a martial appearance. Wearing a blue coat, the orange ribbon of the Order of the Black Eagle, high riding boots and military insignia, the first Chancellor of the Second Reich looked like a conquering warlord. The dazzling appearance of Otto Eduard Leopold von Bismarck-Schönhausen matched the glittering surroundings of the Galerie des Glaces at the Palace of Versailles, for so long the symbol of French military strength and now the scene of her ritual humiliation.

Before an audience of German princes and invited dignitaries, the King of Prussia, Wilhelm I, formally accepted the crown of the newly united German Empire. It was Bismarck himself who delivered the proclamation:

> We Wilhelm, by the Grace of God, King of Prussia, and after the German Princes and free cities have unanimously appealed to us to renew the Imperial dignity, which has been in abeyance for more than sixty years, hereby inform you that we regard it as our duty to the whole Fatherland to respond to this summons of the allied German Princes and free cities to assume the German Imperial title.

Otto von Bismarck, described by Hans-Ulrich Wehler as 'the first man in Germany to practise charismatic rule',[1] was without question the outstanding political strategist of the day, 'the directive genius of German history between 1862 and 1890',[2] a combination of 'swift intuitive judgement, vehemence and intensity'.[3] It would take just nine years serving as minister-president and foreign minister for his leadership to move the state of Prussia from the staging-post of 1862 as an established German power and an emerging great power to a position of central importance in European affairs. At issue is whether Bismarck possessed a clear mental map of the direction and timing of the unification process, whether he benefited from an exceptionally favourable international constellation or if, in fact, he was chiefly a highly skilled opportunist A further problem concerns our view of history itself. Much of what follows in this opening section concerns kings and statesmen, chancellors and mass armies. The ordinary person is largely missing from the story, although we will turn to that perspective in later chapters. Was Germany created from above by 'great men', or did the drive for a German nation-state come from below, fuelled by powerful economic and social forces above and beyond the control of any statesman, even Bismarck?

To be sure, he was fortunate to have at his disposal the burgeoning economic and social infrastructure of the emerging industrial powerhouse. Although a significant proportion of her population was employed in agriculture, Prussia also enjoyed domination of the Zollverein, or customs union, substantial natural mineral resources in the Ruhr, the Saar and Silesia, with growing numbers of mines, blast furnaces and steelworks reflecting an increasing process of industrialization after 1850.

Yet the deployment of this resource needed all the skill and judgement that Bismarck possessed in abundance. Favourable diplomatic configurations at crucial periods also played their part but perhaps, above all, Bismarck was able to manage, at least to an extent, the moments when Prussia's progress would be put to the test in warfare, the most severe examination of a nation's resources and resolve. In the words of American academic Gordon Craig:

> If he had never risen to the top in Prussian politics, the unification of Germany would probably have taken place anyway, but surely not at the same time or in quite the same way as it did. Whatever may be said about the movement of economic forces, there is no burking the fact that the decision concerning the form unification would take was made, not in the area of economic and social policy, but on the battlefield.[4]

Or, as Bismarck himself had so famously put it in a speech to the Landtag's budget committee on 30 September 1862:

> Prussia must gather and consolidate her strength in readiness for the favourable moment which has already been missed several times; Prussia's boundaries according to the Vienna treaties are not favourable to a healthy political life; not by means of speeches and majority verdicts will the great decisions of the time be made – that was the great mistake of 1848 and 1849 – but by iron and blood.

Yet for the new Chancellor, the personal satisfaction at the moment of unification was little more than a veneer beneath which lay weariness, political tension and ill health. Despite the immense power and prestige constitutionally assigned to the head of the new imperial executive, Bismarck ended the unification year in sombre mood. As Lothar Gall notes in his magisterial biography of Bismarck, the Chancellor confided in a letter written on Christmas Day 1871: 'I am weary, and while still bound up with the life of this world I begin to appreciate the attractions of peaceful repose. What I should like most is to leave the stage for a seat in one of the boxes.'[5] As he prepared to accept the imperial crown, Wilhelm also visibly lacked enthusiasm. As Blackbourn notes: 'Germany existed on paper, but it lacked widespread legitimacy as well as seasoned institutions.'[6]

Perhaps Bismarck's uncertainty between the desire for the tranquil existence of a country squire and his need to exercise charismatic leadership on a European level can also be discerned in the restless and sometimes turbulent nature of the country he now led. A nation that would achieve renown for its glorious cultural achievements, scientific progress and technological innovation had been created through wars of unification. Many possible developments, none of them preordained, lay in the future path of the new country, but its ultimate fate would also be sealed on the battlefields of Europe. The military journey began in Denmark in 1864.

## 1.2 conflict with Denmark, 1864

The Duchies of Schleswig-Holstein had traditionally been ruled by Denmark, a nation still regarded in the mid-nineteenth century as a significant Baltic power but with her greatest days in the past. However, by 1860 Holstein had a population of around half a million people who were almost exclusively German-speaking. Schleswig also contained a German element, so that the future of the Duchies became an increasing focus of German nationalist and anti-Danish sentiment. In addition, Schleswig-Holstein's important naval base at Kiel offered the attractive prospect of strategic control of the Baltic and the North Sea. The increasingly passionate interest of the German people in Schleswig-Holstein was stimulated by the fierce clash between German and Danish nationalism in a sensitive frontier area, the complex relationships between Germans and Danes, the conflicting views of the majority of the German Confederation with the carefully managed ambitions of Prussia and the anxiety of the 'imperially overstretched' Austria that it should not be left behind in the changing configuration of European power. Meanwhile, measures taken by the Danes, such as the forced introduction of Danish into the schools of parts of Schleswig, were seen as antagonistic and only raised the international tension.

Within days of his appointment as minister-president of Prussia in September 1862, Bismarck asked War Minister Roon to request from Moltke, chief of the Prussian General Staff since 1857, a plan for military action against Denmark. Yet the notion that Bismarck had a clear sense of what was ahead needs to be treated with care. It is often assumed that Bismarck had fixed his attention upon the annexation of the duchies throughout the crisis of 1863–4 in order to round off Prussian territory in North Germany. While Bismarck undoubtedly appreciated the strategic importance of Schleswig-Holstein for Prussia, it is not certain that annexation was his primary objective. It was not until the late winter of 1864 that he finally opted for that solution. Some authorities have claimed that a primary consideration was the use he could make of the crisis to benefit Prussia in the struggle with Austria. It is more likely that a pragmatist like Bismarck was initially uncertain as to the use he could make of the Schleswig-Holstein affair. His success in gaining Austrian support has often been presented as one of Bismarck's great diplomatic achievements, but in fact agreement with Austria was not unduly illusive.

## 1.3 the Schleswig-Holstein crisis

Matters came to a head in November 1863 when the King of Denmark, Friedrich VII, died without leaving an heir to the throne. With prior international agreement the throne was passed to a Dane, Christian of Glucksburg, who, within days, had signed a new constitution which affected the status of Schleswig and Holstein and raised issues regarding the previous constitutional agreement reached in 1852.

However, his position was challenged by the German Prince of Augustenburg, who had the support of German nationalists, the majority of the German Confederation and the Diet. Bismarck's assessment was that despite the arousal of German nationalism it was not in Prussia's interests to install a new grand duke who would be likely to oppose Prussian interests in the Diet. Bismarck's alternative strategy was to secure the agreement of Austria to work alongside Prussia in the Austro-Prussian military alliance of January 1864 to secure the Duchies by force of arms. Bismarck's tactic was to assure the Austrians of his conservative commitment to the treaty of 1852. Privately he remarked that Prussia had hired Austria and that she was now working for the King of Prussia. In addition, Bismarck had established a firm pretext for intervention – namely, the November constitution binding Schleswig with Denmark which violated the guarantees made to Austria and Prussia in 1852. It was on this basis, and with Denmark lacking military support from any of the great European powers that, in the winter of 1864, troops from Austria and Prussia assailed the medieval fortifications of the Danes with snow on the ground and an icy drizzle biting in from the North Sea to the west and the Baltic in the east.

## 1.4 the Danish military campaign, 1864

The first unification war was a campaign that has been neatly termed by military historian Arden Bucholz 'a small war in the snow',[7] but which was also, in the same author's words, 'a long and difficult campaign, full of mistakes'.[8] The Danish reserves faced the emerging power of the Prussian military machine. The nature of the winter campaign meant that the Danish fleet was effectively neutralized. The unevenness of what followed offered a chilling insight into the difference between an essentially agricultural force and, in relative terms, the industrial mass army of an emerging industrial nation. Brave but naïve, many of the Danish soldiers had only the most rudimentary preparation before they faced the Prussian Army with its superior numbers and rapid-firing breech-load rifles. Under Moltke's dynamic leadership the evolution of the Prussian general staff into a 'learning organization' and the 'futures thinking' of senior figures in the Prussian army led to an innovative approach in key areas such as logistical support, map-making techniques and war-game exercises. The provision of top-quality training in military shooting, gymnastics, artillery and fortifications provided a 'knowledge advantage' that would weigh heavily when deployed against more traditional forces. All of this was underpinned by a highly successful education system, a further vital ingredient in what was becoming an intoxicating mixture.

The Danish reserves, 50 per cent of their army, contained men who were either too old to fight or at the other extreme completely raw, untested and naïve. A general lack of training and cohesion made them no match for the Prussians. It was an uneven conflict between an agriculturally based army, using traditional close-order, muzzle-loading bayonet charges, and an industrial army, equipped with rapid-firing breech-load rifles. The superior technology, organization and leadership of the Prussian army made the simple bravery of the Danish forces seem even more poignant amid the bloody carnage visted upon the Scandinavian winter and spring.

## 1.5  the Treaty of Vienna

By July 1864 Denmark's brave but intrinsically limited resistance was at an end. Bismarck attempted to offer Prussian control of the Duchies for a rather vague commitment to help Austria in Northern Italy. This was unacceptable to the Austrian Emperor Franz Joseph but a compromise came when Bismarck offered joint ownership of the Duchies which were formally surrendered to Austria and Prussia under the Treaty of Vienna of October 1864. This passed Schleswig, Holstein and Lauenburg to the King of Prussia and the Emperor of Austria. Within two years the two leaders would be at war.

## 1.6  chronology of the Schleswig-Holstein issue

| | |
|---|---|
| **1852** | The Treaty of London sets out terms for the relationship of Schleswig-Holstein to Denmark, and subjects the Duchies to international regulation |
| **1863** | |
| 15 November | Death of the Danish King Friedrich VII without an heir, followed by the accession of Prince Christian IX of Schleswig-Holstein |
| 18 November | Christian IX signs a new constitution which conflicts with the terms of the 1852 agreement. Christian's position is challenged by the German Duke August of Augustenburg, who was recognized in Germany as the Duke of Schleswig-Holstein |
| 24 December | Without a formal declaration of war, German Confederation troops from Saxony and Hanover entered Holstein and Lauenburg – the Danes withdraw their forces into Schleswig |
| **1864** | |
| January–February | An alliance of Austria and Prussia occupies Holstein (January) and Schleswig (February), leading to war against Denmark |
| 18 April | Austro-Prussian forces storm Danish fortifications at Duppel |
| 20 April–25th June | London conference on the Schleswig-Holstein crisis |
| 26 June | Resumption of Austro-Prussian war against Denmark |
| 20 July | New armistice signed |
| 25 July | Peace conference opened in Vienna |
| 1 August | Preliminary peace signed |
| 30 October | Treaty of Vienna cedes control of Schleswig, Holstein and Lauenburg to Austria and Prussia |
| November | Bismarck pushes the Diet into withdrawing federal forces from Holstein, leaving Austria and Prussia in control. |

## 1.7 the Gastein Convention, 1865

Although ostensibly the Austro-Prussian military intervention had 'settled' the Schleswig-Holstein issue, in reality the question of the long-term future of the Duchies actually became a source of rising tension between the two powers, leading Bismarck to comment acidly that 'our tickets are on diverging lines' and the Austrian foreign minister to conclude that his pro-Prussian policy of 1864 had been a serious mistake. Indeed when war broke out between Austria and Prussia in 1866 the immediate issue was the question of the future of the Duchies. Despite Austria's assistance Bismarck had no intention of loosening Prussia's grip over the Duchies and he remained convinced that Austria would not sustain its interest in an area that did not directly concern her.

Temporary respite seemed to have been offered with the signing of an Austrian compromise proposal under the Gastein Convention of August 1865 which placed Holstein under the administration of Austria and Schleswig under Prussian authority. The duchy of Lauenburg was bought by Prussia, which also secured new military and naval bases in Holstein. William Carr offers this analysis of why Bismarck was prepared to sign the Gastein Convention: 'The most likely explanation is that Bismarck was not ready for war and simply accepted a favourable offer which loosened Austria's hold over the duchies and avoided all reference to Duke Frederick. Bismarck's determination to force Austria out of Holstein and dominate Germany remained unchanged.'[9] A further insight is provided by David Blackbourn who states: 'Bismarck's policy towards Austria, for all its tactical twists and turns, was more single-mindedly bent on a particular outcome than his policy towards France or the southern states. Nothing is inevitable, but it is hard to see the Gastein Convention as anything other than a truce before the willed conflict of 1866.'[10]

## 1.8 conflict with Austria, 1866

While some historians have claimed that Bismarck had already charted the course of events, many others feel that he was not necessarily full of belligerent intent. It seems most likely that the new minister-president was not immediately fixed on a course of war with Austria. He was a much more multi-faceted, nuanced diplomat than his sometimes direct or even beligerent statements suggest. War was obviously one solution to the Austrian issue and probably the most likely outcome as Bismarck scanned the horizon. However, he cannot be accurately depicted as a bloodthirsty and aggressive Junker itching to commit Prussia to war to satisfy his personal ambition. In fact, he saw war only as a final resort when all hope of a peaceful solution had been exhausted. His diplomatic instincts and personal religious convictions, added to his sense of caution, meant that there was no immediate change of direction in Prussian policy when Bismarck assumed power. In foreign affairs he continued the policy pursued by Count Bernstorff, Prussian foreign minister since 1861, of antagonism with Austria, while making overtures to Russia.

It is clear in retrospect that Bismarck was able to take advantage of an exceptionally favourable international situation. What Klaus Hildebrand called the 'Crimean moment' – the weakening of Britain and Russia after the Crimean War of 1854–56 – provided a window of opportunity for the advancement of German unity. In the words of A. J. P. Taylor, 'Both Russia and Great Britain had virtually eliminated themselves from the European balance; this gave the years between 1864 and 1866 a character unique in recent history.'[11]

Events now moved quickly, with an informal visit by Bismarck to Napoleon at Biarritz in October 1865 designed to shore up the position of France in the event of war. Although the meeting did not lead to any binding agreement it was enough to convince Bismarck that if Venetia could be secured for Italy then Napoleon was likely to remain on the sidelines in the event of a Prussian war with Austria.

As tension between Austria and Prussia over the Duchies reached new heights in 1866, Bismarck was able to conclude that from Britain, Russia and Italy only the Italians could not be counted upon to keep out of a war between Prussia and Austria. This was effectively neutralized when Italy formed an alliance with Prussia in April 1866. This stipulated that in the event of war between Prussia and Austria within three months, Italy would join in and take Venetia. On 21 April amid rumours of Italian troop movements, Austria took the dramatic step of mobilizing her armies in the south.

This was enough to convince the cautious Prussian king that he had no choice but to order mobilization of his troops. As John Breuilly explains:

> It took a great deal of Bismarck's energy to persuade the king to break at last with Austria, the old and legitimate ally both in Germany and against France. Possibly it was one reason why Bismarck avoided war in the summer of 1865. Once the king was persuaded that Austria sought to deprive Prussia of her rightful standing in Germany, and that Austrian mobilisation represented a serious military threat, he agreed to war. It was typical of William that he now pursued the war in a spirit of self-righteousness and the next big problem Bismarck faced was persuading him to bring the war to a rapid end before international complications could develop.[12]

American academic Dennis Showalter provides an interesting alternative critique of the way the king's part in the decision-making process that led up to the war with Austria has generally been characterized by historians.

> William – as usual – emerges as a more or less inert force, needing either the repeated galvanic shocks administered by his minister-president or the clearly presented calculations of his chief of staff to impel him into action. William, in fact, was accustomed to making his own decisions, and regarded both Bismarck and Moltke as what they were under the Prussian constitution: royally appointed officials who served at his pleasure.[13]

This hierarchy is also reflected in the document that follows, a communiqué from Moltke on the possibility of a war between Prussia and Austria.

**SOURCE**

MEMORANDUM FROM HELMUTH VON MOLTKE, BERLIN, 2 APRIL 1866.

As a political question, the war against Austria, its probability or inevitability, lies outside the scope of my judgment. But from my standpoint I believe I must express the conviction that the success or failure of this war essentially depends on our reaching a decision about it sooner than the Austrians, and if possible, right now.

One advantage for us, which cannot be overstated, is that we can advance our army on five railroad lines and thereby have it essentially concentrated on the Saxon-Bohemian border within 25 days.

Austria has just one railway leading toward Bohemia, and allowing for the troops it already has in Bohemia and Galicia, and assuming further that its cavalry is already on the march, then it requires 45 days to assemble 200,000 men.

If Bavaria joins Austria, then it is not so much its army as the use of its Regensburg-Pilsen-Prague railway line that will be disadvantageous for us, since this shortens the above-mentioned Austrian concentration by about 15 days.

If the mobilization of the Prussian army is ordered right now, then Bavaria – so ill-prepared for war in terms of arms, mobilization, and the concentration of its approximately 40,000 men near Bamberg – will in all probability not be ready when the first battle between Austria and Prussia has been fought. Deploying the Bavarian armed forces can hardly serve the purpose of laying siege to Coblenz, or Cologne, or even Erfurt, or of seizing Prussian territory, but more probably of waiting for a successful outcome and then showing up as an armed power on the side of the victor.

For us it all depends on defeating this one enemy Austria, [and] to this end this we have to muster all [our] forces, and if anybody should ask for my opinion, we have to enlist not only the VIIth, but also the VIIIth Army Corps.

*Source*: Helmuth von Moltke, *Moltkes militärische Werke* (1896–1912).

## 1.9 war with Austria, 1866

There can be no doubt that engaging in a war with Austria was a high-risk operation. Many contemporaries held the view that following the rather muddling performance of the Prussian forces in Denmark, Austria had every chance of success in 1866. The allegiance of states from the German Confederation including Saxony, Hanover and Hesse-Cassel with Austria made the situation even more challenging. So it may have been with some trepidation that the German officers gathered at the Königswarder memorial to oversee the departure of their units from Berlin, with forty military trains per day leaving the capital for Bohemia through the first five days of June. In fact the war was over by 22 July 1866. Although the Battle of Königgrätz is rightly regarded as the decisive episode in the war, several other exchanges are worthy of attention and remind us that both sides paid a heavy price in their terrible conflict.

### the key battles of the Seven Weeks' War

| | | |
|---|---|---|
| Battle of Custova | 24 June | Austrian forces in the south brought to a standstill by the Italians, leaving Archduke Albrecht's army in no position to move north against Prussia |
| Battle of Nachod | 27 June | 5-hour battle in hot, humid conditions. Austria lost more than 7,000 men at a rate of almost 20 per minute |
| Battle of Trautenau | 27 June | Poor leadership meant that few of the Prussian battalions were actually able to engage with the Austrians, and although Austrian casualties were heavy this was the only Prussian battlefield defeat in the war with Austria |
| Battle of Skalitz | 28 June | Austria suffered its heaviest casualties of the war. Bucholz provides vivid descriptions of men drowning when trying to cross the river to escape or being burnt to death in house-to-house fighting[14] |

## 1.10  the Battle of Königgrätz (Sadowa), 1866

More than half a million soldiers took part in the decisive engagement between Königgrätz and Sadowa in Bohemia on 3 July 1866, evocatively described by the *Times* correspondent W. H. Russell, when he saw the Austrian army, with their bands playing, assume their positions in 'Squares and parallelograms of snowy white, dark green, azure and blue on the cornfields like checker work of a patchwork quilt'.[15] The scene may have looked picturesque but the reality was a slaughter in which the Austrians suffered 64,000 killed, wounded and taken prisoner. Under Moltke's strategic command 280,000 Prussian soldiers and 900 guns overcame Benedek's forces of 245,000 men and 600 guns. The lightning defeat of Saxony, Austria's ally, at the outset of the war, the fact that the Prussian breech-loading needle gun fired four or five times per minute compared to the single shots of the Austrian's muzzle-loading counterpart, the robustness of Moltke's strategic planning and the failure of the Austrian commander Benedek to utilise a potentially favourable defensive position, all contributed to the Prussian victory. However, Richard Evans contends that what was subsequently depicted as the next smoothly executed move in a preordained plan was in fact more haphazard: 'far from being the perfectly planned and executed operation of Prussian historical legend, Moltke's victory at Königgràtz was, like most battles, a tale of muddle and confusion, in which the great general was only saved from humiliation by the opportune arrival of the Prussian Second Army led by the heir to the Prussian throne.'[16]

Nevertheless it was with some satisfaction that by the afternoon of 3 July Moltke reported to the King 'The campaign is decided, Vienna lies at your Majesty's feet.' In the evening the Prussian generals sat down together for a celebratory game of whist. The card players were in ebullient mood. The day's events on the Bohemian heights of Chlum had unfolded to their complete satisfaction. Craig comments that 'Inflamed by their triumph',[17] the Prussian military and monarchy were now ready to push on to Vienna. Bismarck's task was to rein in the very people on whom he had depended to crush Austria. It was a challenge elegantly summarized by Bismarck in a letter written to his wife in July 1866: 'If we are not excessive in our demands and do not believe that we have conquered the world, we will attain a peace that is worth our effort. But we are just as quickly intoxicated as we are plunged into dejection, and I have the thankless task of pouring water into the bubbling wine and making it clear that we do not live alone in Europe but with three other Powers that hate and envy us.'[18]

Gall's analysis is that 'The real power of the empire was smashed at Königgrätz and a complete conquest of the country only to be staved off by political means with the conclusion of a swift peace.'[19]

In a brief but disastrous campaign Austria had suffered 52,000 men killed and wounded, approximately 20 per cent of their total fighting force. This compared to 9,000 Prussians. The victories over Denmark and Austria reflected a period of rapid development for the Prussian army. Specialization of labour, high-quality training and preparation, a rapidly expanding railway network, meticulous attention to battle details such as the wording of military orders, detailed planning and technical innovation all played a major part in the emergence of the Prussian army as a major force.

## 1.11 the aftermath of the war with Austria

Bismarck's political success in using his powers of persuasion to curb King Wilhelm's militaristic enthusiasm was helped by an outbreak of cholera among the Prussian troops and the fact that lines of communication were already sorely stretched. Rather grudgingly the King agreed to an armistice signed on 22 July, which was followed by preliminary peace terms at Nikolsburg and the final peace settlement, the Peace of Prague, signed on 23 August. This brought substantial gains to Prussia and concluded the first substantial political unification of the German states to the north of the River Main. Although this stage produced considerable initial satisfaction it was also soon evident that nationalist and liberal tendencies within Prussia wanted to take the process of unification to its ultimate conclusion. Bismarck had already begun the process of engineering the military support of the southern states in a commitment to side with Prussia if she came under attack. In 1867 the commercial development of the new Zollparlament as an extension of the Zollverein marked a further step forward for Prussian ambition.

William Carr sees the Austro-Prussian war as 'a power struggle for mastery in Germany, an eighteenth-century war fought with nineteenth-century weapons'.[20] The shattered remnants of Benedek's army scurrying for cover on the banks of the Elbe heralded the triumph of Bismarck's anti-Austrian policy. He had masterminded the crucial break with the traditions of Prussian diplomacy as the means of dividing the parliamentary opposition that was threatening to force the Prussian Government into a cul-de-sac when he came to power in September 1862. He had strategically manoeuvred the Austrian Government into circumstances in which it felt obliged to assume the responsibility for beginning the war even though it lacked the resources to claim victory.

In the wake of the Prussian victory over Austria large sections of the German people took part in an unprecedented outpouring of national sentiment. The momentum towards German unification had substantial energy from the top and from the bottom.

## 1.12 the North German Confederation

The creation of the North German Confederation in 1867 left the south German states in a perilous position. Still historically committed to Austria, to all practical intents and purposes they were beholden to Prussia in military and economic terms. Hans-Ulrich Wehler states that the expansion of Greater Prussia was viewed by the government in Berlin as providing

> the best possible solution to the problem of uniting Germany while excluding Austria. The Austrian defeat in the German 'civil war' and the creation of the North German Confederation confirmed these calculations. The opinion was often enough expressed that a war fought in a common cause would soon overcome any resistance by the South German states to a Prussian-dominated Germany. It was also bound to have the effect of uniting the nation.[21]

The new North German Confederation was a federal state (Bundesstaat) as opposed to a federation of states (Staatenbund). It excluded Austria as well as the south German states of Bavaria, Baden, Hesse-Darmstadt and Wurttemburg. Prussia annexed Schleswig-Holstein, Hesse-Kassel, Frankfurt, Hanover and Nassau. Bismarck's constitution of the North German Confederation allowed territorial rulers to retain the management of their own internal affairs while the head of the Confederation, the King of Prussia, presided over foreign affairs and army issues. The largely impotent parliament (Reichstag) was complemented by an upper house, the Federal Council (Bundesrat), effectively dominated by Prussia. This constitution was to provide a template for that of the subsequent German Empire.

## 1.13 chronology of the war with France and its consequences, 1868–71

| | |
|---|---|
| *1868* | |
| | A revolution in Spain deposes the monarch, Isabella II, creating a vacancy for the Spanish throne |
| *1870* | |
| June | Bismarck secures the consent of Kaiser Wilhelm I to Prince Leopold of Hohenzollern-Sigmaringen's candidacy for the Spanish throne |
| July | Following negotiations between the French envoy in Prussia, Benedetti and Wilhelm I at Bad Ems, Wilhelm tells the French that he will not object if the Hohenzollern nomination is withdrawn. However, French Foreign Minister Gramont now insists on written guarantees and a letter of apology from Wilhelm I to Emperor Napoleon III |
| | The Prussian king telegraphs a report of his discussions with Benedetti to Bismarck. Bismarck subsequently releases a carefully edited version of the Ems dispatch. The edited version creates the impression that the French envoy had been brusquely treated by the German emperor. The doctored telegram causes outrage in France, prompting Napoleon to declare war |
| 16 July | Mobilization of Bavaria and Baden on the Prussian side |
| 17 July | Mobilization of Württemberg on the Prussian side |
| 19 July | France declares war even though her military preparedness is behind the Prussian army |
| August | The Battle of Spicheren is greeted as a German triumph even though the Germans take heavy casualties. |
| | At Wissembourg both sides take heavy casualties but the superiority of German numbers carries the day. At the Battle of Froeschwiller-Woerth, towards the end of August, France suffers more than 25,000 killed, wounded and taken prisoner |
| 1–2 September | Crushing and decisive Prussian victory over France at the Battle of Sedan and the capture of Napoleon III |

| | |
|---|---|
| October–November | Negotiations with the south German states at Versailles |
| 9 December | Proposals for constitutional change accepted by the North German Confederation |
| *1871* | |
| 18 January | Proclamation of the German Empire at Versailles |
| February | Provisional peace terms with France stipulate the annexation of Alsace-Lorraine to Germany. This was to leave a bitter legacy for Franco-German relations |
| 10 May | The Peace of Frankfurt |

## 1.14 origins of the war with France, 1870–71

### the Hohenzollern candidature

By 1870 Bismarck was ready, once again, to use his instinct for power politics to 'engineer a war at a precise juncture which suited his plans'.[22] France remained as the clear obstacle to the southern states being absorbed into Lesser Germany. While it could be argued that conflict between Prussia and France was highly likely, the exact location of its immediate origins came from an unexpected quarter. The cause was a disputed succession in Spain.

When the Spanish throne fell vacant in 1868 it was offered to the Hohenzollern candidate Prince Leopold. In the face of French objections the candidacy was withdrawn but France pushed further and demanded a pledge that the candidature could never be renewed. When Prussia stood its ground the French found themselves in a position where a declaration of war seemed to be the only face-saving option. When the military test came the southern states stood by their alliances with Prussia. Bismarck had manipulated the provocative Hohenzollern candidature for the Spanish throne and clumsy French lapses in protocol to illicit a French declaration of war. Craig states: 'It cannot be said that Bismarck wanted a war in 1870, but, thanks to the crisis that he had encouraged, to Gramont's maladroitness in handling it, and to the passions it released in French opinion, that was what he got'.[23]

**SOURCE A**

ORIGINAL TEXT OF THE EMS TELEGRAM, FROM HEINRICH ABEKEN TO BISMARCK, 13 JULY 1870.

His Majesty writes to me: 'Count Benedetti spoke to me on the promenade, in order to demand from me, finally in a very importunate manner, that I should authorise him to telegraph at once that I bound myself for all future time never again to give my consent if the Hohenzollerns should renew their candidature. I refused at last somewhat sternly, as it is neither right nor possible to undertake engagements of this kind à tout jamais. Naturally I told him that I had as yet received no news, and as he was earlier informed about Paris and Madrid than myself, he could clearly see that my government once more had no hand in this matter.' His Majesty has since received a letter from the Prince. His Majesty having told Count Benedetti that he was awaiting news from the Prince, has decided, with reference to the above demand, upon the representation of Count Eulenburg and myself, not to receive Count Benedetti again, but only to let him be informed through an aide-de-camp: That his Majesty had now received from the Prince confirmation of the news which Benedetti had already received from Paris, and had nothing further to say to the ambassador. His Majesty leaves it to your Excellency whether Benedetti's fresh demand and its rejection should not be at once communicated both to our ambassadors and to the press.

*Source*: Eric Wilmot, *The Great Powers 1814–1918* (1992).

## SOURCE B

BISMARCK'S TEXT OF THE EMS TELEGRAM, EDITED FOR PUBLICATION.

After the news of the renunciation of the hereditary Prince of Hohenzollern had been officially communicated to the Imperial government of France by the Royal government of Spain, the French ambassador further demanded of his Majesty, the King, at Ems, that he would authorise him to telegraph to Paris that his Majesty, the King, bound himself for all time never again to give his consent, should the Hohenzollerns renew their candidature. His Majesty, the King, thereupon decided not to receive the French ambassador again, and sent the aide-de-camp on duty to tell him that his Majesty had nothing further to communicate to the ambassador.

*Source*: as source A.

## SOURCE C

BISMARCK, FROM *REFLECTIONS AND REMINISCENCES* (1898).

I went on to explain: 'If in execution of His Majesty's order, I at once communicate this text . . . not only to the newspapers but by telegraph to all our embassies it will be known in Paris before midnight . . . and will have the effect of a red rag on the French bull . . . Success, however, depends essentially upon the impression which the origination of the war makes upon us and others: it is important that we should be the ones attacked.

*Source*: as source A.

## QUESTIONS

1  What diplomatic impact would the original text of the Ems telegram have made?
2  How does this compare to the diplomatic impact of the second, edited text?
3  Which specific elements of the Ems telegram did Bismarck remove?
4  Why did Bismarck make these amendments?

## 1.15  the Battle of Sedan, 1870

As the slightly chill autumnal mist lifted over the fields of Sedan, in north-eastern France, King Wilhelm I of Prussia was able to take advantage of a superb vantage point in a forest clearing to witness his moment of triumph. The Prussian monarch was joined by his leading generals and his political strategist Otto von Bismarck, flanked by a glittering array of German princes. Meanwhile, on the battlefield they surveyed, the circumstances of the French Emperor could hardly have been more different. Appalled by the carnage visited upon his countrymen, Napoleon personally ordered the raising of a white flag. This was the most significant battle of the Franco-Prussian War, culminating in the armies of Emperor Napoleon III, under the military command of Marshal MacMahon, laying down their arms to Prussia's Third Army. The emperor was taken into captivity at Wilhelmslöhe. More than 100,000 French soldiers were taken prisoner amid the final collapse of the Napoleonic regime. On 2 September Emperor Napoleon III's capitulation was formally accepted. Finally, on 3 September the French troops watched through driving rain as their emperor, followed by his extensive wagon train, rode off into captivity. The Prussian victory had been comprehensively sealed and the moment of German unification was almost at hand.

## 1.16  the Peace Treaty of Frankfurt am Main

The humiliation of France was completed with the signing of the Peace of Frankfurt signed by Bismarck for Germany and by Jules Favre the French Foreign Minister.

On 10 May the two countries concluded a treaty in which France ceded Alsace (except Belfort) and German Lorraine, including the fortresses of Metz and Strasburg. In addition, France was obliged to pay a war debt of 5,000 million francs, starting with 1,000 million francs in 1871. The final indignity was that France was also subject to military occupation.

Alsace and Lorraine had passed from the Holy Roman Empire to France during the seventeenth century. Following the victory at Sedan Bismarck fuelled demands through the press for the cession of these two strategic areas to Germany. Bismarck played on the fact that a German dialect was spoken in Alsace and a section of Lorraine but there is no doubt that he was more interested in the military and strategic implications of securing the salient in the certainty of future French hostility. A subdued France had to accept the surrender of one-third of Lorraine and the whole of Alsace. France retained the fortress at Belfort but did agree to pay an indemnity totalling 5,000 million francs, with 1,000 million due in 1871 and the rest within three years. It was agreed that the payments would be accompanied by the progressive withdrawal of the troops of German occupation. To the surprise of many observers France paid the indemnity in full by 1873 and all occupying troops were withdrawn.

To the immediate signs of French recovery Bismarck added his concern that fear of Prussian strength could lead to an overwhelming alliance against the new Germany.

In the words of Richard J. Evans:

> The new country had been formed 'not by an act of free will on the part of its citizens' but rather by a 'revolution from above'. It was forged in the heat of battle, and imposed by force. It was incomplete, excluding many ethnic Germans from its boundaries, and it was divided, including many people of other nationalities as well as different confessions, classes and regional groups.[24]

Lothar Gall states that:

> what is often referred to even today simply as Bismarck's creation turned out to have been one of the shortest-lived political creations of all time . . . Bismarck achieved only a very limited measure of control over his creation and over the problems and trends of development inherent in it . . . He ultimately found himself in many respects faced with a situation that was insoluble for him on his terms. In the end, perhaps like every major actor on the stage of history, he was really no more than a sorcerer's apprentice.[25]

chapter **2**

German society, 1871–90

## 2.1 the nature of German society

It was easy to be positive about the new creation. When the new German Empire came into existence in January 1871 it covered a geographical area exceeding 200,000 square miles stretching from the borders with France and Belgium in the west towards the Tsarist Russian Empire in the East, including lands which now belong to Poland. The dynamism that characterised this new state was reflected in the fact that the population of approximately 41 million in 1871 had risen to almost 65 million by 1910. The sense of a modern, rapidly developing society is reflected in the following extract.

**SOURCE**

HERMANN VON HELMHOLTZ: EXCERPTS FROM A SPEECH GIVEN ON THE OCCASION OF HIS APPOINTMENT AS PRO-RECTOR OF THE UNIVERSITY OF HEIDELBERG, 1862.

If we count as well the studies of historical sources, the sorting through of all the scrolls and papers piled up in state and city archives, the gathering of all of the notes scattered in memoirs, collections of letters, and biographies, the decoding of all of the documents written in hieroglyphics and cuneiform; if we take all of the rapidly growing systematic overviews of minerals, plants, and animals – those alive today and those from before the great flood – there unfolds before our eyes a dizzying mass of learned knowledge. In these disciplines alone, the research expands to the same degree as the tools of observation, with no limit in sight.

*Source*: 'Ueber das Verhältniss der Naturwissenschaften zur Gesammtheit der Wissenschaft', in *Vortäge und Reden von Hermann von Helmholtz* (1896).

In 1878 the fabled American novelist Mark Twain reported back to a friend his impressions of a visit to Germany: 'What a paradise this land is! What clean clothes, what good faces, what tranquil contentment, what prosperity, what genuine freedom, what superb government!'[1]

Yet from the outset the process of unification was clearly incomplete. In the words of Richard Evans: 'Germany was not united in 1866, nor was it in 1871. Millions of Germans remained outside the Reich, not only in Austria but also further afield, in areas of settlement all over East-Central Europe . . . the German Reich, then, really was created by 'Blood and Iron'. It was the product of violence, not of any natural process.'[2] Three minority groups of non-Germans were of particular importance.

The Danes of Schleswig-Holstein and the inhabitants of Alsace-Lorraine were rendered German citizens after the wars of 1864 and 1870–71, respectively. A still larger group of outsiders were the seven million Poles who had been the subject of sporadic attempts to 'Germanize' them and who suffered from a long-standing German assertion of superiority. Beyond these national issues, a further fissure came as a result of religious differences. Despite a broad decline in church attendance and expression of religious conviction, a deep and serious fracture between Protestant and Catholic Germany was easily visible. Protestantism, the faith of approximately 60 per cent of the population, spanned a broad spectrum, from the Prussian aristocracy, through the traders and craftsmen of small towns and villages, to areas of peasant farming, such as Bavarian Franconia. Catholicism accounted for approximately 40 per cent of the total population, with heavy concentrations in Bavaria, southern Baden, Wurttemberg, Prussian Westphalia, the Rhineland and in Prussian Poland and Silesia in the east. In broad terms, the Catholics tended to be more agrarian than their more industrial Protestant counterparts, a tendency that further fuelled division with Catholics, sometimes depicted as 'backward' or 'superstitious'. Such prejudice was at its most acute during Bismarck's *Kulturkampf*, a campaign that led to the development of what has been labelled 'ghetto Catholicism'. It is worth noting at this point that the German Jews were largely able to avoid this process. The extract that follows shows the outlook of the German Protestant Association.

**SOURCE**

DANIEL SCHENKEL, EXCERPTS FROM *THE GERMAN PROTESTANT ASSOCIATION*, 1868.

The dissolution of Protestantism would pose not only an immense religious, but also a terrible national and political danger. We have an entirely benevolent attitude toward Catholicism, provided it does not pursue goals inimical to culture and does not seek to renew the horror of Jesuitical intolerance and priestly mania for persecution; it may continue its religious and cultural-historical mission unobstructed, as long as it does not keep us Protestants from pursuing our own. However, the religion of the modern world is Protestantism: only it has understood Christianity in a way that the nations that have come of age are able to understand and adopt in the long run. It is our belief that the future belongs to Protestantism to the same degree that it is able to realize its principles in the life of nations and states, and to cast off the theological fetters with which he, the youthful giant, constrained his still-awkward limbs already three centuries ago.

*Source*: Daniel Schenkel, *Der Deutsche Protestantenverein und seine Bedeutung in der Gegenwart nach den Akten dargestellt* (1868).

Beyond these ethnic and religious divisions, further tension came though differences in social class. The rapid industrialization and urbanization of the nineteenth century helped to create a working class that became increasingly politicised, particularly under the rallying cry of Marxism and around the organized activities of the Social Democratic Party of Germany (SPD). In the same way that the external allegiance of Catholics to Rome caused a negative reaction within German society, the affiliation of the socialists to their international class comrades was at best difficult for many to accept, and at worst, a source of unbridled anxiety, even though by 1912 the SPD advocated constitutional reform rather than the violent overthrow of the Kaiserreich. And in the same way that the Kulturkampf only furthered the Catholic cause, so too did the campaign against the left produce a counterproductive result, to the extent that in the 'red election' of 1912, the Socialists made spectacular gains, achieving one-third of the popular vote and becoming the largest party in the Reichstag. For these reasons, then, it could be argued that differences of ethnicity, religion and class meant that the newly unified state remained in some respects a divided nation, although the same point could reasonably be made about some of the other major European powers such as France and Russia.

## 2.2 the political system: the constitution, the Emperor, the Chancellor, the Bundesrat, the Reichstag, the States

Prussia accounted for approximately 60 per cent of the territory and population of the new Germany. Therefore some of the fundamentals of the new constitution are hardly surprising. The structure and constitution of the Reich inevitably reflected the autocratic and dynastic hallmarks of the Prussian victory. Officially sovereignty rested with twenty-two rulers – four kings, six grand dukes, four dukes and eight princes, who combined with the senates of three free cities in an act of association. Therefore the new German Reich can be seen as an alliance between the ruling princes of Germany, supported by the recently triumphant Prussian military machine and with the enthusiastic support of middle-class nationalists, whose backing could now be channelled through the popular plebiscite.

# key elements of the constitution

## the Emperor
- Always the King of Prussia
- Had power to appoint and dismiss the Chancellor
- Could dissolve the Reichstag
- Controlled foreign policy
- Could conclude treaties and alliances
- Could declare war and make peace
- Supreme warlord of all the armed forces of the Empire
- Had the right to interpret the constitution
- Supervised the execution of all Federal laws

## the Chancellor
- Chief imperial officer of the Reich
- Post normally combined with Prussian Minister-President – the basis of substantial power
- Accountable to the Emperor
- Determined the outline of Reich policy
- Chaired sessions of the Bundesrat
- Not bound by resolutions passed by the Reichstag – votes of no confidence could not remove them from office
- Chancellors did need to secure Reichstag support for their own legislative proposals
- Could appoint and dismiss State Secretaries in the various government ministries

## the Bundesrat (Federal Council)
- The Federal Council – The Bundesrat epitomized the federal basis of the Empire
- Comprised 58 members nominated by state assemblies – an assembly of ambassadors from the member states
- The executive body of the Empire – wielded considerable power
- Consent was required in the passing of new laws
- Could veto constitutional changes
- A vote of 14 against a proposal constituted a veto
- Prussia held 17 of the 58 seats, Bavaria had 6, the smaller states one each
- In practice the smaller states did not oppose Prussia on constitutional issues
- Bundesrat meetings were held in private and were presided over by the emperor or the chancellor

## the Reichstag (Imperial Diet)
- The National Parliament
- Elected by universal male suffrage over 25 years of age
- Although some active individuals, including Louise Otto and Hedwig Dohm, were calling for the vote for women, there was very limited support for female suffrage apart from within the labour movement

- Shared legislative power with the Bundesrat
- Could accept or reject legislation but limited capacity to initiate new laws
- State Secretaries, responsible for government ministries, were excluded from the Reichstag
- Imperial ministers were not accountable to the Reichstag and normally sat in the Bundesrat
- Members were unpaid
- Could approve or reject the budget. These budgetary powers would be of some significance in the constitutional development of Germany.

### the States
- Each state retained its own constitution
- The states retained authority over matters such as education, cultural issues, direct taxation and welfare

## 2.3 the political parties

### a brief guide to the main political parties

#### the Progressive Party
A new liberal group founded in January 1861. Within two months of the military victory over Austria the Progressive Party split, with supporters of Bismarck breaking away to form the National Liberal Party

#### the Social Democratic Party of Germany (SPD)
Two major working-class parties were established in the 1860s – the General Union of German Workers, founded by Ferdinand Lasalle, and the Social Democratic Workers' Party, created by August Bebel and William Liebknecht. In 1875 these parties combined to form the Social Democratic Party of Germany (SPD)

#### the Centre Party (Deutsche Zentrums-partei)
Formed in 1870 by members of the Prussian lower house to represent the interests of the Catholic minority who constituted almost 40 per cent of the nation's population

#### the German Conservative Party and the Free Conservatives
The right-wing Conservative Party chiefly represented landowners while the Free Conservatives represented a broader geographical and social base with industrialists, bankers and commercial interests offering them support

#### national minority parties
These included parties representing the Poles, Danes and Alsatians

**the Freethinking party (Freisinnige Partei)**
This party contested elections for the first time in 1884 as a merger of the Progressive Party and the Liberal Union. In 1892 a further split saw this party divide into the Freethinking People's Party and the Freethinking Union

**farmers' parties**
The Bavarian Farmers' League and the Farmers' League contested elections in 1898

**the Economic Union (Wirtschafts Vereinigung)**
This party was formed to contest the elections of 1907

table **2.1 election results, 1871–90**

|  | 1871 | 1874 | 1877 | 1878 | 1881 | 1884 | 1887 | 1890 |
|---|---|---|---|---|---|---|---|---|
| the National Liberals | 125 | 155 | 128 | 99 | 47 | 51 | 99 | 42 |
| the Centre Party | 63 | 91 | 93 | 94 | 100 | 99 | 98 | 106 |
| the Social Democratic Party | 2 | 9 | 12 | 9 | 12 | 24 | 11 | 35 |
| the German Conservative Party | 57 | 22 | 40 | 59 | 50 | 78 | 80 | 73 |
| the Free Conservatives | 37 | 33 | 38 | 57 | 28 | 28 | 41 | 20 |
| the Progressives | 47 | 50 | 52 | 39 | 115 | 74 | 32 | 76 |

*Source*: Eric Wilmot, *The Great Powers: Europe 1814–1918* (1992).

## 2.4 Wilhelm I: King of Prussia (1861–88), Emperor of Germany (1871–88)

By the autumn of 1858 Friedrich Wilhelm's mental health had declined to the extent that at the age of 61 his brother Wilhelm became Prince-Regent. He carried with him the expectation of liberal hopes, which had been invested in his predecessor back in 1840, and indeed the elections of 1858 witnessed a resurgence of liberalism in the new parliament. However, Wilhelm was obstinately defensive of the notion of the preservation of Hohenzollern authority. He succeeded as king when Friedrich Wilhelm died in January 1861 and made it clear that he regarded the Prussian army as the cornerstone of his dynastic authority and sought to strengthen its power. William Carr describes the new monarch as: 'a pious, sober-minded and deeply conservative ruler, typically Hohenzollern in his belief that strong government and military power were the twin bases of the Prussian state'.[3] Wilhelm has been depicted as unimaginative, indecisive, typically representative of the Hohenzollern dynasty in his conservatism, but not a reactionary. Within a year he had made the significant appointment of General Albrecht von Roon as minister of war and charged him with the crucial and ultimately contentious task of masterminding the necessary reform of the Prussian army. This was a crucial milestone in the path to unification that would culminate in the new king becoming the first German Emperor, but it paled into insignificance compared to Wilhelm's appointment of Otto von Bismarck as Prussian Minister-President and then ultimately Chancellor of Germany.

## 2.5 the Chancellor

Under the terms of the German constitution, the Chancellor was appointed by the emperor and remained in office subject to imperial support. The Chancellor was the chief imperial officer and exercised the executive power invested in the Emperor and the Bundesrat. Chancellors were under no obligation to act upon resolutions passed by the Reichstag and could not be removed by a vote of no confidence from the Reichstag. Normally, the office of chancellor was combined with the post of Prussian minister-president and the fact that the Prussian office derived substantial real authority would not be lost in Bismarck, as his political career unfolded. Even when he entered the Chancellery, Bismarck was always eager to ensure that he preserved the closest possible links between Prussia and the Empire. In 1857 illness rendered Friedrich Wilhelm IV incapable of ruling and a regency was established under Wilhelm I. Bismarck was sent as Prussian ambassador to St Petersburg and subsequently Paris. In 1862 the King encountered serious difficulties with the Prussian parliament over army reforms and Bismarck was recalled and appointed as Prime Minister. Although the King had some personal reservations about the appointment of Bismarck, he had a clear view of his abilities. At the relatively young age of 48 the Junker and former diplomat had assumed control of the direction of Prussia's affairs. He was appointed Minister-President and Foreign Minister, posts he would retain for 28 years. He would bring formidable gifts to these positions. In the words of David Blackbourn, Bismarck was 'an almost wholly political animal, lacking the caution or baggage of conventional opinions possessed by most Prussian conservatives'.[4]

### biography of the first Chancellor of Imperial Germany, Otto von Bismarck

| | |
|---|---|
| 1815 | Born on 1 April on the Schönhausen estate, near Magdeburg, to a family of the Prussian landed nobility |
| 1822–27 | Educated at the Plamann Institute, a boarding school in Berlin, which he later described as a 'prison' which 'ruined my childhood' |
| 1827–1830 | Attended the Friedrich Wilhelm Gymnasium |
| 1832 | Sat his school-leaving examination |
| 1832 | Attended the University of Göttingen to read law |

| 1833 | Transferred to the University of Berlin – but did not find the university education to his liking. Commented that "I am still frequently visited by the desire to swap the pen for the plough and the briefcase for the game bag.' Successfully sat law examinations, and subsequently, civil service entry examinations but without great enthusiasm |
|------|--------------------------------------------------------------------------|
| 1837 | Fell in love with the daughter of an English clergyman, but this relationship proved short-lived |
| 1839 | His mother dies at the age of 49. Requested a discharge from the civil service and embarked on a plan to farm the family estates with his brothers in Pomerania |
| 1844 | Applies to resume his civil service training |
| 1845 | His father dies, leaving Otto the estate at Schönhausen. Commented that he could 'skin my game with the precision of a butcher, ride quietly and boldly, smoke great big cigars and cordially and cold-bloodedly drink my guests under the table' |
| 1847 | Married Johanna von Puttkamer, a woman he described as of 'rare intelligence and rare nobility of mind who is at the same time extremely charming ' |
| 1849 | Elected to the Prussian parliament with a reputation as an ultra-conservative |
| 1851 | Appointed Prussian envoy to the Diet of the German Confederation in Frankfurt |
| 1858 | Friedrich Wilhelm IV suffers a stroke and Prince Wilhelm becomes Prince Regent |
| 1859 | Appointed ambassador to St Petersburg |
| 1861 | Death of Friedrich Wilhelm IV and accession of Wilhelm I |
| 1862 | Appointed Prussian ambassador in Paris in May. Appointed minister-president of Prussia in September. Makes 'iron and blood' speech to the Landtag's budget committee. Appointed Prussian foreign minister in October |
| 1864 | Schleswig-Holstein crisis culminates in Prussian victory and the signing of the Treaty of Vienna. |
| 1865 | Constitutional crisis after compromise plan over army reform fails.<br>Gastein Convention with Austria. Accorded status of hereditary count |
| 1866 | Prussian victory over Austria |
| 1867 | Constituent Reichstag elected and passes constitution of North German Confederation. Appointed Bundeskanzler of North German Confederation. Acquires substantial estate at Varzin in Pomerania with endowment from the Prussian Landtag |
| 1870 | Exploits the vacancy of the Spanish throne to promote the Hohenzollern candidature and provoke war with France |

| | |
|---|---|
| 1871 | Proclamation of the new German empire. Bestowed with the hereditary title of prince and becomes Reich chancellor. Receives, as a gift from Wilhelm, the Sachsenwald, outside Hamburg, which becomes his estate at Friedrichsruh. In March, the new Centre Party becomes the second largest party in the Reichstag, but the abolition of the Catholic Section of the Kultusministerium signals the start of the Kulturkampf |
| 1873 | The economic boom comes to an end with the 'Great Crash'. The May Laws are passed by the Prussian Landtag. Formation of the Three Emperors' League |
| 1874 | Survives assassination attempt at Kissingen |
| 1875 | Damaged by the 'War-in-Sight' crisis |
| 1878 | Exploits two assassination attempts against the emperor by launching a campaign against the Socialists. Hosts the Congress of Berlin |
| 1879 | Tariff law passed by the Reichstag |
| 1880 | Becomes minister of trade |
| 1881 | Accident insurance bill is introduced in the Reichstag Three Emperors' Agreement signed |
| 1882 | Triple Alliance formed when Italy joins the Dual Alliance |
| 1883 | Medical insurance law passed by the Reichstag |
| 1884 | Renewal of Three Emperors' Agreement |
| 1886 | Herbert von Bismarck becomes state secretary of the Foreign Office |
| 1887 | Germany concludes secret Reinsurance Treaty with Russia. Doctors confirm that the crown prince has cancer |
| 1888 | (9 March) Death of Wilhelm I and accession of Friedrich III (15 June) Death of Friedrich III and accession of Wilhelm II |
| 1889 | Old age and disability insurance law passed by the Reichstag Striking miners in Westphalia illicit sympathetic response from the new Kaiser |
| 1890 | Following disagreement with the Kaiser, writes a letter of resignation (18 March) which is formally accepted on 20 March. On 29 March leaves Berlin following an elaborate ceremony which he referred to as a 'first-class funeral', and headed for his estate at Friedrichsruh |
| 1894 | (27 November) death of Johanna |
| 1897 | Kaiser Wilhelm II visits Bismarck on his estate |
| 1898 | Dies on the evening of 30 July |

*Source*: Adapted from Katharine Anne Lerman, *Bismarck: Profiles in Power* (2004) and Edgar Feuchtwanger, *Bismarck* (2002).

## 2.6 the German economy and the process of internal unification

The economic strength associated with Germany has traditionally seen emphasis placed on the rapid industrialization that characterized the 1850s. Recent research suggests a longer gestation period with a clearer understanding of the importance of the 1840s to economic growth, principally through the Saxon textile industry and the railways. It is now believed that the German economy grew at something like 2.5 per cent a year in the period 1850–73. Railways, coal, iron and textiles were at the forefront and the proportion of the population occupied in factories grew from 4 per cent in 1850 to 10 per cent in 1873. In Prussia, coal production increased eightfold between 1849 and 1875, with even more pronounced growth in raw iron and steel. During the 1860s major new chemical companies such as Bayer and BASF were founded. The following extract indicates the innovative outlook of Carl Friedrich Benz. Benz (1844–1929), an engineer from Karlsruhe, was a pioneer in automobile construction. In 1885, he built the first three-wheeled carriage propelled by a combustion engine. In this excerpt from his memoirs, the co-founder of the Daimler-Benz Corporation recalls how his experience with a rudimentary bicycle in 1867 spurred his ambition to design a comfortable, self-propelled vehicle.

**SOURCE A**

CARL FRIEDRICH BENZ, *A NEW BICYCLE* (1867).

It was 1867. One day a friend of mine, printing-house owner Walter, paid me a visit. He had just returned from a journey to Stuttgart. There he had seen the elegant racing machine [i.e., bicycle] and – because he was not so steady on his feet – would not rest until he owned it. But, alas, it was easier to buy the machine than to ride the heavy contraption. During almost all of his attempts, riding degenerated into falling. Therefore, he was quickly fed up with this odd sport and looked for a new buyer. Since he knew about my 'quirks,' he must have sensed the aficionado in me. I inspected the curious thing and was immediately taken with it. Actually, it had little in common with today's bicycle except, of course, the two wheels. These were made of wood and held together with iron hoops. In a very primitive set-up, the saddle was mounted on an elongated spring between the front and back wheels. The front wheel, with a diameter of about 80 cm, was slightly bigger than the back wheel and was powered by pedal cranks, which were directly attached to it.

After as little as 14 days of the most demanding trials, I accomplished what my friend had never learned – mastery of the bike. Yet it was by no means a small effort to keep my balance on Mannheim's bumpy cobblestones. But the gamboling workhorse had to obey; yes, I even expected it – or, I should say, myself – to repeatedly tackle the ambitious task of covering long distances in the countryside (e.g. Mannheim to Pforzheim).

Whenever I stopped off at some inn and leaned my heavyweight bike against a corner – I have never in my life passed up a good inn – many curious folk, adults and children, gathered around the large, awkward machine. And no one knew whether they'd rather make fun of the heavy vehicle and its badly sprung saddle or admire the skillful balancing of the 'trick rider on only two wheels'.

Source: Carl Friedrich Benz, *Lebensfahrt eines deutschen Erfinders. Erinnerungen eines Achtzigjährigen* (1925).

Further evidence of the pace of technological development is shown in this extract from a letter written by the inventor, Werner von Siemens, in May 1881, in which he describes the opening of the first electric tramway in Berlin.

**SOURCE B**

WERNER VON SIEMENS, LETTER OF 12 MAY, 1881 TO PROFESSOR WIEDEMANN OF LEIPZIG

Today the small electric trolley in Lichterfelde was officially tested and approved at last. The only problem was, and still is, that the speed of the trolley cars has to be reduced in keeping with the regulations. The inspectors would only permit 20 km/h, whereas the cars, fully loaded with 20 passengers, reached 30 to 40 km/h even uphill! However, I think that people will get accustomed to the higher speed!

Source: Conrad Matschoß, (ed.) *Werner von Siemens. Ein kurzgefaßtes Lebensbild nebst einer Auswahl seiner Briefe* (1916).

In construction, more than a million new buildings were erected in the period from 1852 to 1867 and in the traditional German cities ancient walls were taken down with new buildings in their place. The rise of the urban population led to a corresponding growth in domestic-related industries such as furniture, household goods and kitchen items. Huge corn mills and the specialized infrastructure of the brewing industry also developed rapidly, carrying with them related items such as sugar production.

In contrast, the Austrian economy was encumbered by extensive areas of economically limited agricultural regions.

## national symbolism

There was a limited emphasis upon national values or symbols in the new empire, although there was some significance in the widely held commemoration of the Battle of Sedan, the military victory over France, although this waned somewhat after 1890. An official national anthem was not introduced until 1922. The colours selected for the national flag were black, red and white – effectively a compromise between Prussian and German symbols.

## the railways

Whilst Bismarck may at this stage have been uncertain as to the real prowess of the Prussian army, he was confident that the technological strength of

Prussia would provide significant advantages. Rapidly developing railroad and telegraph companies and improvements in roads and turnpikes stimulated by the customs union or Zollverein of 1834 all strengthened Prussia's position. In 1845 there had been approximately 3,280 km of track in Germany. By 1860 the figure had increased to 11,633. Between 1850 and 1875 around 25 per cent of all state investment went into the railway industry, so that the vast expanse of Prussia became manageable for trade and personal travel. As Eric Wilmot puts it: 'the railways acted as a binding agent, bringing together the scattered territories of Germany. Prussian military chiefs were quick to see their potential for the rapid mobilization of troops and equipment. As a result the railways were constructed to a strategic plan determined by the needs of the army.'[5]

## progressive economic legislation

With the enthusiastic support of the National Liberals, the largest party in the Reichstag and the Free Conservatives, a flurry of progressive legislation was passed by the Reichstag during the first decade of unification. A uniform coinage and currency was created and in 1873 Germany adopted the gold standard. 1875 saw the creation of the Reichsbank and in 1879 an imperial court of appeal was established, underpinned by modernizing reforms to the legal system.

## the development of an urban society

Hagen Schulze offers this summary of the rapidly changing German society: 'Before the backdrop of its economic triumphs, Germany took the final steps in its transformation from an agrarian to an industrialized nation. Across the landscape that fifty years earlier had been dotted with farming villages and sleepy provincial towns there now sprawled giant industrial tracts and acres of new housing.'[6]

The extract that follows reveals that concerns about the environmental impact of the industrialization process were present in the nineteenth century as well as in the modern epoch.

**SOURCE A**

PETITION BY THE CITIZENS OF ULM, OCTOBER 1862.

Recently, the burning of pit coal, especially Mießbach coal, in larger enterprises here, such as beer breweries, malt kilns, and tobacco factories, has gotten so far out of hand that some domiciles are virtually surrounded on all sides by such installations. For example, in the surroundings of the co-signers Teichmann and Baur there are no fewer than six of these fires, namely Winkler's malt kiln toward the east, the beer breweries Hohe Schule and Breite, the tobacco factory of the Bürglen brothers, and the breweries Pflug and Löwen toward the south and west. During strong winds or when fog compresses the smoke, phenomena that are known to be only too common in this town, the houses in proximity to such fire-installations end up floating in a sea of smoke. Not only does this cut off the inflow of fresh air entirely, but because Mießbach coal contains a lot of sulfur, a pestilential stench spreads, which penetrates all openings, makes it unbearable to remain even inside the houses, and is indeed harmful to health. Moreover, the smoke and fumes that rise from the chimneys carry very fine particles of ash and soot, which settle on the wallpaper in rooms and soil curtains and furniture. But if the wind is unfavorable, it is utterly impossible to remain in courtyards and gardens. Now, we are well aware that neighbors must tolerate a good deal from one another. On the other hand, though, it must just as surely be affirmed that everything, including the right to the indulgence of others, must have its limits. If one person has the right to dispose freely over his property, the other person has the right to demand that he will not be impeded in the use of his own property. If one person can lay claim to his activities for his purposes, the other person rightfully demands the possibility of being able to live alongside him a life that is in keeping with the needs of his well-being.

*Source*: Franz-Josef Brüggemeier and Michael Toyka-Seid (eds), *Industrie-Natur. Lesebuch zur Geschichte der Umwelt im 19. Jahrhundert* (1995).

In 1850 only six German cities had a population exceeding 100,000. By 1870 this number had reached eleven. Rapidly developing cities such as Cologne, Dresden and Leipzig joined more established centres such as Berlin, Hamburg and Munich. The extract that follows reveals that the impact of urbanization after 1870 was even felt in the relatively parochial circumstances of village life: in this example, a settlement near Lübeck in northern Germany.

**SOURCE B**

Urbanization of village life near Lübeck after 1870.

Soon after the Franco-German War and the political unification of the German states, a change set in. At first, the change was barely noticeable, because the substance of what had grown slowly over centuries was robust. In the first decade after the war, things did not look much different in the city and the village. But then the new tendencies caught on all the more rapidly and thoroughly. Each year brought further changes, and soon nobody could escape the new circumstances of life. Even in the village one felt the desire to build, something that was characteristic of those years. At first several large factories were built a little further upstream. Initially, they just sat there rather curiously, with their tall brick smokestacks in the middle of cow pastures. It was not long, though, before houses in the style of the factory were built right next to them [the smokestacks], and the green of the meadows disappeared underneath huge piles of coal, rubble, and garbage. Together with the factories came people to the village who had never been seen there before, except in their Sunday best as day-trippers. They were droves of workers – the kind who differ from rural and skilled tradesmen at first sight, because they had no training except for in a few mechanical tasks, because they felt no occupational spirit, because they belonged to that class which was subsequently called Proletarians. Since the journey to the city was a long one, the need soon arose to create dwellings for these workers in the village itself. And because there was nothing suitable there, the first meager apartment houses were put up. Tall, bare, multi-floor buildings stood isolated in the middle of fields. Poor families lived there side by side in squalor, without any comfort; an unkempt, quickly dilapidating backyard adjoined directly. The space between the houses was teeming with children. But they were the children of a new population. The poverty of these people was different from the poverty of the village farmworker; The industrial workers seemed to be degenerate; if they were really poor, it seemed as though foul-smelling poverty was their natural element. The men were not brought up in the tradition of any particular occupation, the women were not housewives and mothers, and the children were little vagabonds who stole fruit from the gardens and trampled on the grain in the fields.

Source: Karl Scheffler, *Der junge Tobias. Eine Jugend und ihre Umwelt* (1927).

Meanwhile, in the economically significant Ruhr, the population of Dortmund, Essen and Bochum increased between four and six times in a single generation. Frankfurt, Hamburg and Bremen were associated with commerce, Kiel with military infrastructure and Bonn and Königsberg with educational developments. The Ruhr, the Saarland, Upper Silesia and Saxony owed the rapidity of their growth to the new industrial processes of the age, but these areas often contained some of the most difficult housing conditions, with exploitative rents, overcrowded houses and unsanitary conditions. These grim circumstances led directly to a growing sense of political awareness and class consciousness among the working class, so that a sense of injustice increasingly prevailed in urban centres. In response, industrialists and mine owners constructed housing 'colonies' partially in an attempt to control the workforce. In the capital, Berlin, 50 per cent of all houses in 1875 had only one heated room. Thousands of Berliners lived five to a room or worse and 10 per cent of the population lived in cellar dwellings. Such conditions meant that sporadic outbreaks of cholera and typhus, as well as more persistent threats such as pneumonia, scarlet fever, diphtheria and tuberculosis, haunted the existence of the urban masses. It was not until the 1870s that public waterworks designed to provide for all began to develop. The deadly nature of the threat to those who lived in the densest housing with the least adequate water and sewerage provision was dramatically underlined in the infamous Hamburg cholera outbreak of 1892, where the poor were those who suffered most. Although life expectancy was gradually improving, the figure for a man born in the 1870s was still only 36.5 and for a woman, 38.5.

The harsh nature of these conditions served to accentuate the contrast between the grim backstreets and dreary apartments inhabited by the working class and the impressive town houses and villas of the rapidly increasing bourgeoisie. From its inception, therefore, the new nation-state was one characterized by class division. At the top of the structure were the landowning aristocracy, followed by the established middle class, consisting of well-educated professionals and civil servants and the burgeoning ranks of the new middle-class entrepreneurs. This section of society provided the bedrock of political support for the German liberal parties. On the next level down were the hardworking craftsmen and artisans whose specialist skills were threatened by the nature of the industrial revolution. Finally came the growing mass ranks of the industrial proletariat, responsible for generating much of the new-found wealth and yet at this stage unable to share its benefits. Their increasing class-consciousness and politicization helped so fuel the development of political parties, movements and newspapers that stood up for the rights of the new working class.

## 2.7 Bismarck's domestic policy

The sheer extent to which Bismarck developed his personal authority has attracted considerable criticism. Heinz Gollwitzer contends that Bismarck concealed his power 'beneath the cloak of monarchical tradition, which he wore as the King's servant and Imperial Chancellor with considerable decorum and skill'.[7]

Hans-Ulrich Wehler states that Bismarck:

> balanced traditional and modern elements in a combination that was typical of Bonapartism. For example, he combined an absolutist-style military policy with state interventionism on behalf of vested interests and underpinned it by plebiscitary approval. Through a policy of war up to 1871 and later, in the 1880s, of social and economic imperialism, he sought to stifle internal problems by diverting attention to the sphere of external affairs. Through it all he lived off an undeniable and heightened charisma derived from his role in the founding of the German Empire.[8]

In the words of one of Bismarck's liberal contemporaries, Ludwig Bamberger: 'One had to have been there to be able to testify to the power this man exerted over all those around him at the height of his influence. There was a time when no one in Germany could say how far his will extended . . . when his power was so rock-solid that everything trembled before him.'[9]

Despite this sustained emphasis on 'charismatic Bonapartism', recent analysis by Katherine Lerman takes a rather different perspective:

> Bismarck's prestige and authority were so great after 1871 that they have tended to obscure many of the theoretical and practical limitations to his position within the political system . . . His dependence on the monarch's confidence, the theoretical sovereignty of the states, the need to secure parliamentary majorities, the collegial nature of the Prussian government, the political independence of the army and the significance of the court as a centre for political intrigue all imposed limits on his freedom of action.[10]

Neither interpretation is easy to dismiss. After all, part of Bismarck's skill was for him to overplay the obstacles he faced and to understate his own influence.

He often confessed that he would be all too willing to leave the political arena, but his conduct when he did finally depart centre stage suggests that this was not necessarily sincere. His working relationship with the Emperor was skilfully depicted as one of loyalty and service, but at the same time the Chancellor knew how much the Emperor depended upon him and his navigational skills through moments of crisis.

## the National Liberals, the 'liberal era' and the issue of tariffs

Beyond the issue of the extent of Bismarck's personal authority is the nature of the policies he pursued. Substantial attention had been paid to the notion of the 'liberal era' of 1871 to 1878, a period when Bismarck relied on support from the National Liberals in the Reichstag and when a series of progressive measures of economic unification seemed to point the way to an accompanying growth in the strength of liberal idealism and parliamentary independence. Unifying developments in the railways, banking, currency and postal systems seemed to illustrate this relationship. In fact, the electoral success of the National Liberals, with their increase from 125 seats in 1871 to 155 seats in 1874, gave Bismarck acute course for concern, as did the corresponding demise in the Conservative representation from 57 to a dismal 22. It seems more accurate, then, to view the period from 1871 to 1878 as a pragmatic stage, when Bismarck necessarily depended on National Liberal support in the Reichstag without losing the desire to reorientate his policy towards conservatism when the opportunity presented itself in the Reichstag.

Therefore, despite the importance and value of the legislation passed during this spell, Bismarck's break with the National Liberals and his accompanying shift to the conservatives cannot be seen as a surprise.

When he moved into the Chancellery Bismarck sought to combine Germany's obvious military strength with a corresponding degree of financial security, stability and protection. He envisaged that the Reich could receive finance from the substantial income generated by the customs and tariffs of the Zollverein. In addition, the states of the empire would make additional contributions to the national coffers, based on the relative size of their population. The reluctance of the states to support these arrangements meant that Bismarck began to explore other avenues that could generate income. These financial aspects could not easily be separated from the overarching influence of the new German constitution. A further consideration was that as a member of the wealthy Junker class, Bismarck had a natural aversion to methods of direct taxation. He therefore prepared to explore proposals such as a potentially lucrative government monopoly on certain spirits, beer and tobacco. However, the Reichstag, with its liberal parliamentary majority, steadfastly blocked Bismarck's suggestions. Increasingly, as the 1870s progressed, Bismarck was motivated by his desire to escape from what he saw as a restrictive dependence on the National Liberals. The corollary of this was to devise a different parliamentary base for his government. Bismarck manipulated the public fear of revolution and ruthlessly used the National Liberals' opposition to his anti-socialist legislation to damage the party's standing. This dual approach aimed at diminishing both the National Liberals and the socialists.

Further conflict over the military budget of 1874, only resolved by Bismarck's threat to call new elections and a compromise that fixed the budget for seven years, served to heighten the sense that his relationship with the National Liberals was of limited duration. However, the real turning point in his relationship with the National Liberals came in 1878 over the issue of trade policy. Initially Bismarck had been willing to back the free-trade policy espoused by the liberals. However, the economic dislocation of 1873 onwards saw Germany's trading rivals erecting domestic trade barriers of their own. Naturally, many of Germany's powerful industrialists and agrarians now began to agitate for the introduction of domestic trade tariffs. This demand for protection gathered particular momentum in 1875–76 and presented Bismarck with an opportunity to exploit support for the protectionist issue, potentially generate much needed income and damage the National Liberals. In the Reichstag elections of 1878 the National Liberals lost 29 seats, with a Conservative increase leading to a new configuration in the parliament that was much more favourable to Bismarck.

The protective tariff law of 1879 was passed in the Reichstag by a majority of the two conservative parties, the majority of the Centre Party and a bloc of right-wing National Liberals. Not least amongst the benefits for Bismarck was the fact that the tariff issue had divided the National Liberals. Those who still supported free trade now moved to the Progressives. The National Liberals who were left behind supported Bismarck's tariffs but crucially he no longer relied upon them. Bismarck had successfully managed his transition to the Conservative camp. The industrialists and the agrarians were happy to back the Chancellor. This was the so-called 'alliance of steel and rye' that would serve Bismarck for the remainder of his period in office, while the National Liberals suffered as a consequence of these developments and from the political fall-out of the assassination attempts upon the Emperor in 1878.

Outlining his aims before the Reichstag in 1881, ten years after he had assumed the Chancellorship, Bismarck was in wistful mood: 'From the beginning of my [ministerial activity], I have often acted hastily and without reflection, but when I had time to reflect I have always asked: what is useful, effective, right for my fatherland, for my dynasty – so long as I was only in Prussia – and now for the German nation?'[11] The campaigns against the Catholics and the Socialists waged by the Chancellor rested on what Bismarck perceived as the threat posed by 'internal enemies' of the state, or Reichsfeinde. Given the negative characteristics of these policies, it is important to note that Bismarck was also directly responsible for pioneering social welfare legislation. Some of the key policies are outlined in Table 2.2.

table **2.2 Bismarck's social welfare legislation**

| 1881 | Emperor Wilhelm I makes a speech announcing Bismarck's social insurance plans |
|------|------------------------------------------------------------------------------|
| 1883 | Introduction of Sickness Insurance |
| 1884 | Introduction of Accident Insurance |
| 1889 | Introduction of Old Age and Disability Insurance |

These policies were not universally acknowledged at the time or subsequently by historians. The contemporary perspective of the socialists was that Bismarck was merely offering 'crumbs from the rich man's table' rather than the kind of wholesale reform advocated by the left. Many historians have assumed that Bismarck can only have had ulterior motives for this social programme.

However, Mary Fulbrook offers a more nuanced picture: 'These welfare measures were not purely the result of Machiavellian considerations or bread-and-circuses policies on the part of Bismarck'.[12] The genuine material distress emanating from the depression of the 1870s accentuated the gulf between rich and poor and aroused concern across a broad spectrum, not just on the left. The growing momentum for reform was supported by both Catholic charities and the Christian Social Movement. Bismarck's drive to suppress the socialist movement was combined with a disconcerting tendency to alleviate some of their social concerns. However, it is essential to recall that Bismarck showed more genuine interest in the construction of prestige projects in the capital city, such as the development of the Kurfurstendamm and the leafy suburb of Berlin-Grunewald than he was able to muster for the plight of those left homeless by the acute housing shortage that faced the inhabitants of the capital city after 1871.

**SOURCE A**

THE DIFFICULT CIRCUMSTANCES OF A LARGE WORKING-CLASS FAMILY LIVING NEAR FRANKFURT AM MAIN IN 1877.

At the time these notes were recorded, the family whose domestic situation we will describe consisted of the following seven persons:

| | | |
|---|---|---|
| Head of the household | 44 years old | } married since 1859 |
| his wife | 38 years old | |
| Joseph, the eldest son | 16 years old | |
| Adam, the second son | 15 years old | |
| Magdalene, the elder daughter | 9 years old | |
| Georg, the third son | 5 years old | |
| Christiane, the younger daughter | 2½ years old | |

Apart from these five surviving children, N. had also had two sons who died before their first birthday, and a third one who had succumbed to spinal tuberculosis at the age of 10. These children would now be 13, 11, and 7 years of age. Before long, N. will become father to a ninth child.

N. can be regarded as more or less typical of the penniless day laborers living in the Feldberg villages [in the Taunus region]. He owns neither fields nor livestock and lives in a little rented house made of clay and half-timbering, which he owned in the past but was forced to sell because of his debts. He still has use of all rooms in the house: a living room (3.88 m long, 3.50 m wide, and 2 m high), which accommodates the common bed for him, his wife, and his youngest daughter, as well as the children's bedstead for the youngest son; and an unheatable, very damp room (3.88 × 3.75 × 2.17 m), in which the two older sons and the eldest daughter sleep in one bed. The cottage also has a small barn used for storing potatoes and a pantry; N. manages to grow some herbs and a bit of lettuce in a small garden measuring about 25 square meters. In the usual fashion, the kitchen is identical to the hallway. There is no separate wash-boiler; water is heated in one of the cooking pots. As the inventory shows, kitchen utensils in general, as well as home furnishings, are very meager. The situation is even worse in terms of clothing. The inventory shows that most of their clothes were already purchased second-hand.

*Source*: Gottlob Schnapper-Arndt, *5 Dorfgemeinden auf dem Hohen Taunus* (1883).

If Bismarck did regard the working class as a docile and biddable group that could be drawn towards the comforting paternalism of the State, he was misguided. Although his reforming legislation may have diminished the more revolutionary elements of Social Democracy, and led some German workers to develop a limited degree of loyalty towards the Empire, he was unable to reverse the progress of the Social Democratic Party at the ballot box. By 1890 there were in excess of a million Social Democratic voters and the party had secured 35 seats in the Reichstag. Bismarck's grasp of the nature and severity of the social problem was limited and the ills of the factories and mills with their long hours, exploitation of children and lax attitudes towards safety were not addressed, ensuring that the radicalization of factory workers would continue.

## SOURCE B

THE CHALLENGES FACED BY A LARGE FAMILY LIVING IN DRESDEN AROUND THE 1880S AND SURVIVING ON AN INCOME OF 1,000 MARKS PER ANNUM.

Starting with our first child, I began depositing money into savings accounts. The child was only two years old, but money was already going into a school account, for I had told myself that if I only started [saving] when the money was needed, it would be too late . . .

And how fortunate that was! We had five children at two-year intervals. When the fifth child was three months old, the third one, a sweet little girl of four and a half, caught diphtheria and unfortunately died, despite the doctor's efforts.

That cost a lot of money, because the second child also fell seriously ill. I went to the savings bank with a heavy heart, but was glad that the money was available, and I withdrew from the contingency fund the amount needed to pay for the doctor, the pharmacy, and the funeral. Three years later, the same misfortune befell us: the youngest child, a three-year-old boy, fell ill. After being sick for one day, the dear boy was taken from us.

In this instance, we also had to take money from the contingency fund. However, I never lost my courage, thank God, to continue saving, even though the money disappeared time and again in such a sad way. I thought that one day it would be used for something good after all. After opening my savings accounts, I immediately saw to it that my husband and I joined the 'Dresden General Health Insurance Company', so that in case of illness the doctor and the pharmacy would be free of charge, and a bit of sick pay would be granted to us as well. This included a death benefit How nice it was when the account statements arrived and all the money was there. – When the children started school, they were admitted to a . . . savings plan. I put away the deposits from the money I had available for board. Each confirmation disbursement was wonderful, like hitting the jackpot. The money was then used for educational purposes; the children were allowed to learn what they felt like.– But the most important thing, however, was that my loved ones were very modest; great was the delight on birthdays when sausages and buns were served for breakfast, along with a bag full of goodies that grandmother bought from the confectioner for 15 pennies.

Source: Augusta Petri-Dresden, 'Aus dreißigjähriger Erfahrung', in Wie wirtschaftet man gut und billig bei einem jährlichen Einkommen von 800–1000 Mark? (1900).

There is an obvious contrast between Source B and Source C, in which a young woman from the German nobility recalls her life in the capital, with grand balls, skating and cycling.

## SOURCE C

LIFESTYLE OF THE NOBILITY.

In those days, a house ball occurred as follows: the leader, a gentleman close to the family, was invited for dinner at some point before the event. The list of dancers was discussed with him at length; and if there was still a need for gentlemen – no shortage of candidates here – he told ardent dancers to call on the following Sunday. The dance sequence and the cotillion were drawn up. The next day, a number of things had to be ordered: the folded dance programs, with pencils attached to the side, which listed the dances on one half and the names on the other, and accessories for the cotillion, ribbons . . .

The first waltz sounded exactly half an hour after the scheduled time, and the leader opened the dance with the host family's daughter. The first waltz, the dance immediately following the festive dinner, and the cotillion were – in ascending order – the three 'most important dances.' If a dancer asked you for one or even more of these dances, this was significant; if you agreed, this constituted encouragement.

During this decade, each family in our circle that gave a ball tried to secure Mr. Neumann as the pianist . . . If I am not mistaken, he received six marks an evening and, of course, was provided with a tasty supper and a bottle of wine.

There were two variations on dinner: either a warm festive banquet was served to guests sitting at long tables by elegant servants, who were borrowed from acquaintances or hired temporarily (waitresses would have seemed petit bourgeois in those days); the dancing gentlemen felt that this arrangement was the more restful and comfortable. More common and fashionable was to have the male dancers serve the ladies sitting with them at small tables from a cold buffet; this was our preferred way. In some good families there was only red and white wine, but most of the time champagne was offered, in our family as well. After supper, the small contingent of fathers attending the ball disappeared, but the mothers remained till the very end. Mothers who danced were only found in the chicest families; in others, the younger mothers were invited for one stationary dance at most. In our circles, however, mothers were necessary. It was only when one mother was ill that a friend's mother took a young girl under her wing.

*Source*: Marie von Bunsen, *Die Welt, in der ich lebte. Erinnerungen 1860–1912* (1959).

## 2.8 the Kulturkampf

In William Carr's memorable phrase, 'The new Reich was hardly in existence before it was shaken to its foundations by a great conflict between Church and State, the so-called Kulturkampf.'[13] It may be the case that this deeply damaging episode in German history was linked to the nature of the foundation of the Reich itself. As Richard Evans observes:

> Religious and racial discrimination were built into the fabric of the Empire from the very beginning. Founded on power and force, the Empire not only stigmatized those whom it conceived to be its internal enemies, it also created a myth of external power and force by the very fact of its existence. The temptation to prioritize these factors in foreign policy in pursuit of this myth was eventually to prove too strong to resist.

Several elements in the development of the Catholic Church from the 1860s onwards can be identified as contributing to the fissures that emerged between Church and State. The Syllabus errorum of 1864 indicated that the pontiff could find no common ground with 'progress, liberalism and recent civilization'. The 'militant' nature of the Catholic movement in Southern Germany in the 1860s, the Pope's assertion of his spiritual powers and a church governed by the ecclesiastical hierarchy and the Vatican Council of 1870 with its pronouncement of the dogma of papal infallibility, all added to the estrangement of the Roman Catholic Church from Bismarck's new creation. This prompted Bismarck to launch a bitter and protracted assault against Catholicism, predominantly in Prussia but throughout the Empire. The work of the leading German authority

Wolfgang Mommsen has depicted the make-up of the new empire as flawed from the beginning. Catholics were excluded and were treated like second-class citizens. Evans notes that 'Mommsen's research has revealed the full extent and scale of Bismarck's cataclysmic struggle with the Catholic Church.'[14]

While the papal pronouncements that predated the creation of the Reich were significant it was political and pragmatic considerations, rather than theological positions, that prompted Bismarck to move from his initial position of strict impartiality towards outright hostility. Crucial to the unfolding of events was the formation of the Centre Party created in 1870 by members of the Prussian lower house. This sought to cater for a minority of almost 40 per cent in the new Protestant state who held the Catholic faith. Drawing from the full range of social classes, from rich to poor, the party's campaign for social reform was led by its dynamic spokesman, the former minister from Hanover, Ludwig Windthorst. Although Bismarck did not come out against the Centre Party on its inception, the party's support for intervention against the entry of Italian troops into Rome in 1870 and their attempts to include religious guarantees in the imperial constitution convinced Bismarck that this was a sectarian party. Put simply, Bismarck came to believe that the Centre Party's allegiance was to Rome rather than Berlin.

Bismarck's considerations also extended to Poland where the Chancellor was aware that the Catholic Church and school authorities were doing what they could to preserve the use of Polish in schools, at the expense of the German promoted by Bismarck. With this in mind, anti-Catholic legislation began to stem from the Prussian Landtag and the Reichstag in 1872–73. In 1872 the Reichstag banned the Jesuit order from creating establishments within Germany and authorized governments to expel Jesuits from the Reich on an individual basis. The pressure was increased with the passage of the May Laws by the Prussian Landtag in 1873. From now on, state authorities had the power of veto over church appointments and all candidates for the priesthood had to spend three years at university before attending seminary school. A year later Prussia introduced civil marriage and stipulated that births, deaths and marriages were to be notified to the civil registration rather than the church authorities. This law was extended to the remaining states in 1875. Under legislation of 1874 the states could restrict the freedom of movement of the clergy and expel offending priests from Germany. As the struggle reached its climax in the middle of the 1870s Germany witnessed the unedifying spectacle of bishops being issued with wanted notices. In 1875, all religious orders in Prussia, apart from nursing orders, were dissolved.

By now, the struggle had divided the country. Bismarck was backed by the National Liberals and Progressives, and enjoyed popular support for his policies in North Germany. He faced opposition from the conservatives and a minority of liberals. In addition to solid Catholic resistance, the Chancellor knew that the emperor had grave concerns about the Kulturkampf while the Empress actually sympathized with the Church. Yet it was within the Church itself that resistance was most emphatic. Pope Pius IX condemned the legislation in 1875 but it was the general perception of a faith-based movement bravely resisting persecution that was most telling. The fortunes of the Centre Party were boosted rather than damaged by the campaign, with a doubling of its vote in 1874 and an increase to 100 seats in the Reichstag elections of 1881. Bismarck's pragmatism told him that he needed to change track. The opportunity to do so came with the death of his old adversary, Pope Pius IX, on 7 February 1878. His replacement, the conciliatory figure of Leo XIII, wanted to reconcile some of the differences between Church and State. Preliminary discussions between the Chancellor and Monsigneur Masella took place at Bad Kissingen in the summer of 1878. Meanwhile, two attempts on the life of the Emperor shifted the emphasis away from the Catholic Church and towards the Socialists. It was now their turn to face the wrath of the Chancellor. David Blackbourn offers a long-term perspective on the impact of the Kulturkampf:

> The Kulturkampf left a powerful legacy among German Catholics, a sense of being branded as pariahs that reinforced the existence of a separate German subculture. Yet, just as the Centre Party came in from the cold, so Catholics also came slowly to accept the new Germany, led by the professional and business classes. . . . For all the continuing strength of local loyalties on the one hand and supranational allegiance to Rome on the other, Catholics in the Empire came to feel more German with the years.[15]

## 2.9 the campaign against socialism

As the upheaval of the Kulturkampf came to an end, a new struggle between the state and an organized section of German society began. The fresh assault, this time against the Social Democratic Party, reached its peak with the passage of the anti-socialist law of 1878. As with the Catholics, the perception of the Socialists from the corridors of power in Berlin was of a group who had chosen to place themselves outside the general sphere of Bismarck's Germany. The formation of the Social Democratic Party in 1875 aroused deep-rooted fears among the ruling classes, who regarded the new group as a 'party of subversion'. It seems clear that Bismarck was genuinely alarmed by the internationalist alliances of the socialist movement, but it is equally true to say that he was also flagrantly opportunistic in stampeding popular opinion against those who failed to support his anti-subversion measures.

Ostensibly, Bismarck's genuine fears seemed to be borne out by two assassination attempts against the Emperor in 1878. On 11 May a 21-year-old plumber named Max Hödel, who had briefly belonged to the socialist party but had subsequently been expelled, made an assassination attempt on the Emperor in which no one was actually hurt. An insight into Bismarck's opportunist thinking is provided from the text of a telegraph sent by him within hours asking: 'Should we not take the opportunity to present an immediate proposal against the socialists and their press?'[16]

A legislative proposal presented to the Reichstag looked hasty and opportunistic and was rejected by 251 votes to 57, with only the Conservatives prepared to support it. On 2 June a second, much more serious attempt was made on Wilhelm's life, raising genuine concerns that the 81-year-old Emperor might not survive. This time the deed was carried out by Karl Nobiling, an eccentric academic who craved attention. Again, Bismarck's political instincts rather than genuine concern for the old man were the first to come to the fore. The Reichstag was dissolved, with Bismarck's keen political antennae telling him that the German public would be alarmed and affronted by the savagery of the attack on the emperor. Bismarck's biographer Lothar Gall provides an interesting alternative to the 'opportunistic' depiction of Bismarck's behaviour. He contends that 'The second assassination attempt found him not in a mood of cool calculation but in an exceptional situation. He saw himself surrounded by mistrust and by political opponents who, he believed, were looking only to outmanoeuvre him once and for all.'[17]

Whatever conclusion is reached as to Bismarck's motivation and state of mind, there is no doubt that the election campaign that followed was saturated with wild propaganda and outright repression. The liberals who had 'failed to protect the emperor' against the 'red assassins' were portrayed as 'unpatriotic' and the outcome in the Reichstag was that the two Conservative parties gained 600,000 votes and 37 seats between them, while the National Liberals lost 130,000 votes and 29 seats, despite the fact that during the election campaign they had moved to support anti-socialist legislation. The anti-socialist bill that Bismarck demanded was passed in the new Reichstag by 221 votes to 149, with the support of the National Liberals and the Conservatives, and in the face of opposition from the Socialists, the Poles and the Progressives. The key elements of the bill were as follows:

- socialist and communist meetings, societies and publications were banned
- the police were given powers to expel socialist agitators
- each state was given the option of declaring a state of siege in the event of socialist disturbances for a period of up to one year

Crucially, however, the bill carried no direct embargo on elections or on freedom of speech in the Reichstag and state assemblies. This meant that the socialists were able to weather the initial storm and ultimately stage an electoral resurgence. Initially, the Socialist vote declined from 493,000 in 1877 to 312,000. Yet by 1884 it had risen to 550,000, with a corresponding rise in Reichstag seats to 24. While Bismarck's legislation undoubtedly caused severe distress amongst the Socialists it also inadvertently caused their ranks to pull together in an almost spiritual renewal of their comradely faith. The real impact of more than a decade of harassment and persecution was to strengthen the siege mentality of the German working class. Despite the early evidence that the Socialist electoral support had been effectively repressed, by 1884 the radicalized and emboldened party had regained its confidence and continued to rise in the Reichstag until it exceeded one million votes in 1890. The party printing presses were more active than ever, but acted with relative impunity from outside Germany's borders. Party congresses could be held overseas while within Germany the party operated covertly but effectively. These processes merely heightened party discipline, loyalty and camaraderie. The socialists entered the new century as a tightly structured, highly organized party of the masses, leaving Bismarck's objective of bringing the working class to order in tatters and making the integration of the working class seem highly unlikely.

This perspective is underlined in this extract from a police report of 1889 describing the conflict in the workplace caused by the issue of strikebreaking, in this instance, in an iron foundry in Hamburg.

**SOURCE**

On the evening of September 14, with the words, 'You deserve to be thrown into the Elbe [River],' the molder August Arnold Dahl supposedly attempted to coerce the molder Grüttner to stop his recently commenced work at the iron foundry on Steinwärder. Dahl maintains that he told Grüttner that, as a young person, he should be ashamed of himself first for accepting assistance for half a year from colleagues who had been forced out, and then signing on after all, even though many older colleagues, who were married and in some instances had many children, were still unemployed. Besides, Grüttner was apparently so drunk that evening that it seems unlikely that he could have even the slightest recollection of the exchange. The witness Grüttner insists under oath that Dahl did use these words. The prosecutor deems Dahl guilty of attempted coercion on account of the witnesses' testimony and requests a sentence of two months imprisonment based on extenuating circumstances. The defense counsel, Dr. R. Gieschen, pleads for an acquittal, because there was certainly no attempted coercion. The court pronounces a verdict of guilty and sentences the accused to one month in prison.

*Source: Hamburger Echo* (20 December 1889).

## 2.10 the deaths of Emperor Wilhelm I and Crown Prince Friedrich III: the succession of Wilhelm II

Although his monumental reign was drawing to its natural conclusion as he entered his 91st year Wilhelm I clung tenaciously to his office and to life itself, but when he developed pneumonia and a kidney infection at the start of March 1888 it was clear that he did not have long to live. On 8 March he discussed matters of state with Bismarck for the last time. The next day a tearful and red-eyed chancellor formally announced Wilhelm's passing to the Bundesrat and the Reichstag. While Wilhelm's personal relationship with the Chancellor had been tempestuous, there can be no doubt as to the closeness of the ties between them. At the royal mausoleum in Charlottenburg Bismarck left roses on the coffin and for his own epitaph on the tomb he chose the words 'a faithful German servant of Kaiser Wilhelm I'. It seems that successive generations of historians have been happy to confine Emperor Wilhelm to the margins of their textbooks. A colourless character, easily outwitted by his deft Chancellor, he has been portrayed as economical, moderate and unpretentious. However, even the negative accounts of Wilhelm I acknowledge the continuity and stability he had provided. However, his death gave way to a period of rapid change. His son Friedrich III, who succeeded him, died in June of the same year, of cancer of the throat. He was in turn succeeded by his son, Wilhelm II. Stability, it would soon transpire, was not a characteristic that seemed to have been passed through the Hohenzollern DNA, from grandfather to grandson.

## 2.11 the resignation of Bismarck

Bismarck's official departure from the German political stage was marked by a formal ceremony at the Lehrter railway station in Berlin on 29 March 1890. With a military band playing, imperial flags waving and before an audience of senior politicians and army generals, the slightly stooped man of 75 left the scene after what he acidly described as a 'first-class funeral'. He departed Berlin and went into reluctant retirement where, from the vantage point of a converted hotel with its extensive wine cellar, the embittered old man would look on with some scepticism as those he had left behind attempted to fill the power vacuum his dramatic departure had created. Although in formal terms it was Kaiser Wilhelm I (1871–88) who had been proclaimed Emperor with all the trappings of a traditional monarch, it had been his servant, Bismarck, who actually made most of the important decisions. The charismatic Chancellor bestrode European politics and assumed a degree of internal power far beyond the paper limits of the constitution. Such was his power that some historians have spoken of a 'chancellor dictatorship'. Skilfully combining the posts of German Chancellor and Prussian Prime Minister, Bismarck enjoyed authority far beyond the theoretical limits of the constitution. Behind a façade of monarchical tradition the charismatic and wilful chancellor accumulated huge authority.

What was the lasting significance of his departure? In the words of the American academic Gordon Craig:

> When the great star fell, many Germans had a chilling presentiment that their country had suffered an irreparable loss and that it would not soon again be governed with such intelligence and assurance. Time was to prove them correct, although it must be said that the mistakes of Bismarck's successors might have been less disastrous if he had not contributed to the difficulties of their task by leaving them an anachronistic political system in which he had sought – in the case of liberalism with success – to stifle every progressive tendency.[18]

With Bismarck ushered from the stage a new era dawned. In the words of John Rohl:

> Kaiser Wilhelm II set out to 'charismatise' the Hohenzollern monarchy. By his ubiquity, his innumerable speeches, parades, swearing in of recruits, 'nailing' of flags and unveiling of monuments, Wilhelm II wanted to turn the Imperial throne into the 'bulwark of the Reich idea', not least in order to take the wind out of the sails of the growing Bismarckian movement.[19]

The new Kaiser did not conceal his unease with the men who had occupied pivotal positions in the Prussian government and imperial administration in Berlin, during the Bismarck era. In January 1890 he told the Grand Duke of Baden: 'These ministers are not my ministers, of course they are the ministers of Prince Bismarck.' Despite this he must have been pleasantly surprised when the only major figure to follow the old Chancellor out of the door was the Foreign Secretary, Bismarck's own son, Herbert von Bismarck.

James Retallack offers this helpful analysis of the transition from the Bismarckian period to the Wilhelmine era:

> Wilhelm's dismissal of Bismarck from the Reich chancellory on 20 March 1890 was correctly seen at the time as a sea change in German politics. To many it was a presumptuous and premature act, undertaken by a young ruler who had been on the throne less than two years. How would the empire operate under anyone who lacked Bismarck's will of iron? This feeling of unease upon 'dropping the pilot' was understandable and incidentally, one that Bismarck deliberately cultivated. But Wilhelm appeared determined to be a 'social Kaiser' who would alleviate the suffering of his most underprivileged subjects.[20]

## 2.12 an assessment of Bismarck

SOURCE A

His constitutional arrangements for the Empire amounted to a 'system of evaded decisions' in which the lines of responsibility were left fatally unclear, and proper arrangements for the running of the Reich were never made. He left a bourgeoisie unused to political responsibility, an upper class reluctant to modernize, a lower middle class hostile to liberal constitutional values, and a proletariat alienated from the mainstream of society and politics.

*Source*: Richard J. Evans, *Rereading German History: 1800–1996* (1997).

SOURCE B

That he was a great man is undeniable. He towered above contemporaries. . . . No other German exerted so profound an influence on German history in the nineteenth century. . . .Like all great men he had serious defects and limitations.

He was petty, vindictive and ruthless in his treatment of those who stood in his way. . . . His most serious limitation was that he was cast in the mould of the eighteenth century. To him government was essentially a function of rulers and officials, not of peoples.

*Source*: William Carr, *A History of Germany, 1815–1990* (1991).

## SOURCE C

Bismarck left behind him as his political heritage a nation without any political education, far below the level which, in this respect, it had reached twenty years earlier. Above all, he left behind a nation without any political will, accustomed to allow the great statesmen at its head to look after its policy for it. Moreover, as a consequence of his misuse of the monarchy as a cover for his own interests in the struggle of political parties, he left a nation accustomed to submit, under the label of constitutional monarchy, to anything which was decided for it, without criticising the political qualifications of those who now occupied Bismarck's empty place and who with incredible ingeniousness now took the reins of power into their own hands.

*Source*: Max Weber, 1917, quoted in William Carr, *A History of Germany, 1815–1990* (1991).

## SOURCE D

For some years it is the domestic calculations and effects of Bismarck's policy that have dominated historical debate. Neutralizing the liberal opposition, ending the constitutional conflict, preserving the substance of the Prussian political system – these have been seen as crucial to the course of unification. The strong version of this argument presents Bismarck as a Bonapartist. That means, he was willing to break with monarchical legitimacy, balance himself above the social classes, wield the weapon of mass suffrage on behalf of conservative authority, and use foreign policy for domestic purposes.

*Source*: David Blackbourn, *History of Germany 1780–1918: The Long Nineteenth Century* (1997).

## ESSAY QUESTION

To what extent would you agree that Bismarck was the 'flawed giant' of German history in the nineteenth century?

# foreign policy, 1871–90

## 3.1 Bismarck's foreign policy: an introduction

From 1871 to 1890 German foreign policy fell under the personal control of Bismarck. His unquestionable diplomatic abilities and his proud track record of military victories in the period of unification meant that, as Reich chancellor and Prussian foreign minister, there were no significant constraints on the exercise of his political will. If the notion that Bismarck controlled German foreign policy has broad acceptance, what can be said about his primary objectives? From 1871 Bismarck's most pressing objective in foreign policy was to preserve and defend the new Reich and to guard against any attempts by the other European powers to undo his creation. It may be that Bismarck's much-vaunted 'alliance system' did not come about as quickly or as comprehensively as has often been assumed. Rather it could be seen as something that gradually became more complex, evolving from his initial tactic of moving to isolate France, whose unshakeable hostility towards Germany after the war of 1870–71 he now considered to be a permanent feature in the international arena. However, it was not until the 1870s drew to a close that Bismarck fully recognized the value of a stable international framework in which Berlin could enjoy good relations with all the major powers, with the exception of France. It was only in the 1880s that the treaties he made with the other European countries can be said to have appeared as systematic, and even then the system bore the signs of improvization rather than permanence and therefore may be more accurately seen as a series of stopgaps rather than a planned, cohesive and permanent system of alliances. While the aggrandizement of Prussia brought continuity between Bismarck and his predecessors, the brutal cynicism, the willingness to go for broke at moments of crisis, his tactical audacity and the ability to see further than the next move on the complex diplomatic chessboard gave the new Minister–President a very distinctive character from those who had served before him.

## 3.2 Franco-German rivalry

For all Bismarck's skill as a diplomatic strategist it soon became clear that one of the central presumptions upon which he founded his foreign policy was fundamentally misplaced. The victory at Sedan and the crushing terms of the peace treaty seemed to indicate that France would remain in a subdued state for a long time to come. Yet the speed of the French recovery astounded both friends and foe alike. As Paul Kennedy points out:

> France was immensely rich in terms of mobile capital, which could be (and systematically was) applied to serve the interests of the country's diplomacy and strategy. The most impressive sign of this had been the very rapid paying off of the German indemnity of 1871, which, in Bismarck's erroneous calculation, was supposed to cripple France's strength for many years to come.[1]

The economic historian T. Kemp summarizes French economic progress as follows:

> This period saw a great development in banking and financial institutions participating in industrial investment and in foreign lending. The iron and steel industry was established on modern lines and great new plants were built, especially on the Lorraine ore field. On the coalfields of northern France the familiar ugly landscape of an industrial society took place. Important strides were made in engineering and the newer industries. France had its notable entrepreneurs and innovators who won a leading place in the late nineteenth and early twentieth century in steel, engineering, motor cars and aircraft. Firms like Schneider, Peugeot, Michelin and Renault were in the vanguard.[2]

France's economic revival was not lost on the other powers. From the east, Russia was able to recognize that the resurgent French would make a formidable ally. In July 1891 a French military delegation visited the Russian naval base at Kronstadt and French loans to Russia were stepped up. Meanwhile, the Tsar conferred Russia's highest decoration on the French President. The attraction between Russia and France was assisted further by Germany's unwillingness to renew the Reinsurance Treaty with Russia in the wake of Bismarck's resignation in 1890. In August 1891 the French exchanged letters with Russia in which they agreed to act together 'on all questions likely to upset the general peace'. This Franco-Russian entente was extended a year later with the secret military convention of August 1892. The full commitment of an Alliance was now virtually inevitable. James Joll highlights the logic behind such an agreement:

> A rapprochement between France and Russia, in spite of the differences of political system between the Third Republic and the tsarist autocracy had been a logical consequence of the new balance of power established

in 1870. As Karl Marx had put it at the time of the Franco-Prussian War, 'If Alsace and Lorraine are taken, then France will later make war on Germany in conjunction with Russia.' The annexation by Germany of the two French provinces meant that there could be in the long run no reconciliation between France and Germany; and although at some

table **3.1 a comparison of the economic and social resources of Germany and France, 1850–1914**

|  | Germany | France |
|---|---|---|
| **Population** |  |  |
| 1851 | 33.4 | 35.8 |
| 1881 | 45.2 | 37.4 |
| 1891 | 49.0 | 38.3 |
| 1901 | 56.4 |  |
| 1913 | 66.0 | 39.7 |
| population of largest city | Berlin<br>1850 – 419,000<br>1900 – 1,889,000 | Paris<br>1850 – 1,053,000<br>1900 – 2,714,000 |
| **agricultural output** |  |  |
| output of grain crops<br>(annual averages, million quintals) | 1885–94 – 304.6<br>1905–14 – 457.9 | 1885–94 – 160.1<br>1905–14 – 171.9 |
| output of wheat<br>(thousands of metric tons) | 1913 – 5,094 | 1913 – 8,690 |
| **industry** |  |  |
| output of coal and lignite<br>(annual average for quinquennia,<br>million metric tons) | 1890–94 – 94<br>1895–99 – 120<br>1900–04 – 157<br>1905–09 – 201<br>1910–14 – 247 | 1890–94 – 26<br>1895–99 – 31<br>1900–04 – 33<br>1905–09 – 36<br>1910–14 – 40 |
| pig iron (annual production,<br>million metric tons) | 1880 – 2.7<br>1910 – 14.8 | 1880 – 1.7<br>1910 – 4.0 |
| output of steel (million metric tons) | 1890 – 2.2<br>1900 – 6.6<br>1910 – 13.7 | 1890 – 0.7<br>1900 – 1.6<br>1910 – 3.4 |
| motor vehicles, commercial<br>and private (thousands) | 1910 – 10 | 1910 – 38 |
| railway mileage (km) | 1880 – 33,838<br>1900 – 51,678<br>1913 – 63,378 | 1880 – 23,089<br>1900 – 38,109<br>1913 – 40,770 |
| merchant ships registered by<br>country (thousand tons) | 1880 – 1,104<br>1910 – 2,890 | 1880 – 920<br>1910 – 1,452 |
| value of external trade<br>(millions of francs) | 1870 – 5,669<br>1900 – 8,807 | 1870 – 5,741<br>1900 – 10,380 |

moments the French government and public temporarily forgot about the lost provinces, the hope of recovering them was always likely to ensure that in a European war France would join the side opposed to Germany.[3]

In January 1893 the Franco-Russian Alliance was agreed and in December 1893 the Franco-Russian military convention came into force. Although the terms of these agreements were kept secret their existence was widely known. It was also apparent that the Dual Alliance of France and Russia would, in the event of war, be pushed into confrontation with the Triple Alliance of Germany, Austria-Hungary and Italy. Britain's position remained unclear, and it is arguably the central achievement of French diplomacy that by 1904 the position had changed to the extent that France and Britain had become much closer, whereas Germany's isolation had been heightened.

## 3.3 the Three Emperors' League, 1873

France's dramatic and surprising resurgence in the wake of her defeat in 1871 made Germany's relations with her neighbours to the east even more important. Bismarck's analysis of relations with his eastern neighbours in the aftermath of the Franco-Prussian war was clear. He wanted to restore the old understanding with both Austria-Hungary and Russia and heighten the isolation of France. In 1872 the emperors of these three great powers held initial meetings and discussions. This was not without difficulty. The growing tension between Austria and Russia dominated the proceedings. While there was plenty of rhetoric about the three emperors defending monarchy against republicanism and socialism in a 'Holy Alliance' there was little more concrete to emerge. The Austrian Emperor Franz Joseph would not put his name to the military convention agreed to by the Tsar and Wilhelm I. The loose agreement that emerged from these talks was known as the *Dreikaiserbund*, or Three Emperors' League. The emperors agreed to consult on matters of common interest or in the event of a third power disturbing the European peace. Beyond this, there was little to suggest that the ties between the three emperors could not be easily undone. The first test would come in 1875.

## 3.4 theisolation of France, French recovery and the 'War-in-Sight' crisis

The combination of crushing military defeat and humiliating peace treaty served to heighten the assumption that France, as a defeated power, had been permanently humbled. This was soon dispelled. France made an economic recovery which startled her friends and disturbed her rivals. The final payment was made in September 1873. How long would it be before the opportunity for revenge presented itself?

## the 'War-in-Sight' Crisis, 1875

By 1875 it seemed clear that events at home and abroad had not followed the path that Bismarck had hoped for. Domestically, the Kulturkampf was causing tremendous upheaval and on the international scene, the recovery of France caused Bismarck great concern. He was able to conjure up the notion of a conspiratorial agreement against the new nation-state stirred by the French and utilizing the resistance of the German Catholics. While he ruled out the notion of a pre-emptive strike against France he believed it might be possible to intimidate the French and make them reconsider their rearmament strategy. To that end, an embargo was placed on the export of horses to France – in the conventions of nineteenth century warfare, this was normally a prelude to mobilization. Then, on 5 April 1875 the *Kölnische Zeitung* carried a piece entitled 'New Alliances' followed three days later by the publication in the highly influential newspaper the *Berliner Post* of a sensational article asking 'Is war in sight?', which offered the conclusion that war was indeed likely, given the increases in the size of the French armed forces. Whether Bismarck directly inspired these articles remains in doubt, but the press certainly was in line with his policy towards France.

Then, through diplomatic channels, it was hinted to France that there were some in the German corridors of power who were talking of a preventative strike against the French. All of this was intended to frighten and isolate the French but in fact the reverse happened. When the French looked to Britain and Russia for protection and positive assurances, they were forthcoming. A change of government in Britain in 1874 contributed to the strength of feeling that Bismarck, in the private words of Disraeli, 'must be bridled', leaving Bismarck in no doubt that the international latitude he had enjoyed in the past could not be taken for granted. Bismarck was left with no choice but to assure the Russians that rumours of a strike against France could be discounted. The Chancellor had been put very firmly in his place. The significance of the crisis was that Bismarck took the lesson from the episode that future wars would bring about the intervention of Russia and Britain, in contrast to the position in the 1860s. On a personal note, Bismarck found the whole episode humiliating and irritating but it sharpened his sense that he must, in Gall's words:

> not only take into account the peculiarly exposed position of the Reich at the heart of Europe . . . he must also make increased allowance for the mistrust and the fears that the emergence of this new power in central Europe had aroused in many quarters. The policy of the Reich, Bismarck now realized, must henceforth proceed with the utmost

caution. It must try to avoid anything that might even remotely suggest to the most hyper-critical observer intentions of an aggressive nature.[4]

## 3.5 the Near-Eastern crisis, 1877–78

The 'War-in-Sight' crisis revealed the fragility of the Three Emperors' League and brought home to Bismarck in the sharpest sense the need to avoid a war on two fronts. It underlined the fact that the international situation could easily leave Germany badly exposed. The danger that Bismarck now appreciated so keenly presented itself in a conflict he had hoped to avoid, in the Balkans and between two countries he had hoped to keep in step with, Austria and Russia. Between 1875 and 1877 the Sultan of Turkey, whose empire embraced this combustible area of Europe, faced revolts in Bosnia-Herzegovina, Bulgaria, Serbia and Montenegro. Initially the League held firm when the people of Bosnia-Herzegovina revolted in 1875 and Austria-Hungary and Russia stood together to impose reforms on the Turkish Sultan of the Ottoman Empire. However, the conversion of the Russian Tsar in November 1876 to the cause of Pan-Slavism in the wake of harsh Turkish reprisals in the region did not bode well for the future of the Emperors' League. From now on Russia would defend the Slav peoples even if this went against the wishes of Austria. Austria feared that Slav nationalism could damage her own multinational empire and was apprehensive about Russian intervention in the region.

Here was Bismarck's dilemma – Russia and Austria-Hungary were clearly bound to disagree in the future over the Balkans – but both would look to Germany for support. To his credit, Bismarck skilfully manoeuvred through the next few months, assuring both sides that he wanted to see a balance between the two states and victory for neither. In January 1877 Russia came to terms with Austria-Hungary in return for a Russian assurance that no large Slav state would be created in the Balkans. Meanwhile Austria-Hungary promised benevolent neutrality in the event of a Russian attack on Turkey. Russia declared war on Turkey in April 1877 but the conflict lasted longer than they had expected and it was not until the spring of 1878 that the Russians imposed the stringent terms of the San Stefano Treaty on the Turks. The proposed treaty caused widespread unease among the powers, particularly for the proposal of the creation of a large Bulgaria, seen as a potential Russian satellite, on the strategically important Aegean Sea. Britain dispatched the fleet to the straits, Austria expressed her feelings over Russia's breach of the agreement over Bulgaria. War seemed inevitable, but Russia's experience in Turkey had convinced her that a further conflict with Austria and Britain was out of the question. Therefore an international congress was called for Berlin in June 1878.

## 3.6 the Congress of Berlin, 1878

Russia had been militarily stretched in Turkey and this was reflected in her willingness to accept Bismarck's offer of his services as an 'honest broker' following Bismarck's speech to the Reichstag on 19 February 1878 in which he offered to mediate in the mounting crisis. The powers came to the conference table at an international Congress in Berlin, held from 13 June to 13 July 1878. Bismarck was convening one of the great diplomatic occasions of the nineteenth century, a glittering, full-dress meeting of the European powers. The status and powerful symbolism of Bismarck's central position was not lost on the German public or on the celebrated historian Otto Pflanze, who commented that the choice of Berlin was 'symbolic of the position to which Bismarck's diplomacy had elevated the Prussian capital in merely fifteen years'.[5] Interestingly, it is now clear that Bismarck's preferred location was Paris and that his instinct was to downplay his own role in the event for tactical reasons. Once the conference began, Bismarck played an energetic, positive role, particularly in resolving the issue of Bulgaria. The gulf in stature between Bismark and his European counterparts was now apparent. Although Bismarck could not command affection from his rivals, his diplomatic skills, linguistic fluency and willingness to take an impartial line made him the dominant figure and natural host, even though he was not as uninterested in the Balkans as he implied. Despite his abilities he was unable to satisfy all the expectations of his guests in Berlin. Most significantly, Russia departed in disgruntled spirits feeling that the corrections to the terms of the Treaty of San Stefano, seemed to favour Britain, its main imperialist rival, who gained Cyprus, and Austria, its main opponent in the Balkans. The Russians felt the reserve they had displayed in 1870–1871, had not been rewarded in 1877–1878.

## 3.7 the alliance with Austria-Hungary, 1879

Although the Congress of Berlin meant that war was avoided in the first instance and the revision of the San Stefano Treaty was accepted by all of the European powers with the exception of Russia, the reality was that the Three Emperors' League was unable to withstand the fallout caused by the Near Eastern crisis. Russian frustration at the turn of events since the war with Turkey and dissatisfaction over the outcome of the Congress of Berlin were reflected in an outbreak of anti-German sentiment in the Pan-Slav press. The Tsar's personal antipathy towards Bismarck, whom he referred to privately as a 'frightful scoundrel', added to the sense that relations between Germany and Russia had reached a crossroads. From the German perspective, Bismarck seemed willing and able to heighten the growing sense of ill-feeling between the two powers. In January 1879 Bismarck highlighted in the Reichstag the aspects of the Tariff Bill which were most damaging to Russia. A ban on the import of 'diseased' Russian cattle further damaged relations.

The corollary of this was to strengthen relations with Austria, and Bismarck wasted no time in meeting the Austrian Foreign Minister Andrássy to discuss a formal alliance with Austria-Hungary. The outcome was a defensive alliance which committed Germany and Austria-Hungary to resist Russian aggression. However, if Germany or Austria-Hungary went to war with a third party, the other partner would remain neutral unless Russia intervened. In terms of two likely scenarios, Germany was bound to help Austria-Hungary in the event of a Russian attack, but Austria-Hungary was not obliged to support Germany against France. Although the alliance was initially intended to last for five years, the option of renewing the agreement was repeatedly taken up so that the alliance was in existence until 1918. For Austria, the diplomatic isolation she had endured since the Crimean War was over. Although Bismarck presented this alliance as a long-standing aim since the war of 1866, it is more likely that he took the pragmatic view that the best way to preserve the delicate balance in the Balkans was to be firm towards Russia at this point, without in any sense committing Germany to a final choice between Austria and Russia. In fact, Bismarck's long-standing objective was to secure ongoing agreement between Germany, Russia and Austria-Hungary in the Balkans and beyond.

## 3.8 the Three Emperors' Alliance, 1881

Bismarck understood the importance of repairing the breach with Russia, and as this political instinct coincided with Russian anxiety at her diplomatic isolation, it did not take long for the two powers to come back together. However, while the Russians were eager to find a settlement this was not so forthcoming from the Austrians. The new foreign minister in Vienna, Haymerle, felt that an alliance with Britain was a more attractive proposition. However, a change in the British political configuration saw Gladstone enter Downing Street and his anti-Austrian instincts prevailed. The outcome, much to Bismarck's satisfaction, was the signing of the Three Emperors' Alliance concluded in June 1881. Whereas the original *Dreikaiserbund* of 1873 was a relatively flimsy commitment to the monarchical principle, the new arrangement, a secret treaty of three years' duration, was much more precise. The key terms can be summarized as follows:

- if either Germany, Russia or Austria went to war with another power, the others would remain neutral
- the three signatories would keep the Black Sea closed to foreign warships
- no territorial changes in the Balkans would be made without prior and mutual agreement
- the Balkans would be divided into 'spheres of influence', with Russian interests paramount in the eastern section and Austria prevailing in the western region

- Russia accepted Austria's right to annex Bosnia-Herzegovina
- Austria acknowledged Russian ambitions to re-create a large Bulgarian state

While the alliance pleased the Russians and confirmed Bismarck's prediction that 'the Russians would come to us once we had pinned the Austrians down', it had its limitations. Although Bismarck had satisfied the Austrians in 1879 and the Russians in 1881 he could not maintain this balance indefinitely and the fundamental antagonism between them could not be spirited away by diplomatic sleight of hand. When the rivalry between Austria and Russia was reignited as the 1880s drew to a close, the Three Emperors' Alliance went the way of the Three Emperors' League – into the past.

The central weakness of the alliance, then, was the question of its durability. Although it was renewed in 1884, the flaring up of the Balkans question in a new dispute over Bulgaria meant that Bismarck's central task of managing the complex alliance system would remain as challenging as ever.

## 3.9 Germany's colonies in Africa

Until 1884 Bismarck's vision for the development of German foreign policy did not appear to extend to Africa. He once remarked that 'my map of Africa lies in Europe', and yet between 1884 and 1885 Germany acquired the foundations for a colonial empire in Africa with South-West Africa, Togoland, the Cameroons, German East Africa and some islands in the Pacific. Several factors coalesced to lead to this change in outlook. The European partition of Africa that gathered such momentum in the 1880s was more than just a fad. Economic pressures, the rapid extension of overseas trade, and the rise of colonial pressure groups such as the Kolonialverein, founded in 1882, helped to create a climate in which a clear correlation seemed to exist between colonial development and national prestige. The truth was that despite these acquisitions, colonialism was of little direct importance to Bismarck. He encouraged trade in Africa but the associated administrative costs were met by chartered companies and investors, not from the coffers of the Reich. Trade remained the imperative and no military bases were established in Africa under Bismarck. In any case, it was in Europe that events continued to dominate Bismarck's attention.

## 3.10 the Triple Alliance, 1882

Ostensibly, there seemed little prospect of an agreement between Germany and Austria and their near-neighbour Italy. Bismarck had a traditionally low opinion of the Italians, remarking that they had a substantial appetite but poor teeth. Austria had little desire to move closer to the Italians. However, in 1881 the Italians responded to the French occupation of Tunis, which thwarted their plans for colonial expansion in North Africa by making overtures to the Austrians for an alliance. It was Bismarck who recognized in these circumstances that there might be some value in an alliance with the Italians. Acutely aware of the rising tide of Pan-Slavism in Russia, he feared that a Franco-Russian agreement was increasingly likely. A move towards Italy would deprive France of an ally and would secure Austria's potentially exposed southern flank. These were the considerations that led to the signing of the Triple Alliance in 1882. The terms lasted for five years and stated that if any of the signatories were attacked by two or more powers, the other would lend assistance. In the event of a war between Austria and Russia, Italy would remain neutral. If France attacked Germany, Italy would offer support to Germany and Austria would remain neutral. If Italy were attacked by France without direct provocation then Germany and Austria would offer support.

While the Italians were statisfied with what was seen as a prestigious coalition, the international situation remained fraught with difficulty for Bismarck. He had viewed the agreement as a device to rein in Italian ambitions in North Africa in a similar fashion to the way he had manoeuvred the Austrians over the Balkans. However, it would be safe to conclude that Italian ambitions in Africa were not reoriented to the extent that Bismarck had hoped. In addition, the direction of German policy combined with Bismarck's conservative domestic policy meant that England now seemed in a position that presented a potential problem for Germany. In international terms the power of Austria and Italy was limited. The possibility of a war with France meant that the avoidance of a Franco-Russian alliance was more important to Bismarck than ever.

## 3.11 the Balkans and the crisis in Bulgaria

The Three Emperors' Alliance of 1881 had given Russia and Austria the ability to consolidate their respective spheres of influence in the Balkans. However, while Austria flourished in Serbia, the situation for the Russians in Bulgaria was much more troubled. In 1885, Prince Alexander of Bulgaria began to take an increasingly independent line, symbolized by his unilateral action in engineering the union of Eastern Roumelia with Bulgaria without Russian consent. While Russia spoke sternly of a return to the status quo, events seemed to be escalating beyond control when in November 1885 Serbia launched a pre-emptive strike against Bulgaria. Bulgaria not only emerged triumphant from this conflict at Slivinitza but then began planning for the invasion of Serbia. A stark Austrian warning to the Bulgars that if they crossed the frontier they would meet Austrian troops there staved off a Bulgarian offensive but strained Austro-Russian relations to the limit. The very commitments that Bismarck had hoped would avoid conflict in the Balkans now seemed to be embroiling the powers in a situation where a general war could result from a local dispute. Bismarck was forced into informing Austria that Germany could not fight Russia over this issue. A further crisis in Bulgaria in 1886 brought Austro-Russian relations to their lowest point. It was in this context that Bismarck's fear of France and of a Franco-Russian alliance became particularly acute. Under the pressure of events in the Balkans, the Germans were forced to renew the Triple Alliance in 1887 on terms that were more favourable to Italy than those of 1882. Although the Triple Alliance had been renewed, the crisis in the Balkans meant that the Three Emperors' Alliance was damaged beyond repair. It must have been clear to Bismarck that Austro-Russian rivalries in this volatile region were ultimately irreconcilable. It was with this in mind that he turned to Russia.

## 3.12 the Reinsurance Treaty, 1887

Events in the Balkans in 1885–86 highlighted the irreconcilable differences between Russian and Austrian interests in the Balkans, shattered the Three Emperors' Alliance and meant that this central element of Bismarck's alliance network could not be renewed when it expired in the summer of 1887. From the outset it was made clear in St Petersburg that the Russians would not sign an agreement with Austria. Amid intimations that an agreement between Russia and France might be forthcoming, Bismarck pressed for a commitment from the Tsar, but it was only with some reluctance that Alexander III signed the Reinsurance Treaty in June 1887. The central provision of the treaty was established in Article 1:

> If one of the high contracting parties [Russia or Germany] should
> find itself at war with a third Great Power, the other would maintain
> a benevolent neutrality, and would try to localize the conflict. The
> provision would not apply to a war against Austria or France resulting
> from an attack on one of these two powers by one of the high
> contracting parties.

In fact, the degree of reinsurance provided by the treaty was somewhat limited. Russia would only guarantee neutrality if France attacked Germany. If Germany was the aggressor, Russia would not guarantee to remain on the sidelines. Similarly, if Austria-Hungary attacked Russia then Germany would remain neutral. However, if Russia had committed the aggression then Germany would assist Austria-Hungary. Although early interpretations of the Treaty called it a 'masterpiece' it is now accepted by most historians that Bismarck himself did not regard it as of the greatest importance and in the immediate future the treaty did little to enhance Russo-German relations. Nevertheless, the Reinsurance Treaty was one of the final throws of Bismarck's diplomatic dice, and the work he had put into it was unravelled in 1890 under the auspices of the new, impulsive emperor. Gordon Craig's analysis is that the new Kaiser's failure to renew the Reinsurance Treaty was of considerable significance:

> One can argue plausibly that the first foreign political action taken in
> . . . the Wilhelmine New Course was the most crucial of all those made
> between 1890 and the outbreak of the First World War and that it set
> in train the whole chain of calamity that led toward that catastrophe. If
> this is true, however, it has to be noted that, on this occasion, William II
> played an essentially passive role, the decisive force being exerted by the
> Foreign Ministry.[6]

## 3.13 sources: evaluation of Bismarck's foreign policy

**SOURCE A**

Bismarck has long enjoyed a formidable reputation in the field of foreign affairs. His apologists claim that he was largely responsible for preserving peace in Europe for twenty years; he did not want war himself, so it is argued, and he prevented others from going to war by enmeshing the Great Powers in such an intricate diplomatic web that war became too perilous an undertaking, That is to exaggerate his influence. A factor of equal importance was the desire of the powers to avoid a major war in Europe . . .

No one would deny that Bismarck was a past master in the diplomatic arts . . . by cleverly exploiting and fostering the rivalries among the powers he prevented the formation of any hostile coalition against Germany and obtained for his country an assured place at the top table. These are solid achievements. But, equally, it cannot be denied that his policies ended in failure. His bullying tactics, however successful in the short term, were bitterly resented, especially by the Russians and poisoned international relations in this period . . . he conceived of international relations as nothing more than an exercise in power politics.

*Source*: William Carr, *A History of Germany, 1815–1990* (1991).

**SOURCE B**

It was a policy that was bound up with a particular period of European history . . . in essence this was no longer his world. His world remained that of the old Europe of the powers, as reconstituted in 1815, the year of his birth; it remained that of a diplomacy schooled in that Europe and taking its bearings from it, a diplomacy of which he was himself a near-perfect exemplar. . . . These were the premises on which he had implicitly based his views and actions for the past forty years. He himself had not infrequently operated on the very edge of them, particularly during the 1850s and 1860s. To such tactics he owed many of his successes, which had stemmed from a kind of 'brinksmanship' that deliberately went to extreme lengths. . . . Now, however, as the 1880s drew to a close, the foundations of the whole thing threatened to shift decisively – not so much as a result of concerted attacks and calls for change, more as a result of that creeping process of economic and social transformation that even within states was beginning to invalidate the old order to an ever-increasing extent.[8]

*Source*: Lothar Gall, *Bismarck, The White Revolutionary: Volume 2, 1871–1898* (1990).

**SOURCE C**

The chancellor's use of foreign policy for domestic purposes – banging the colonial drum in 1884, whipping up a war scare in 1887, attempting the same thing in 1890 – was a further sign of weakness rather than strength, as well as an ominous pointer to the future. Add to these problems the inbuilt tensions between the Empire and Prussia, and it is clear that Bismarck left his successors a troubled system, designed by and for one man, over which even he had lost control.

*Source*: David Blackbourn, *History of Germany 1780–1918: The Long Nineteenth Century* (2003).

Bismarck's control of German foreign policy and his multidimensional grasp of the complexities of international relations once attracted much admiration from diplomatic historians despite more recent scholarly criticism of his 'crisis management without real prospects'. Nevertheless, if Germany came to occupy a semi-hegemonial position in Europe after 1871, it is important to emphasise that this was not a result of Bismarck's diplomacy alone. The other powers of Europe could not fail to be impressed by Germany's economic and demographic growth after unification; and Bismarck himself later emphasised that his efforts to prevent hostile coalitions would have failed without 'the German military organisation . . . and without the respect which we instil'. . . .

The inability to reach any understanding with France after 1871 as well as the recurring tensions in the Balkans both represented major threats to the Reich's security that Bismarck, for all his imagination and talent, could never resolve . . . by the late 1880s Bismarck was increasingly constrained by a very different international environment. It appeared less and less likely that conflicts could be consigned to the periphery of Europe; and a system of checks and balances designed to maintain the status quo in Europe appeared increasingly obsolete. . . . The division of Europe into two, mutually hostile armed camps in 1914 cannot be explained without reference to Bismarck's foreign policy initiatives.

*Source*: Katherine Anne Lerman, *Bismarck: Profiles in Power* (2004).

## QUESTIONS

1 Consult sources A–D. To what extent do they provide conflicting views of Bismarck's foreign policy?

2 Using sources A–D and your own knowledge, explain whether you consider Bismarck's foreign policy to have been a success in the period 1871–90.

## 3.14 the impact of the resignation of Bismarck on German foreign policy

The year 1888 was the 'year of the three emperors'. The death of Wilhelm I on 9 March 1888 at the age of 90 was closely followed by the passing of his successor, Friedrich III. Although the royal doctors had ruled out cancer when they examined the heir to the throne in May 1887, by the time of his succession he was critically ill. Although Friedrich III briefly carried hopes for a liberal era, he was already sorely incapacitated, and so after his death on 15 June 1888, the throne was passed to Wilhelm I's 28-year-old grandson, Wilhelm II.

For so long Bismarck had been at the helm of German foreign policy, but in the high summer of 1888, when the restless and exuberant new emperor, Kaiser Wilhelm II, ascended the throne, it was clear that this was about to change. Edgar Feuchtwanger offers a fascinating insight into Bismarck's now perilous position; 'many were wondering if he was merely clinging on to power for its own sake. Among the political elite doubts and intrigues were rampant, labyrinthine and poisonous.'[7] As Bismarck remarked in the second volume of his memoirs, written in 1891, but not published until after his death: 'I take the view that, during the twenty-one months when I was his Chancellor, the Emperor stifled his inclination to be rid of an inherited mentor only with difficulty until it exploded.' Bismarck's departure represented a pivotal moment in German history even though the central element of the old campaigner's foreign policy, the understanding between Austria, Russia and Germany, was in ruins and the gravitational pull between Russia, Britain and France was becoming more pronounced. Without Bismarck the foreign press wondered aloud and with some anxiety about European's destiny. It would not be long before some of those anxieties were borne out.

# chapter 4

# Wilhelmine Germany, 1890–1914

## 4.1 interpretations

While there is general agreement that Germany in this period was a modern, dynamic, energetic society, issues concerning its governance remain. Wilhelmine Germany has attracted a range of perspectives that are fascinating in their range and breadth. At one extreme the Canadian historian Stuart Robson 'wondered aloud whether the established elites in Wilhelmine Germany could successfully have organized a cake-sale, let alone a ruthless, determined, coherent defense of the established order'.[1] Such a damning appraisal seems borne out by the oft-quoted observation of the British diplomat Lord Haldane who famously remarked in 1912 that, 'when you mount to the peak of this highly organized people, you will find not only confusion but chaos'. However, there is an alternative perspective that needs to be given equal consideration.

Historians have, perhaps, been guilty of emphasizing the most bizarre, unattractive and damaging aspects of the Wilhelmine period at the expense of a more balanced perspective. Recently, however, a group of American historians including Joachim Remak and Jack Dukes

> have suggested that Wilhelmine Germany was far less backward, authoritarian and outwardly aggressive than has been supposed. . . . Within this 'other' Germany one finds cities that were vibrant and wholesome; universities and research institutions imbued with progressive spirit; a free press able to check authoritarian excesses; a stabilizing and socially integrative army that provided a fruitful learning experience for its recruits; a progressive social ethos that combated religious and sexual discrimination; and a foreign policy that was modest and moderate in comparison with the strident and threatening postures assumed by French, British and Russian diplomats. . . . The tendency has been to force the reader to choose between two Germanies – one virulent, the other benign.[2]

As you read what follows consider which perspective you find most compelling.

## 4.2 Leo von Caprivi and the New Course, 1890–94 (1831–99)

No historian has done more to develop our understanding of the Wilhelmine period than John Rohl. One of Rohl's early findings was that the Kaiser's most important prerogative was his control and intervention in all personnel appointments. As Wilhelm remarked in 1891, 'I always have a good luck at my men beforehand.' This did not necessarily mean that Wilhelm was also able to put in place a clearly defined vision or programme based on the appointment of a succession of appointees with a uniform or consistent political agenda. On the contrary, Christopher Clark has argued that his appointees reflected 'the eclectic composition of his personal acquaintance, rather than a consistent preference for individuals with a specific political outlook'.[3] Isobel Hull, in her important work on the entourage of Wilhelm II, argues that the Kaiser tended to select men with 'a military aura wrapped around a courtier's soul'.[4] It seems that the Kaiser's approach to ministerial appointments could sometimes be rather cavalier. Holstein, a key official in the 1890s, noted in a letter that the 'Kaiser has the habit of selecting his ministers like mistresses'. It could be argued that William had merely appointed a sychophantic clique that served only to feed his ego and separate him from political reality.

Of vital importance in the Kaiser's choice of personal appointments was the position of the chancellor, who could be appointed or dismissed by the emperor at his discretion. The chancellor was the emperor's key instrument in ensuring good relations with the parliament or Reichstag. When breaches occurred between the chancellor and the Reichstag the chancellor could take the measure of dissolving the Reichstag and calling fresh elections. Caprivi came to the Chancellery as a middle-aged army general with substantial administrative experience. It had been hoped that a military figure would provide an impression of authority. Wilhelm personally selected Caprivi from a list of generals because he was seen as an amenable man who would do what he was told. In fact, once in office he soon displayed a mind of his own. In his maiden speech to the Prussian Landtag he expressed his desire to steer 'a new course'. James Retallack observes that people responded with some relief to the fact that 'the new chancellor, Leo von Caprivi, seemed willing to challenge the power of the agrarian Junkers and to pursue a foreign policy that was less devious than Bismarck's'.[5]

It soon became clear that Caprivi was an energetic, reforming administrator who adopted a conciliatory policy towards the Socialists, Poles and Centrists and generally a policy of non-alignment, so that initially he received a good deal of support for his 'New Course' from the Reichstag. Much of this new legislation was Caprivi's personal policy.

## domestic legislation, 1890–94

- *Finance Bill*. Progressive income tax introduced (1890)
- *Rural Administration Reform and modernization* (1890)
- *Social welfare*. Restricted Sunday working and hours of labour for women and children (1891)
- *Arbitration of industrial disputes*. Courts set up with workers' and employers' representatives to settle disputes. Anti-socialist laws from Bismarck's era lapsed (1891)
- *Reform of the Tariff Act of 1879*. Germany was obliged to reduce her tariffs on cattle, timber, rye and wheat in order to gain overseas markets for German industrial exports in return (1892). A series of commercial treaties guaranteeing Germany markets for industrial exports were signed in return for reductions in tariffs on rye, wheat, cattle and timber. Between 1891 and 1894 treaties were concluded with a host of countries, including Russia, Austria-Hungary, Switzerland and Italy. These measures brought down the general cost of living and therefore secured support for the government from the socialists for the first time. On the other hand, the unease of German Conservatives aroused by Caprivi's conciliatory tone in 1890 was now inflamed by the tariff reforms
- *Army Bill*. Increased peacetime army by 84,000. Reduced military service from 3 to 2 years. This infuriated the German Conservatives. The Reichstag could now debate the army grant every 5 instead of 7 years (1892)
- *Prussian School Reform Bill*. This aimed to restore church influence in education and allow Polish to be used in schools in Posen and West Prussia but was dropped when the emperor intervened directly in the dispute this proposal caused.

Despite, or perhaps, because of, this legislative energy, Caprivi's time in office came to an end within four years of his appointment. The Agrarian League of 1893 portrayed Caprivi as a 'socialist' who was willing to bring financial ruin to wheat farmers. By 1894 the embattled Chancellor faced mounting opposition not just from powerful agrarian forces but from the German Conservatives, who were increasingly alarmed by the inexorable rise of socialism and the legislative direction of the Caprivi era. When the Chancellor also angered the Kaiser by refusing to draft a law against subversive elements, his influence was coming to an end. Behind his back the Kaiser was prepared to use grossly insulting language about Caprivi, describing him as a 'sensitive old fathead'. Against this background of an unsatisfactory personal relationship between the two men it was not entirely surprising when Caprivi tendered his resignation at the end of 1894.

## 4.3 the development of the German economy

Although the impatient new emperor was prepared to send Caprivi the way of Bismarck in 1894, the outgoing general's commercial treaties had helped

Germany to enter the twentieth century with every confidence. By 1900, Germany had become Europe's leading industrial nation. An indication of the rapidity of this process is indicated by the fact that the population of 49 million in 1890 had reached 66 million by 1913. Germany became internationally renowned for its rapid industrial growth and technological progress. Coal, iron and heavy engineering had provided the powerful foundation stones but during the period of industrial 'take-off' were supplemented by fast-moving technological progress in steel, chemicals, shipping and electrical engineering. To these highly successful industries could be added hugely important developments in areas such as agriculture and textiles. The massive engineering combines of Bosch and Siemens typified the qualities of efficiency and innovation synonymous with German industry. Major breakthroughs such as the electric dynamo and the petrol engine were made in Germany. Industrial strength was matched by cultural excellence. German citizens were able to enjoy top-class theatre, opera and classical music. The next extract shows that actors, musicians and other visual artists could attain a position in higher social circles, although gender remained a major barrier to upward mobility.

**SOURCE A**

In the course of the century, actors have attained a higher standing than ever before. But not the entire class of actors. Much depends on the theater where the individual works. Here in Berlin, as in Vienna, members of the court theater occupy the highest ranks. Above all, the male actors socialize in solid middle-class society, and it is not rare for them to be quite popular . . .

When it comes to the female members of court stages, their status vis-à-vis society varies considerably, depending on the circles in which they conduct their affairs – and I am not using the word in its disreputable sense here. In general, particularly among the more orthodox bourgeois families, there is still mistrust towards female members of playhouses . . .

Today, the famous virtuoso is virtually the only one to whom all doors are open. His art secures his influence, which even extends to the women of the elegant classes – and in the salon it is the women who determine the status of all those not belonging to the circle of equals by way of birth.

Among visual artists, architects, painters, and sculptors, portrait painters play the foremost role in society, provided that they have the necessary reputation. Some of them have received special honors from the court and have even enjoyed the privilege of invitation to exclusive social events in a smaller circle. That also constitutes a carte blanche for entry into elegant society. In this context, the vanity of women is very important. If a painter enjoys the reputation of having a flattering brush, he will be treated with special kindness and spoiled almost as much as a famous violinist or pianist.

Social intercourse between the court and all types of artists is not particularly lively. Representatives of the latter are certainly invited to grand celebrations, but the kind of exchange seen between artists and persons of the highest standing in Munich during the rule of Maximilian has never developed here in

Berlin. Much more active relations to individual painters and sculptors were maintained by the court of the Crown Prince and then Emperor Friedrich; after all, the now widowed Empress practices this art herself.

*Source*: Otto von Leixner, *1888 bis 1891. Soziale Briefe aus Berlin. Mit besonderer Berücksichtigung der sozialdemokratischen Strömungen* (1891).

The spirit of civic progress was perhaps reflected in the opening of zoological gardens in Cologne, Hamburg and Dresden in the early 1860s. Library provision was impressive, literacy rates were high, the leading national newspapers were forthright and independent, and Germany's ancient universities enjoyed an international reputation. From this healthy knowledge base stemmed rapid advances in medicine and public health. Compulsory immunization against smallpox in 1874, the foundation of the German Paediatric Society in 1883, the availability of a diphtheria serum in the early 1890s and general improvements in hygiene and living conditions caused a fall in infant mortality, from around 25 per cent in the 1870s to less than 15 per cent in 1912. The German language became synonymous with international scientific discourse. Yet at the same time, education for those from an underprivileged background was often jeopardized by harsh economic realities, as shown by this extract describing the damaging impact of the demands of child labour on young people in the Prussian province of Pomerania.

**SOURCE B**

Even if one only considers the number of hours that children are employed, it can surely be said without further observation that children aged eight to fourteen years simply cannot cope physically with such prolonged periods of work. When it was time to thin out the turnips, which usually took four weeks in these parts, the children at my school, after being dismissed, trotted home as soon as they were out of my sight. Barely five minutes later, they appeared on the double, breakfast sandwiches in hand, at the gathering point, where the supervisor already awaited them. Then it was off to the turnip field – and not exactly at a leisurely pace. They ate breakfast while marching. . . . Back at the village around noon, you could see the children wandering out to fields again at 1 p.m. They returned at 9 o'clock at night. On some days when there was no school, the children, I was told, had to show up at 5:30 a.m. Have I really gone too far in saying that such working hours have an adverse effect on the health of eight-year-old children or children with weak constitutions? An eleven-year-old girl had to be sent home from the field because she fell ill. Is such work advisable for healthy children if it makes weak ones sick? Let's look at weather conditions. In damp, cold wind or rain the working children easily catch cold; in drought conditions they frequently suffer from headaches and sore knees. One can see how, during school, some boys cannot hide that they have sore knees; they often clasp and squeeze them. According to my diary, I received the following reports of illness during the turnip-thinning season: one child sick for five days, one child for three days, two children for two days each, and two for one day each. What's more, I recently had to send several girls out of class, repeatedly, on account of nausea. The prolonged, exhausting work has made their bodies more susceptible to illnesses: scarlet fever and the measles currently keep two-thirds of the students out of school. Thinning out turnips, however, is not the children's only work in the fields; it is preceded by planting potatoes and followed by thinning out cabbage . . . we soon become convinced that our children are overburdened with agricultural work throughout the whole summer.

*Source*: Teacher Gossow, in *Pommersche Blätter für die Schule und ihre Freunde* (1887).

## the rise of the urban society

In towns, urban tram networks, trains, the bicycle, the typewriter, carbon paper, department stores and mail-order catalogues all reflected the passage of German society into what could truly be called an age of modernity. In 1888, the first year for which figures are available, Germans made 155 million phone calls and by 1904 the number reached a billion. In the pre-war period the country appeared exceptionally dynamic, with a population reaching 68 million by 1914, an increase of 60 per cent compared to the period of unification. The population contained a large proportion of young people and this population was becoming increasingly urban. By 1910 more than 60 per cent of Germans lived in towns, with 20 per cent residing in the 48 'big cities' with populations exceeding 100,000. Berlin's population exceeded 2 million by 1907. By 1914 Hamburg's population had reached almost a million and cities including Breslau, Cologne, Dresden, Liepzig and Munich had passed the half-million mark. As Blackbourn states: 'In short, Germans were moving to towns in unprecedented numbers, and continuing to move, with effects on every aspect of life.'[6]

## 4.4  Wilhelm II and the issue of personal rule

Amid the atmosphere of youthful exuberance that marked the succession of the young Emperor, few Germans lamented Bismarck's passing and in Wilhelm II they seemed to have a Kaiser whose personal energy and aspirations seemed synonymous with the qualities and ambitions of the German nation itself. We will now examine the nature of his government.

Wilhelm II often declared with some disdain that he had never bothered to read the German constitution, although the document he neglected invested him with substantial powers. The constitution of the 'Kaiserreich' referred to the emperor as the 'all highest person' and the 'supreme warlord'. The emperor exerted absolute control over the government, the armed forces, the diplomatic network and the civil service. This was the framework for an autocratic, semi-absolutist state. The instruments of power were within the reach of the Kaiser and his advisers providing they had the ability to grasp them. An autocratic ruler could easily work outside the democratic niceties of the constitution. Was this Wilhelm's intention?

John Rohl has stated that 'gradually William II ... created a government and an administrative apparatus of his own choosing' in which 'pliant tools of the imperial will' were appointed to 'all key offices'.[7] Rohl claims that by 1897 William II had worn down resistance to his personal rule among the bureaucrats in the Wilhelmstrasse. In her pioneering study of the 'entourage of Kaiser Wilhelm II', Isabel Hull claims that the Emperor's ministers were 'like panes of glass ... they were to shelter the Kaiser from hostile winds and at the same time allow his policies and his alone to shine through without distortion'.[8]

## the personal rule of Wilhelm II

In the summer of 1900 the royal yacht *Hohenzollern* carried the Emperor from Germany to the North Sea accompanied by his substantial personal entourage. Those who had been with the *Reisekaiser* (travelling Emperor) on earlier voyages knew that their royal master had a penchant for physical jerks, practical jokes and elaborate or even, at times, dangerously debauched and bizarre fancy-dress parties. Accompanying Wilhelm as usual was Philip Eulenburg, for many years his closest friend and confidant. It was Eulenburg's photograph which normally occupied pride of place on the Kaiser's desk in the royal hunting lodge at Rominten. However, on the night of 15 July, Eulenburg locked himself into his cabin and wrote a secret letter, addressed to the German Chancellor von Bülow, describing in vivid detail how the Kaiser had thrown a terrifying fit of rage. Eulenburg reported: 'H.M. is no longer in control of himself when he is seized by rage. I regard the situation as highly dangerous and am at a loss to know what to do.' He added that the Kaiser's personal physician was 'utterly perplexed' by his behaviour, and came to the disturbing conclusion that being on the yacht with the Emperor was like 'sitting on a powder keg'.[9]

Eulenberg's letter has provided additional evidence for historians who have tried to compose a complex psychological profile of the last kaiser. The impression has not been favourable. Born with a badly withered left hand and plagued by a recurring ear infection, William's physical difficulties probably left their psychological mark. Some historians have claimed that his distant mother instilled in him a sense of inferiority. Wilhelm's frequent bursts of irrational behaviour have been attributed in some part to the traumatic circumstances of his difficult birth. In adult life Wilhelm took pleasure in turning the ornate rings on his good hand inward, enabling him to deliver a painful handshake to unsuspecting diplomats or dignitaries. On more than one occasion, members of Wilhelm's inner circle were subject to damaging blackmail demands which implicated Wilhelm himself. In 1896, for example, Philip Eulenburg was blackmailed by the owner of a Viennese bathhouse, and in 1908 members of the inner circle were involved in a protracted court case which received national attention. Contemporaries found Wilhelm's behaviour difficult and hard to predict. In 1888 Bismarck remarked that 'the Kaiser is like a balloon, if you don't keep fast hold of the string, you never know where he'll be off to'.[10] Both contemporaries and historians have speculated about Wilhelm's state of mind.

English historians of the Second Reich – led by John Rohl – have maintained that there is still a great deal to learn about Wilhelm, and that his personal neuroses exerted an important and direct impact on the decision-making process in pre-war Germany. They claim that Wilhelm stamped his personality on the period 1890–1914, and that therefore their 'palace perspective' – concentrating on the Emperor and his court – is the correct one. They believe that the more light they can shed on Wilhelm's personality the better our understanding will be of German society in this vital period.

Meanwhile, a group of German historians, led by Hans-Ulrich Wehler, offer a totally different viewpoint. Wehler has described Wilhelm as a 'shadow emperor' (*Schattenkaiser*) without say or influence in pre-war Germany. He says that Wilhelm reigned but did not rule. He sees Wilhelm as an irrelevance, lacking the ability to direct policy, command the respect of senior figures in the army or influence the real decision-makers. Wehler accepts that in 1890 the Kaiser launched a brief, unsuccessful bid to establish personal power but that after this date he abandoned this 'anachronistic game' and contented himself with making outspoken yet ultimately irrelevant speeches. After the departure of Bismarck a power vacuum existed which Wilhelm II was unable to fill. Wehler contends that the glamour of the Berlin court and its trappings of power represent a powerful illusion which has beguiled historians fascinated by the Kaiser's personality. Beneath this veneer, he claims, the Emperor was increasingly out of touch and isolated. From this it therefore follows that the Kaiser's personality is also irrelevant, he exerted no real influence whether he was in a good mood or a bad mood. Wehler states that there is nothing more of interest to be discovered about the Kaiser. Historians like Rohl, who continue to search the archives for further information on the shadow emperor, are – according to Wehler – wasting their time in writing 'personalistic' accounts.

Wehler's alternative perspective represents a 'structural' approach. He believes that real influence was in the hands of powerful elite groups, members of which did not necessarily hold elected office but pulled strings behind the scenes. Such groups consisted of powerful industrialists, wealthy landowners, pressure groups and press barons. The shared objective of these powerful blocs was to prevent Germany's rapid industrialization being accompanied by genuine democracy. Most of them feared the growth of left-wing political parties and the mass participation of the working classes in the political system. For this reason they carried out a programme of social integration, or *Sammlungspolitik*, by which they hoped to manipulate German society into accepting their continued domination. They used their influence to steer Germany towards a programme of colonial expansion for overseas markets (world policy, or *Weltpolitik*). This was sustained by the construction of a huge battle fleet and ultimately led to war and attempts at overseas conquest. The massive production of ships was intended to boost the economy, reduce unemployment and the damaging consequences of fluctuations in the normal economic cycle and persuade the working class to remain loyal to the ruling elite rather than voting for the socialist parties. For their own self-preservation and personal profit, the elite favoured an increasingly ambitious armaments programme and aggressive foreign policy. They believed that success in this area would satisfy the population at large and preserve their position. The Kaiser, Wehler maintains, was merely a mouthpiece for this policy and, when it failed, a scapegoat.[11] In Rohl's words, Wehler is engaged in 'writing the history of the Kaiserreich without the Kaiser' or 'Wilhelmine Germany without William'. Rohl argues that the reality is that Wilhelm established an autocratic, semi-absolutist state in which his personal influence was paramount.[12]

## the nature and development of the political parties

Voting behaviour was strongly influenced by factors of class, race and religion. Increasingly the political parties became polarized between parties of the left and the right at the expense of the centre. While support for the Socialist party increased, there was also increasing representation for extreme nationalist and anti-Semitic groups. German society came to have the largest socialist party in Europe but also the largest army. The fact that the Kaiser was notoriously close to leading military figures enhanced the feeling that the wishes of the population at large were not necessarily represented by the State. Hans-Ulrich Wehler states that the central dilemma was that Germany's rapid economic and social development into a modern industrial society was not accompanied by similar progress in the political sphere. Rather Germany retained a political system which was outdated and anachronistic. The middle and working classes were increasingly influential and demanding but this trend was not reflected in political developments because of the hostility of the traditional ruling elites.

The verdict of some historians on the Kaiser's administration has been that the country was the most economically successful in Europe, but also one of the worst governed. The feeling is that the glamour of the court in Berlin has tended to distract attention from the chaos that the Kaiser, politicians, confidants and the military created in their struggle for power. While there is broad agreement among historians that the German government in the Wilhelmine era was ineffective, the question of who was actually in charge remains the subject of intense debate.

## 4.5 Hohenlohe and the policy of concentration, 1894–1900 (1819–1901)

Historians have had relatively little that is positive to say about Caprivi's aging successor. A Bavarian aristocrat, he was already older when he was appointed to the highest office than Bismarck was when he retired. Although his political outlook was regarded as relatively liberal, Wilhelm was prepared to overlook this as he saw him as a mere figurehead whom he could easily control and manipulate. His age, indecision and naturally evasive personality meant that he was unable to exert firm leadership during what can be characterized as a period of transition. Remaining Liberals from the Caprivi era were soon dismissed and the initiative passed to key ministers such as Miquel and Koller. Johannes von Miquel was a former banker and co-founder of the National Association. He brought energy, dynamism and a sense of purpose to the government. He became a powerful figure in the Berlin administration and at one point was described by Wilhelm as 'the greatest Finance Minister of the century'.[13] Miquel and Koller became associated with a 'policy of concentration' that led to reactionary anti-left measures such as the Subversion Bill (1894) and anti-union legislation (1899). These measures were opposed by the middle-class parties. It was a measure of Bülow's growing influence over the monarch that he was able to damage Miquel's standing before the Emperor to the extent that Miquel shouldered the blame for the economic slowdown after 1900, and he was forced out altogether by Bülow after he became Chancellor in 1900.

Meanwhile, Hohenlohe's main contribution was to restrain the Kaiser who, during the period of reaction, talked wildly of subverting the constitution and removing the workers' vote. As early as 1895 Wilhelm was writing critically of Hohenlohe and praising Bülow, whose blatant flattery of the Kaiser made it certain that he would replace Hohenlohe. By 1900 the old man was widely ridiculed for his senility and he was equally weary of serving such as unpredictable master. However, his term of office had lasted long enough for the succession prospects of General Waldersee to have faded; when he resigned, the more moderate, but relentlessly sycophantic Bernhard von Bülow took over.

## 4.6 Baron von Bülow, 1900–09 (1849–1929)

A more formidable and politically astute character than his predecessor, Bülow came from the landed aristocracy. His extensive experience in the diplomatic service and Foreign Office left him expert in the arts of personal charm and flattery. Sycophantic in his dealings with the Emperor, he became known to his enemies as 'the eel'. Bülow's appointment as Chancellor in 1900 brought the Kaiser's personal favourite, 'the man with my absolute confidence', to a position of unparalleled power. Bülow relentlessly fostered his personal relationship with Wilhem and used this power base to enhance his control over the rest of the Kaiser's appointments. The corollary of this was the increased coordination between civilian and military authority in imperial Germany.

Beyond Bülow's personal flattery he did display a degree of independence as Chancellor. He helped to put a stop to the reactionary policies instigated under Hohenlohe. Instead he advocated a policy of rallying together Germany's disparate social groups in a *Sammlungspolitik*. The loyalty of the German people would be secured by the building of a prestigious fleet and the promotion of the Kaiser as a charismatic leader. In addition, Bülow restored tariffs to their pre-1892 level but resisted pressure from the Agrarian League to raise them much higher. Even so, in the 1903 election working-class resentment of higher tariffs enabled the Socialists to increase their votes by almost a million. Bülow also faced opposition from the Centre Party over tax reforms and colonial policy. In 1907 he dissolved the Reichstag and ran an election campaign on issues of defence and national security. After this election Bülow relied on a bloc of support from the Conservative and National Liberal Parties. In 1908 he allowed Wilhelm's notorious *Daily Telegraph* interview to go ahead and an extract from this highly damaging episode is shown below. When a storm blew up in the aftermath of the interview Bülow appeared to be willing to put the blame for this on the Emperor's personal style of government.

## the *Daily Telegraph* interview

**SOURCE A**

His majesty honoured me with a long conversation, and spoke with impulsive and unusual frankness. 'You English' he said, are mad, mad, mad as March hares. What has come over you that you are so completely given over to suspicions quite unworthy of a great nation? What more can I do than I have done? . . . I repeat', continued His Majesty, 'that I am a friend of England, but you make things difficult for me. My task is not of the easiest. The prevailing sentiment among large sections of the middle and lower classes of my own people is not friendly to England . . . I strive without ceasing to improve relations, and you retort that I am your arch-enemy. You make it hard for me. Why is it?

*Source*: *Daily Telegraph*, 28 October 1908.

**SOURCE B**

WILLIAM CARR'S COMMENTARY ON WHY THE *DAILY TELEGRAPH* INTERVIEW WAS SO DAMAGING.

ii) It was full of the Emperor's usual inept comments and was certain to offend the maximum number of people in the shortest possible time. . . . All the major parties, including the Conservatives, vehemently attacked the chancellor and his officials for their ineptitude in allowing the article to be published; nor did they spare the Emperor, who was severely censured for meddling once more in matters which were the proper concern of the government. . . . In fact William acted with constitutional propriety on this occasion. When Stuart-Wortley sent him the article, the Emperor passed it on to Bulow for approval. The latter was too preoccupied. . . . Most likely he only glanced at it casually before passing it on.

*Source*: William Carr, *A History of Germany, 1815–1900* (1987).

However, Bülow's apparent reprieve was short-lived and despite the extent of the personal rapport between the two men, or perhaps because of the depth of feeling between them, Wilhelm was unable to forgive his formerly loyal servant. Once Wilhelm's depression over this incident lifted he was determined to see Bülow removed. In 1909 Bülow submitted his resignation after his Finance Bill had been rejected by the Reichstag. To his surprise this was immediately accepted and he left the government to be replaced by Theobald von Bethmann-Hollweg.

## 4.7 Theobald von Bethmann-Hollweg, 1909–17 (1856–1921)

Bethmann-Hollweg had risen through the ranks of the Prussian administration but it was with some reluctance that he moved to the higher echelons of the government. When he was made Prussian Minister of the Interior in 1905 he confided in a friend that the post was 'thoroughly repugnant'.[14] In 1907 he was appointed Secretary of State in the Imperial Office of Internal Affairs and two year's later Bülow's dismissal placed Bethmann in contention for the highest position.

Bethmann-Hollweg was not Wilhelm's first choice and surprisingly, Bülow was able to put forward the claim of Bethmann-Hollweg as his successor. Once Wilhelm accepted the idea he was typically enthusiastic: 'He is true as gold. A man of integrity, also very energetic, he will straighten out the Reichstag for me. Besides, it was with him in Hohenfinow that I shot my first roebuck.'[15] Once again, Bethmann-Hollweg was unable to enthuse about his promotion; 'Only a genius or a man driven by ambition and lust for power can covet this post. And I am neither. An ordinary man can only assume it when compelled by his sense of duty.'[16] Gordon Craig concludes that Bethmann-Hollweg was a 'careful and energetic administrator, an effective negotiator, and a man of courage and honour in time of crisis'.[17] Bülow's old tactic of shielding the emperor from ministerial contact was abandoned by Bethmann-Hollweg, and government ministers were now allowed time to make their formal presentations (*Vortrage*) to Wilhelm.

However, like Caprivi, Bethmann lacked creative talent and his intellectual and political horizons were narrow. His knowledge of foreign affairs was initially limited, although he soon came to have a clearer understanding of international politics. In other areas, too, he lacked verve and assurance. He was intelligent enough to see that the German political system was in need of reform but he was too conservative in his views, and too opposed in principle to the idea of parliamentary government, to favour any fundamental change in the existing system. During Bethmann-Hollweg's administration the Socialists became the largest single party in the Reichstag (1912), and in foreign policy he presided over the disastrous July Crisis of 1914. In 1917 Bethmann-Hollweg came under intense pressure from the Supreme Command led by Hindenburg and Ludendorff, and Wilhelm was obliged to accept his resignation even though he was reluctant to do so.

## 4.8 the Zabern incident

On the eve of war attention was briefly focused on the small town of Zabern in Alsace. The Alsace-Lorraine region had endured poor relations with Germany since the war of 1871. In 1913 a young German lieutenant made insulting remarks about the civilian inhabitants and encouraged his men to treat them harshly. When the citizens of Zabern protested and organized demonstrations, the commander of the regiment, Colonel von Reuter, had almost 30 of the protesters locked up in the cells of the barracks. The matter caused some consternation in Germany because the principle that only civilian courts or the police could interfere with the liberty of citizens appeared to have been so brusquely violated. However, when the matter was raised in the Reichstag, the minister of war rejected the concerns on the basis that commanding officers in the army were accountable to the emperor and not the Reichstag. Although a vote of censure against Chancellor Bethmann-Hollweg for his handling of the matter was passed by the Reichstag, the vote seemed to have no immediate consequence. Although some of the officers concerned were transferred elsewhere, the commander of the regiment in Zabern was acquitted by a court-martial of a charge of illegal arrest. The War Minister and senior army officers did not hide their contempt for parliament and made it quite clear that they would never allow the army to be directly accountable to them. Although the Zabern incident damaged relations between the inhabitants of Alsace-Lorraine and the occupying German army, its real significance was in what it revealed about German society. Although criticism of the army was made openly in the Reichstag, it was clear that the Chancellor could ignore a parliamentary vote of censure. The army appeared contemptuous of the criticisms made of it. Above all, the Kaiser himself seemed to encapsulate the militaristic values that the Zabern incident had rather crudely highlighted. Nevertheless, the incident paled into insignificance when it was set against the crisis of July 1914.

## 4.9 Interpretations of the nature of German society in 1914

The emphasis on the negative, pathological aspects of Wilhelm's rule can distract attention from the outstanding industrial, cultural and scientific achievements of the German nation in the early part of the twentieth century. Some of its many qualities can be expressed simply – in broad terms, the streets were clean, the trains were on time and illiteracy was almost unheard of. German citizens enjoyed the finest public school system and the most progressive social insurance programme in the world. In the period 1900–25, more than one-third of the Nobel prizes awarded for chemistry and physics went to German scientists. The archaeological discovery by Heinrich Schliemann of the site of Homeric Troy became a prestigious centerpiece of the Berlin Museum.

Yet there has remained a tendency for people to have to make a stark choice between this image of dynamism, culture and sophistication and the rather crude, bombastic and intolerant society reflected in some of Kaiser Wilhelm's most notorious public excesses.

A step beyond this rather over-simplified choice may be for historians to concentrate on the 'many Germanies' available for scrutiny through regionalized studies, or through examination of particular social groups. It may be that this reveals a society that was increasingly sophisticated, well-educated, articulate and politically aware. For example, closer scrutiny of the German scientific community, or of life on the university campus, might reveal a dazzling image of modernity and progressive thought. On the other hand, a focus on the alternative and less favoured might also reveal a socially divided society with diverse groups such as Poles, Jews, women, and artists all losing out compared to those allocated a more valued role in the Germany of Wilhelm II.

Leaving these thoughts aside, what of contemporary opinion? Appropriately enough, it is easy to find evidence of a society ill at ease with itself. In a document prepared in Britain in 1909 the verdict was that 'the ultimate aims of Germany surely are, without doubt, to obtain the preponderance on the continent of Europe', to be accompanied by 'a contest with us for maritime supremacy'. To many Germans on the eve of war, this was a scenario that could be embraced. As one nationalist exclaimed in 1913: 'Let us regard war as holy, like the purifying force of fate, for it will awaken in our people all that is great and ready for selfless sacrifice, while it cleanses our sole of the mire of petty egotistical concerns.'[18] Yet in the same year, Gustav Wyneken made this plaintive plea: 'When I view the radiant valleys of our fatherland which spread out here at our feet, I can only wish: May the day never come when the hordes of war rage through them. And may the day also never come when we are forced to carry war to the valleys of a foreign people.'[19] Perhaps the war years would remove the sense of division and unite the German people behind the colours?

## 4.10 sources: Wilhelm II: personal ruler or shadow emperor?

### the views of historians

**SOURCE A**

Most people were impressed by the new ruler's vitality, his openness to new ideas, the diversity of his interests, and his personal charm. As his Court Marshal wrote later, William was 'a dazzling personality who fascinated everyone who appeared before him. He was well aware of his ability to do this and developed this talent with much effort and refinement to an extraordinary perfection.

*Source*: Gordon Craig, *Germany 1866–1945* (1981).

**SOURCE B**

A good deal has been written about William's 'Personal Rule' and there can be little doubt that his strong desire to decide everything himself represented an important element in his character. Even more important was the fact that, with the monarchy beset by manifold problems, a focal point was needed. If the existing power structure was to be saved from the impact of a changing industrial society, William II had to be turned into a people's Kaiser whose charisma would help to reduce internal tensions and secure Germany's position as an admired and respected world power.

*Source*: V. R. Berghahn, *Germany and the Approach of War in 1914* (1973).

Kaiser Wilhelm II – far from standing alone against the enclosed corps of officialdom – was served by more than two thousand court officials and servants, was surrounded by a vast, hierarchically structured court society, was in possession of unrestricted 'powers of command' in all military matters, and above all was in a position to corrupt and to force into a relationship of subservience the whole Reich and state civil service by means of his absolute control over appointments, honours and even marriage plans. A symbol of this is the fact that the German Reich Chancellor, Chlodwig Prince zu Hohenlohe-Schillingsfurst, the 'highest official' of the Reich, the Kaiser's 'prime adviser', was constitutionally authorised by the Reichstag to receive a salary of only 54,000 marks per annum. Secretly an extra 120,000 marks were passed to him each year from the funds of the crown.

Source: John Rohl, *The Kaiser and his Court: Wilhelm II and the Government of Germany* (1996).

Our image of Wilhelm II remains overwhelmingly negative. Recent studies of the reign describe him as a 'suitable case for [psychiatric] treatment', an 'abominable emperor' with an 'incoherent, narcissistic personality', a 'psychically disjointed', 'offensive' and 'sadistic' bully who took pleasure in the humiliation of others and felt a 'cool alienation' from other human beings, a 'tedious', 'deranged', puffed-up, vainglorious and self-overestimating fool'. . . . The mocking, denunciatory, even diabolising tone of much historiographical comment on Wilhelm is one of the most distinctive and striking characteristics of the field. One need not approach the subject with rehabilitation in mind to feel that there is something excessive and misplaced about such language. . . . Wilhelm's understanding of power and how it should be exercised was not the outlandish confection of a deranged mind. It was acquired in part from a familial setting uniquely disturbed by power-political conflicts, and in part from Bismarck, the titan who loomed so large over Wilhelm's political education'.

Source: Edgar Feuchtwanger, *Bismarck* (2002).

It was not just the public's 'loss of monarchical conviction' that was detectable in the Wilhelmine epoch. Lost in its 'political shape', 'social atmosphere' and rhetorical behaviour were 'natural authority' and role model function for the future. In the 'democratic current' the monarchical aura suffered continually and to a degree that had not even been experienced during the revolution of 1848–9. The *Kreuz-Zeitung* commented in 1913: 'Never in the history of the German people, the most monarchical people in its conviction and character, its customs and habit, has the monarchical thought been so attacked, has the monarchy faced such a strong front of open and hidden opponents as in this most recent past.

Wilhelm II did not succeed in developing new, more sophisticated, and politically convincing forms of leadership-aesthetic, suitable for an industrial nation.'

Source: Bernd Sosemann, in Annika Mombauer and Wilhelm Deist, *The Kaiser: New Research on Wilhelm II's Role in Imperial Germany* (2003).

The files not only reveal with how much commitment and decisiveness Wilhelm exercised his 'personal rule' in this respect. They also show how densely the Kaiser's diary was crammed with this kind of public engagement and what a huge effort was afforded to his domestic and foreign trips. . . . In the Reichstag, within the political parties and the public, the Kaiser's reputation had suffered to such an extent that what still remained of the already corroded 'royalist capital' now threatened to dissolve further even in conservative and generally monarchist circles.'

*Source*: ss source E.

## ESSAY QUESTION

'Wilhelm II: Personal ruler or shadow Emperor?' With reference to each of the sources and your own knowledge, explain which interpretation you regard as most convincing with regard to the period 1890–1914.

# chapter 5

# Germany and the origins of the First World War, 1890–1914

## 5.1 Wilhelm's war?

With the German war effort in a state of terminal collapse in November 1918, it was with some relief that the anxious and depressed Kaiser received news that he was to be offered sanctuary. A Dutch nobleman, Count Betinck, offered to house the royal refugee in his castle at Amerongen. The Kaiser crossed the border from Germany into the Netherlands during the night of 9 November 1918. He appeared to be safe. The abdication of Wilhelm II, Emperor of Germany, was complete. However, the search for someone who could take the blame for the outbreak of a war that had lasted for more than four years had only just begun. Seven months later the peacemakers at Versailles delivered this scathing verdict on the role played by the Kaiser in the outbreak of the war: 'The Allied and Associated Powers publicly arraign Wilhelm II of Hohenzollern, former German Emperor, for a supreme offence against international morality and the sanctity of treaties.'

Although Wilhelm was never directly punished and lived out his exile in the Netherlands until his death in June 1941, it is sometimes maintained even today that the First World War can justifiably be called the 'Kaiser's War'. While it is still true to say that Germany remains the government most directly held responsible for the war, and there is ample evidence that Wilhelm personally embraced the militaristic, chauvinistic and aggressive values that sorely damaged international relations in the pre-war period, there is a clearer sense now of the paradox between the assertion that Wilhelm and his cohort personally mapped out the path to war and our understanding of the sometimes chaotic nature of Wilhelm's leadership style. Was Wilhelm personally responsible, or should there be a broader sharing of guilt for what could be regarded as the greatest mistake in modern history? We will now examine whether the label the 'Kaiser's War' still bears any resemblance to historical fact.

## 5.2 the aims of German foreign policy

In the same way that the allied arraignment of the Kaiser offered a clear-cut assertion of German war guilt, it could be argued that the historical perspective initially veered towards an explanation that presented German foreign policy as a consistent, purposeful drive for world power. The notion that Germany's task was world policy, the aim was world power and the instrument was the navy seemed to contain the essential ingredients of the Kaiser's outlook, and it was argued that these elements sustained Wilhelm and his circle on the path to war.

Much of the pioneering work in this area was carried out by Fritz Fischer, who was able to cite the Potsdam War Council of 1912 as a pivotal moment in a planned war, and the Chancellor's memorandum of September 1914 as proof of the expansionist tendencies that prevailed in the Kaiser's court and amongst his military entourage. Fischer's initial contention was that the German political and military leadership had actively planned for war and had deliberately raised the stakes during the July crisis of 1914 knowing that the outcome could be a general European conflagration. In addition, the numerous episodes between 1900 and 1914 in which Germany ham-fistedly dealt with France, Britain and Russia in a series of clumsy pieces of diplomatic ineptitude could be seen as supporting evidence of Germany's intention to assert herself on the world stage at all costs. The work of Fritz Fischer has been summarized by Klaus Epstein as demonstrating that the ruling circle 'succumbed during the First World War to a collective megalomania which expressed itself in utterly unrealistic war aims and a grotesque inability to see the world as it actually was'.[1]

It is interesting to note that more than forty years after the publication of 'Germany's Aims in the First World War' there is much of Fischer's work that remains of the highest value. Nevertheless, it also seems fair to say that some of his interpretations have been subject to a useful degree of refinement. For example, Epstein contends that Fischer 'tends to exaggerate the . . . continuity and consistency of "Germany's drive for world power", and misunderstands the complex figure of the Chancellor, Bethmann-Hollweg.'[2] There is now a growing consensus that German policy at this time can also be characterized as muddled, contradictory and uncertain.

Two important alternative interpretations should also be borne in mind at this stage. Some academics have argued that it was predominantly domestic factors that drove Germany to act the way it did. The Reichstag elections of 1912 in which the socialists emerged triumphantly as the largest party in the Reichstag are of central importance in this thesis. This moment of crisis convinced the Kaiser and his advisers that their efforts to constrain socialism had come to nothing. To make matters worse, as the country lurched to the left, and with Bethmann-Hollweg unable to pass legislation through the Reichstag, the international situation could hardly have been worse. The policy of Weltpolitik seemed in tatters; an expensive programme of naval expansion had failed to close the gap on Great Britain. The Moroccan Crisis of 1911 had underlined the extent to which Germany was isolated from its European neighbours. With problems on all sides, a tempting panacea presented itself. A victorious European war would unite the country behind the throne, rendering previous diplomatic aberrations obsolete and sweeping away enthusiasm for socialism at the expense of a rallying to the colours behind the banner of the Hohenzollern throne. An alternative viewpoint by historians, including David Kaiser and Niall Ferguson, has deliberately shifted emphasis away from domestic pressures. They have claimed that Berlin drew its motivation from a geopolitical and military perspective that placed Germany in an increasingly perilous situation. With her enemies encircling and growing ever stronger, Germany faced a steady and ultimately irreversible deterioration in her international standing. Time was therefore of the essence. A test of strength, a showdown, a reckoning with her enemies could not be postponed indefinitely.

## 5.3 Bülow, the pursuit of Weltpolitik and the policy of the 'free hand'

Given the burgeoning nature of the German economy towards the end of the nineteenth century, it was perhaps inevitable that the country began to look with some ambition towards the wider markets and potential of Africa and the Far East and embark upon a policy of Weltpolitik. Naturally, the Germans looked at the vast expanse of the British overseas Empire and felt that they were entitled to close the gap. As Bernhard von Bülow, the future Chancellor, observed in a famous speech in 1897: 'We do not wish to put anyone in the shade but we do demand our place in the sun.' During the last decade of the nineteenth century there were several indications that Germany intended to live up to the spirit of Bülow's declaration. In 1897, Germany occupied the harbour of Kiao-Chow, which gave her a strategically important coaling station in the Far East. In the Spanish-American war of 1898, Germany pressured Spain to sell the Carolines, Pelews and Marianne islands to her. A year later, with British consent, Germany acquired most of the Samoan islands. These individual incidents were not particularly significant, but assessed together from the perspective of her European rivals, Germany's restless desire to be a world power could be clearly discerned.

Despite these acquisitions, it can be argued with some force that when Bülow became Chancellor in 1900, Germany already lacked the freedom of manoeuvre that he believed existed. Germany's firm commitment to Austria-Hungary in 1879 meant that any rapprochement with Russia was always likely to be tenuous, given the volatile nature of the Balkans. From the British perspective, Germany's eagerness to assert herself on the world stage manifested itself in a foreign policy that was at best cumbersome and on other occasions completely offensive. Nevertheless, as the new century dawned Britain was seriously contemplating an alliance with Germany. The rise of Russia and the tsar's interest in China, furthered by her acquisition of the strategic naval base at Port Arthur, prompted the British to see Germany as an important counterweight to Russian ambition in the Far East. Between 1898 and 1901 Britain made three attempts to foster an alliance with Germany. However, the response from Germany was lukewarm and Bülow's appointment as Chancellor made a deal with Britain even less likely. Bülow had no great faith in the value of a commitment as firm as an alliance with Britain. It seems likely that he believed that Germany could steer its own course and achieve its world status with the construction of an immense fleet. Meanwhile Britain would face significant problems dealing with France and Russia. In William Carr's words: 'All things considered, Germany's policy of the "free hand" seemed correct. Germany must avoid new commitments and remain friends with both Russia and Britain as long as possible. Skilful diplomacy would reap a rich harvest. . . . As the German ambassador in London remarked in 1901, "If people in Germany would only sit still, the time would come soon when we can all have oysters and champagne for dinner".'[3]

Unfortunately, the skilful diplomacy outlined in this rosy scenario was often lacking. With Bülow in the Chancellery, it did not take long for the hard bargaining of the Germans and the scepticism of the British to result in an end to the negotiations between the two powers. Above all, it was Germany's expansionist naval policy after 1897 that convinced the other powers that Germany meant to have its place on the world stage. It was the naval aspect of Germany's development that most alarmed the British and which undoubtedly encouraged the British, French and Russians to form the Triple Entente in 1907. In addition, the often crass conduct of German diplomacy undoubtedly contributed to the development of a scenario that ultimately came to look very alarming from the German perspective.

## 5.4 the Kruger telegram

The conduct of German foreign policy in the Wilhelmine era can legitimately be characterized as clumsy and inept. Whilst the programme of rapid naval expansion was bound in itself to create some disquiet, it was the insensitive handling of other issues, both great and small, that cumulatively created a widespread sense of unease. An example of this came with German intervention in South Africa, an area which Britain justifiably regarded as vital to its strategic interests. In December 1895, Jameson, an agent of Rhodes, invaded the Transvaal, deploying 800 men in an attempt to seize Johannesburg. Wilhelm II responded wildly to the Jameson Raid and insisted on immediate action. There was intemperate talk of declaring a protectorate over the Transvaal and sending troops to the Republic. His advisers in the Wilhelmstrasse managed to calm the Kaiser with the alternative suggestion that he should display his feelings through a congratulatory telegram to Kruger, President of the Transvaal Republic. News of the Kruger telegram was well received in Germany, where nationalist sentiment echoed Wilhelm's resentment of Britain and welcomed Germany's outspoken protest as a sign that Germany was now playing a more pivotal role in world politics. The truth was that this piece of diplomatic activity was inept and ill-judged. The German response had done nothing to impede future British action in South Africa but anti-German sentiment in Britain was certainly heightened as a result of the Kaiser's impetuous actions.

## 5.5 the Far East and the Boxer Rebellion

European attention switched to the Far East when the foreign legations in Beijing came under siege from the Chinese in what became known as the Boxer Rebellion. While the European powers were generally motivated by the defence of their growing commercial interests in the region, the murder of a German diplomat and Wilhelm's contentious claim of a 'Yellow Peril' prompted the Emperor to intervene directly in shaping the German response. He demanded an international expedition under the command of General Waldersee to restore law and order and bring the rebels to heel. Wilhelm's outspoken demands for a ruthless approach from his soldiers to make the name 'German' feared showed the Emperor's personal capacity for causing diplomatic damage. Meanwhile, the Russians had used the Boxer Rebellion to justify their own invasion. The Germans now sought to pre-empt a British move in the Yangtze basin by persuading them to sign the Yangtze Agreement in October 1900. The two signatories renounced further territorial ambitions in China and promised to maintain an 'open-door' policy, with talks to take place if other nations disturbed the status quo. Britain recognized an opportunity to use the agreement against Russia and in 1901 a further crisis looked likely when Russia insisted on retaining political control in Manchuria before withdrawing troops. Britain looked to the Germans for a firm response. However, the Germans were not prepared to risk armed conflict in Europe for the sake of their Chinese investments. In the spring of 1901 Bülow declared officially that Russian action in Manchuria was outside Germany's concern. Britain determined that she would look elsewhere for an ally, terminating the negotiations with Germany and instead signing an alliance with Japan in January 1902.

## 5.6 the Dogger Bank incident, 1904

The Entente Cordiale of 1904 settled Anglo-French colonial disputes in North Africa and agreed to leave Siam as an independent buffer state between French Indo-China and British possessions in Burma. However, the real significance of the agreement was that it laid the groundwork for further co-operation in the future.

The German view was that the Entente was superficial and would crumble as soon as it was put to the test. The opportunity Germany was looking for presented itself shortly after war had broken out between Japan and Russia in the Far East in 1904. As part of the Russian fleet made its way from the Baltic to the Far East, shots were fired at some British fishing boats on the Dogger Bank in the North Sea. Russia was quick to apologise for the sinking of these vessels, claiming that they had been mistaken for Japanese submarines. Germany, however, was eager to take advantage of the situation. Amid a brief but powerful upsurge of anti-Russian sentiment in Britain, the German government proposed to the Russians a continental league against Britain. German intentions were made clear with the suggestion that France might also wish to join the league.

However, Delcassé steered a skilful course through the crisis, urging mediation between Britain and Russia and advising Russia to pay the compensation which the British were demanding. The Dogger Bank incident was short-lived, but it had further discredited Germany and offered evidence that the agreements between France, Britain and Russia were based on fairly firm foundations. The rather clumsy conduct of German foreign policy in this period was typified by the handling of the Dogger Bank incident.

## 5.7 the First Moroccan Crisis, 1905

Chancellor Bülow's influence on foreign affairs was possibly at its height in the conduct of the First Moroccan Crisis of 1905. It now seems clear that Germany's decision to intervene in events in Morocco rested less on economic factors, as was once thought, than on considerations resulting from the changes which had taken place in the European balance of power since 1904. Bülow, supported by Holstein in the Foreign Office, wanted to use the Moroccan crisis as a pretext for either a preventative war against France or, at least, the destruction of the as yet untested Entente Cordiale. It was his calculation that pressure should be applied to France at her most vulnerable point, Morocco. The crisis began in February 1905 when France demanded further concessions from the Sultan over Morocco. Seeing an opportunity to harass the French, Bülow and Holstein decided on a flamboyant gesture of German influence based on a visit by the Kaiser to Tangier during his spring cruise in the Mediterranean. Wilhelm was by no means enthusiastic to pursue this line. Reluctantly he gave way and in March 1905 landed at Tangier where he was received by the Sultan's uncle. It was during this three-hour meeting that the Kaiser made it clear that Germany considered Morocco an independent state and expected her to stand up to the French.

Although no signs of international support for Germany's aggressive stance were forthcoming, Bülow insisted that an international conference on Morocco would have to be held. His hints that Germany would resort to war led to the resignation of the French Foreign Minister. When the conference was held at Algeciras in January 1906 Germany's isolation over Morocco became clear. Although the crisis came to a peaceful conclusion, the conference enabled Great Britain and France to come together for military discussions. Germany had intended to drive France and her partners apart, yet the opposite was achieved. In the words of Sir Edward Grey, the British Foreign Secretary, in February 1906, 'If there is a war between France and Germany, it will be very difficult for us to keep out of it. The Entente and still more the constant and emphatic demonstrations of affection ... have created in France a belief that we shall support them in war. If this expectation is disappointed, the French will never forgive us. There would also I think be a general feeling that we had behaved badly and left France in the lurch.'[4]

Isobel Hull offers a broad view of Germany's perilous position: 'In 1905/06, the aura of peace and prosperity which had graced Wilhelm's reign was suddenly dashed. The great hopes of world power, of economic expansion and of conservative, domestic stability were replaced by greater fears. The Moroccan Crisis, which Germany had engineered in order to break up the newly formed entente cordiale, ended in a chilling demonstration of Germany's diplomatic isolation. ... Domestic politics offered no respite from this gloomy picture. 1905 found Germany embroiled in the worst labor unrest since the beginning of Wilhelm's reign.'[5]

## 5.8 the alliance system

Both at the time the events took place and with hindsight, there has been a clear view that the European alliance system had a damaging impact on the general pre-war climate. Many Germans felt that France and Russia, supported by Great Britain, were deliberately following a malign policy designed to encircle their country. At the same time, the powers of the Entente were alarmed by Germany's rapid programme of naval expansion, the Kaiser's various bellicose statements and the clumsy and sometimes arrogant diplomacy that seemed to mark her conduct in this period. Therefore France, Russia and Britain may have felt that their coming together was a fundamentally defensive instinct.

### the nature of the Alliance system as it developed at this time

| | | |
|---|---|---|
| 1882 | the Triple Alliance (Germany, Austria and Italy) | Following the German–Austrian treaty which had been signed in 1879, Italy had joined the German–Austrian alliance in 1882 and this was known as the Triple Alliance. This was renewed in 1907 and 1912 |
| 1893 | the Franco-Russian Alliance | In 1890 Germany allowed the Reinsurance Treaty with Russia to lapse. In 1891, partly as a consequence of this, came the Franco-Russian Entente, in which the signatories agreed to consult each other in the event of threats of aggression to one of the powers. In 1892 came the Franco-Russian Military Convention and then the full Alliance of 1893 |
| 1902 | the Anglo-Japanese Alliance | Britain strengthened its position in the Far East by signing a defensive alliance with Japan |
| 1904 | the Entente Cordiale (Great Britain and France) | Not as formal an agreement as a full-scale alliance. This Entente was intended to resolve previous colonial differences, particularly over Egypt and Morocco. This came in the same year as the Dogger Bank incident in which Britain's relations with Russia were badly strained following the sinking |

Niall Ferguson sees the German perception of the alliance system as crucially important:

> Why did the Germans act as they did? The best answer which can be offered by the diplomatic historian relates to the structure of European alliances, which had clearly tilted against Berlin since the turn of the century. Russia, France and England had all been able to find issues on which they could agree, but Germany had repeatedly failed (or chosen not) to secure ententes. Even such allies as they did have the Germans had doubts about: declining Austria, unreliable Italy. It can therefore be argued that the Germans saw a confrontation over the Balkans as a means of preserving their own fragile alliance, possibly also creating an anti-Russian Balkan alliance and perhaps even splitting the Triple Entente. Such calculations were by no means unrealistic. As events proved, there was good reason to doubt the Triple Alliance's dependability; and the Triple Entente was indeed fragile, especially where England was concerned.[6]

## 5.9  the Balkans

The general European mood of tension and distrust that characterized the pre-war years led to a situation in which the actions of each of the great powers were often construed as malign by their fretful rivals. Nowhere was anxiety more acutely felt than in the besieged Austro-Hungarian Empire. Having observed the rapid disintegration of the Ottoman Empire and rising demands for Slavic independence, the Austrians were increasingly on the defensive, particularly in the Balkans, a region in an inflamed state as the new century began. As the authority of the Turkish Empire waned, the independent Balkan states were becoming increasingly volatile. Above all, Austria saw Serbia as the driving force of Slav nationalism, a problem which one day would have to be confronted if Austria was to avoid complete collapse. In Berlin, the German elite recognized that the fate of their closest ally was inextricably linked with their own future. Yet, in the same scenario that had challenged Bismarck for so long, the Germans also had to deal with Russia's apparent sponsorship of Slav nationalism, through their Pan-Slav policy, which seemed to make conflict with Austria inevitable. Paradoxically, however, the state visit of Emperor Franz Joseph to Russia in 1897 actually marked the start of a ten-year period in which disagreement over the Balkans between Russia and Austria became much less pronounced. Nevertheless, the antagonistic racial policy pursued by the Hungarians aroused considerable unrest among the Croats and Serbs who lived within the Dual Monarchy. By 1903, Serbia had emerged as a critical force in the Balkans. The upsurge in Serbian patriotism was fuelled by the murder of King Alexander Obrenovich of Serbia in 1903. This dynasty, which had enjoyed fairly positive relations with Austria, was now replaced by the Karageorgevich family, which had historic links with Russia. From this moment, Russian influence developed in Belgrade and Serbian patriotic clubs were established in Bosnia and Hungary. Despite this, the period 1904–07 has been described as the golden age of the Austro-Russian Entente. While Austria focused on its manifold domestic issues, Russia was preoccupied in the Far East and its ultimately humbling conflict with Japan. Yet by 1907 Europe's division into two power blocs, the Triple Alliance and the Triple Entente, was clearly apparent. As Russian attention moved increasingly from the Far East and towards Europe, the Balkans became increasingly tense and volatile. In particular, Austria had decided that the time to take vigorous action in defence of her empire could no longer be put off. The testing ground would be Bosnia-Herzegovina.

## 5.10 the annexation of Bosnia-Herzegovina

The decision to annex Bosnia-Herzegovina in the autumn of 1908 was taken by the Austrian Foreign Minister, Aehrenthal. The precarious position of Germany within the logic of the European alliance system meant that Germany had little choice but to back the Austrians, despite the obvious damage this would do to the future relationship with Russia. In the words of Chancellor Bülow: 'our position would indeed be dangerous if Austria lost confidence in us and turned away . . . in the present world constellation we must be careful to retain in Austria a 'true partner'.[7] The annexation provoked indignant protests from Russia and Serbia, but Germany remained steadfastly behind the Austrians. In the spring of 1909 Germany suggested to Russia that they should formally acknowledge the annexation. When Russia baulked at this proposal, the Germans underlined the suggestion in terms that virtually constituted an ultimatum. The Germans had calculated that after the military debacle with Japan in 1904–05, the Russians were in no position to go to war over Bosnia. Russia had been backed into a corner and was left with no choice but to acknowledge the annexation. Although this episode highlighted Germany's commitment to the alliance with Austria-Hungary, the humiliation of Russia meant that she had been pushed firmly in the direction of her two willing suitors, the French and the British.

It now seemed likely that in the event of an Austrian war with Serbia, Russia, France and Germany would also become involved. It could be argued that, from this point, Germany's room for manoeuvre was sorely limited.

## 5.11 the naval race

Wilhelm II's fascination with naval matters was well known. The 'supreme warlord', whose favourite dress uniform was that of the British Admiral of the Fleet, was determined to reverse the long-standing German tradition that had seen the nation as fundamentally a land-based power to the detriment of her naval standing. In 1888, the German army comprised 19,294 officers and 468,409 non-commissioned officers and men in peacetime, which contrasted with the naval strength of only 15,480 men and a fleet of 18 armour-clads, 8 large and 10 small cruising vessels. On the eve of war, in 1913, the navy comprised 2,196 officers and 59,991 non-commissioned officers and men. In addition, the naval regulations of 1912 stipulated that the fleet would consist of 61 capital ships, 40 small cruisers, 144 torpedo boats and 72 submarines. These figures reflected the view of Grand Admiral Tirpitz expressed in 1895 that 'In my view, Germany will, in the coming century, rapidly drop from her position as a great power unless we begin to develop our maritime interests energetically, systematically and without delay.'[8] This outlook was sustained by Tirpitz in February 1899: ' In view of the changes in the balance of power in Asia and America, the Navy will, in the coming century, become increasingly important for our defence policy, indeed for our entire foreign policy.'[9] It was no surprise, then, that in 1900 William proclaimed: 'Just as My Grandfather reorganised his Army, I shall unswervingly complete the task of reorganising My Navy so that it shall be in a position, internationally, to win for the German Reich that place which we have yet to achieve.'[10] Fritz Fischer stresses the importance of the navy to the realization of Germany's strategic objectives: 'The slogans which William II proclaimed vociferously and which Bülow adopted without resistance, though in a somewhat smoother form, were world policy as a task, world power as the aim and naval construction as the instrument.'[11]

table **5.1  the relative naval strength of the major European powers, 1914**

|  | France | Great Britain | Russia | Austria-Hungary | Germany | Italy |
|---|---|---|---|---|---|---|
| Dreadnoughts | 14 | 24 | 4 | 3 | 13 | 1 |
| Pre-Dreadnoughts | 9 | 38 | 7 | 12 | 30 | 17 |
| Battle cruisers | 0 | 10 | 1 | 0 | 6 | 0 |
| Cruisers | 19 | 47 | 8 | 3 | 14 | 5 |
| Light cruisers | 6 | 61 | 5 | 4 | 35 | 6 |
| Destroyers | 81 | 228 | 106 | 18 | 152 | 33 |
| Submarines | 67 | 76 | 36 | 14 | 30 | 20 |

table **5.2  military and naval personnel of the major European powers, 1890–1914**

|  | 1890 | 1900 | 1910 | 1914 |
|---|---|---|---|---|
| France | 542,000 | 715,000 | 769,000 | 910,000 |
| Great Britain | 420,000 | 624,000 | 571,000 | 532,000 |
| Russia | 677,000 | 1,162,000 | 1,285,000 | 1,352,000 |
| Austria-Hungary | 284,000 | 255,000 | 322,000 | 345,000 |
| Germany | 504,000 | 524,000 | 694,000 | 891,000 |
| Italy | 284,000 | 255,000 | 322,000 | 345,000 |

## 5.12  sources: the impact of the Kaiser on foreign policy

**SOURCE A**

THE LIMITATIONS OF POWER.

(i)   He berated the Foreign Office for not showing despatches to him promptly, but he does not seem to have realised that sometimes, as in 1909, 1911 and 1914, important ones were not shown to him at all. A court official said to the Chief of the Military Secretariat 'It is extraordinary that in every department the Kaiser should have someone about who deceives him.'

(ii)  Behind William's favourite pose of iron resolve, there was an acute lack of self-confidence, combined with an obstinate desire to have how own way . . . At critical moments, as in 1907, 1908 and 1918, this lack of confidence and staying power became a complete loss of nerve, accompanied by such physical symptoms as giddiness and shivering.1

*Source*: M. Balfour, *The Kaiser and His Times* (1972).

**SOURCE B**

There were periods when Wilhelm II became totally obsessed with one idea to such a degree that everything touching upon it even remotely, produced in him a violent rage . . . it was at this stage, surely, with his utterly relentless pursuit of one goal and angry determination to brook no opposition, that Kaiser Wilhelm's personality had the greatest impact on policy making. The pressure for an Army Bill in 1891–3, the demand for a crusade against 'subversion' in 1894–5, the obsession with naval expansion from 1895 onwards, his adoration of his grandfather in 1897, culminating in the 'lackeys and pygmies' speech . . . the thirst for revenge during the China expedition of 1900, the unbounded fury against Britain in December 1912 (quite possibly leading to a decision to go to war in eighteen months) are all good examples – and there are many others – of such moods affecting the direction of German policy.

*Source*: John Rohl, *Kaiser Wilhelm II: New Interpretations* (1982).

THE IMPACT OF THE KAISER ON THE CONDUCT OF GERMAN DIPLOMACY.

The main cause of alarm was William's lack of tact. Holstein wrote to Eulenburg that 'the chief danger in life of William II is that he remains absolutely unconscious of the effect which his speeches and actions have upon Princes, public men and the mass'. He astonished the British Ambassador by the way he talked about the diminutive King of Italy whom he always referred to as 'the Dwarf' while calling the Queen 'a peasant girl' and 'the daughter of a cattle thief'. He was capable, when in the middle of a reception for Prince Ferdinand of Bulgaria, of calling him 'the cleverest and most unscrupulous ruler in Europe'. He later made fun of Ferdinand for being 'festooned with decorations like a Christmas tree'.

*Source*: as source A.

**SOURCE D |**

The outbreak of war in August 1914, for which Bethmann-Hollweg's risk policy was largely responsible, soon proved a great challenge to Wilhelm's concept as Commander-in-Chief of the navy. While he more or less completely left operations on the land-fronts to the Supreme High Command, he at least tried to direct naval operations himself. Unfortunately, he was never able to fulfil this task. More important in this respect was his inability either to develop a convincing strategic concept against the Grand Fleet with his naval advisers or to give his admirals a free hand in naval operations in the North Sea, where the Royal Navy's distant blockade had trapped the Kaiser's splendid vessels. Instead, not wanting to risk the High Sea Fleet, he almost continuously wavered with regard to all questions of naval operations as well as naval strategy.'

*Source*: Michael Epkenans, in Annika Mombauer and Wilhelm Deist, *The Kaiser: New Research on Wilhelm II's Role in Imperial Germany* (2003).

**ESSAY QUESTION**

With reference to the sources and your knowledge, examine the nature of the impact of Kaiser Wilhelm II upon the conduct of German foreign policy in the period 1890–1914.

## 5.13  the Second Moroccan Crisis, 1911

One characteristic of German foreign policy at this time was a readiness to become involved in matters that ostensibly were not their direct concern. Clearly the intent was to demonstrate to the other European powers that Germany had emphatically arrived on the scene as a great power which was entitled to be consulted on matters great and small. A second, related objective may have been to place sustained pressure on the members of the Triple Entente. If sufficient pressure was exerted, during moments of crisis, it might be the case that tension between members of the alliance might come to the surface. This was the case when France responded to reports of disorder by sending troops to Morocco in April 1911. The German Secretary of State for Foreign Affairs, Alfred von Kiderlen Wachter, let it be known that he felt that France had breached the terms of the 1906 Algeciras Act. Despite the reluctance of both Wilhelm II and Chancellor Bethmann-Hollweg to become involved, Kiderlen insisted on sending the gunboat *Panther* to the Moroccan port of Agadir. Kiderlen seemed to personify the aggressive, sabre-rattling, even bullying characteristics that characterized the least satisfactory elements of German foreign policy. As this extract from a memorandum to the Kaiser of 3 May 1911 reveals, the high-ranking official believed that this was an opportunity to intimidate France and to make a successful impression at home:

> By seizing a (territorial) pawn, the Imperial Government will be placed in a position to give the Moroccan affair a turn which would cause the earlier setbacks (of 1905) to pass into oblivion . . . to obtain tangible advantages for Germany . . . (from the) liquidation of the Moroccan question would be important also for the future development of political conditions at home.[12]

However, it soon became apparent that the outcome of the second Moroccan Crisis was not what the German leadership had anticipated. Kiderlen's 'thumping on the table' led to France withdrawing from conference talks with Germany. At the Mansion House dinner on 21 July 1911, Lloyd George warned Germany that Britain would not be dictated to where her vital interests were at stake:

> If a situation were to be forced upon us, in which peace could only be preserved by the surrender of the great and beneficent position Britain has won by centuries of heroism and achievement, by allowing Britain to be treated, where her interests were vitally affected, as if she were of no account in the Cabinet of Nations, then I say emphatically that peace at that price would be a humiliation intolerable for a great country like ours to endure.[13]

After protracted negotiations, the Moroccan question was resolved in November 1911, when Germany recognized France's rights to establish a protectorate in Morocco, in return for which Germany received 275,000 square miles of Congolese jungle. In a confidential letter to the Premier of Wurttemberg on 16 November 1911, Chancellor Bethmann-Hollweg explained why Germany had negotiated an end to the crisis rather than resorting to force:

> Had I . . . allowed the war stage to be reached, we should now be somewhere in France, while the major part of our fleet should lie at the bottom of the North Sea and Hamburg and Bremen would be blockaded or under bombardment. The German people might well have asked me why? Why all this – for the fictitious sovereignty of the Sultan of Morocco?'[14]

German foreign policy in the first decade of the twentieth century has been characterized as crude, aggressive and reckless. The Moroccan Crisis of 1911 and the escalating conflict in the Balkans merely added to the sense of malaise. Relations with France and Russia were poor, while the naval race acted as an impediment to any improvement in relations with Britain, without ruling out the possibility of a rapprochement between the two sea powers.

Psychologically, the argument that Germany was being systematically encircled by her rivals seemed to go hand-in-hand with the argument that the time to break through the malign circle might be drawing closer. The sense of time running out was compounded by the shattering domestic events of 1912. The Reichstag elections of that year saw the emergence of the Social Democrats as the single largest party in the Reichstag. It is not hard to imagine the paranoia that may have spread through the royal court and the military hierarchy as they contemplated the national political scene. An interesting alternative view thrown up by recent research has suggested that Bethmann-Hollweg was, in fact, more perturbed by the Conservative Party whom he accused of trying to destroy him. It may be that the success of the left in the 'red election' of 1912 handed the Chancellor an opportunity to exploit this weakening of the conservative position.

It was against these darkening storm clouds that the Kaiser and his military commanders convened a special meeting at Potsdam in December 1912. It has been claimed that at this meeting the Kaiser was persuaded that war was inevitable. Moltke is said to have advised the Kaiser to launch an immediate 'preventative' war against France and Russia. However, Admiral Tirpitz wanted the great struggle to be postponed for 18 months, which would allow extra time to widen the strategically significant Kiel Canal, so that Germany's battleships would have easy access to the North Sea. A further question concerns the exact nature of the link between the conduct of domestic and foreign policy. Was a sense of domestic crisis driving the ruling elite towards a high-risk foreign policy?

When the contents of this secret meeting were first revealed by historians who discovered notes and diary entries referring to it, they caused a sensation. The meeting itself was depicted as the 'Potsdam war council'. Was this title justifiable? Was the meeting really as significant as it first appeared and, if it was so important, why was a key figure such as the Chancellor, Bethmann-Hollweg, not present when such apparently momentous decisions were being made?

Some of the key extracts are reproduced below.

**SOURCE A**

THE KAISER.

If Russia were to support the Serbs. . . . If Austria were to invade Serbia, war would be inevitable for us. . . . The fleet, of course, would have to face the war against Britain.

GENERAL VON MOLTKE, CHIEF OF THE GENERAL STAFF.

In my opinion war is inevitable, and the sooner the better . . . the popularity of a war against Russia as outlined by the Kaiser, should be better prepared.

**SOURCE C**

ADMIRAL VON TIRPITZ.

Postponement of the great struggle by one-and-a-half years.

**SOURCE D**

GEORGE ALEXANDER VON MULLER, CHIEF OF THE NAVAL CABINET, VERDICT ON THE SIGNIFICANCE OF POTSDAM MEETING.

Pretty much nil.

**SOURCE E**

WILHELM II'S DESCRIPTION OF THE CHANCELLOR'S FRAME OF MIND, TO ADMIRAL MÜLLER.

He has 'accustomed' himself 'to the idea of . . . war.'
(Note: Bethmann-Hollweg was not present at the meeting.)

*Source*: all taken from John Traynor, *Europe 1890–1990* (1995).

## the significance of the Potsdam Conference

A range of historians including Fischer and Rohl regard the meeting that took place on 8 December 1912 as a major staging post on the German path to war. It is striking to note that when it was agreed at Potsdam that war would be postponed while work on the widening of the Kiel Canal was completed over an 18-month period, this project culminated in the summer of 1914, the very moment when war broke out. The conference also signalled an increased level of German military readiness, with a new Army Bill planned to be introduced into the Reichstag in 1913. Antagonism towards Russia in the popular press seemed to signal that the population were being mentally prepared for war. Financial reserves were consolidated in the wake of Potsdam and courses at the Prussian military academy were reduced in length, a further sign that war was looming.

On the other hand, Wolfgang Mommsen claims that the so-called 'war council' did not make any decisions of note other than to agree to naval and military increases which had already been contemplated. He contends that the press campaign against the Russians was short-lived. Most significantly he has argued (though this is contested by other authorities) that Bethmann-Hollweg was not informed of the decisions taken until much later. Finally, Rohl's monumental research on Wilhelm II has made it difficult to conclusively reject the significance of the conference.

**QUESTION**

With reference to the sources presented here and your own knowledge, prepare the case for and against the importance of the Potsdam war council in the conduct of German foreign policy and the origins of the First World War.

## 5.15 the July Crisis

### Sunday 28 June 1914: the assassination of Franz Ferdinand

In late June 1914 Kaiser Wilhelm II spent the day under the blazing sun racing his yacht *Meteor* at Kiel. Meanwhile, several hundred miles to the south, Archduke Franz Ferdinand – heir to the throne of Austria-Hungary – was spending his wedding anniversary with his wife, Countess Sophie, on a state visit to Sarajevo. Ostensibly they received a warm welcome and the fine weather allowed them to drive through the crowded streets in an open-topped car. However, Sarajevo was the capital of the former Turkish province of Bosnia, a state inhabited by Slavs but occupied since 1908 by the Austro-Hungarian Empire. A southern Slav terrorist organization consisting of ultra-nationalist officers and student intellectuals (calling itself the 'Black Hand' gang) regarded the Austrian prince as the figurehead of an occupying empire which stood in the way of Slav independence. Within this radical group, and beyond the direct control of the Serbian government, was Gavrilo Princip, who had decided to lead an assassination attempt against the Austrian prince. As the car moved through the streets of Sarajevo, Prinzip was able to breach the rudimentary security and step out of the crowd and on to the running board, and at point-blank range he fired several shots. A few minutes later the royal couple were dead.

### Wilhelm's response to the assassination of Franz Ferdinand

Wilhelm II was still aboard his yacht when Admiral Muller, the Chief of the Naval Secretariat, pulled alongside in a launch and shouted that he had a telegram to pass across. His response was initially considered and he wondered whether it would be good form to call off the race. His mind would now have to turn to much weightier decisions.

Why did an isolated act of terrorism in an area of which few Europeans have even heard lead to a prolonged and widespread political crisis throughout July? It is unlikely that any period in the history of mankind has been subject to more intensive historical research than that between 28 June and 4 August 1914.

### the role of Bethmann-Hollweg in the July Crisis

The role played in the crisis by the Chancellor, Theobald von Bethmann-Hollweg, has aroused intense debate. The traditional persepctive saw the

Chancellor as a peace-loving, liberal statesman who evoked comparisons with Abraham Lincoln. Bethmann-Hollweg was praised for his valiant efforts to keep the radical militarists at bay and prevent them from indoctrinating the Kaiser with their warlike talk. This view portrays the chancellor as a helpless victim of circumstances beyond his control, trying at all costs to avoid war but being dragged to the brink by inflexible military strategies, belligerent generals and a headstrong Emperor.

## the Fischer thesis

Fritz Fischer's formidable study, *Griff Nach der Weltmacht* (Grasping at world power), published in 1961, presented a radically different picture of Bethmann-Hollweg. Fischer placed the Chancellor much closer to military extremists like General Ludendorff. He claimed that Bethmann-Hollweg had far-reaching war aims which followed closely the ideas put forward by leading German industrialists and by the radical lobbying of the Pan-German League. These ideas, Fischer argued, were there for all to see in an influential memorandum of 9 September 1914 in which Bethmann-Hollweg stated that the aim of the war must be the security of the German Empire in the West and in the East for the foreseeable future, with France permanently weakened and Russia pushed as far as possible from the German frontier, and her rule over non-Russian subject peoples broken. Fischer was convinced that these ideas must have been formulated before the war had begun. Moreover, he provided damaging evidence of close personal links between the Chancellor and Walther Rathenau, director of the powerful German electrical combine: AEG. Fischer found evidence to show that Rathenau was a regular guest at the Chancellor's magnificent country estate in Hohenfinow and argued that his expansionist ideas came to exert a powerful influence over the Chancellor.

There is no doubt that long before the July Crisis the Chancellor found himself full of doubts and apprehension. Overlooking the park of his estate near Berlin, the gloomy Chancellor told his son that there was no point in planting new trees, for the Russians would soon be there. Germany's international isolation cannot have relieved the Chancellor's growing sense of pessimism. As a gloomy military memorandum of May 1914 put it: 'At the moment Italy is still on the side of the Triple Alliance and Emperor Franz Joseph's personality still holds the hotch-potch Danubian monarch together. . . . But for how long? Will these things perhaps not change in favour (of the Entente Powers) quite soon?'[15]

## the handling of Serbia in the July Crisis

This growing sense of urgency tinged with gloom and pessimism was heightened by the events in Sarajevo of 28 June 1914. When Kaiser Wilhelm II received an official report on the assassination from the German ambassador in Vienna, his reaction was less restrained than it had been when he had first heard the news on his yacht. The aggressive comments which the Kaiser scribbled in pencil in the margins of the memorandum have become history in themselves. 'Now or never' exclaimed the Kaiser, 'The Serbs will have to be straightened out and soon.' Wilhelm II had set the tone for the regime's reaction and had personally added a powerful, personal momentum to events.

The crucial question was whether action against Serbia could be carried out without Russian intervention. The critical contribution of the military at this stage was to urge the Kaiser to meet this risk head-on and launch a preventative war against Russia. They argued that with Russia still a few years away from being at full military capacity, a much greater chance of victory was to be had in 1914 than a few years later.

## the ruling elite in Berlin

In his book *Germany and the Approach of War in 1914*,[16] Volker Berghahn estimates that within Germany no more than 12 people were consulted over the main decisions. Moreover, the crucial steps in the July Crisis were made by individuals within the Court, the German Foreign Office and the General Staff. The leading industrialists, despite their power and influence, do not appear to have been consulted at this stage.

## Austria and the 'blank cheque'

The Austrian monarchy reacted to the assassination with more restraint than their German counterparts. Rather than seeking out immediate revenge, Emperor Franz Joseph made it clear that he would prefer to hear the results of an inquiry into the assassination before approving any action against the Serbs. Only Conrad, the chief of the General Staff, proposed immediate action. Meanwhile Berchtold, the Austro-Hungarian foreign minister, was concerned that Germany 'would leave us in the lurch' and this prompted Franz Joseph to write a personal letter to Wilhelm II asking for clarification of the German position at the highest level.

Count Berchtold's personal envoy was sent to deliver the letter in person, and after lunch with the Kaiser in the Royal Palace, emphatic clarification was forthcoming:

> I gave the autograph letter and the enclosed memoir into the hands
> of His Majesty. In my presence the Kaiser read both with the greatest
> attention. The first thing he assured me was, that he had expected
> some serious step on our part towards Serbia, but that at the same time
> he must confess that the detailed statement of His Majesty made him
> regard a serious European complication possible and that he could
> give no definite answer before having taken council with the Imperial
> Chancellor.
>
> After lunch, when I again called attention to the seriousness of the
> situation, the Kaiser authorised me to inform our gracious Majesty that
> we might in this case, as in all others, rely upon Germany's full support.
> He must, as he said before, first hear what the Imperial Chancellor
> has to say, but he did not doubt in the least that Herr von Bethmann

Hollweg would agree with him. Especially as far as our action against Serbia was concerned.'[17]

This offer of support to Austria from the Kaiser was so wholehearted that it has become known as the 'blank cheque'. It represented a key step in unlocking the complex mechanisms of treaty obligations which would ultimately unleash a world war. The Kaiser, without obtaining prior approval from the Chancellor but assuming it would be given later, had personally issued full, unconditional support to the Austrians and had underlined this 'blank cheque' with the advice that the Dual Monarchy should not hesitate to take action against the Serbs. As Wilhelm prepared to set sail for Norway on the evening of 6 July he told the industrialist, Krupp, 'This time, I shall not chicken out.' Krupp regarded this more as a rather strained show of bravado than genuine aggression but nevertheless, the Kaiser's nervous energy was having a profound effect on those around him.

Bethmann-Hollweg probably recognized that the 'action' against Serbia which the Kaiser envisaged could easily trigger the whole process of alliance commitments and lead to a major war. The Chancellor devised an alternative plan which at least obtained some breathing space but with the militarists pushing for more strident action. Wilhelm II explained the plan to officials with some enthusiasm: 'the Austrian Government will demand the most far-reaching satisfaction from Serbia and will, as soon as this is not given, move its troops into Serbia'. Russian intervention was regarded as highly unlikely 'because the Tsar will not lend his support to royal assassins and because Russia is at the present moment, militarily and financially totally unprepared for war'.

## the ultimatum to Serbia

Now it was up to the Austrians to draw up a definitive ultimatum to Serbia. Fatally, it took until 19 July for the Austro-Hungarian ministerial council to approve a suitably worded ultimatum. A further delay was caused when the Austrians realized that between 20 and 23 July, Raymond Poincaré, the French President, would be on a state visit to St Petersburg. If the ultimatum were presented to Serbia during this period, then there was every possibility that the response would come not just from the Serbs alone but as a coordinated move from Serbia, her protector Russia and Russia's ally, France. The ultimatum would have to be shelved until Poincaré left Russia. Yet even before Poincaré arrived in St Petersburg the Russians had cracked the cipher used by the Austro-Hungarian Foreign Ministry and had a clear idea that the Austrians were planning some sort of decisive action against Serbia. Nevertheless, when the ultimatum was finally delivered to Serbia on 23 July, its harsh terms and 48–hour time limit for a reply sent shock waves through the foreign offices of Europe. The hard-pressed Serbs skilfully produced a reply which, while conciliatory in tone, did not meet all of the demands. The Serbian reply was delivered to the Austrian representative moments before the 6 p.m. deadline on 25 July. Its contents were scarcely considered. Following prior instructions, the Austrian official immediately announced his dissatisfaction and returned to Vienna on the 6.30 p.m. train. Austria announced that it had broken off relations with Serbia, but the real intentions behind the smokescreen of the ultimatum had been laid bare.

## Bethmann-Hollweg and the approach of war

Meanwhile, in Germany, Bethmann-Hollweg remained at the helm, lamenting the delays in the Austrian response and realizing the risks inherent in his plan. He began to sink into his familiar melancholy. According to one source, Bethmann-Hollweg said on 7 July: 'An action against Serbia can lead to world war.'[18] A week later he admitted that he was taking 'a leap into the dark', but this constituted his 'gravest duty'.[19] By now Bethmann-Hollweg seemed to think that there was no way out: 'Secret intelligence gives a shattering picture . . . the military might of Russia is growing fast.'[20] By 25 July it was becoming painfully apparent that Russia and Britain were not prepared to stand by and observe the defeat of Serbia. Universal diplomatic condemnation of the ultimatum and the way it had been handled by the Austrians ensured that Bethmann-Hollweg's over-elaborate plan had failed. Over his shoulder the harassed chancellor could sense Moltke and the other leading military figures gathering against him. By 26 July they had all returned to Berlin. Their time had come.

The struggle between the General Staff and the civilian politicians lasted for three days. The prospect of a swift military victory resolving Germany's complex foreign and domestic problems was an intoxicating one, and the optimism of the General Staff ensured that the military now gained the ascendancy over the civilians. The Chancellor exclaimed that he now saw the 'force of fate, stronger than the power of humans, hanging over Europe and our people.'[21] On the same day Bethmann-Hollweg informed the Kaiser of his new priorities: 'in all events Russia must ruthlessly be put in the wrong.'[22]

## mobilization of troops and declarations of war

The events of the last few days of July and the first few days of August now took on an alarming European dimension. On 28 July Austria-Hungary declared war on Serbia and shelled Belgrade, although general mobilization against Russia had not yet occurred. When the French took the precaution of recalling soldiers from Morocco the Germans warned that further steps would force Germany to proclaim the 'state of imminent danger of war' which directly preceded mobilization. In Russia, two alternative decrees – one for partial mobilization and one for general mobilization – had already been signed by the Tsar. Germany's firm warning to Russia now followed, but backfired since the Russian Foreign Minister, the War Minister and the Chief of Staff unanimously agreed to respond with general mobilization. The Tsar only hesitated because of the intervention of Wilhelm II. Evidence that the Kaiser was now beginning to have second thoughts is provided by his personal telegram to his cousin the

Tsar which ended: 'I am exerting my utmost influence to induce the Austrians to deal straightly to arrive to a satisfactory understanding with you. I confidently hope you will help me in my efforts to smooth over difficulties that may still arise. Your very sincere and devoted friend and cousin Willy.'[23]

It may be that for their conduct in the last days of July and the first days of August, Europe's decision-makers should be burdened with a collective responsibility because they had allowed the control of events to slip from their grasp and assume an inexorable momentum. In his analysis of the leaders involved in the July Crisis, the Italian historian Luigi Albertini was alarmed by 'the disproportion between their intellectual and moral endowments and the gravity of the problems which faced them, between their acts and the results thereof'.[24] On 27 July Edward Grey – the British Foreign Secretary – sent an urgent message to Bethmann-Hollweg asking Germany to persuade the Austrian government to accept Serbia's reply to the ultimatum. In return, Grey was urging the Russians to act with restraint. The telegram was passed to the Kaiser, who replied that the Serbian response had indeed removed grounds for war but nevertheless recommended that Austria should occupy Belgrade and stay there to provide some guarantee that the Serbs would fulfil their promises. However, while the civilian Berchtold was weighing up the Kaiser's 'halt in Belgrade' proposal, General Conrad was being reminded by Moltke (the chief of the German general staff) that any further delay in Austrian action against the Serbs would have disastrous consequences. It is no wonder that such conflicting advice had Berchtold in despair, to the extent that he is said to have exclaimed: 'Who actually rules in Berlin, Bethmann or Moltke?'[25] Austria's subsequent announcement that it was too late to delay operations against Serbia suggests that the advice of the German military was now carrying more weight. On 30 July Austria-Hungary ordered general mobilization for the next day. Russia immediately followed suit. At noon on 31 July news of Russian general mobilization became known in Berlin. The news moved the civilian and military factions in Germany together. Bethmann-Hollweg was satisfied that the press would be able to bring together the German people in a wave of anti-Russian patriotism. The generals knew that their demands for full German mobilization could no longer be resisted. Allegations in the German press that Russian patrols had trespassed onto German soil on 2 August ensured that left-wing opposition to the war was brushed aside amid alarmist talk of the imminent invasion by the 'Russian barbarians'. On 1 August Germany declared war on Russia and mobilized her troops. The harsh logic of the alliance system meant that on 3 August Germany also declared war on France.

Germany's military strategy, based to a considerable extent on a plan drawn up by General Schlieffen, made it unlikely that Britain would remain neutral. In the expectation that it would be several weeks before the Russian mobilization would take full effect, Germany's soldiers would outflank the French army by marching through southern Belgium. This was in direct violation of the Treaty of London, Britain's guarantee to Belgium made in 1839. Britain declared war on Germany on 4 August. The chain was complete.

## 5.16 sources: interpretations of the origins of the First World War

**SOURCE A**

How important was the general mobilisation of the Russian army on 31 July? At first glance it would seem to have been crucial since Russia's move was answered immediately by Germany's mobilisation and within two days by the outbreak of war. Even without the Russian mobilisation there is, however, every reason to doubt whether by 30 July a European conflict could have been avoided since, as Russian diplomats stressed, by then Austria and Germany had gone too far to retreat without serious damage to their prestige and to the stability of their alliance. . . . Study of the July Crisis from the Russian standpoint indeed confirms the now generally accepted view that the major immediate responsibility for the outbreak of the war rested unequivocally on the German government.

*Source*: D. C. B. Lieven, *Russia and the Origins of the First World War* (1983).

**SOURCE B**

At the center of the dispute stands the German Chancellor, Theobald von Bethmann-Hollweg, the civilian head of the German federal government. Some historians, with Fritz Fischer in the lead, have argued that Bethmann seized upon the assassination as the pretext to launch a long-planned war of aggression, whose goal was German hegemony on the European continent. The preponderance of evidence, however, now suggests instead that the chancellor pursued a somewhat more cautious policy, which grew out of his anxiety over the future of the Austrian monarchy, whose survival, he believed, did justify the risk of a European war. Bethmann was strengthened in this belief by the country's leading soldier, the chief of the army's General Staff, Helmuth von Moltke . . .

The thinking of both Bethmann and Moltke betrayed as well the malaise that was rife among Germany's political and social elites over the country's domestic future – particularly over the dramatic growth of the world's most formidable Socialist party.

*Source*: Roger Chickering, *Imperial Germany and the Great War, 1914–1918* (1998).

**SOURCE C**

This sense that men were carried away by the tide of history tempts us to look for historical forces which will explain the decisions of individuals as part of a broader and inevitable historical process, or at least as part of a wider landscape than that provided by the view from the chancelleries of Europe. The problem of relating these broader explanations to the individual decisions taken in July 1914 remains a major historiographical and philosophical problem which may indeed be insoluble.

*Source*: James Joll, *The Origins of the First World War* (1984).

## SOURCE D

Two things are clear. First, while the Fischer controversy is now itself a part of history . . . it still provides the framework within which the origins of the war are discussed by both German and non-German historians. . . . Some rejecting the so-called 'primacy of domestic policy' have tried to reinstate the decisive importance of international politics for the outbreak of war. . . . More persuasively, historians have underlined the interdependence of foreign and domestic policy. . . . Even among those who emphasize the role played by domestic considerations, there has been debate over whether Germany really faced internal crisis in 1914 – and whether this was true of Germany alone. . . . There is still a good case for arguing that Germany bore a major share of responsibility for the war. But any such argument must be grounded in the volatile international situation of the time and set against a realistic analysis of how other powers behaved.

*Source*: David Blackbourn, *History of Germany 1780–1918: The Long Nineteenth Century* (2003).

## SOURCE E

Rohl has argued that the destruction of much of the documentation which would have allowed historians to piece together German decision-making during the July Crisis amounts to a cover-up. . . . We can never establish with certainty when the German decision for war was taken because so much of the documentation which would have helped to establish the answer has been destroyed. However, it seems most likely that the decision was taken in response to the assassination of Franz Ferdinand. The Kaiser interpreted his friend's murder as 'a dreadful blow' and he, Moltke, Bethmann and the Prussian War Minister Falkenhayn were all resolved to back Austrian demands for retribution from Serbia, even at the risk of a European war. Konrad Jarausch has argued that the Germans were pursuing a policy of calculated risk in 1914, designed to secure a massive diplomatic victory over the Entente powers, while avoiding war. However, this position is no longer tenable given the evidence which has recently emerged indicating that even the allegedly peace-loving Bethmann was working for war during the crisis . . .

Germany was the only power which was actively working for a European war in 1914. She was doing so because the Reichsleitung, and particularly the military component within it, believed that the international balance of power was shifting inexorably against Germany. This was compounded by their fear of Russia and a perception that Germany was destined to lose their arms race against the Entente. Domestic factors were only peripherally involved. The July crisis was regarded as offering Germany a last chance to achieve a European hegemony. The fact that this view was based on misperception makes German decision-making in 1914 all the more catastrophic for Europe and tragic for Germany.

*Source*: Matthew S. Seligmann and Roderick R. McLean, *Germany from Reich to Republic* (2000).

The consensus has for many years been that it was the German government that wilfully turned the Balkan crisis of 1914 into a world war. Yet that is surely to understate the shared responsibility of all the European empires. For one thing, the Austrian government could hardly be blamed for demanding redress from Serbia in the wake of the Archduke's murder. . . . It is true that when the Kaiser first informed the Austrian ambassador that Germany would back Austria, he explicitly stated that that support would be forthcoming 'even if it should come to a war between Austria and Russia'. But an offer of support conditional on Russian non-intervention would have been quite worthless . . .

Without doubt, the German generals eagerly seized the opportunity for war and delayed their own mobilization only in order that Russia would appear the aggressor. Yet German anxieties about the pace of Russia's post-1905 rearmament were not wholly unjustified . . .

The French generals, whose belief in the morale-building benefits of the offensive was second to none, were scarcely less eager for war. They had no intention of standing by while Germany defeated their Russian ally, but planned instead to invade southern Germany through Alsace-Lorraine as soon as hostilities began.

Where the Kaiser erred most egregiously was in believing that the encirclement of Germany had been carefully planned by the Entente powers, above all by Great Britain. In reality, neither Edward VII nor his successor George V had remotely considered this possibility; nor had politicians in either the Liberal or the Conservative Party.

*Source*: Niall Ferguson, *The War of the World: History's Age of Hatred* (2006).

## ESSAY QUESTION

With reference to all of the sources presented here and your own knowledge, explain the extent to which:

(a)  Wilhelm II and
(b)  Germany

can be held directly responsible for the outbreak of the First World War.

chapter **6**

# the First World War, 1914–18

## 6.1 mobilization for total war

It was August 1914 and German mobilization was in full swing. The political tension of July had been replaced by feverish military preparation. Two million reservists were on the march, in their field-grey uniforms and distinctive spiked helmets. The standard issue for each man included a greatcoat, groundsheets, tinned corned beef, a box of coffee beans, two small bags of biscuits, a prayer book, a song sheet and 90 rounds of rifle ammunition. Within just 16 days more than 2,000 trains bound for the front crossed the Hohenzollern Bridge at Cologne.

The military chiefs of staff knew that the effective performance of their land armies would depend upon the logistic support they received. In the words of William Carr, 'Victory in the field under modern conditions called for total mobilisation of a country's economic potential.'[1] Everything would have to be geared towards the war, with much of the European continent becoming a battlefield, while behind the lines resources of arms and bread had to be made available to the troops.

### how well equipped was the German economy to wage war?

The German economy was one of the most powerful and best balanced in Europe. Germany produced twice as much steel and cotton goods as her nearest competitors (Britain and France, respectively). Her coal production matched Britain's and her electricity output surpassed Britain, France and Italy. Germany's performance in modern economic activities such as the production of synthetic materials, dyes, drugs and fertilizers was uniformly impressive. German technology was already renowned in areas such as plastics, printing, photography, precision instruments and cables. Substantial government investment in heavy industry and shipbuilding had led to rapid technological development. German companies such as Siemens, Krupp and AEG enjoyed an international reputation and areas such as the Ruhr, Alsace-Lorraine and Silesia were highly productive industrial regions. Germany had become a modern, prosperous, self-confident nation. This image was enhanced by the country's excellent education system. Of 160,588 recruits for the German armed forces in 1908, only 39 were classified as illiterate. This led to an educated workforce which, in a further show of industrial development, came to reside increasingly in towns and cities as opposed to the countryside. Compared with some of her less developed rivals, Germany appeared to be blessed with a well-educated, forward looking and increasingly sophisticated workforce.

However, not all aspects of the German economy were so well placed. In 1914 the Reich had to import almost half of its foodstuffs and raw materials. A critical area of weakness concerned materials essential for the waging of war. Germany faced a shortage of the hardening agents needed for the production of top-quality steel and needed to import rubber, nitrates, petroleum and a range of oils and fertilizers. To make matters worse, historians have been unable to detect evidence of substantial economic planning in the years immediately before the outbreak of war. Most historians now agree that Germany was not ready for war economically in 1914 and that within a year, Germany faced a serious manpower shortage in industry following the drafting of many skilled male workers into the armed forces. The critical point here is that Germany did not organize her economic resources as quickly or as efficiently as has previously been depicted. This was partly due to the administrative incompetence of the Kaiser and his administrators, although it is probably fair to say that each of the main protagonists neglected the economic dimension in their plans for war, partly because of assumptions over the duration of the conflict. However, in his introduction to *The War Plans of the Great Powers* Paul Kennedy highlights the importance to German military planning of the big industrialists and armaments manufacturers. He states that 'a primitive form of "military-industrial complex" had stoked up and exploited the arms race to satisfy the needs of the vast armaments industry and to divert public attention from domestic political questions'.[2]

## the extent of national unity in 1914

The decision makers in Berlin and St Petersburg recognized that securing popular support for the war in the country at large was every bit as important as ensuring that there were enough troops, guns and bullets at the front line. The physical and economic mobilization of the nation had to be accompanied by a psychological preparation of the whole population. Jay Winter highlights the importance of consent:

> Consent was essential because the war was so costly; and however powerful the instruments of propaganda and censorship, consent was never produced by force. . . . It came from the core of civil society itself . . . the need to see the conflict through to victory also depended on the vilification of the enemy as the incarnation of evil. The cultural politics of hatred flourished in total war, creating the conditions for atrocity and genocide.[3]

In his study of the mood of 1914, James Joll provides a note of caution at the outset. He states that 'the analysis of . . . beliefs and attitudes and of the accumulated mentality of a nation is a very difficult task. To establish anything which can be called the "mood" of Europe in 1914 is probably impossible. We lack the detailed study of opinion for most countries, even where the material for it exists and is accessible.'[4] However, it is clear that a vital element in the process of psychological mobilization was for each government to convince its people that the other side was to blame for the outbreak of hostilities. The news of Russia's general mobilization at the end of July enabled German Chancellor Bethmann-Hollweg to ensure that 'in all events Russia must ruthlessly be put in the wrong'. A sustained effort was being made by the government to create a mood of war enthusiasm.

As the German soldiers left for the front, thousands of civilians crowded the streets to wave them off and attend open-air services. Admiral Müller enthused that 'the mood is splendid'. On 4 August Emperor Wilhelm II delivered an electrifying speech to a packed and enthusiastic Reichstag in which he declared that Germany had drawn its sword for war with a clear conscience. Eager to take advantage of the prevailing hostility towards the Russians, Wilhelm exclaimed, 'I know no parties any more, only Germans!' The speech was greeted with cheers and applause from all sections of the Reichstag. The left had clearly decided that at this time of national crisis it was necessary for them to rally around the throne, suspend their opposition to the Kaiser, and join in the patriotic struggle against Russia. It was agreed that for as long as the war lasted there would be a political truce, the so-called *Burgfriede*, or 'truce of the fortress'. In the same momentous Reichstag session, Chancellor Bethmann-Hollweg claimed that Germany was the victim of unprovoked aggression. The Chancellor argued that 'we are not driven by the pleasure of conquest; an inflexible will inspires us to preserve what God has given us for ourselves and for all future generations. . . . With a clear conscience and with clean hands we take up arms in self-defence that has been forced upon us.'[5]

The war credits, the finances needed for the struggle, were passed unanimously, with the Reichstag allocating 5 billion marks to the war effort. The Reichstag was happy to leave the running of the war to the Emperor and his advisers and did not even meet again until December 1914. The attitude of the socialist and left-wing parties was of particular importance. In late August 1914 the Berlin Police President described the 'elated spirit' in the Reich capital and went on to say that 'even in the north and east of Berlin [working-class districts] which were formerly hardly responsive to patriotic emotion, masses of black-white-red flags are displayed'.[6] A number of trade unions voluntarily renounced the right to strike. The authorities felt that the likelihood of socialist dissent had been reduced by the simple fact that many working-class activists had already been 'called to the colours' and had left for the front. Nevertheless, the government invoked the Siege Law of 1871 which meant that a virtual state of martial law was introduced. Newspaper editors and their journalists showed that they were prepared to shelve their normal critical stance. For example, the magazine *Simplicissimus* abandoned its satirical approach and took a much more patriotic line. The popular newspaper the *Hamburger Fremdenblatt* became a loyal supporter of the German military high command.

A country which in 1912 had seemed to be increasingly politically divided between a burgeoning socialist movement on the one hand and an increasingly volatile emperor on the other now seemed to enjoy a greater degree of political unity than at any time since the unification of 1871. The feeling of political fervour was so intense that people would later refer to 'the spirit of August 4' to evoke the mood of national solidarity which prevailed at the start of the war. Letters and diaries are an important source for historians of this period, although it is worth remembering that most of this type of evidence comes from the middle classes and above, whereas the working classes were less likely to keep a diary.

There is ample evidence of war enthusiasm in these contemporary accounts. A Leipzig historian described a 'single great feeling of moral elevation, a soaring of religious sentiment, in short, the ascent of a whole people to the heights'.[7] The writer Carl Zuchmayer exclaimed: 'I have experienced such a physical and moral condition of luminosity and euphoria two or three times since, but never with that sharpness and intensity.'[8] The novelist Thomas Mann stated that 'only the enemies of the spirit opposed the war which would leave Germany stronger, prouder, freer, happier'.[9]

Even in areas where there were substantial numbers of non-German citizens there were displays of popular support for the war. Contemporary reports on Germany's Polish population in Upper Silesia referred to 'unanimous enthusiasm among the local Poles'. Equally encouraging from the government's point of view would have been this account from the predominantly industrial and working class Ruhr. Written by a coal miner, it reported 'high went the waves of enthusiasm in the days of the mobilisation. Never have I heard the song *Deutchland Über Alles* sung more passionately than at this time!'[10]

It is not surprising, given the positive flavour of much of this correspondence, that many historians have supported the notion that the outbreak of war was greeted with general enthusiasm. Recently however, as historians have delved deeper into regional studies, they have begun to question this assumption. In a recent study of the mood of 1914 Richard Bessel points out that less attention has been paid to those who displayed panic and anxiety rather than enthusiasm and patriotism. He describes how thousands of Germans queued to withdraw savings and bought large amounts of food which they then hoarded. Meanwhile, shopkeepers raised their prices, adding to the feeling of concern and alarm. In many areas petitions were drawn up, asking for particular groups of young men such as those who worked on family farms to be excused military service. Bessel argues that the majority of the peasant population were very reluctant to see young men being called away from the land at harvest time. Equally, there was very little enthusiasm at the prospect of increased taxes which the war would demand. Bessel concludes that the German people were not enthusiastic about war in general but that they did generally support a war involving a defensive struggle against tsarist Russia and the promise of a quick and relatively painless victory over France in the west.[11]

Jay Winter and Blaine Baggett offer this conclusion on the mood of 1914:

> To understand their lives, and the world they passed on to us, we need to go back to that moment in 1914 when, in a sense, the twentieth century began. When we look at their faces, so hopeful, so fresh, so full of possibility, we can see some of what might have been, as well as some foreshadowing of what was to be.
>
> The history of the Generation of 1914 is a story of decency betrayed, of the gap which separated the narrow vision of the men in power and the open hearts of the millions who followed. To contrast the outlook of the leaders with the humane responses of the multitude – the people who really knew the war at its worst – is to begin to form some sense of the waste and tragedy of the Great War.[12]

While there is no doubt that many German soldiers went to the front line with a degree of enthusiasm, there is an abundance of evidence to show that this good will was very quickly put to the test amid the harsh realities of trench warfare. This extract, written in September 1914 by a young law student from Leipzig, illustrates the point: 'This ghastly battle is still raging – for the fourth day! Up till now, like most battles in this war, it has consisted almost entirely of an appalling artillery duel. I am writing this letter in a sort of grave-like hole which I dug for myself in the firing-line. The shells are falling so thick today, both before and behind us, that one may regard it as only thanks to the special mercy of God if one comes out of it safe and sound.'[13]

To what extent did the German government mobilize popular support for the war in August 1914?

**SOURCE A**

EXTRACT FROM BETHMANN-HOLLWEG'S ADDRESS TO THE REICHSTAG, AUGUST 1914.

A tremendous fate has fallen upon Europe. While we have endeavoured to maintain the prestige of the German Empire in the eyes of the world, we have lived for 44 years in peace . . . in this work of peace we have become strong and mighty – therefore we are envied. We have suffered with long-enduring patience, while in the East and West, under the excuse that Germany is lusting for war, hatred for us has been nourished and fetters wrought wherewith to bind us. The wind which blows there has now become a storm. We desired nothing but to live on in peaceful toil . . . our sword shall only leap from its sheath in defence of a just cause . . .

I repeat the words of the Kaiser: 'we enter the struggle with a clear conscience! The hour of great trial has struck for our nation. But we look forward to it with absolute confidence. Our army is in the field, our fleet is ready, and behind them the entire German nation.

## SOURCE B

In 1914 popular support for the war effort was not universal, but the relatively few voices raised against the war were drowned by a chorus of approval in the popular press, in the churches and even among organised labor. What the rest of the population thought is not so clear, but the masses in the towns and in the countryside took the war in their stride, thereby enabling the major belligerents to mobilise without the fear of internal popular opposition. Of course the war they all supported was not the war they were to fight, but few had the prescience to realise what they were getting themselves into by rallying round the flag in 1914 . . . But in some instances there was little war enthusiasm at all. The most famous instances of flag-waving occurred in capital cities. This is unsurprising since these were also centers of rail traffic, and therefore staging points for mobilised soldiers, who were indeed given a noisy and emotional send-off when they went to fight. But what about the villages and country towns where the bulk of Europe's population lived?

There seems to have been much less to-do about the outbreak of war in such places. In France and Germany, Russia and Austria, conscription was a 'normal' experience; men who left were just doing what they had done many times before'.

*Source*: J. M. Winter, *The Experience of World War 1* (1988).

## SOURCE C

Using sources from the city of Hamburg, he found that the *Hamburgische Correspondent*, a respectable middle-class paper, reported that the news of the mobilisation had been received in 'silent earnestness'. Ulrich also found the diary of a member of the Socialist Youth League which contained the following passage: 'Excitement among the population which expressed itself in a panicky run on savings banks and grocery shops. Most people were downcast, as if they were to be beheaded on the following day'. In addition, there is the response of an older Social Democrat in Hamburg who wrote on the day the Reichstag voted the war credits: 'In front of the trade union offices in Besnbinderhof many comrades assembled day after day. We watched the commotion rather dumbfounded. Many asked themselves: "Am I mad or is it the others?"'

*Sources*: Volker Berghahn, citing the findings of Volker Ulrich, in *History Sixth Magazine* (May 1988).

ADMIRAL MÜLLER, 1 AUGUST 1914.

The morning papers reprint the speeches made by the Kaiser and the Reich chancellor to an enthusiastic crowd in front of the Schloss and the Chancellor's Palace. Brilliant mood. The government has succeeded very well in making us appear as the attacked.

*Source*: V. R. Berghahn, *Germany and the Approach of War in 1914* (1983).

**SOURCE E**

The declaration of war was greeted with a bewildering mixture of patriotic euphoria and anxiety about day-to-day concerns. August 1914 saw an outpouring of patriotic enthusiasm which has fascinated historians ever since and which gave Germans 'the intoxicating illusion that the social rifts of the past had disappeared . . . a less prominent place in the popular memory of August 1914 was occupied by the expressions of anxiety, bordering on panic, about everyday concerns'.

*Source*: Richard Bessel, *Germany after the First World War* (2001).

**SOURCE F**

THE MOOD IN AUSTRIA: THE VIEWPOINT OF THE BRITISH AMBASSADOR IN VIENNA.

The British ambassador noted that the Austrian reaction to the news of a breach with Serbia was to 'burst into a frenzy of delight, vast crowds parading the streets and singing patriotic songs till the small hours of the morning.' An Austrian socialist added, 'The party is defenceless. . . . Demonstrations in support of the war are taking place in the streets. . . . Our whole organisation and our press are at risk. We run the risk of destroying thirty years' work without any political result.'

*Source*: James Joll, *The Origins of the First World War* (1984).

**SOURCE G**

RECENT RESEARCH ON 'CROWDS OF PANIC AND DEPRESSION'.

Historians engaged in local histories on First World War Germany have suggested, however, that the mood of the population in July and August 1914 cannot be adequately explained by the adjective 'enthusiastic' . . . there were long queues in front of the banks throughout Germany, as people attempted to withdraw their money, or change their paper money into coin. . . . There were also long queues in front of food stores, as people attempted to hoard foodstuffs. Prices rose dramatically. . . . One of the most striking examples of crowds of panic was the refugees fleeing the war in the east. Already before the declaration of war some 'mostly well-to-do residents' in the areas bordering Russia, had fled their homes . . .

There were three areas in Germany where there are almost no accounts of any enthusiastic or even curious crowds in the first two weeks of the war: in the countryside, in the working-class areas of large cities, and in the areas near the border. We have little evidence on the mood in the countryside. Yet it is telling that there are no accounts anywhere of enthusiasm: the local correspondents for the larger newspapers simply chose not to report on the mood of the population in the countryside. It is likely that if there had been any enthusiasm they would have written about it. What evidence there is does not speak of enthusiasm. Benjamin Ziemann could not find any enthusiasm in the rural areas of southern Bavaria. . . . In the countryside around Halle, according to one local minister, 'a deeper impression was made upon the small land owners by the taking of their horses than by the marching out of the reserves.' In the countryside in Bavaria, 'a deep concern has overtaken the families of most of our peasant families. . . . The sons, horses and wagons have been requisitioned by the military authorities, and the harvest is waiting.'. . . . The Danish population in Schleswig-Holstein likewise displayed little enthusiasm.

Source: Jeffrey Verhey, *The Spirit of 1914: Militarism, Myth and Mobilization in Germany* (2000).

## 6.2 the Schlieffen Plan

Count Alfred von Schlieffen was born in 1833 and admitted to the Prussian General Staff in 1865. General Ludendorff described Schlieffen as 'one of the greatest soldiers who ever lived'.[14] Paul Kennedy describes his personality thus: 'proud, reserved and sarcastic, he drove himself as ruthlessly as his staff and his capacity for work seemed limitless. He frequently continued his labours until midnight, and then spent a couple of hours reading military history to his daughters.'[15] But as he laboured into the small hours, the monacled general was devising a plan which would ultimately determine the fate of the country he worked so hard to serve.

German military planning in the period preceding 1914 rested almost entirely on the Schlieffen Plan. James Joll observes:

> The one state whose military plans involved immediate aggressive action as soon as mobilisation was proclaimed was Germany. German strategy on the outbreak of war had been determined in its general lines by the plan for a two-front war prepared by General von Schlieffen, the chief of staff from 1891–1906. He had been working on various versions of it since 1892 when he took the crucial decision to begin the war with an attack in the west rather than the east. The plan was given its final form at the end of 1905, just before Schlieffen's retirement and at the moment of Russia's greatest weakness.[16]

American academic Gordon Craig argues that 'the daring of this conception must arouse a reluctant admiration and it is probably true that, if this plan had been carried out in its original form and under the direction of an energetic and stubborn commander-in-chief, it would have achieved an overwhelming initial success'.[17]

On the other hand, there are many compelling weaknesses in the plan. First, it was based on the invasion of France, although that country might not have been directly involved in the causes of the war. It involved a clear transgression of the territorial rights and neutrality of Belgium and Luxembourg, leaving some historians to condemn the plan as 'immoral'. It rested on the assumption that France would be quickly defeated, although this premise was undermined by the fact that from 1911 onwards, the French general staff were well aware of the broad character of the plan. Paul Kennedy states that the plan showed 'almost reckless indifference to British intervention'.[18] Finally, the German historian Gerhard Ritter draws this damaging conclusion: 'the gamble of the Schlieffen Plan was so great that it could only succeed as a result of a direct surprise advance by the Germans or by a sudden assault on Belgium. In the opinion of the General Staff, Germany was therefore obliged by purely technical necessities to adopt, before the whole world, the role of a brutal aggressor – an evil moral burden which, as is well known, we have not got rid of even today.'[19]

Important recent work by Terence Zuber has shifted historical thinking on the Schlieffen Plan, contending that there never was any such single, neat entity. Instead Schlieffen produced a variety of operational sketches, outlines and memoranda. Some were more sharply focused than others, while some envisaged hypothetical force structures and manpower levels that were not actually available at the time. A document of this type was drafted in 1906, and published in book form by Gerhard Ritter in 1960. This is the document that most historians have in mind when they discuss the Schlieffen Plan. In actual fact, the 'plan' was little more than a memorandum, similar to a variety of other documents prepared during Schlieffen's tenure. Therefore, rather than a plan, Schlieffen had only constructed a development scheme for the German forces. Zuber contends that it was only towards the end of the war, within the officer corps itself, with an eye on the final reckoning of events, that so much emphasis was placed on the Schlieffen Plan. So although Schlieffen was, for the convenience of others, depicted as the guiding force of the German military operation, Zuber claims that his plan carried less actual significance than has generally been assumed.[20]

## 6.3 the Western Front, 1914–15

Implementation of the German strategy in August 1914 seemed to have got off to a good start as three German armies swept through Belgium and into France. Success seemed assured as the French armies fell back and the government withdrew from Paris. However, it was at this moment that the inherent weaknesses of the German operation soon began to show themselves. Carr's analysis is that the plan was a 'gambler's throw dictated by Germany's need to win the war before the numerical strength of her opponents led to her defeat'.[21] The fundamental problem was that Germany was never able to call upon enough men to actually make the plan work. Even when the German army was fully mobilized in 1914 it fell short of the eight army corps essential for the plan's success. The operation of the plan depended to a large extent on the leadership of von Moltke, a highly-strung, neurotic personality whose nervous disposition seemed unlikely to stand up to the tribulations of war. His cautious approach meant that before success was achieved in France, Moltke was already diverting troops to repel a French offensive in the Rhine and to resist the Russians in the east. This left the German First Army under Kluck short of the men he needed to encircle Paris. By September 1914 the German army found itself confronted by the newly arrived British Expeditionary Force. The entry of these troops was in itself a major factor in slowing down the execution of the German strategy.

Moltke's faith in the plan, which was limited at the outset, now disappeared altogether. His nerve collapsed, but it did not help matters that the Supreme War Lord, Wilhelm II was equally incapable of providing firm leadership. By the end of September 1914, Moltke had suffered a breakdown, lost his command and been replaced by Falkenhayn, the Minister of War. Germany's hopes of a quick victory in the west (the very essence of the Schlieffen Plan) had been dashed. With the Germans on one side and the French and British on the other, the two sides now dug themselves in along a 400-mile Western Front from the North Sea to Switzerland. On no other occasion in history was the simple human process of digging with spades to have such heavy consequences. As the trenches took shape and the machine guns were assembled, the process of attrition was set to begin. It would be the scene of slaughter on an unparalleled scale. In general, historians have worked on the assumption that the calculation on both sides was that victory would be at hand by Christmas 1914, although the early slaughter of thousands of enthusiastic young German students who had joined in during the initial wave of patriotism indicated that no easy victory would be possible.

Recent research by John Horne and Alan Kamer in their *German Atrocities and a History of Denial* has shed new light on the behaviour of German troops when hostilities broke out in 1914. Germany sent a million men into Belgium in August 1914. Belgian neutrality was first violated early in the morning of 4 August 1914 when troops under the guidance of General von Emmich crossed the border between Aachen and Malmédy. While the General declared that Belgium was not regarded as an enemy and the German army merely wanted unhindered passage, he warned that any hindrance would be harshly dealt with. Yet the Belgians, spurred on by King Albert's call for national unity, were ready to offer resistance while they waited for the assistance that they believed would soon be forthcoming from France and Britain. Horne and Kamer's research reveals that the 'first mass executions of civilians took place on 5 August, and by 8 August nearly 850 civilians had been killed and about 1,300 buildings deliberately burned down'.

When the 14th Brigade . . . were repulsed on 5 August, they fell back on the village of Soumagne on which they vented their frustration. They placed the inhabitants under armed guard in the church. Male victims were selected and shot in a field in front of women and children. The execution squad bayoneted the bodies to ensure that no one survived; one injured victim, covered by corpses, lived to tell his story to the Belgian commission of inquiry. . . . Three hundred to 400 survivors were used as a 'human shield' by the Germans as they entered Liège on 7 August. Some were kept on the bridges of the Meuse without food for several days to prevent the Belgian artillery destroying the crossings. . . . As some units retreated . . . to Battice . . . they pillaged and burned 146 houses, farms and the church, and killed 33 inhabitants . . .

Bülow and the Kaiser condemned Belgian civilians on 9 August for nothing less than a 'popular uprising'. A source in Bavaria accused civilians in one area of Belgium of conducting a 'People's War' (*Volkskrieg*). 'This was the message of the 'solemn warning' issued on 12 August by the German commander-in-chief, Moltke. He accused the Belgian population of illegally participating in fighting and committing 'atrocities' against German soldiers, and threatened that any individual who acted similarly in the future would be . . . 'immediately shot according to martial law'. On 18 August, the German government condemned the French for 'organizing a war in which the whole population takes part' and threatened dire consequences if it continued. Even before the mass invasion got under way, the notion of mass civilian resistance obsessed the German government and Supreme Command.[22]

## 1915

As 1914 gave way to 1915 a pattern began to emerge that would become all too familiar. In the face of several offensives launched against them by the British and the French, the Germans were able to hold the line, inflicting substantial losses on their opponents. However, the opposite also held true. Germany was also unable to achieve any significant breakthrough in 1915. Offensives on either side were invariably repelled, with huge casualties and with only small tracts of land changing hands. The elaborate trench network, the substantial defence systems, the industrial scale of the shelling taking place and the apparent failure of the leaders on either side to worry unduly about the loss of human life, meant that a process of protracted attrition set in, with stalemate appearing more likely than victory. Meanwhile, what of the anticipated campaign on the high seas?

## 6.4 the war at sea

One of the ironies of the First World War was that despite the huge amounts of money and resources ploughed into the German Navy before the war began, and the importance of the naval race in exacerbating the Anglo-German rivalry that helped to create the conflict in the first place, the German fleet remained in port for a large part of the war.

Within the context of the naval conflict itself, it did not take long for the Entente powers to gain the upper hand. Significantly, Germany's colonies quickly fell into the hands of their enemies. Although initially German cruisers caused considerable damage to Entente shipping, it did not take long for this element of the German armoury to be disabled. Somewhat surprisingly, the expensively assembled and prestigious ships of the German high-seas fleet remained in port. A sharp debate ensued, with Tirpitz advocating a full-scale engagement with the British while the Kaiser sided with those who wanted to hold the fleet in reserve, until the time was right. This meant that the fleet fulfilled a defensive role but was unable to challenge the blockade imposed by the British. The only major engagement between the British and German fleets took place at the Battle of Jutland on 31 May 1916. Although the British fleet took heavy losses, the advantage was not pressed home and so the engagement remained inconclusive.

Indirectly, the lack of direct action at sea meant that the frustrated Tirpitz channelled much of his energy into advocating the unrestricted submarine warfare that would do so much to bring a reluctant United States into the First World War. On 7 May 1915 the Lusitania, a British liner owned by Cunard, was attacked off the Irish coast en route to New York from Liverpool. The American press roundly condemned this act of 'mass murder' in which 128 Americans formed a significant proportion of the 1,198 casualties. At this point, President Wilson refused to be stampeded into war but an attack on an unarmed passenger steamer, the *Sussex*, in March 1916 prompted Wilson's most strongly worded message so far: that if Germany did not immediately abandon submarine warfare against passenger and freight-carrying vessels the United States would cut off diplomatic relations. Germany now made the 'Sussex pledge', which promised that merchant vessels would be granted traditional rights of stop and search, instead of being attacked without warning. These developments meant that there was a brief respite in the submarine campaign.

## 6.5 the Western front, 1916

From the German perspective, a scenario in which Germany was gradually brought to its knees not by some sweeping military manoeuvre but by a steady erosion of its resources seemed to be a real possibility. It was this consideration that led Falkenhayn to conclude that time was of the essence. Germany would have to seize the initiative rather than risk being smothered by the greater resources of Britain and France. This led Germany to launch a massive offensive against the French at Verdun in the spring of 1916. For five months Germany inflicted unending pressure on the French lines. More than 300,000 French troops died in the process of defending Verdun, but the German casualties of 280,000 men were on a similar scale. By June 1916 Falkenhayn felt he had no option but to bring the offensive to an end. Meanwhile the British military command planned to respond to the bloody offensive at Verdun with an attempt of their own to break the deadlock. They calculated that a British attack on the Somme would not just relieve pressure on the beleaguered French but also provide the vital breakthrough that would represent a crucial turning point in the war. The British strategists believed that a 7-day, 24-hour bombardment of the German lines at the Somme would render the German positions defenceless. When the bombardment came to an end it would therefore be a straightforward task for the British soldiers to walk across 'no man's land' in an immense line and occupy the trenches of the shattered German troops. Yet within an hour of the offensive being launched on 1 July 1916, it became clear that the British army leadership had made a miscalculation on a catastrophic scale. Even in the context of the slaughter taking place elsewhere, the casualty figures at the Somme beggar belief. Within one hour, almost 60,000 British troops had fallen – killed, missing or injured – before the positions of the German machine guns. The terrible logic of the First World War meant that rather than bringing this to an end, after such an appalling day, the slaughter would continue for months.

By October 1916, Britain had lost 420,000 men, with gains of no more than a few miles. At the same time, Germany had lost 450,000 troops to the slaughter. From the perspective of Woodrow Wilson's White House, both sides now seemed to be culpable, but Wilson's avowed commitment to neutrality would become more difficult when tested by the German campaign of unrestricted submarine warfare. It seemed that neither side was willing to do anything other than to continue a war of attrition that seemed to have no end in sight. It was only as autumn turned to winter and the incessant rain made movement through the muddy morass of the Western Front impossible, that the carnage on the Somme came to an end. No land of any significance had changed hands. Meanwhile, in the East, a further titanic struggle was taking place.

## 6.6 the Eastern Front, 1914–15

With Germany placing so much emphasis in August 1914 on the need to attack France through Belgium, the Russians had a relatively free hand to launch two offensives of their own. The initial Russian thrust against Austria-Hungary meant that most of Galicia was in Russian hands by December, with the Austrians in disarray. It was an early sign for the Germans of the difficulty of having the ailing monarchy as their partner.

Meanwhile the second Russian offensive was launched against East Prussia, the symbolic heartland of the Junker class. Alarmed by this sudden development, the Kaiser, whose influence was soon to dwindle, persuaded a reluctant General Moltke to immediately send two divisions to the East. This was a fatal development. By the time the divisions arrived in the east, it was too late for them to have any immediate impact. Crucially, the armies in the west had been undermined at a moment when everything depended on the rapid achievement of their goals. Moltke, neurotic and uncertain was immediately overwhelmed by these developments. His personal collapse meant that he was replaced by Falkenhayn as the minister of war.

In some respects the Eastern front, where Germany and Austria-Hungary confronted the massed forces of the Russian army, has received less attention from historians than its western equivalent. For that reason, Winston Churchill once described the conflict as 'the unknown war'. Despite this apparent neglect, there can be no doubting the importance of the war with Russia for Germany at this time. The deaths inflicted in the east formed a higher percentage of German casualties than was the case in the west until the end of 1916. Furthermore, until the turn of 1916–1917 the Russians had captured a greater number of German prisoners than the British and French combined.

## the Battle of Tannenberg, 25–30 August 1914

The uncertain start to the war led to important personnel changes. Paul von Beneckendorff von Hindenburg had retired from German public life in 1911 but was recalled to duty in the crisis of 1914 with the words, 'I am ready.' He was appointed commander of the Eighth Army in East Prussia with his newly appointed chief of staff, a dour, uncompromising character, Erich Frederick Wilhelm Ludendorff. It would not be long before the name of the sleepy village of Tannenberg became a word synonymous to the Germans with the military brilliance of Paul von Hindenburg, the 'Hero of Tannenberg'.

German strategy in the east was based on the knowledge that the attacking Russian armies would be split by the immense network of water known as the Masurian Lakes. The initial battles on the Eastern Front took place in a region of lakes, forests, marshes and poor roads. Despite the apparent Russian advantage in numbers they soon outran their logistic support and the rudimentary nature of their secret messages meant that they were easily picked up. The Russian commander Samsonov launched his attack at the centre of the German forces but the troops he deployed were tired and hungry. Russian provision for their wounded men was hopelessly inadequate. Despite Germany's numerical disadvantage, a major German counter-attack at the end of August trapped Samsonov's army with the consequence that 70,000 Russian troops were killed or injured and nearly 100,000 taken prisoner. The first of the two Russian invading armies had been comprehensively defeated. The German casualties of 15,000 looked relatively small. Samsonov was left, lost in the swamps and woods, wheezing and in despair. His sense of failure was so acute that he shot himself, but in his absence a further 60,000 Russian troops were lost in the following month.

## the Masurian Lakes, 1914–15

In September 1914 the second invading Russian army came to grief at the Masurian Lakes. Hindenburg's reputation soared and a further victory in February 1915, known as the winter battle of the Masurian Lakes, sealed his elevation to almost mythical status and expelled the Russians from East Prussia. Despite these stunning victories, a conclusive moment had not been reached. Nevertheless, the aura of Russian invincibility was brought to an end, with losses of almost a quarter of a million men, although Russia had sufficient resources to absorb those heavy casualties and continue the struggle. As 1914 came to an end the Eastern Front was stabilized along the line of Russia's western frontier running from the Baltic southwards to Romania.

## 6.7 the Home Front and the impact of the war on the German economy

Two elements of the war, a progressively heightened perception of food shortages that pervaded the cities, towns and countryside, and increasing distress over casualties at the front line, can be seen to have steadily sapped national morale on the home front. The first factor stemmed from food shortages, which in turn led to very high levels of inflation. This had the further damaging consequence of wiping out the value of peoples' life savings. As normal food supplies dried up, increasing numbers of people resorted to the black market. Those who sold food in this way were able to charge very high prices. Faced with this problem, the government felt that it had no choice but to introduce bread rationing, which it did in 1915.

Several factors led to a crisis in food supply. First, it soon became clear that insufficient planning had taken place before 1914. Secondly, the allied blockade on German shipping and trade soon began to take its toll. The critical factor here was that the government decided that it needed to take control of food supplies. Although the government was trying to deal with the situation, it had actually opened itself up to a tremendous amount of criticism in taking over the regulation of the war economy.

Innovative historian Niall Ferguson describes the commonly observed idea that Germany was starved into defeat as

> one of the most tenacious in modern European historiography. Yet it is almost certainly wrong. . . . German per capita consumption of potatoes and fish was actually higher in 1918 than in 1912–1913. Much criticism has been heaped on the German wartime system of food rationing but it is at least arguable that Britain's laissez-faire approach was more wasteful and inefficient. The Germans introduced bread rationing in January 1915 and established a War Food Office in May 1916. . . . Germans certainly went hungry. Instead of the sausages and beer, they had to make do with nasty ersatz products and East European wine. . . . But the evidence that anyone starved – much less the fantastic figure of 750,000 still cited by some otherwise sensible historians – is not to be found'.[23]

Despite Ferguson's valuable analysis it seems accurate to say that by the middle of 1916, with the Battle of the Somme imminent, a sense of war-weariness began to pervade German society. Perceived food shortages and industrial disputes meant that the war enthusiasm which may have existed in some quarters in 1914 was now a thing of the past. There is also substantial statistical data to support the case that the war progressively impoverished the working class, especially after 1916. A decline in real wages, food shortages and an increase in the price of basic foodstuffs went hand in hand with a gradual radicalization of the working class.

## the Hindenburg Programme and the Auxiliary Service Act

The Battle of the Somme exerted unprecedented strain on the German economy. From the terrible summer slaughter inflicted on the British army on the morning of 1 July 1916, to the rain-drenched stalemate of November, the loss of life and material costs on both sides was almost unimaginable. By the summer of 1916 General Erich von Falkenhayn's position as Chief of the General Staff was increasingly vulnerable. At the end of August the Kaiser succumbed to pressure from the military command and the Chancellor and Falkenhayn was replaced by the 'hero of Tannenberg', Field Marshal Hindenburg. This placed the ageing general at the head of the army supreme command (OHL, *Oberste Heeresleitung*), supported by the assertive character of General Ludendorff, who was appointed Quartermaster General. In practice, many historians have concluded that Ludendorff became the dominant figure in this new partnership. As Ferguson puts it: 'Notoriously, the authority of both the Chancellor and the Kaiser declined during the war; the military came to dominate, with the Supreme Command of Hindenburg and Ludendorff constituting after 1916 a "silent" (i.e. unstated) military dictatorship. In practice, Ludendorff came to be the sole master of German strategy and much else besides.'[24]

This was of the highest importance. Ludendorff was an outspoken critic of domestic political reform and rejected any notion of a negotiated, 'honourable' peace in favour of the quest for a victorious, annexationist victory, regardless of the strain this would inflict on the German people. As this outcome became progressively more remote, civilian life was marked by food shortages, profiteering and a black market. In the aftermath of the cataclysmic struggle on the Somme, the government introduced the Hindenburg Programme in an attempt to bolster arms production. Yet no attempt to increase efficiency could mask the naked fact that Germany's resources were ultimately unequal to the task. Under the Auxiliary Service Act, direction of labour was introduced for all males from the ages of 17 to 60. Although women and children were excluded from this measure and the right of the working population to change jobs was preserved, children were used to form 'salvage' teams to rescue and reuse materials, and a campaign to recruit female labour was also launched. In addition, a Supreme War Office was established with sweeping powers over industry and labour. Patriotic cooperation from the trade unions and workers' committees was unable to stave off shortages of coal and transport, but by the early summer of 1917 there was substantial improvement in iron and steel output and a threefold increase in munitions production.

Under this far-reaching law the military hoped to establish a basis for the total mobilization of Germany's labour reserves. However, this measure could not resolve the central dilemma of the German wartime economy. Put simply, the problem was that most of the young men had gone to the front. This meant that the only way for the factories to meet their targets was for soldiers to be recalled from the front. German agriculture suffered just as badly. Total mobilization had two very damaging and immediate consequences. As well as the departure of thousands of young men, most farms also suffered from the removal of hundreds of thousands of horses to the front line. This meant that the responsibility of running the farms was passed to women, who lacked the physical strength needed for so much of the farm work. This meant that production levels fell, the morale of farm women declined and the price of foodstuff increased. The insatiable demand for manpower by the German military directly undermined the capacity of the German economy to supply the goods needed to sustain the war.

## the 'turnip winter', 1916

Widespread harvest failure in 1916 led to the so called 'turnip winter' of 1916–17, when in some areas food shortages became desperate. Roger Chickering offers a bleak appraisal of what this actually entailed for the hard-pressed German people:

> Hunger became the overwhelming fact of life on the home front, and it retained this status despite a number of attempts to temper it. Attention turned initially to another root vegetable, which rivalled the potato in versatility and nutritiousness but was more resistant to the weather. For humans and animals alike, this ersatz potato was the turnip. It was baked, fried, boiled and put into soups. It was dried and ground into flour for use in war bread. It was used to make coffee, marmalade, a variety of other pastes, and in countless other capacities. . . . So omnipresent was the vegetable in the German kitchen that the term 'turnip winter' was sufficient to invoke the misery of early 1917: most Germans found the taste of this hard warrior to be execrable.'[25]

Clearly, the impact of the war was being felt in the stomachs as much as in the minds of the German people. The fact that the government had taken such direct responsibility for food supplies and rationing meant that it was now blamed for the shortages. Bessel says that 'in failing to provide the basic necessities to the working population, Germany's war-time rulers had broken the unspoken contract they had made with the German people at the outbreak of the war'.[26] His conclusion is that 'almost all Germans were materially worse off during the First World War than they had been before 1914'.[27]

## casualty figures

The most obvious effect on wartime morale was the massive and mounting level of casualties. On average, the German army suffered 465,000 casualties a year. This was bound to impact on the mood within the army itself but also on those left grieving at home. One observer noted that on a train compartment the soldiers had written: 'The war is for the wealthy . . . the people provide the corpses.'

Before 1914 the strength of the German army was set at roughly 1 per cent of the total population. However, by 1913, as political tension mounted and the naval race was lost, the military build-up was accelerated. The army, which had stood at 622,483 in 1910 increased to 2,931,756 and to 4,357,934 by January 1915. During the four years of the war, the average size of the army was roughly 6,372,000. Of this figure, around 4,183,000 served in the field army (*Feldheer*) while 2,189,000 served behind the lines and within the Reich (*Bestatzungsheer*). The total number who served between August 1914 and July 1918 was 13,123,011, which amounted to around 19.7 per cent of Germany's 1914 population. Therefore, virtually one in five Germans experienced military service.

The casualties suffered by the German forces were immense. More than 14 million registered cases of illness, and a figure of those reported wounded of around 4,814,557 illustrate the strain placed on the German people. Approximately two million German soldiers were killed (see table 6.1). This figure can be broken down as follows:

table **6.1 German army casualties in the First World War**

| Army | 1,900,876 |
|---|---|
| Navy | 34,836 |
| Colonies | 1,185 |
| Missing in action | 100,000 |

Source: Richard Bessel, *Germany after the First World War* (2001).

Therefore German casualties averaged around 465,000 per year, or 3.5 per cent of the total who served. Inevitably, as the war dragged on, these high casualty figures began to weaken the resolve of the remainder of the army. There is evidence that the military authorities were deeply disturbed by the depressing contents of many of the letters being sent home. By the autumn of 1917 up to 10 per cent of the troops being transported from the Eastern Front to the west had deserted. The male civilian death rate was higher in 1918 than it had been in 1914. There were sharp increases in the rates of TB, pneumonia and severe influenza. In the influenza epidemic of 1918, 72,721 men and 102,130 women perished.

## 6.8 the Eastern Front, 1916–17

Germany had entered the war with a strong sense of self-belief, and although the early victory she had craved and anticipated was proving illusive, the conviction that ultimate victory would be achieved remained strong through

1915. This sense of optimism was boosted by a major German victory in the early summer of 1915. In May, Austria and Germany combined forces to drive the Russians out of Galicia and secure all of Poland, Lithuania and Courland. Austria-Hungary's previously weak position had been supported and the Russians had suffered a further quarter of a million troops killed, wounded or taken prisoner. With the opportunity to strike a mortal blow against Russia presenting itself, the Germans once again made strategic decisions that ruled out a decisive victory in the east. Hindenburg and Ludendorff's attacking instincts were curtailed by Falkenhayn, who as Chief of the General Staff, was aware of pressing needs elsewhere. Resources of men and material were also needed in the Balkans, where in October 1915 a joint Austro-German army launched a successful offensive against Serbia. Important though this was, the more fundamental point was that as 1915 came to a close, the decisive victory German had strived so hard to bring about remained outside her grasp. The Russians, with an immense reservoir of men, had suffered huge casualties but were still not beaten. Indeed 1916 would see a new Russian offensive against the German positions. For these reasons, Richard Pipes concludes that:

> For all its brilliant battlefield successes . . . the German campaign of 1915 must ultimately be classified as a strategic defeat, because it failed to attain its military purpose and because it lost precious time. The debacle of 1915 may well have been Russia's greatest, if unintended, contribution to Allied victory.[28]

Germany's failure to secure a decisive advantage meant that the civilians on the home front had to make a much deeper, more gruelling commitment to the war than they might have initially anticipated.

## 6.9 the Treaty of Brest-Litovsk, 1918

Although the Versailles settlement has received substantial historical attention, its equivalent in the east, the Treaty of Brest-Litovsk, has been aptly named the 'forgotten peace'. The setting for the treaty was the small provincial town of Brest-Litovsk, close to the Russian border with Germany. It was here that Leon Trotsky, the representative of the newly installed Bolshevik government and self-styled revolutionary Peoples' Commissar for War, came face to face with the aristocratic representatives of the German officer corps. On paper, it seemed that Lenin was simply fulfilling his promise that the Bolshevik government, which had seized power in Russia in November 1917, would immediately withdraw Russia from the First World War. However, despite Lenin's hope that Germany would dissolve into the same workers, soldiers and sailors' ferment that had enveloped Russia, it soon became clear, that for the time being at least, he was mistaken. It was now apparent that with Germany still in the hands of the old military and political establishment, all the territory gained by Russia in the 300 years of Romanov rule was at stake. Trotsky, by nature arrogant and self-confident, set off for the talks optimistic that he would be able to stave off Germany's territorial demands and sign only an honourable peace.

A brilliant writer, orator and revolutionary strategist, he was totally inexperienced in the realm of diplomacy and foreign affairs. The German academic Fritz Fischer indicates the exacting nature of Trotsky's task:

> Lenin's victory over Kerensky on November 6 and 7, 1917 could not but seem to the German government to be the crown of their military and political campaign against Russia since the autumn of 1914. At last the Russian colossus had collapsed under the pincer movement of military pressure and the social revolution fostered by Germany through the Bolsheviks . . . the new rulers in Petersburg were in a dilemma: on the one hand they had come to power under the slogan of peace, and they therefore needed an immediate end to hostilities. . . . On the other hand, they could not accept peace at any price, for fear of strengthening the right-wing Social Revolutionaries and the Mensheviks . . .

The German government saw the Bolsheviks' dilemma and decided to exploit it ruthlessly, in order not only to secure the comprehensive solution in the east for which it had so long been working, but also by concluding a separate peace with Russia, to decide the issue in the west and thus achieve the whole of their war aims.'[29]

Therefore when the flamboyant, multilingual representative of the workers came face to face with the German delegation, it was soon pointed out to him that it was Russia that had little room for manoeuvre. In the words of a private comment amongst German and Austrian delegates, 'There is only one thing for them to choose now – under what sauce are they to be devoured.' Or, as General Hoffman stated: 'The Russian delegation talks to us as if it stood victorious in our countries and could dictate conditions to us. I would like to point out that the facts are just the reverse: that the victorious German army stands in your territory.'[30]

Adam B. Ulam offers this summary of the cost of the treaty to Russia, imposed by the victorious Germans:

> On 1 March the Soviet delegates again reached Brest-Litovsk . . . to sign the most humiliating peace in Russia's modern history . . . on March 3 the treaty was signed. Russia had lost the Ukraine, Finland, her Polish and Baltic territories. In the Caucasus she had to make territorial concessions to Turkey. The treaty placed the German sphere of occupation close to Petrograd, which on its other side was perilously close to Finland, where the Finnish Bolsheviks were being ejected by the nationalists with German help. Three centuries of Russian territorial expansion were undone.'[31]

In March 1918 Trotsky, for the Bolsheviks, signed a peace treaty that represented disastrous territorial terms for the Russian state. The war on the Eastern Front was over. However, the campaign in the West remained in the balance.

## 6.10 the Western Front, 1917–18

### the United States' entry into the war

The absence of sustained naval conflict did not mean that events in the high seas were completely peripheral to the conflict as a whole, not least because it was clear that Germany's policy of unrestricted submarine warfare was instrumental in bringing the United States into the conflict in April 1917. Although the impact of American involvement was not immediately felt, there is no doubt that within twelve months, the weight of American commitment, energy and resources took a heavy toll on the correspondingly diminishing morale of the German armed forces. In addition, these developments exacerbated the vulnerable position of Chancellor Bethmann-Hollweg, who had consistently opposed the policy of unrestricted submarine warfare in the face of military 'experts' who contended that the tactic could deal a decisive blow to the British, and who argued that even if America was endlessly provoked, the likelihood of American troops actually arriving to do battle on European soil was extremely remote. Crucially, the energetic and well-resourced troops of the United States now began to exert their influence.

### 1918

When Russia's war effort came to a dramatic end with the Bolshevik Revolution in the late autumn of 1917 and the subsequent Peace of Brest-Litovsk signed in March 1918, the Germans saw one last opportunity to take the initiative in the west. By the spring of 1918, more than fifty divisions had been moved to the west and over three and a half million men assembled to take part in a springtime 'victory' offensive. Such was the weight of numbers that the Germans were able to achieve some significant advances with the objective of driving the British back towards the sea. However, this initial success was misleading. By early summer, the offensive had ground to a halt and the military initiative would never be regained on the Western Front. It was not just the immediate failure of the offensive to achieve its breakthrough that was so damaging. By July 1918, the United States had deployed a million troops to the Allied cause. This coincided with the French under Foch launching their own counter-offensive, which sent the Germans into reverse. On 8 August British troops were able to overrun the German positions at the Somme, taking more than 15,000 men prisoner. The endgame was drawing near.

## 6.11 collapse

Historians agree that the decisive turning point in the undermining of national morale came after the failed spring offensive of 1918. It was now becoming clear that further action was likely to result merely in fresh casualties rather than a genuine military breakthrough. By the early summer of 1918 a combination of an Allied counter-offensive, an emerging influenza epidemic, the sheer weight of American resources being brought to bear after their entry into the war in April 1917 and further military casualties led to a gradual crumbling of German resolve, both at home and in the field. In July 1918 the German commander, General Ludendorff, complained of the increasing incidence of unauthorized leave, acts of cowardice, and refusal to follow orders in the face of the enemy on the Western Front. In a last-ditch attempt to preserve the dwindling 'fighting spirit' of the troops, the Army Supreme Command introduced stiffer punishments for the so-called *Druckeberger*, or shirkers. Despite these measures, it is now clear that in the final few months of the war the German army was disintegrating. The sense of hopelessness and defeatism in the German army was now profound. Such sentiments are reflected in the following extract from a government report of October 1918: 'Among the working masses the belief is widely held that large-scale desertions are daily occurrences and that one can no longer reckon with a serious capability of military resistance. The masses are supported in this belief by numerous soldiers on leave who, perhaps in order to boast, report about the lack of discipline.'[32]

Within weeks of this gloomy prognosis the German war effort was in a state of virtual collapse. In November 1918 the Kaiser slipped away to the sanctuary of a Dutch castle, leaving the military leadership to make an ignominious exit of their own. General Ludendorff, theoretically second only to Hindenburg in the German military establishment, donned false whiskers and spectacles and made his escape to a place of sanctuary in Sweden. Rather than face the consequences of their failure, the military leadership abandoned their responsibilities and left the civilians to pick up the pieces. Instead of admitting their mistakes it was maintained that the military had been 'stabbed in the back'. This distorted perspective held that the troops and their leaders had held firm at the front line but had been fatally undermined by the combination of the socialists, anti-war campaigners and deserters who lacked patriotism and the will to carry on.

Following the sudden collapse of the German war effort it was agreed that the details of the peace settlement would be drawn up at a conference to be held in the New Year. The Great War had cost the lives of more than 8 million men while over 21 million others were wounded. Russia lost 1.75 million men and the Germans almost 2 million. Nevertheless, it is important to point out that even as defeat loomed in the late autumn of 1918 the German troops largely retained their discipline, despite the comprehensive nature of the final outcome. When the guns finally fell silent on the Western Front on 11 November 1918, the German troops still held the line from Antwerp to the Meuse.

In *Germany After the First World War* Richard Bessel includes this vivid account of the scene when the first German troops from the front line arrived back in Berlin in December 1918:

> From the Heidelberger Platz onward, the streets were black with
> people. A great excitement lay upon them. The tension grew. People
> thought they heard distant drum-beats. A wave of shouts rolled along
> the streets. The stewards formed a chain to hold back the mass of poor

people. And now the trumpets were indeed approaching. And then came the sight that caused many in the crowd to weep. Men as well as women, moved by a feeling of humanity's common fate, remembering the long war and all the dead. Did the people see the troops? They were looking at the long war, at victories and at the defeats. Before them a piece of their own life was marching past, with wagons and horses, machine-guns and cannons.[33]

# the Weimar Republic, 1919–29

## 7.1 interpretations

### introduction

Interpretations of the Weimar Republic are fraught with difficulty, and even the selection of where to begin and where to mark its end can be to some degree contentious. To illustrate the point, it might be instructive if we were to begin our examination of the Weimar Republic by avoiding, albeit temporarily, the traditional step of exploring its traumatic origins and instead listing the names of some its most outstanding citizens. We could mention, for example, the lasting impact of the artist Käthe Kollwitz, the painter Max Leibermann, the novelist Thomas Mann and the scientist Albert Einstein. In war and politics, the monumental figures of the career soldier Paul von Hindenburg or the politician Gustav Stresemann had an enormous impact on the whole epoch. In the broader sphere, the industrialist Carl Duisberg, the philosopher Theodor W. Adorno, the avant-garde cultural and architectural achievements of Walter Gropius or Georg Grosz, or reforming figures such as Agnes Neuhaus, Alice Salomon or Gertrud Baumer are all worthy of substantial attention. Each of these figures can be said to have made substantial contributions to the development of German society. Yet the Weimar Republic represents transience, a teetering on the edge of the economic abyss, political crises, and even a tendency to look back at the troubled Wilhelmine period in a nostalgic, rose-tinted manner.

The brief era of the Weimar Republic, therefore, represents a particular challenge to historians. Its difficult infancy, marked by bloody and abortive revolution and the psychological challenges of a lost war and the Versailles peace settlement, have led to the characterization of the period as a traumatic birth leading to inherent structural weaknesses and ultimate collapse. It has been easy to see the Weimar Republic as doomed to failure from the outset, lurching from one crisis to the next. Alternatively, the end of Weimar in 1933, with the violently irrational, catastrophic outcomes of the National Socialist period, has meant that other interpretations have used a reverse projection, understanding Weimar by looking at what succeeded it or what it gave birth to. The roots of the 'German' problem have been detected by some in the early years of the Weimar Republic, or even with its antecedents in the Wilhelmine era or the Bismarck period. It has been hard for Weimar to stand alone and be judged on its own strengths and weaknesses. Strong contrasts are also apparent within the social and cultural milieu of Weimar. The avant-garde cultural life of the Weimar Republic, a brief 'golden age' of cultural achievement and the forces of economic modernization can be seen in one perspective, while another valid alternative could accentuate social upheaval and political breakdown. While some observers welcomed the modernizing influence of American society, through areas such as jazz music, fashions and cinema, others condemned the urbanization of German society, lamenting its decadence and lack of moral compass. If we momentarily consider Adolf Hitler at this juncture we can see a politician who, during the most difficult period of the Weimar Republic, made claims to modernity through his innovative propaganda techniques and campaign style, while the same figure also cynically appealed to a deep-rooted desire to return to the values of a traditional, pastoral society. With these interpretations in mind, we will examine the nature of the German Revolution of 1918–19.

## 7.2 the German Revolution, 1918–20

It could be claimed that the short-lived German Revolution began on 28 October 1918 when sailors at the Schillig roadstead near the naval port of Wilhelmshaven refused to put to sea for a last-ditch cruiser raid in the English Channel. With rumours of armistice negotiations in the air, the sailors, whose morale, amidst particularly difficult and cramped conditions, was already perilously low, refused to embark on what they regarded as a futile mission. When the crews of the cruisers, *Thuringen* and *Helgoland*, dampened their fires and mutinied, the naval authorities responded by arresting all of the sailors who had disobeyed orders. However, the mutiny quickly spread to Kiel, and as the old political order crumbled in the face of defeat, disorder became nationwide. On so many occasions, when the military had been put to the test, the German forces had come through, obeying orders and displaying cohesion, loyalty and discipline. Yet by November 1918 the difficulties facing the soldiers, sailors and the country at large were legion. The front-line troops, who had sacrificed so much and had remained in the trenches following orders to the last, now faced a traumatic, disorientating period with an abrupt transition from war to peace. The sudden acceptance of defeat completely staggered the German people, who had grown accustomed to the relentlessly optimistic propaganda messages of the wartime period. It is hard to imagine the experiences of the troops, many of whom had witnessed the most disturbing violence, and suffered severe personal injury or lasting psychological damage. As the war effort crumbled, workers' and soldiers' councils, similar to those that had been so significant in revolutionary Russia, sprung up in the larger cities across the country, where shortages of food and a sense of disorder were particularly acute.

Amidst these conditions, the radicalization of opinion at both extremes of the political spectrum which had taken place through the catalyst of war now accelerated, although it could be argued with some force that the popular mood was one of war-weariness rather than revolutionary fervour. Nevertheless, those individuals moving to the forefront of political movements on the extreme left and right now found more fertile ground for their beliefs to spread. A key moment in this period of social upheaval came on 8 November with the establishment under Kurt Eisner, a Jewish journalist and left-wing socialist, of the Bavarian Democratic and Socialist Republic. This brought home to Chancellor Prince Max of Baden how serious the situation had become. The willingness of Eisner to support the revolutionary tide was not shared by all members of the Independent Socialists (USPD), some of whom advocated parliamentary methods over revolutionary insurrection. The extent to which the left was divided over tactics was underlined by the fact that the Majority Socialists, led by Ebert and Scheidemann, were totally opposed to violent revolution. They emphatically supported parliamentarianism and law and order. The USPD had broken away from the Majority Socialists in 1917 as an anti-war faction and contained within their ranks a combustible mixture of radicals, reformers, idealists and labour leaders. This division among the left would be of lasting significance.

Against this background of upheaval and street disorder the Kaiser came under sustained pressure to abdicate. The Chancellor, Prince Max of Baden, now believed that only the abdication of the Kaiser would stave off a civil war, but Wilhelm II stubbornly attempted to hold on to the crumbling vestiges of his own position. At noon on 9 November Prince Max took the decision to announce the abdication of the emperor. At this point Hindenburg and Ludendorff's successor, General Groener, made it clear to the Kaiser that he no longer had the support of his generals or his ministers. It was on this note that the embittered Kaiser slipped away into exile in the Netherlands, never to return. Although it could be argued with some conviction that the Kaiser's personal authority had long since disappeared, the removal of the monarchy from the German constitutional system heightened the sense that the most profound changes to the political landscape were under way.

Amid the fast-moving chaos of November 1918, Prince Max, acting outside the realms of the constitution, transferred the Chancellor's post from himself to Ebert. With the Emperor gone, the circumstances under which the new republic was proclaimed were somewhat bizarre and symbolically damaging. When Scheidemann, of the Majority Socialists, was told over his lunch that the Spartacists on the extreme left of the political spectrum were about to proclaim a soviet republic, Scheidemann reacted instinctively by rushing on to the balcony of the Reichstag to address the crowd in the streets below, ending his speech with the words 'Long live the great German republic!'

The early months of the Weimar Republic were a curious mix of political idealism and cynical brutality. The backdrop of a traumatic defeat in war and the subsequent historic burden for a proud military nation of a lost war, combined with the grim practical realities of demobilization, food shortages, epidemics of sickness and sheer exhaustion made it difficult for those who were trying to carve a new constitutional path to go about their work unhindered. So when Chancellor Ebert called for elections to a National Assembly at Weimar, these were immediately boycotted by the new German Communist Party (KPD).

In January 1919 the Spartacist (*Spartakusbund*) faction of the socialist movement, that would take the initiative in the formation of the KPD, launched an armed uprising in Berlin. This event was spontaneous rather than planned. The Spartacist leaders, intellectual Marxists who had closely followed events in Russia, believed that Germany's dire circumstances had not yet created the preconditions for a successful armed uprising. Karl Liebknecht and Rosa Luxemburg completely rejected the notion of a non-socialist parliamentary republic, and on that basis had broken away from the USPD, contending that the pursuit of socialism through parliament was a 'risible petty bourgeois illusion', while civil war would merely represent 'the class struggle by another name.'

Rather than come to terms with the democratic intentions of Ebert and his colleagues, the Spartacists wanted to create a Marxist state, but only when the time was ripe. It was not until the events of early January saw promises of armed support from the Berlin shop stewards that the left-wing intellectual Rosa Luxemburg reluctantly agreed to go along with the majority in her movement and take part in a full-blown uprising.

However, the Spartacist movement was small, ill-organized and mismanaged, and they had sorely underestimated the power of the right to resist their revolutionary plans. In the middle of this was the new Chancellor, Ebert who in the first instance lacked the physical means to resist the Spartacists out on the streets of Berlin. Ebert calculated on the support of the Freikorps, a collection of disgruntled ex-soldiers and right-wingers, to crush the Spartacists. In what is referred to as the Ebert–Groener Pact, Ebert made a deal with General Groener to enlist his support in putting down the Marxist uprising. However, there can be little doubt that Ebert did not expect the violent settling of scores with the radical left that now took place in his name. On 10 January 1919 the Communist positions in Berlin came under sustained attack from the Freikorps. Within three days of horrendous street fighting the uprising had been crushed. The brutal murders of Sparticist leaders Rosa Luxemburg and Karl Liebknecht, by officers from the Horse Guards Division, highlighted the fact that democracy had relied on brute force to protect itself while the working-class movement was disastrously divided, a factor that would eventually come to the assistance of the extreme right. The deployment of the Freikorps units against the left spread from the capital to become a national phenomenon.

Meanwhile, the intensity of the violence in Berlin meant that the government decided to convene its National Assembly in the more tranquil surroundings of the historic university town of Weimar. An interim law of only ten paragraphs set out the essential constitutional elements of the republic based on the authority of the Reichstag, the President and the Republic. On 11 February the National Assembly elected Friedrich Ebert as the first President of the Reich, who in turn asked Scheidemann, the SPD deputy, to form a government. Within days the Reich Cabinet was appointed, composed of the Weimar coalition of Majority Socialists, Democrats and the Centre Party. Conan Fischer states that there

> is a near consensus that the series of compromise agreements between republican and imperial interests contained the seeds of disaster, for the old guard was at best resigned to the revolutionary settlement, at worst hostile. From its bastions within the Reichswehr, heavy industry, agriculture, the judiciary, and civil service, so the argument runs, imperial society was well-placed to compromise the orderly functioning of the republic and, as the Great Depression struck, to plot its overthrow – and all of this before the National Socialists had really become a force to reckon with.[1]

Meanwhile, the violence that scarred the streets of Berlin was mirrored by events in the Bavarian capital, Munich, where Kurt Eisner was murdered by a right-wing extremist. At the end of April hundreds of workers and the leaders of the communist movement in Bavaria were shot dead by local Freikorps soldiers amid bitter street fighting in what amounted to a short civil war. The politicians who were charged with bringing stability to the embryonic republic now faced the difficult task of dealing with the further trauma of the peace conference. For this, the focus would switch from the beleaguered German cities to the relative tranquillity of the magnificent French palace at Versailles, from where, as fate would have it, the new leaders of Germany would return with the heavy burden of the dictated peace settlement.

## recent interpretations of the German Revolution

From the outset the German Revolution of 1918–20 has been a controversial topic for historians, although the intense debate has not been able to shift the basic motif of failure that characterizes the discussion of Weimar's birth and brief life. Writing in 1979, Sebastian Haffner condemned the Republic's fundamental failure to create the 'proletarian democracy' that the Social Democratic (not Communist) masses demanded, with the use of former front-line troops against the revolutionary workers in a misguided effort to restore stability. In the words of Conan Fischer:

> In summary, the revolution's leaders allegedly failed to harness adequately a powerful popular movement that could have underpinned the new republic, instead relying on cooperation with the new pre-war elite to secure order. They did so to ensure that the new domestic and international settlement accommodated as far as possible the complex and diverse range of interests that constituted German society. However, this process of accommodation afforded the revolution's

enemies the opportunity to strike back at the Republic . . .

It is almost too easy to find reasons for the eventual failure and collapse of Weimar. However, it is also too simplistic to dismiss the revolution as a charade or a feeble compromise and in this regard many accounts, no doubt with an eye to the National Socialist future, become over-deterministic or indulge in various forms of wish fulfillment. In fact, the revolution reflected pretty accurately the reformist potential already present in Wilhelmine society and, beyond that, the more radical ambitions of the democratizing forces in that society. Given the circumstances of defeat, the immediate imposition of indemnities on the provisional Republic, and the enormous energies expended in accommodating the occupation regime in the west of the country the revolution was in many regards a remarkable achievement.[2]

## 7.3  the Versailles Treaty

### main points of the Versailles Treaty

- Northern Schleswig ceded by Germany to Denmark
- Holstein remained part of the German Empire after a plebiscite
- Posen and West Prussia were ceded to Poland. This was referred to by Germans as the 'bleeding border'
- The important port of Danzig was taken out of German hands and given the status of a free city
- The Memel region was ceded to Lithuania
- Eastern Upper Silesia was ceded to Poland
- Huttschin territories were ceded to Czechoslovakia
- Alsace-Lorraine was ceded to France
- Saarland was placed under the control of the League of Nations and was occupied by France
- The Rhineland was occupied by Allied troops and became a demilitarized zone for Germany
- Eupen-Malmédy was ceded to Belgium
- The Ruhr district belonged to Germany but was occupied by France and Belgium in 1923
- These areas remained part of the German Empire following a plebiscite

The First World War finally came to an end on 11 November 1918 when the Germans formally surrendered to the Allies. The armistice was signed at 5 a.m. in a railway carriage in a forest clearing at Compiègne. The peace took effect at 11 a.m. when the guns finally fell silent on the Western front. The sudden collapse of the German war effort took everyone by surprise, and so it was agreed that the details of the peace settlement would be drawn up at a conference to be held in the New Year. Germany would be obliged to send

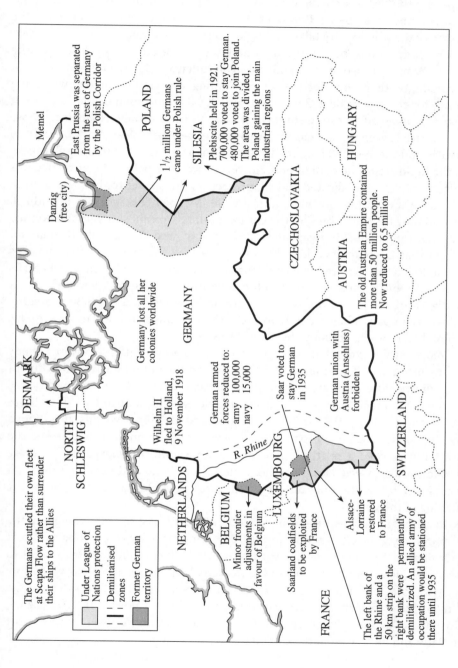

The Germans scuttled their own fleet at Scapa Flow rather than surrender their ships to the Allies

Under League of Nations protection

Demilitarised zones

Former German territory

DENMARK

NORTH SCHLESWIG

Memel

Danzig (free city)

East Prussia was separated from the rest of Germany by the Polish Corridor

POLAND

1½ million Germans came under Polish rule

SILESIA

Plebiscite held in 1921. 700,000 voted to stay German. 480,000 voted to join Poland. The area was divided, Poland gaining the main industrial regions

Germany lost all her colonies worldwide

GERMANY

Wilhelm II fled to Holland, 9 November 1918

German armed forces reduced to:
army    100,000
navy    15,000

CZECHOSLOVAKIA

HUNGARY

AUSTRIA

The old Austrian Empire contained more than 50 million people. Now reduced to 6.5 million

German union with Austria (Anschluss) forbidden

Saar voted to stay German in 1935

R. Rhine

NETHERLANDS

BELGIUM

LUXEMBOURG

SWITZERLAND

Minor frontier adjustments in favour of Belgium

Saarland coalfields to be exploited by France

Alsace-Lorraine restored to France

FRANCE

The left bank of the Rhine and a 50 km strip on the right bank were permanently demilitarized. An allied army of occupation would be stationed there until 1935

map **4 – the main terms of the Treaty of Versailles**

representatives to receive and agree to the terms, but they would not be invited to take part in the meetings or discussions. Nevertheless, Germany fully expected the peace settlement to be based on the principle of 'peace without victory' announced by US President Wilson; a principle which had been at the centre of the preliminary talks leading to German surrender.

The horrendous casualty figures and the enormous physical cost of the Great War had two major political consequences. First, and perhaps not surprisingly, they combined to create among the victors an overwhelming desire for revenge against Germany. Secondly, it would soon become apparent that the so-called victors were physically and economically exhausted. Those who desired revenge were particularly keen to see Kaiser Wilhelm II brought to justice, and the slogan 'Hang the Kaiser' seemed to dominate the popular press in the build-up to the conference. However, two days before the armistice was signed, the Kaiser abdicated and slipped across the border to the Netherlands, where he was to live out his political exile. Meanwhile, General Ludendorff, second only to Hindenburg in the German military establishment, had donned a disguise and made his escape to a safe haven in Sweden. Ludendorff could not accept that Germany had lost the war and placed the blame on the socialists in the Reichstag. Before his hasty departure he commented: 'I have asked His Majesty to bring those circles into the government to whom we mainly owe it that we are in this position. We will therefore now see these gentlemen assume ministerial posts. They are now to make the peace which must now be made. They shall now eat the soup they have brewed for us.'[3]

Many of the factors that were to dominate the peace settlement were already falling into place. The trauma of defeat had led the old political establishment to abdicate responsibility, leaving the representatives of German's embryonic democracy to face the stigma of accepting defeat and punishment. The desire for revenge felt by the people of France and Britain was only heightened by the Kaiser's exile. Pressure for severe anti-German measures from the press represented a relatively new but highly significant ingredient. In these circumstances it was clear that the Americans – who had occupied the high moral ground as the only disinterested party – would play a key role in the making of the peace.

Russia's dramatic withdrawal from the war in the east served to heighten the importance of the US entry in April 1917. Having played such an important part in swinging the balance of the war towards the Allies, America now sought to play an equally important role in the peacemaking process. Woodrow Wilson, 62 years old, leader of the Democratic Party and, since 1912, President of the United States of America, arrived in Brest on 13 December 1918. The French President, Raymond Poincaré, sent his own train to bring Wilson from the port to Paris and he arrived in the capital to a hero's welcome.

J. A. Thompson highlights the importance of Wilson's mission:

> Woodrow Wilson was the first American President to leave the
> Western Hemisphere during his period of office, and, as befitted him,

the circumstances in which he did so were neither casual nor frivolous. He went to Europe in late 1918 to take part in the peace conference following a war that the United States had played a crucial part in bringing to a decisive end. His aim was to secure a peace that accorded with the proposals he had set out in his Fourteen Points address of January 1918 and in other speeches – a peace that would be based upon justice and thus secure consent, that would embody liberal principles (the self-determination of peoples as far as practicable, the prohibition of discriminatory trade barriers) and that would be maintained by a new international organisation in which the United States, breaking its tradition of isolation, would take part – a league of nations that would provide a general guarantee of "political independence and territorial integrity to great and small states alike."[4]

The French people made their gratitude to America clear but it was also apparent that they expected the American President to support them in their desire for revenge. Wilson's steadfast refusal to commit himself to the French point of view and his clear commitment to his Fourteen Points highlighted the fact that there was a substantial difference between the French, with their desire for revenge, and the Americans, who stood for a more abstract 'peace without victory'.

The polarity of these positions meant that the stance adopted by Britain would be absolutely vital. The importance of public opinion in influencing the politicians was heightened by the fact that a general election was being fought out in December 1918. It was difficult for any politician to resist climbing on to the popular bandwagon of 'Hang the Kaiser' and 'Make Germany Pay' which was being whipped up by the popular press in the build-up to the election at home and the peace conference in Paris.

## a summary of Woodrow Wilson's Fourteen Points

1 Open covenants of peace, openly arrived at, after which there shall be no private international understandings of any kind.
2 Absolute freedom of navigation upon the seas . . . alike in peace and in war.
3 The removal, so far as possible, of all economic barriers.
4 Adequate guarantees given and taken that national armaments will be reduced to the lowest point consistent with domestic safety.
5 A free, open-minded and impartial adjustment of all colonial claims, based upon a strict observance of the principle that the interests of the population concerned must have equal weight with the equitable claims of the government whose title is to be determined.
6 The evacuation of all Russian territory and . . . a settlement of all questions affecting Russia.
7 Belgium . . . must be evacuated and restored.

8 All French territory should be freed and the invaded portions restored, and the wrong done to France by Prussia in 1871 in the matter of Alsace-Lorraine . . . should be righted.

9 A readjustment of the frontiers of Italy should be effected along clearly recognisable lines of nationality.

10 The peoples of Austria-Hungary . . . should be accorded the freest opportunity of autonomous development.

11 Romania, Serbia and Montenegro should be evacuated; occupied territories restored; Serbia accorded free and secure access to the sea; . . . and international guarantees of the political and economic independence and territorial integrity of the several Balkan States should be entered into.

12 The Turkish portions of the present Ottoman empire should be assured a secure sovereignty, but the other nationalities which are now under Turkish rule should be assured . . . an absolutely unmolested opportunity of autonomous development, and the Dardanelles should be permanently opened as a free passage to the ships and commerce of all nations under international guarantees.

13 An independent Polish State should be erected which should include the territories inhabited by indisputably Polish populations, which should be assured a free and secure access to the sea.

14 A general association of nations must be formed under specific covenants for the purposes of affording mutual guarantees of political independence and territorial integrity to great and small states alike.

*Source*: Ruth Henig, *Versailles and After (1919–1933)* (1984).

## the Versailles settlement

The preliminary peace conference was opened at the French Foreign Ministry on the Quai d'Orsay on 18 January 1919 and concluded when the peace terms were presented to the German delegation in May. On 7 May 1919 representatives of 27 nations crowded into the dining room of the Trianon Palace Hotel, at Versailles, to see the terms of the peace treaty being handed to the German delegation. When the German politicians were ushered in to hear their fate, Georges Clemenceau, the French Prime Minister, was the first to speak. He addressed the German delegation as follows:

> This is neither the time nor the place for superfluous words. You see before you the accredited representatives of the Allied and Associated Powers, both small and great, which have waged without respite for more than four years the pitiless war that was imposed on them. The time has come for a heavy reckoning of events. You have asked for peace. We are ready to grant it to you. I must of necessity add, that this second Peace of Versailles which is now to be the subject of our discussions, has been too dearly bought by the peoples represented here, for us not to be unanimously resolved to use all the means in our

power to obtain every lawful satisfaction that is due to us. There will be no verbal discussion, and observations must be submitted in writing. The plenipotentiaries of Germany will be given fifteen days in which to submit their written observations on the entire treaty.[6]

The peace terms, with drastic implications for Germany, were handed over in a large, white, folio volume. The recipient – the head of the German delegation, Count Brockdorff-Rantzau – accepted the folder with a bow and began his reply.

To the astonishment of the onlookers, he delivered his reply sitting down. The discourtesy was intentional. 'We are under no illusions', he stated, 'as to the extent of our defeat and the degree of our powerlessness. We know that the strength of German arms is broken. We know the intensity of the hatred which meets us, and we have heard the victor's passionate demand that as the vanquished, we shall be made to pay, and as the guilty, we shall be punished.' It was now, with a note of defiance, that Brockdorff-Rantzau raised his objections. 'We are required to admit that we alone are to blame for the war: such an admission on my lips would be a lie.' The German politician told the Allies that he was 'far from seeking to absolve Germany from all responsibility for this World War, and for its having been waged as it has'. However, 'we emphatically deny that Germany, whose people were convinced that they were waging a war of defence, should be burdened with sole responsibility'.[6]

Although 32 states were officially represented, the whole conference only came together six times. Ultimately the talks were dominated by the 'big four': President Wilson of the USA, Prime Minister Lloyd George of Great Britain, Premier Clemenceau of France and Prime Minister Orlando of Italy. Much of the historical verdict on the manner in which the negotiations were carried out has been critical. The historian Sally Marks describes how the big four 'proceeded in slipshod fashion without agenda, minutes, or any record of decisions until the secretary of the British delegation, the supremely efficient Colonel Sir Maurice Hankey, insinuated himself into their midst and rescued them from disaster. Even then, the agenda darted from topic to topic, and the big four were startlingly erratic in either accepting, ignoring or rejecting expert reports.'[7]

The range of problems facing the main protagonists was immense but the range of agreement was narrow. Relations between Wilson, Lloyd George and Clemenceau began coolly and deteriorated. Clemenceau, nicknamed 'the Tiger' and with a fearsome appearance that matched his reputation, soon made it clear that he was not impressed by Wilson's idealism: 'God gave us the Ten Commandments and we broke them, Wilson gave us the Fourteen Points. We shall see.'[8] When Wilson showed the strain and fell ill on 3 April Clemenceau was scarcely able to conceal his delight. This personal animosity, combined with the range of technical problems in constructing a complex peace settlement, meant that the conference was unlikely to emerge uncompromised. The historian Anthony Lentin, in his book *Guilt at Versailles*, highlights the practical problems encountered by Wilson in seeking to implement the worthy ideal of national self-determination. 'He was ignorant, when he promised Italy the South Tyrol, that its population was Austrian. When he approved the boundaries of Czechoslovakia, he had no idea that they contained three million Germans. When he assented to the incorporation of Transylvania within Romania, he was unaware of sanctioning an act of annexation.'[9]

Ultimately the complexities of the problem were pushed aside in order to produce a finished treaty. After four months of argument the treaty was hurriedly brought together at the end of April. Germany's outspoken resentment at the manner in which the terms had been dictated to them only served to harden the position on both sides, and the only amendments made to the treaty were minor ones. On 28 June 1919 the conference finally came to an end when the Germans signed the treaty in the Hall of Mirrors in the glittering Palace of Versailles. The very room that had been the scene of German's unification and triumphant victory over France in 1871 now symbolized national humiliation. The fate of Germany had been decided and when the terms were made public they dismayed the German nation.

## extracts from the terms of the Versailles Peace Treaty

Article 42: Germany is not to maintain or construct any fortifications either on the left bank of the Rhine or on the right bank to the west of a line drawn 50 kilometres to the east.

Article 45: As compensation for the destruction of the coal mines in the north of France, and as part payment towards the total reparations due, Germany gives to France the coal mines of the Saar. At the end of 15 years, its inhabitants shall be asked under which government they wish to be placed.

Article 80: Germany acknowledges and will respect strictly the independence of Austria . . . she agrees that this independence will be inalienable.

Article 102: The Principal Allied and Associated Powers undertake to establish the town of Danzig . . . as a Free City. It will be placed under the protection of the League of Nations.

Article 119: Germany renounces in favour of the Principal Allied and Associated Powers all her rights and titles over her overseas possessions.

Article 160: By a date not later than 31 March 1920, the German army must not consist of more than seven divisions of infantry and three of cavalry [i.e. not more than 100,000 men].

Article 231: The Allied governments affirm, and Germany accepts, the responsibility of Germany and her allies for causing all the loss and damage to which the Allied governments and their peoples have been subjected as a result of the war.

Article 232: The Allied governments recognise that the resources of Germany are not adequate to make complete reparation for all such loss and damage. . . .

But they require, and Germany undertakes, that she will make compensation for all the damage done to the civilian population of the Allied powers and to their property during the war.

Article 428: As a guarantee that the treaty shall be carried out, the German territory to the west of the Rhine will be occupied by . . . Allied troops for 15 years.

*Source*: Alan Sharp, *The Versailles Settlement: Peacemaking in Paris 1919* (1991).

## analysis of the Treaty of Versailles

**SOURCE A**

The fundamental significance of Versailles . . . was emotional rather than rational. Allied statesmen, urged on by the pressure of public opinion, had made peace in a spirit of revenge. The cries of 'Hang the Kaiser' and 'squeezing the German lemon until the pips squeak' were indicative of the desire not merely for a guarantee of future security, but for the national humiliation of Germany . . . The Germans saw every difficulty in subsequent years as a further indignity that they alone must suffer as a result of the hated Treaty of Versailles.

*Source*: Anthony Wood, *Europe 1815–1960* (1986).

**SOURCE B**

It was a wise precept of Machiavelli that the victor should either conciliate his enemy or destroy him. The Treaty of Versailles did neither. It did not pacify Germany, still less permanently weaken her, appearances notwithstanding, but left her scourged, humiliated and resentful. It was neither a Wilson peace nor a Clemenceau peace, but a witches' brew concocted of the least palatable ingredients of each which, though highly distasteful to Germany, were by no means fatal.

*Source*: Anthony Lentin, *Guilt at Versailles* (1984).

**SOURCE C**

Severe as the Treaty of Versailles seemed to many Germans, it should be remembered that Germany might easily have fared much worse. If Clemenceau had had his way, instead of being restrained by Britain and America, the Rhineland would have become an independent state, the Saarland would have been annexed to France and Danzig would have become an integral part of Poland . . . However, the Germans as a nation were not inclined to count their blessings in 1919 . . . Most of all they resented the moral stigma of sole war-guilt which they did not feel . . . Finally, the fact that the treaty was not negotiated but dictated to Germany and signed in humiliating circumstances made it certain that the German people would accept no responsibility for its fulfilment. To the discerning it was clear from the beginning that the Versailles settlement would last only as long as the victorious powers were in a position to enforce it on a bitterly resentful people.

*Source*: William Carr, *A History of Germany, 1815–1945* (1991).

GERMANY AND THE VERSAILLES TREATY.

Far more energy, it has been observed, was expended in denying war guilt than in addressing adequately the very legitimate concerns of the Allied powers. Similarly, it has been claimed, the avoidance of reparations, even at the cost of undermining orderly economic life, periodically took precedence over genuine efforts to comply with a reparations schedule that Germany had agreed. Revanchist sentiment within the new Reichswehr – a successor to the Imperial Army in all but name – added to the desolate picture.

*Source*: Conan Fischer, *A Very German Revolution* (2006).

### QUESTIONS

1 To what extent do the historians whose views are reflected here support the view that Germany was harshly dealt with at the Versailles peace settlement?
2 To what extent do they agree as to the strengths and shortcomings of the peace treaty?

## 7.4 the Weimar Republic, 1919–23

Although the embryonic republic had survived the threat from the radical left, it had been badly compromised by the bloody violence that had taken place in its name and was then challenged by the forces of the extreme right. The conservative–nationalist right condemned the 'shameful peace' settlement at Versailles and argued that the soldiers at the front line had been 'stabbed in the back' by the politically irresponsible agitation of left-wing pacifists. Since the summer of 1919 a group of extremists under the direction of General Ludendorff and Wolfgang Kapp, a former founder member of the Patriotic Party, had planned the violent overthrow of the new government. In March 1920, Freikorps officers launched a pro-monarchist coup d'état in Berlin in an attempt to install Wolfgang Kapp as Chancellor. Without a blow being struck and with the support of army commanders across many parts of Germany, the rebels were able to occupy Berlin. Unable to secure support from the military to quell the putsch, the government and its president were briefly forced out of Berlin, initially to Dresden and then to Stuttgart.

Although troops refused to take action against the Freikorps the success of the putsch was frustrated by the working class, who organized a general strike in Berlin which gained spontaneous and widespread support from workers throughout the country. On 18 March Kapp and the closest members of his entourage fled to Sweden, marking an inglorious end to the putsch. Although the regime survived this threat, evidence that brutal extremism still existed was provided by the assassination of Matthias Erzberger, leader of the Centre Party, shot dead in the Black Forest in August 1921, and Rathenau, the Jewish Foreign

Minister, who was murdered in June 1922, in a disturbing anti-Semitic incident that did not bode well for the future.

These outrages caused great indignation among the general public and led Chancellor Wirth to declare in the Reichstag that the 'enemy is on the right!' These events led to a Law for the Protection of the Republic, but the extremists would not be easily deterred. Clearly, one reason for the existence of this pronounced political extremism was the troubled nature of the new republic's economy.

## 7.5 the Weimar economy

From the outset, the republic faced crushing economic difficulties that in turn fuelled support for those who wanted the exercise in democracy to be strangled at birth. The aftermath of the war placed a heavy burden on the republic and as early as 1919 Germany's internal finances were close to collapse, mainly because the war effort had been financed through short-term loans and by inflating the currency in the belief that when victory came the vanquished enemy would pay the war debts. The bleak alternative scenario of defeat left the republic with a massive internal debt in excess of 140,000 million marks and with a currency which had lost over one-third of its pre-war value. In addition a trade deficit, the difficulty of attracting foreign investment, and the shattering loss of the Saarland and Upper Silesia added to the scale of the economic problem. With monetary inflation and a falling mark, successive chancellors failed to address the fundamental but unpalatable issues of balancing the budget and stabilizing the currency.

### the Weimar economy, 1919–23

**1919**

| | |
|---|---|
| June | The Treaty of Versailles obliged Germany to pay reparations to the victors. However, a total figure was not reached at this conference |

**1921**

| | |
|---|---|
| March | At the London conference, Germany proposed a significant scaling-down of the reparations figure put forward by the Allies in January 1921. Angered by the additional German conditions that the Rhineland be evacuated and Upper Silesia restored, the Allies occupied three towns in the Ruhr, claiming that Germany was already in breach of the agreement by not making an interim payment of £1,000 million |
| April | The Reparations Commission finally presented its report. It recommended a total bill of £6,600 million (132 billion marks), which was to be delivered in annual payments of £100 million (2 billion marks), with additional payments equivalent to the value of one quarter of all German exports |

*1922*

By the start of the year it was obvious that Germany was going to have to default on its payments. Consequently, the Reparations Commission granted relief on the first payments of the new year. However, the French felt strongly that Germany could pay but simply did not want to. The Treaty of Rapallo, with its provision for economic co-operation between Germany and Russia, intensified French suspicion

*1923*

The Paris Conference in January 1923 tried to resolve the reparations dispute but on 9 January the Reparations Commission announced that Germany had deliberately defaulted over coal deliveries. Two days later French and Belgian troops were sent into the Ruhr, the industrial heartland of Germany

The problems of the Weimar Republic reached a peak in 1923. In January, with Germany in default of her reparations payments, French and Belgian troops occupied the Ruhr in order to seize coal deposits. The trauma of defeat in the First World War was echoed in the humiliation of the French occupation of the Ruhr, which devastated the German economy and sparked off the most catastrophic hyper-inflation in its history. Early in 1923 the dollar was worth 18,000 marks, by August it was worth 4,600,000 marks and by November it had reached 4 billion marks. It is hard to underestimate the extent of the damage this caused. Images abound of vast amounts of banknotes being carried around by people whose life savings had become worthless. Printing presses churned out money furiously, but with the outcome that the currency itself became utterly worthless. This profound and protracted disorder in the German economy placed the population in a situation of economic and social crisis. By September, interest rates were raised to 90 per cent. Some stability was restored when passive resistance to the occupation was abandoned and the Rentenmark was introduced. Chancellor Cuno's policy of passive resistance and non-cooperation succeeded in frustrating the French, but meant that this crucial economic region became a beleaguered and blockaded occupied zone. Germany's fragile currency and delicate economy were devastated by the consequences of the Ruhr occupation.

Nowhere was the sense of discontent and rage at the Government's impotence more strongly felt than Munich. It was here that Hitler came to national prominence.

## 7.6 the origins of Adolf Hitler's political ideology

A glance at the names of chancellors who served the Weimar Republic reveals a mixed list. It contains worthy characters, idealists and others who have disappeared from general interest. But the name that stands out is the one who brought the Weimar republic to a close, creating the Third Reich in its place. When Adolf Hitler became Germany's latest Chancellor in January 1933, a change had taken place of much greater consequence that the bankers, agrarians, industrialists, army generals and political fixers who placed him there had bargained for. To be sure, the Weimar Republic had already lurched from its constitutional, democratic principles to a system teetering on the brink of collapse and resting on the use of emergency laws.

Yet within months of his appointment Hitler had brought about the complete and systematic destruction of a modern, civilized society and replaced it with the values of a harsh, totalitarian regime. Justice, freedom of speech, democracy and the rule of law were vanquished. Political parties, the independent press, trade unions and an impartial judiciary passed into history. Germany's parliament, the Reichstag, was reduced to the role of a rubber stamp to endorse Hitler's policies. The police became the instrument of terror rather than the defenders of law and order. All aspects of the media were shaped into the mouthpiece of authoritarianism rather than an outlet for free speech. Why was the Weimar Republic unable to survive, and why did it give way to such an extreme successor?

### German chancellors after the war

*date of assuming office*

| | |
|---|---|
| November 1918 | F. Ebert |
| February 1919 | P. Schiedemann |
| June 1919 | G. Bauer |
| March 1920 | G. Müller |
| June 1920 | K. Fehrenbach |
| May 1921 | J. Wirth |
| November 1922 | W. Cuno |
| August 1923 | G. Stresemann |
| November 1923 | W. Marx |
| January 1925 | H. Luther |
| May 1926 | W. Marx |
| June 1928 | H. Müller |
| April 1930 | H. Brüning |
| June 1932 | F. von Papen |
| November 1932–January 1933 | K. von Schleicher |
| 30 January 1933 | Adolf Hitler |

Why did a country which prided itself on its glorious heritage of fine art, music, literature and political thought come to invest such high office in an ill-educated, racist demagogue whose earlier years had included time spent in a men's doss-house in Austria and in a prison cell in a Gothic castle?

What were the origins of Hitler's political ideology? Hitler derived intense personal satisfaction from his wartime service in the List Regiment. In the words of one of his superiors, 'the List Regiment was his homeland'. For the first time since his mother's death, Hitler felt a sense of belonging. Hitler's biographer, Joachim Fest, writes that life in the army gave Hitler a sense of prestige, while its impersonality suited his temperament. His solitary work as a messenger-carrier between the regimental staff and the front-line trenches meant that he retained his sense of isolation and his eccentric, brooding mannerisms.[10]

Nevertheless, several accounts testify to Hitler's bravery, loyalty and willingness to obey even the most dangerous of orders. Despite these qualities, Hitler was never promoted beyond the rank of private, first class. His adjutant later recalled that Hitler had not displayed 'leadership qualities' and added that Hitler himself had not wanted promotion. Hitler was, in his own way, contented, but this almost idyllic period was abruptly shattered in the autumn of 1918. The acute sense of trauma which accompanied his mother's death was to return in the most painful of circumstances. On the night of 13 October Hitler's regiment faced a British gas attack at Wervick, near Ypres. Within hours, exposure to mustard gas had taken away Hitler's sight. The hysterical and deeply shocked young soldier was taken to the Pasewalk hospital in Pomerania, where his eyesight gradually returned. However, for Hitler worse was to follow. He was still in hospital when on 10 November 1918 he was informed that a revolution had broken out in Germany and that the Kaiser had abdicated. The news of Germany's imminent defeat traumatized Hitler. Contentment had been replaced by deep despair. The next day, the war, and with it, Hitler's sense of purpose, came to an end. At the end of the war he appeared to be a lost soul. The news of Germany's defeat was almost impossible for him to accept. Yet within a year he found a new sense of direction as he stumbled into the political arena, albeit on its most extreme fringes. How was it possible for this socially isolated, obsessive young man to become the most important member of a political party which would eventually become the largest in German history?

In the pre-war period, Munich, the capital of Bavaria, had enjoyed a reputation as a tolerant, cosmopolitan city. However, amid the trauma of defeat it became a more troubled place, a seething stamping ground for demobilized soldiers who struggled to come to terms with their new circumstances. It was within this political ferment that Hitler's political ideology began to take shape, a world-view consisting of a belief in history as racial struggle, virulent anti-Semitism and extreme anti-Marxism, and a conviction that the long-term future of the German population could only be secured through the conquest of *Lebensraum* (Living Space) at the expense of Russia. Exactly when Hitler acquired these ideas remains open to interpretation, but the composite ideology can be clearly seen in his dictated work *Mein Kampf*, written during his spell in prison.

SOURCE A

During these years a view of life and a definite outlook on the world took shape in my mind. These became the granite basis of my conduct at that time. Since then I have extended that foundation very little, I have changed nothing in it . . . Vienna was a hard school for me, but it taught me the most profound lessons of my life.

*Source*: Adolf Hitler, *Mein Kampf* (1925).

SOURCE B

One day when passing through the Inner City, I suddenly encountered a phenomenon in a long caftan and wearing black sidelocks. My first thought was: is this a Jew? . . . But the longer I gazed at this strange countenance and examined it section by section, the more the question shaped itself in my brain: is this a German? I turned to books for help in removing my doubts. For the first time in my life I bought myself some anti-Semitic pamphlets for a few pence . . . As soon as I began to investigate the matter . . . Vienna appeared to me in a new light . . . Was there any shady undertaking, any form of foulness, especially in cultural life, in which at least one Jew did not participate? On putting the probing knife to that kind of abscess one immediately discovered, like a maggot in a putrescent body, a little Jew who was often blinded by the sudden light.

*Source*: as source A.

SOURCE C

EXTRACT FROM A SPEECH MADE BY HITLER AT KULMBACH, 5 FEBRUARY 1928.

The idea of struggle is as old as life itself, for life is only preserved because other living things perish through struggle . . . In this struggle, the stronger, the more able win, while the less able, the weak lose.

## the origins of Hitler's ideology: the views of historians

SOURCE A

We remain in the dark about why Hitler became a manic anti-Semite . . . Hitler's own story, retailed in *Mein Kampf*, tells of his conversion to anti-Semitism after encountering a kaftan-garbed figure with black hair locks in the streets of Vienna. This was probably a dramatisation. Hitler was already reading pan-German anti-Semitic newspapers in his Linz days and was even then an admirer of the Austrian anti-Semite and pan-German leader Georg von Schorerer.

*Source*: Ian Kershaw, *Hitler, Profiles in Power* (1991).

For most of his Vienna years he had no independently thought-out political line. Rather, he was filled with emotions of hatred and defensiveness . . . Alongside these were vague, up welling prejudices against Jews and other minorities . . . He was obsessed by fears of Jew and Slavs . . . His fellows in the home for men did not share his paranoid emotions . . .

In retrospect, Hitler laid claim to an intense intellectual development. During the approximately five years he spent in Vienna, he maintained, he read 'enormously and thoroughly' . . . But it would probably be more accurate to say that the real influences of this phase of his life stemmed not so much from the intellectual realm as from that of demagogy and political tactics . . . His experiences during this phase of his life helped Hitler arrive at that philosophy of struggle that became the central core of his view of the world . . . his belief in brutal struggle, in harshness, cruelty, destruction, the rights of the stranger . . . He learned in that school for meanness in Vienna.

*Source*: Joachim C. Fest, *Hitler* (1974).

**SOURCE C**

Hitler's early life, unlike Stalin's, was not one of hardship and poverty. Contrary to the impression he portrays in *Mein Kampf*, he was neither poor nor harshly treated. His father . . . had a secure income, as well as the social standing of an imperial official, and when he died he left his widow and children well provided for.

*Source*: Alan Bullock, *Hitler and Stalin : Parallel Lives* (1991).

**SOURCE D**

The picture which Hitler gives of Vienna in *Mein Kampf* is not correct. He says that he became an anti-Semite in Vienna, but if you check the contemporary sources closely, you see that, on the contrary, he was very good friends with very many, extraordinarily many Jews, both in the men's hostel and through his contact with the dealers who sold his pictures.

*Source*: Brigitte Hamann, *Hitler's Wein* (1996).

## 7.7 Hitler's rise to the leadership of the National Socialist Party, 1919–24

As we have said, the news of Germany's defeat was almost impossible for Hitler to accept. Yet within a year he found a new sense of direction as he stumbled into the political arena, albeit on its most extreme fringes. This section will enable you to examine Hitler's development of his position from a mere observer of the German Workers' Party in September 1919 to its dominant figure at the time of the 'Beer-Hall Putsch' in November 1923.

## Hitler's rise to dominance within his own party

**1918**

**November**

Following his release from Pasewalk hospital and his recovery from the gas attack which had temporarily blinded him, Hitler made his way to Munich. The city was in turmoil amid the trauma of defeat and a once cosmopolitan and tolerant place became a seething stamping ground for bitter, demobilized soldiers and a variety of extremist cranks

**1919**

**9 January**

A railway mechanic, Anton Drexler, set up the German Workers' Party (DAP) which, as Fest puts it, 'was very small potatoes'.[11] Initial membership was between 20–40 people

**Spring**

The army retained Hitler's services at the end of the war and assigned him to an 'educational unit'. Based at a barracks at Camp Lachfeld, he attended a series of army indoctrination courses and made an impression on other course members with his strongly held views. It was at this point that He first experienced the thrill of seeing groups of people respond to his crude, emotional language and imagery. Hitler was now used as an agent with the task of investigating the various political parties which were springing up amid the chaos of post-war Germany.

**August**

He made his first public comments on the 'Jewish Question' in a 'lecture' to demobilized soldiers organized by the Reichswehr

**September**

Hitler attended a meeting of the DAP. He spoke out at the end of the meeting and was subsequently sent a membership card inviting him to become the 555th person to join. Hitler took a few days to decide to join and became the seventh member of the party's board. At that point the party was just one of more than seventy similar political groups on the extreme right wing of German politics. Hitler returned to his barracks and eagerly set about typing letters and making contacts. He immediately devoted more time to the party than the majority of the other members.

In the same month Hitler set out his first detailed political statement in a letter which contained his early views on anti-Semitism. Before the year was over he had become the party's propaganda chief

**16 October**

Hitler delivered a blistering speech at the party's first public meeting. Afterwards, he had discovered 'I could speak.' Before the end of the year the party had moved into headquarters – a rented room in the Sternecker beer hall. Hitler was dragging the party forward, out of complete obscurity and on to the edge of the public arena

| 24 February | At the Hofbrauhaus in Munich the party announced details of a 25-point programme which Hitler had helped to create. Within a week the party changed its name from German Workers' Party to the National Socialist German Worker's Party (NSDAP) and adopted the swastika as its battle symbol. Hitler's artistic talents were now employed in designing posters and publicity material for party meetings |
| 31 March | Hitler left the Reichswehr and devoted his energies to politics, although his friendship with Ernst Röhm enabled him to retain a useful contact with the army. In a series of speeches over the next few months Hitler repeatedly condemned the Jews in the most extreme terms. He was now developing a link between the Jews and Bolshevism, contending that weak government and poor social conditions in Germany were playing into the hands of the revolutionary Marxists whom he connected with Soviet Russia and world Jewry. Hitler, with his talent for crude simplification and his ability to connect with his beer-hall audience, was becoming the most effective speaker in the party. This set him apart from party 'intellectuals' such as Gottfried Feder and Alfred Rosenberg, who lacked Hitler's emotionally raw appeal |
| December | The NSDAP bought the *Münchener Beobachter* newspaper, which was then renamed the *Völkischer Beobachter* (this became the party's daily newspaper from February 1923) |

| July | Hitler responded to policy differences within the party by offering his resignation on 11 July. He issued preconditions for his return, and these were accepted at a meeting at the end of July which saw Hitler emerge as Party Chairman, with dictatorial powers |
| 3 August | The armed squads which were used to provide protection for party members were formally organized into what was euphemistically called the 'Gymnastic and Sports Section' and which in October was renamed the 'Storm Detachments' (SA) . The SA was deployed to prevent disruption of party meetings and to intimidate political opponents |

| February | Hitler made a speech to the SA in which he claimed that the 'Jewish Question' was his 'single, total and exclusive' concern |
| May | There were 45 party branches, mostly in Bavaria and many |

| | |
|---|---|
| | beyond the direct control of Hitler. By late 1922 total membership was around 20,000 |
| Summer | By the time of the murder of the Jewish German Foreign Minister Walter Rathenau the NSDAP's violent tendencies meant that the party had been outlawed in virtually every German state, with the notable exception of Bavaria. In July, Hitler was briefly imprisoned after violence at an opposition meeting the previous September. By now Hitler was consciously developing his own personality cult amongst his loyal followers |
| 10 October | Hitler was boosted by the decision of Julius Streicher to merge his *Völkisch* group based in Nuremberg with the NSDAP, under Hitler's leadership |
| December | Historian Ian Kershaw states that by now, Hitler had formulated the basis of his personalized world-view, namely, 'the struggle to destroy the power of international Jewry, the struggle to annihilate Marxism, and the struggle to obtain "living space" for Germany at the expense of Russia'[12] |
| *1923* | |
| January | The party organized its first 'Reich Party Rally' in Munich. Speakers at the rally condemned the Weimar government's weakness in the face of the French and Belgian occupation of the Ruhr. The sense of crisis which this created eventually led Hitler to decide that he could attempt a national uprising |
| February | The SA joined with other Bavarian paramilitary groups and became increasingly militarized |
| 1 March | The SA was placed under the command of Hermann Goering. By late 1923 party membership had reached nearly 50,000 |
| November | The Munich Putsch. Hitler led a march through Munich which he hoped would lead to the overthrow of the Bavarian government and to the proclamation of a national revolution. The putsch dissolved amid a hail of gunfire from the Bavarian authorities. Hitler had seriously overestimated his own position. Sixteen of his followers were killed. Hitler fled the scene but was subsequently arrested |

## 7.8 the Munich Putsch, 1923

The trauma of military defeat, revolution, French occupation and hyperinflation transformed the atmosphere of Munich from its pre-war status as a cosmopolitan, tolerant city to its post-war reputation as a centre of violent political upheaval. The brutal repression of the socialist republic had given way to an ultra-right-wing regime which dominated Bavarian politics. By 1923 Adolf Hitler had established himself as the mouthpiece of the numerous right-wing groups which flourished in Munich.

Hitler had now found his niche as the leader of the NNSDAP. By November 1923 he sensed that the time was ripe to make a stand against the continued prominence of communist politicians in central Germany. His ambition was to force the Bavarian government to take armed action against the Communists, which would leave Hitler poised to seize power in Berlin. However, this attempt was stopped in its tracks and it soon became clear that Hitler had badly misjudged the political situation.

In the so-called 'Beer-Hall Putsch', Hitler led his assortment of right-wing followers in a march to the centre of Munich. However, as the following extracts suggest, it took little more than a volley of shots from the well-organized police to scatter the insurgents and ruin Hitler's ambitions.

## SOURCE A

FROM AN OFFICIAL ENQUIRY INTO THE MUNICH PUTSCH (1923).

The column of National Socialists about 2000 strong, nearly all armed, moved on through the Zweibruckenstrasse across the Marienplatz towards the Theatinerstrasse. Here it split up, the majority going down the Perusastrasse to the Residenze, the rest going along the Theatinerstrasse. The police stationed in the Residenze tried to cordon it off as well as the Theatinerstrasse by the Preysingstrasse. Numerous civilians hurried on ahead of the actual column in Residenzstrasse and pushed the police barricade. The ceaseless shouts of 'Stop! Don't go on!' by the state police were not obeyed. Since there was a danger of a breakthrough here, a police section, originally in the Theaterinstrasse, hurried round the Feldherrenalle to give support. They were received with fixed bayonets, guns with the safety catches off, and raised pistols. Several police officers were spat upon, and pistols with the safety catches off were stuck in their chests. The police used rubber truncheons and rifle butts and tried to push back the crowd with rifles held horizontally. Their barricade had already been broken several times. Suddenly a National Socialist fired a pistol at a police officer from close quarters. The shot went past his head and killed Sergeant Hollweg standing behind him. Even before it was possible to give an order, the comrades of the sergeant who had been shot opened fire as the Hitler lot did, and a short gun battle ensued during which the police were also shot at from the Preysingplais and from the house which contains the Cafe Rottenhoffer. After no more than thirty seconds the Hitler lot fled, some back to the Maximilienstrasse, some to the Odeonsplatz. General Ludendorff apparently went on towards the Odeonsplatz. There he was seen in the company of a Hitler officer by a police officer barring the Briennerstrasse, who went up to General Ludendorff and said to him: 'Excellency, I must take you into custody.' General Ludendorff replied: 'You have your orders. I'll come with you.' Both gentlemen were then accompanied into the Residenze.

*Source*: J. Noakes and G. Pridham (eds), *Nazism 1919–1945: A Documentary Reader. Vol. 1: The Rise to Power* (1998).

Hitler's precipitate flight from the Odeonsplatz has often been contrasted unfavourably with Ludendorff's calm and impassive walk through the police cordon to surrender to the officer in charge. It is a matter of taste. One could just as easily argue that Ludendorff behaved in a foolhardy manner, exposing himself to unnecessary risks when bullets were flying whereas Hitler, the seasoned front-line soldier, obeyed the dictates of common prudence and took cover. Actually he was thrown to the ground by the shot that killed Scheubner-Richter (with whom he had linked arms) and dislocated his shoulder. Coward Hitler was not, as his war record proves. But to stay behind with the smell of defeat in the air would have been a romantic gesture out of keeping with his sense of political realism. The 'whiff of grapeshot' was the final incontrovertible proof that the forces of law and order were not on his side and that he could not, therefore, succeed.

*Source*: William Carr, *Hitler: A Study in Personality and Politics* (1978).

## Hitler's trial and the aftermath of the Munich Putsch

Hitler came within inches of a violent death in November 1923. With this narrow escape came the realization that the prospect of an armed seizure of power was completely unrealistic. Hitler and his colleagues went on trial for high treason at a court in Munich in February 1924. During the trial Hitler launched a spirited defence of his actions. He now presented himself as an anti-Marxist. Hitler received considerable press coverage, much of it favourable. Although the putsch had ended in calamity Hitler had managed to turn the trial into a personal triumph, consolidating his position as the dominant figure in the party and establishing himself as the key political figure of the extreme right. Sentence was passed on 1 April. Hitler was fined 200 gold marks and sentenced to five years in prison. However, after serving less than a year in prison in Landsberg am Lech he was released on 20 December. By the time Hitler emerged from prison it was clear that he was indispensable to the party. During his imprisonment the party, under the stand-in leadership of Rosenberg, had virtually disintegrated, completely losing the momentum it had enjoyed until the abortive putsch and splitting into various rival factions. Without Hitler's leadership the party was dead in the water.

The failure of the Munich Putsch taught Hitler a profound lesson about the difficulties of direct confrontation with the power of the state. Although during his confinement he had the time to write his sprawling political autobiography, *Mein Kampf*, Hitler came out of prison in December 1924 knowing that the prospect of a successful armed seizure of power was completely unrealistic. In *Mein Kampf* he made it clear that the strategy employed by the NSDAP would, from now on, concentrate on the ballot box and the drive for seats in the Reichstag. Although the trial in Munich brought him national publicity and unprecedented prominence, this marked a period in Hitler's career when his chances of holding real political power seemed increasingly remote. He emerged from prison to find that the favourable climate in which he had launched his abortive putsch no longer existed. It seemed that the period of political extremism was over. Between 1924 and 1928 the Nazi structure was reorganized, rallies became more elaborate, the SA was reformed, Hitler's authority was consolidated, and a challenge to his authority in 1926 was brushed aside. However, it was not to Hitler's advantage that Germany was now entering a period of economic recovery and political stability. He emerged from prison to find that the favourable climate in which he had launched his abortive putsch no longer existed. It seemed that the period of political extremism was over. Despite the Nazi Party's organisational changes, the results of the 1928 election would confirm that Hitler remained on the margins of German politics. Much of the credit for this was due to the leadership of Gustav Stresemann.

## 7.9 the Weimar Republic and foreign policy

The widespread revulsion at the suffering of 1914–18, combined with a general feeling of war-weariness, served to create an atmosphere which embraced new notions of openness, discussion and morality at the expense of secrecy and power-politics. However, Anthony Lentin, in his book *Guilt at Versailles*, argues that any sense of optimism that European society had embarked on a radical change of direction was in itself dangerous: 'The mirage of the League of Nations as an entity somehow different from the erring states which composed it, the myth of the actual efficacy of peaceful aspirations, was to prove among the most infectious and tenacious of the illusions born of the Peace Conference.'[13]

In addition, Sally Marks makes the important point that:

> The advent of peace was highly relative. The major powers were no longer in bloody collision, but civil war raged in Russia, Ireland, China, Turkey, and briefly in the Ruhr. Foreign troops remained in Russia; the Baltic area was a battleground; and Poland invaded Russia while Hungary marched briefly on Poland, Romania and Slovakia. There was fighting on the Finish frontier and in Fiume; in Silesia Germans and Poles waged an undeclared war; most Balkan borders were aflame; and in Anatolia the Turks fought the Greeks, backed by the British. Yet the world was officially at peace.[14]

The power of the League of Nations to resolve these disputes was not always apparent. In the absence of the United States – whose Senate finally rejected the Versailles Treaty in March 1920 – it was essential that the remaining powers were in agreement on major issues. This was by no means the case. Indeed Ruth Henig points out that the 'repudiation by the United States of the entire peace settlement increased the reluctance of successive British governments in the 1920s to underwrite in any tangible way the European territorial settlement'[15]. While France fretted about Germany, Britain sought to redevelop trade links with her former enemy. Sally Marks points out that the powers had assumed that the treaties would be honoured, although this was emphatically not the case: 'The Dutch refused to relinquish the Kaiser, and Germany did not surrender alleged war criminals. Nor did she disarm on schedule or meet reparations quotas. Austria could not and did not pay reparations. Poland did not accept her frontiers . . . Nothing much happened. The will to enforce the treaties was lacking or at best divided.'[16] Despite, or perhaps because of, these problems, the 1920s were marked by a series of conferences and treaties. As we will see, it was not always the intention at these conferences to uphold the peace settlement.

## The Rapallo Treaty, April 1922

The details of the Rapallo Treaty between Germany and Russia were made known while the great European powers were still in conference in Genoa. The Genoa Conference had marked the limited readmission of Russia into the international community. Russia had been completely isolated by the revolutions of 1917 and the subsequent reluctance of the powers to recognize Lenin's government. The failure of the allies to invite Russia to the Versailles Conference and Lenin's repudiation of tsarist war debts damaged relations even further. At Genoa, while France insisted that Russia should still honour her war debts, Lloyd George made very effort to court Russian favour. Alarmed by this trend, Germany went ahead with her growing commitment to Russia (there had been a secret Russo-German military collaboration in 1921), sending delegates away from Genoa to nearby Rapallo to negotiate with the Russians. On 16 April the terms were made known: the German and Soviet governments reintroduced diplomatic relations and pledged their future co-operation. Germany fully recognized the Soviet government and both powers denounced reparations. In addition, the Rapallo Treaty provided for close economic co-operation. In the future, military co-operation would become just as important.

As Sally Marks explains:

> On the Russian plains, far from the prying eyes of military control commissions, Germany could and did build factories, produce the airplanes, poison gases, and tanks forbidden by the Versailles Treaty, test them, and train military personnel, both German and Russian, in their use. While this mutually beneficial arrangement had its ups and downs, it flourished throughout the twenties and to a lesser degree until the advent of Hitler.[17]

In the short term, the announcement of the Rapallo Treaty increased the difficulties which the Genoa Conference was running into and the negotiations eventually broke down over the insistence by France that Russia should honour its pre-war debts.

## the Dawes Plan, 1924

Further stability came with the Dawes Plan (April 1924), which provided a modified settlement of the reparations issue. Extensive American loans over the next five years boosted German industry and agriculture so that by the start of 1929 its economy was superficially prosperous and stable. Economic prosperity meant that the extremist parties on both the right and left floundered. Against this background, Germany was well placed to re-enter the international community on favourable terms.

## the role of Gustav Stresemann, 1878–1929

Writing in 1989, Jonathan Wright highlighted some of the central issues in our understanding of one of the most important and successful politicians of the Weimar period, the man credited with leading a traumatized nation into a period of relative prosperity and whose untimely death in October 1929 robbed Germany of a figure who represented credibility, authority and stability.

> From being a violent nationalist in the First World War, he became the leading statesman of the Weimar Republic. Together with the French Foreign Minister, Aristide Briand, and the British Foreign Secretary, Austen Chamberlain, he negotiated the Locarno Pact in 1925. This held out the promise of peace after the ravages of war and the turmoil of the immediate post-war period. Yet, over this achievement hangs a question mark. Was Stresemann's goal a peaceful Europe in which Germany was a reliable partner, or was his aim rather the step by step revival of Germany as a great power until it had regained a position of dominance?'[18]

Below we examine the making of one of the most pragmatic politicians in German history. What were the forces that shaped the personality and political complexion of Gustav Stresemann and his influence on German foreign policy?

### the personal background of Gustav Stresemann (1878–1922)

| | |
|---|---|
| 1878 | Born in Berlin, of a modest family background. His father ran a small business bottling beer. Later Gustav established his own business and developed a manufacturers' association in the state of Saxony |
| 1907 | Stood for election as a National Liberal candidate in a poor district of Saxony, and at the age of 28 became the youngest member of the Reichstag |
| 1914 | Although physically unfit for military service he adopted an extremist nationalist stance in the First World War. A member of the Navy League, he became a propagandist for a 'greater Germany', advocating expansion into Belgium and the development of a colonial empire. He also supported the move to unrestricted submarine warfare which, eventually, pushed the United States into the war |
| 1917 | Became leader of the National Liberal Party until its break-up in 1919 |
| 1918 | Advocated harsh peace terms in the settlement with Russia |

| 1919 | Stresemann was denied membership of the new Democratic Party even though most of its members were former National Liberals. Written off by his critics, he responded by founding the German People's Party (DVP). Like its founder, the party's attitude towards the embryonic Weimar Republic was ambivalent. Stresemann was emotionally hostile towards the republic but decided that he could only make an effective political contribution within the party system. It was his pragmatic recognition of prevailing circumstance which also led him to advocate acceptance of Germany's commitments under the Treaty of Versailles. Even so, he was strident in his criticism of the republican leaders, whom he claimed had been duped by Wilson's promises of 'peace without victory'. Stresemann was in favour of submission because he appreciated Germany's military weakness and did not want to risk Allied occupation of the coal-rich mid-Ruhr region. In the long run, it is very clear that Stresemann wanted to see a complete revision of Versailles. |
| 1920 | The DVP benefited from the prevailing anti-Versailles sentiment and obtained 65 seats in the Reichstag |
| 1921–22 | Stresemann led his party in condemning the murders of the Republican politician Mathias Erzberger, leader of the Centre Party (1921) and Walter Rathenau, Foreign Secretary (1922). He advocated firm legislation against the right-wing extremists who carried out these assassinations. Although Stresemann himself was not in office at this time his party was playing an important role in the government, he had come through a turbulent period in Germany's history well placed to offer leadership in Germany's future |

## 1923–29

Against the traumatic background of the occupation of the Ruhr, the leadership of the Republic passed into the hands of a man who was ambivalent about its very fabric. He was unanimously appointed Chancellor in August 1923, placing him at the head of a coalition of the centre parties and the SPD. Stresemann realized that the ensuing deadlock was doing untold damage to the German economy. As Carr has stated, 'Chancellor Stresemann acted upon the simple truth that a government which lacks power cannot play power politics.'[19] In September, Stresemann called off passive resistance unconditionally. Although this was domestically unpalatable, Stresemann had laid the foundations for a successful foreign policy grounded in hard-headed realism. He had also created the impression that Germany was at last being led by a reasonable and rational man who would seek compromise and conciliation rather than conflict. Under Stresemann's leadership at the end of 1923 the German currency was stabilized by the introduction of the Rentenmark, valued at one billion old marks.

## the Locarno Conference, 1925

The Locarno Conference marked a critical turning point in the post-war fortunes of Germany. Two years earlier, Gustav Stresemann had called off passive resistance to the French occupation of the Ruhr. This gesture seemed to many observers to symbolize Germany's new willingness for international co-operation. Stresemann had persuaded many of his opponents that Germany had finally given up her hostility towards the peace of Versailles. He reaped the benefits of this apparent change of heart at Locarno in October 1925. The leading statesmen came together for this vital conference in the picturesque Swiss town on Lake Maggiore, ready to readmit Germany to the international community on equal terms. Yet like most other German politicians, including Hitler, Stresemann wanted to restore German power and free his country from the shackles of Versailles. Indeed Sally Marks had gone so far as to say that 'no man in the Weimar Republic did more to destroy the Versailles Treaty' than Stresemann.[20]

At the time, the Locarno Pact seemed to herald a new era of co-operation and goodwill.

### some key terms of the Locarno Pact

1 The Rhineland Pact. Germany, France and Belgium agreed to respect their mutual frontiers, recognizing them as permanent, including the demilitarized zone of the Rhineland. Britain and Italy acted as guarantors to the agreement

2 It was agreed that French troops would complete their withdrawal from the Ruhr

3 A Treaty of Arbitration between France and Germany provided for settlement of all disputes through the League of Nations

4 Plans were made for German admission to the League of Nations, which took place in 1926

When news of the agreement was announced church bells rang out, fireworks exploded and celebrations carried on late into the night. France seemed to have been offered some guarantee of border security and Germany had shown more goodwill than ever before. Britain was pleased to have made only a limited guarantee to France without undertaking wider obligations, for example in Eastern Europe.

However, in reality Germany was already in breach of the disarmament clauses of the Versailles settlement through her secret military co-operation with Russia. Sally Marks says that 'the real spirit at Locarno behind the façade of public fellowship was one of bitter confrontation between a fearful France and a bitter Germany'.[21] It would not be too long before the true nature of international relations in Europe would once again become the subject of political concern.

The Locarno Pact of December 1925 signified the readmission of Germany to the international community, and indicated that sympathy for France had been exhausted. It was confirmed that French troops would leave the Ruhr and that future disputes between the two countries would go to an independent ruling. Crucially, Stresemann had convinced the powers that he had no warlike intentions and would accept the limitations of the Versailles Treaty. This trend was underlined when Germany was admitted to the League of Nations in 1926. In the same year Stresemann was awarded the Nobel Prize for Peace.

## the Kellogg-Briand Pact, August 1928

The International Treaty for the Renunciation of War as an Instrument of National Policy was signed at the Quai d'Orsay in Paris on 27 August 1928. Fifteen nations signed this renunciation of war, with a subsequent endorsement by 31 additional countries. Confined to two paragraphs, the declaration stated that the signatories would in future seek to resolve disputes only by peaceful means. In practice, countries were still left free to exercise self-defence and fulfil their treaty obligations. The sense of optimism engendered by this show of goodwill was heightened when the US Secretary of State, Frank Kellogg, came to Paris to place his signature next to that of his French counterpart, Aristide Briand. This was taken as a sign that the United States was poised to return to a central position in world affairs, but this was a mistaken notion.

America was to remain aloof from European affairs, and the Wall Street Crash of October 1929 heightened her sense of domestic preoccupation. In the same month, Stresemann, who had risen from his sickbed to sign the Kellogg–Briand Pact, died and Germany too entered a period of intense domestic crisis. The Pact had genuinely represented a moment of international goodwill and stability.

There can be no doubt that Stresemann made a profound contribution to the well-being of the Weimar Republic:

> He steered the republic from its parlous state when he took office
> as Chancellor when it was at rock bottom both politically and
> economically to the point when the great coalition collapsed in
> November 1923, when the republic was well on the road to recovery.
> He combined immense political skill, the personal gravitas of a true
> statesman, prodigious hard work, powerful oratory and a forceful
> personality evoking comparisons in both manner and appearance with
> Winston Churchill.[22]

## the Young Plan

In 1929, under the leadership of the US financier Owen Young, the Allied Reparations Commission came up with a new plan to settle German war reparations. Now Germany would pay less than originally intended, although she would still be obliged to make substantial payments until 1988. The German

Nationalists, led by Alfred Hugenberg, organized a referendum for a law rejecting the Young Plan out of hand. The nationalist viewpoint was that Germany was being asked to saddle future generations with the burden of debt. To win maximum support for his ideas, Hugenberg invited the co-operation of the Nazis. For Hitler this was a golden opportunity to align himself with the more respectable, conservative and upper-class nationalists. Later, he could abandon them.

## 7.10  from economic stability to crisis, 1925–29

### 1925–28

Traditionally this period has been depicted as a period of economic 'boom', but many historians now feel that this has been exaggerated. Agriculture and small industry, in particular, did not enjoy a period of growth and prosperity. More generally, growth in economic activity was modest when compared to US growth rates. By the end of 1927, although Germany's foreign situation had improved, economic circumstances were beginning to deteriorate. Many farmers, small businessmen and retailers were in trouble while prices and wages were rising.

### 1929

By 1929, capital investment was already falling and unemployment never fell below 1.3 million (and had risen ominously to 3 million by February 1929). The success of huge industrial trusts (e.g., I. G. Farben), the massive influx of foreign capital, and developments in the state welfare system all served to hide the structural problems inherent in the German economy. American loans to Europe abruptly collapsed after the share collapse on the Wall Street Stock Exchange in October. The subsequent contraction in world markets meant that Germany's export trade was drastically reduced.

The fact that much German economic growth had been financed by American loans was underlined when the Wall Street Crash of 1929 devastated the German economy. Stresemann died in the same year and month as the crash. It seemed almost fitting that this figure of stability should pass away at the moment when the turbulence of the Great Depression was about to devastate Western Europe. Unemployment, which stood at 900,000 in the summer of 1929, soared to more than 3 million in December 1930, 5½ million by July 1931, and more than 6 million by the start of 1932. The consequences of this catastrophe were profound. The Weimar Republic, having overcome the difficulties of 1923, was now placed under intolerable pressure. It was the economic crisis which led to the political upheaval which culminated in the rise to power of Adolf Hitler.

However, the Great Depression which began in 1929 was to have much more far-reaching consequences. The economic crisis precipitated a shift from democratic, liberal regimes to authoritarian and even totalitarian government in many European countries. In addition, the economic crisis and the authoritarian governments which it helped to produce heralded a period in which international co-operation gave way to acts of aggression and expansionism.

# the collapse of the Weimar Republic, 1929–33

## 8.1 the German economy and the Great Depression

There is widespread agreement that the fundamental turning point in the fortunes of the Nazis came about not through an impassioned Hitler speech, or a carefully choreographed Goebbels rally, but thousands of miles away in the frenzied selling of stocks and shares in the Wall Street Crash of October 1929. In simple terms, it seems likely that if Weimar had not been subjected to the trauma of a world economic crisis on an unprecedented scale, Hitler would have remained in the margins of history. As Laurence Rees explains, in *The Nazis: A Warning From History*: 'Shortly after the election, [of 1928] the economic and political situation in Germany radically changed. First an agricultural depression hit home and then the Wall Street Crash triggered the most serious economic crisis ever encountered in Germany, as the United States called in its loans.'[1] Although the depression which followed the crash devastated the German economy, there was no guarantee that the German people would now turn to Hitler. How was the party able to extend its appeal beyond the fringes of extreme right-wing activity, where it appeared to be marooned as late as the Reichstag elections of May 1928, into the mainstream of German politics, as shown in the Reichstag elections of September 1930?

The success of huge industrial trusts such as I. G. Farben, the massive influx of foreign capital and developments in the state welfare system had all served to hide the structural problems inherent in the German economy. However, when American loans to Europe were abruptly withdrawn after the share collapse on the Wall Street Stock Exchange in October, the subsequent contraction in world markets meant that Germany's export trade was drastically reduced.

Lord Bullock highlights the relationship between the harrowing economic circumstances of the depression period and the political fortunes of the extremists.

Like men and women in a town stricken by an earthquake, millions of Germans saw the apparently solid framework of their existence cracking and crumbling. In such circumstances men are no longer amenable to the arguments of reason. In such circumstances men entertain fantastic fears, extravagant hatreds and extravagant hopes. In such circumstances the extravagant demagogy of Hitler began to attract a mass following as it had never done before.[2]

An additional factor that aided Hitler's rise came in 1929 when under the leadership of the US financier Owen Young, the Allied Reparations Commission came up with a new plan to settle German war reparations. The German Nationalists (DNVP), led by Alfred Hugenberg, organized a referendum for a law rejecting the Young Plan out of hand. The nationalist viewpoint was that Germany was being asked to saddle future generations with the burden of debt. To win maximum support for his ideas, Hugenberg invited the co-operation of the Nazis. For Hitler this was a golden opportunity to align himself with the more respectable, conservative and upper-class nationalists. This was always a cynical arrangement on Hitler's part. As late as July 1932 this marriage of convenience would be renewed with a right-wing alliance between Hitler, Hugenberg and Franz Seldte, the head of the important veterans' organization, the Stahlhelm but Hitler was always careful to maintain his distance and to withdraw when it suited him.

## 8.2 the electoral breakthrough of the National Socialist Party

It seems likely that Hitler would have remained on the margins of German politics forever had it not been for the catastrophic events of 1929. The death of Gustav Stresemann in October of that year coincided with the onset of the most severe economic depression in modern world history. Memories of 1923 returned as the country was plunged into a crisis which was to be more prolonged and more severe than its drastic predecessor. In the winter of 1929–30, Germany felt the full force of a bitter depression. In the urban areas food shortages, poor housing, unemployment, strikes and demonstrations created severe problems. In the Ruhr region a serious industrial dispute culminated in more than a quarter of a million iron and steel workers being locked out without a job or a wage for several weeks.

In the countryside, rapidly accumulating debts, overseas competition, high taxation and bad weather made the lives of many small farmers and fishermen more desperate than ever before. The economic anxiety felt in the countryside was combined with an acute sense of unfairness that the produce of the rural areas was being consumed in an exploitative manner by those who lived in the larger towns and cities. The political repercussions were just as acute. Six months after the Wall Street Crash, Germany lost its last parliamentary Cabinet with the resignation of Müller's socialist bloc in March 1930.

## 8.3 Chancellor Müller

| Date | Event |
|------|-------|
| **1928** | |
| June | 'Great coalition' government formed by Herman Müller (SPD) |
| **1930** | |
| March | The Müller Cabinet resigns. Heinrich Brüning appointed Chancellor of the first Presidential government |
| **1932** | |
| May | Brüning Cabinet resigns. Government of 'national concentration' formed by Franz von Papen, with Schleicher as Defence Minister |
| August | Hindenburg turns down Hitler's demand to be appointed Chancellor |
| September | The Reichstag passes a vote of no confidence in the Papen government. Dissolution of the Reichstag, leading to further elections in November |
| November | Resignation of von Papen cabinet |
| December | Kurt von Schleicher forms presidential government |
| **1933** | |
| January | Schleicher resigns, having lost Hindenburg's support. Hitler appointed Chancellor at the head of a presidential government |

Against an increasingly turbulent economic backdrop, Social Democrat leader Herman Müller's 'grand coalition' had never been able to look secure. A controversial decision to construct a battle cruiser contradicting a pre-election SPD stance and the Ruhr industrial dispute emphasized the growing fissures within the government and left it vulnerable to criticism from both the left and the right. A reliance on American short-term loans, persistently damaging levels of unemployment, disillusionment among small shopkeepers and producers at the power of the large department stores and a degree of alienation at the 'Americanization' of popular culture in the bigger cities were all factors in a general sense of unease, in a climate of 'crisis before the crisis'. When Gustav Stresemann died on 3 October 1929 following a stroke, Germany had lost its only statesman of real stature and Müller had lost a crucial pillar of support. Although Müller survived the first six months of the economic crash, his administration reached breaking point on 27 March 1930, ostensibly over the issue of raised employer contributions to unemployment insurance. By now, the SDP's coalition partner, the DVP, with its strong links with big business and industrialists, had moved sharply to the right and was increasingly critical of the Weimar welfare state. Müller now needed support from Reich President Hindenburg through the deployment of the emergency powers contained in Article 48 of the constitution. When this was not forthcoming, Chancellor Müller tendered his resignation and the Weimar Republic began its slide into terminal destruction.

## 8.4 Chancellor Brüning

Long before Müller's resignation, political manoeuvrings were underway to replace him. Central to these machinations was Major-General Kurt von Schleicher, a rising figure and political fixer in the Defence Ministry who had gained close access to the President. Behind the scenes, Schleicher made overtures to Heinrich Brüning, a conscientious but stern and aloof figure on the right of the Centre Party, to let him know that he was regarded by the President as a potential replacement for Müller, once the Young Plan had been accepted. By the time Brüning had become parliamentary leader of the Centre Party it was made clear to him that he could become the leader of an anti-parliamentary and anti-Marxist government, utilising the emergency powers held in the Constitution. Brüning was appointed as Chancellor on 30 March 1930 and, backed by the naturally autocratic President, relied increasingly on Article 48 of the constitution to push through emergency legislation, but even this could not stave off grave difficulties in his attempts to reduce public spending through emergency decree.

A sweeping finance bill proposed by Brüning was rejected by the Reichstag in July 1930 and, to the delight of the National Socialists, who displayed a sharper understanding of the nation's mounting anger and frustration than Brüning was able to muster, new parliamentary elections were called for September. Three years before Hitler came to power, parliamentary democracy was suspended and replaced by an authoritarian system which rested largely on the powers invested in the ageing president, von Hindenburg. How long would it be before such substantial powers were taken out of the control of the old man and put into the hands of a political extremist?

## 8.5 the Communists

The answer many Germans feared was that power would soon pass into the hands of the Communists, led by Ernst Thalman. In the Reichstag elections of September 1930, the Communists received 77 seats but to many anxious middle-class citizens it was the influence of the 'reds' on the streets of the big cities which was most alarming. Fuelled by economic anxiety and influenced by the government's increasingly autocratic stance, political dialogue and debate were replaced by bitter street battles between the extremes of left and right. Ultimately, it may well be that the frightening prospect of Communist rule was the key factor which led so many powerful groups to lend support to the opposite extreme, personified by Adolf Hitler.

In retrospect, it is clear that the Communists had little prospect of gaining real political power.

The Communists did succeed in gaining the support of an overwhelming number of the urban workforce, frustrating Hitler's protracted and expensive attempts to secure this vital bloc of votes for himself. But too many powerful groups – including the army, the police, the middle classes and the peasantry – felt that they had a great deal to lose if the Communists were to win the day in Weimar Germany. The fact that many people came to see the Nazis as the last bulwark in the fight against Communism was of the utmost value to Hitler's campaign. Indeed, the contrast between the spectre of Communist disorder with the Nazis' promises of law and order, economic stability, the curbing of the unions, the endorsement of traditional values and the promise to crush Marxism was at the very centre of Hitler's success. In addition, the pitched street battles with the Communists furnished Goebbels with the type of propaganda material which he relished. It now seems clear that the electoral success of the extreme left actually helped rather than hindered the Nazi movement. Every step that the Communists took towards the corridors of power made Hitler's presentation of the Marxist threat more potent.

## 8.6 Brüning and the National Socialists

The political earthquake of the September 1930 elections saw the NSDAP move from 12 Reichstag seats and just 2.6 per cent of the vote to 107 seats and 18.3 per cent. This transformed Hitler's position and gave the party a momentum that would be difficult to resist. However, Brüning dismissed calls to admit the NSDAP into a coalition government and a post-election meeting with Brüning and Hitler in October only emphasized the gulf between the two men, leaving Hitler with a deep sense of personal animosity towards the chancellor. In addition, despite an increasing sense of disillusionment with the Brüning administration in German society as a whole, Hitler was still unable to make substantial headway in terms of attracting support from big business, whose leaders, at this stage, in general preferred to offer their support to Hitler's opponents on the conservative right. Even a high-profile address in the distinguished surroundings of the Düsseldorf Industry Club in January 1932 could not hide the fact that the majority of NSDAP funding came from membership dues and admissions to party meetings rather than from the coffers of the captains of industry, although the conspicuous consumption of powerful individuals such as Göring, indicated the degree of corruption that existed in some of the links between the party and industry.

## 8.7 who voted for the National Socialists?

At the height of its electoral appeal in the summer of 1932 the National Socialist Party was a much more broadly based political movement than has previously been acknowledged. The NSDAP is now seen by many experts as more than just a magnet to the middle and particularly lower middle classes. It is now claimed that the party is more accurately seen as the most socially homogenous party in German electoral history in the whole period from 1871 to 1933. This enabled the Nazis to lay claim to be the *Volkspartei* (people's party) – a claim which its rivals could never make. The new consensus is that by 1932 the party was drawing on an unprecedently broad social spectrum of support among Protestant (but not Catholic) voters, including some workers and members of the professional and commercial elites, as well as members of the middle and lower-middle classes.

The working classes were not proportionately represented in the membership or the leadership of the Nazi party, although there was a left-wing faction represented by Gregor Strasser which hoped to attract support from the urban and industrial areas. However, if the definition of working class is extended beyond manual workers to include occupations such as shop assistants, clerks and tradesmen then Nazi support in this area appears much more significant. It is more accurate to say that it was the organised working class, such as trade union members and workers with links to the SPD or KPD who remained resistant to the National Socialists.

table **8.1  Nazi election results, 1924–33**

| date of election | seats in the Reichstag | % |
|---|---|---|
| May 1924 | 32 | 6.5 |
| December 1924 | 14 | 3.0 |
| May 1928 | 12 | 2.6 |
| September 1930 | 107 | 18.3 |
| July 1932 | 230 | 37.3 |
| November 1932 | 196 | 33.1 |
| March 1933 | 288 | 43.9 |

table **8.2  limitations in support of the Communist Party (KPD), 1924–33 (seats)**

| | |
|---|---|
| May 1924 | 62 |
| December 1924 | 45 |
| May 1928 | 54 |
| September 1930 | 77 |
| July 1932 | 89 |
| November 1932 | 100 |
| March 1933 | 81 |

table **8.3  regional variations in support of the National Socialists, 1924–1933 (%)**

| | Berlin | Cologne-Aachen | East Prussia | Koblenz | Lower Bavaria | Schleswig-Holstein |
|---|---|---|---|---|---|---|
| May 1924 | 3.6 | 1.5 | 8.6 | 1.3 | 10.2 | 7.4 |
| December 1924 | 1.6 | 0.6 | 6.2 | | 3.0 | 2.2 |
| May 1928 | 1.4 | 1.1 | 0.8 | 2.1 | 3.5 | 4.0 |
| September 1930 | 12.8 | 14.5 | 22.5 | 14.9 | 12.0 | 27.0 |
| July 1932 | 24.6 | 20.2 | 47.1 | 28.8 | 20.4 | 51.0 |
| November 1932 | 22.5 | 17.4 | 39.7 | 26.1 | 18.5 | 45.7 |
| March 1933 | 31.3 | 30.1 | 56.5 | 38.4 | 39.2 | 53.2 |

Women were not traditionally regarded as natural Nazi supporters. Before 1930 the party was appealing to more male voters than female. However, after 1930 the party gained a greater proportion of female voters and in the Reichstag elections of March 1933, more women than men were voting Nazi. Finally, recent research into electoral results in the larger cities shows that significant numbers in the wealthier suburbs tended to support Hitler. Wealthy businessmen, professional and high-ranking civil servants can be included in this grouping.

## sources: the verdict of historians

### SOURCE A

The supporters who made the NSDAP the largest membership and electoral party in Germany by mid-1932 were animated less by the extreme histrionics of the party's leadership than by calculations of political rationality similar to those that prompted the choices of other voters or political activists.

*Source*: Jane Caplan, 'The Rise of National Socialism', from G. Martel (ed.), *Modern Germany Reconsidered: 1870–1945* (1992).

### SOURCE B

The millions of Germans who voted for Hitler did not do so because they wanted genocide or total war. These aims were by no means in the forefront of Nazi propaganda. For most people, economic anxiety and fear of communism were far more important. However, some social groups were much more likely than others to believe that Hitler and the Nazis could solve their problems. The hard core of Nazi supporters were male, Protestant and broadly speaking, middle class. Women, Catholics and despite strenuous Nazi efforts, industrial workers, were far more resistant, at least until the last, desperate months of the republic when habitual allegiances began to crumble. The NSDAP's youthful, dynamic image attracted young, middle class men. Unlike Weimar's elderly, social democratic and conservative politicians, many Nazi leaders were still in their twenties, when the depression began. . . . But the biggest pool of Nazi voters was in parts of the countryside. In Protestant North Bavaria, the North German Plain and Schleswig-Holstein, debts, foreign competition, high taxes and bad weather caused severe problems for many small farmers and fishermen.'

*Source*: Robin Lenman, *Warwick University History Film*.

### SOURCE C

Until 1928 Nazism was an insignificant political force trying to win factory workers away from Marxism. . . . It was a marginal political movement on the radical right. But under the impact of the slump, the rise of communism and the political stalemate of parliamentary politics the movement began to attract more attention. Nazism became the authentic voice of the small townsman, the anxious officials and small businessmen, the peasant who felt he had a raw deal from the Republic. . . . The Nazi Party was made up and led by people like this: Nazi leaders articulated their fears and desires, and promised to end the crisis. Nazism gave expression to the latent nationalism of the conservative masses by blaming the Allies and reparations for Germany's ills. Above all, Nazism was violently anti-Marxist. It was the only party demonstrably, visibly combating the threat of communism on the streets. Although the violence alienated many respectable Germans, they hated communism more. Social disorder and disintegration seemed a reality in 1932 with six million unemployed. In the chaos Nazism promised to restore order, to revive German fortunes, to bring about a moral renewal, to give 'bread and work'.

*Source*: Richard Overy, *The Road to War* (1989).

**SOURCE D**

Between 1928 and 1930 the Nazi Party had concentrated largely on trying to win over sections of the middle class, notably the peasantry, the artisans and the small retailers. After 1930, while still continuing much of their propaganda for these groups, they revived their pre-1928 efforts to win over the workers. But apart from white collar workers, the majority of workers remained loyal to the Social Democrats and communists and . . . if they became more extreme they tended to move to the Communists rather than the Nazis. . . . The main strength of Nazism lay in the Protestant and predominantly rural areas of the North German Plain stretching from East Prussia to Schleswig-Holstein. Eight out of ten districts with the largest Nazi vote in July 1932 are in this area. Nazism was weakest in the big cities (e.g. Berlin and Leipzig) and in the industrial areas; particularly in predominantly Catholic ones. . . . In the cities it tended to draw most support from upper middle class districts. It was also weakest in overwhelmingly Catholic rural areas.'

*Source*: J. Noakes and G. Pridham (ed.), *Nazism 1919–1945: A Documentary Reader. Vol. 1: The Rise to Power* (1998).

## 8.8 how did Hitler become Chancellor (1932–33)?

### the presidential election of 1932

What Goebbels referred to as the 'chess match for power' began to unfold in the spring of 1932 but in circumstances that did not necessarily appear favourable for Hitler and which resulted in his customary uncertainty when faced with difficult decisions. The expiration of von Hindenburg's seven-year term of office in the late spring of 1932 prompted moves by von Papen to have the ageing Reich President's term in office extended without going to the polls. However, this manoeuvre required a two-thirds majority in the Reichstag which therefore necessitated Hitler's support. The Nazi leadership understood that agreeing to this extension would effectively strengthen the much-loathed Chancellor Brüning's position and so they rejected the proposal on 'constitutional, domestic and moral grounds', opening up the possibility of presidential elections, but exposing Hitler to the difficult prospect of a personal battle with the nationally revered war hero. To step away from the contest would be certain to disappoint his followers and open Hitler to charges of cowardice, but to take on Hindenburg could look like the unseemly action of a political upstart against a figure who was widely respected and seen as above politics. After a month of indecision from Hitler, that had even Goebbels seething with frustration, Hitler's candidacy for the Presidency was announced on 22 February 1932. Before an appreciative audience of 25,000 at the Berlin Sportpalast on 27 February Hitler urged the 'old man' to 'step aside'. During a typically energetic election campaign Hitler spoke in 12 major cities in 11 days. When the results were announced Hitler was somewhat disappointed. Hindenburg had secured just over 49 per cent of the almost 38 million votes cast, leaving him just 170,000 votes short of the absolute majority he needed and necessitating a second round. Hitler's 30 per cent share of the vote contrasted with Thalmann, the leader of the KPD's vote of just 13 per cent. In the second round, as expected, Hindenburg was re-elected with 53 per cent of the vote, while Thalmann dropped to 10 per cent and Hitler's share increased to 37 per cent, a personal vote in excess of 13 million. Further success in the state elections of April 1932 added to the clear sense that Hitler had now mobilized the masses to something approaching its limit. Further progress towards power would need additional tactics. The American authority Thomas Childers indicates what Hitler had achieved at the ballot box. He states that the NSDAP had become 'a unique phenomenon in German electoral politics, a catchall party of protest'.[3] Hitler's burgeoning electoral fortunes did not lead to an improvement in his personal relationship with Brüning. The Chancellor had immediately followed up Hindenburg's re-election with a request in cooperation with the Interior and Defence Minister Groener to 'dissolve all military-like organisations of the NSDAP'. However, the ban on the SA merely heightened the sense of political tension and increased the treacherous chicanery that would ultimately undermine the position of both Groener and Brüning. The figure behind the new machinations was General von Schleicher, head of the army's political bureau, who wanted to see Brüning removed to establish what would have amounted to a military dictatorship, resting on the support of the Reichswehr and with popular backing from the National Socialists but with the ultimate intention of 'taming' Hitler into the bargain. Hitler's price for supporting a new, right-wing cabinet was the immediate removal of the ban on the SA and the calling of fresh elections. A systematic campaign by the Nazis in the Reichstag to undermine Groener culminated in his resignation on 12 May. This development badly damaged Brüning, but the broader picture of calamitous economic collapse did him even more harm. In a shatteringly brusque exchange with the President on 29 May, Brüning was left in no doubt that his resignation was expected. It was forthcoming the next day, leaving Franz von Papen, a sophisticated and aristocratic Catholic, as Chancellor.

## 8.9 von Papen as Chancellor

Von Papen's privileged background, urbane character, close personal connections with industrial leaders and army officers, and his conservative, reactionary tendencies made him a natural choice for those who hoped for a return to the traditional values and authoritarianism that had gained acceptance in the past. It was a measure of the direction the government had taken since Müller's fall that von Papen sought to lead with a 'cabinet of barons' independent of the political parties and with not even a gesture towards parliamentary government. But whereas such values may have represented continuity in the past, on this occasion things were moving very quickly and von Papen's ability to stabilize the country was soon cast into doubt, not least because of the gulf between his style of government and the expressed electoral views of the politically radicalized masses. The lifting of the ban on the SA in June 1932 ushered in an unprecedented wave of violence between the NSDAP and the Communists. A month later the elections of July 1932 saw the Nazi share of the vote increase to 37.4 per cent, making them by some distance the largest party in the Reichstag. Yet despite the massive electoral support gained in the July 1932 elections, the fact remained that Hitler remained on the outside looking in still without any formal experience of political office

With support for the party at record levels Hitler believed he was now in the position to demand the office of Chancellor from the President. While Hindenburg was prepared to offer Hitler the position of Vice-Chancellor he was not willing to take the risk of offering him ultimate responsibility. It was at this point that Hitler was offered, for the first time, the type of political responsibility that he apparently craved. As with the presidential elections, this development again posed questions over Hitler's political judgement.

In the summer of 1932, the President and the Chancellor came to the decision to offer Hitler the position of Vice-Chancellor. It is a measure of Hitler's self-belief and conviction in his own destiny that his calculation was that he had more to lose by accepting the job than rejecting the advances of those that he believed were trying to curb his movement. The extracts below show the reasoning behind this decision and the 'spin' placed on these events by Hitler and Goebbels. What they do not convey is the straightforward fact that when the Reich President flatly refused to hand over the Chancellorship, Hitler suffered his greatest personal setback since the failure of the putsch in 1923.

## 8.10 the period of crisis, August–December 1932

**SOURCE A**

HITLER DEMANDS POWER FROM THE PRESIDENT, 13 AUGUST 1932.

Minutes of the second meeting between Hitler and Hindenburg, taken by Otto Meisner, Head of the Presidential Chancellery.

The President of the Reich opened the discussion by declaring to Hitler that he was ready to let the National Socialist Party and their leader Hitler participate in the Reich Government and would welcome their cooperation. He then put the question to Hitler whether he was prepared to participate in the present government of von Papen. Herr Hitler declared that . . . his taking any part in cooperation with the existing government was out of the question. Considering the importance of the National Socialist movement he must demand full and complete leadership of government and state for himself and his party.The Reich President in reply said firmly that he must answer this demand with a clear, unyielding No. He could not justify before God, before his conscience or before the fatherland the transfer of the whole authority of government to a single party, especially to a party that was biased against people who had different views from their own.

*Source*: J. Noakes and G. Pridham (ed.), *Nazism 1919–1945: A Documentary Reader. Vol. 1: The Rise to Power* (1998).

**SOURCE B**

Goebbels' reaction to the presidential meeting, 13 August 1932
Extract from Goebbels's diary, 13 August 1932.
The Führer is back in under half an hour. So it has ended in failure. He has gained nothing. Papen is to remain Chancellor and the Führer has to content himself with the position of Vice-Chancellor! A solution leading to no result! It is out of the question to accept such a proposal. There is no alternative but to refuse. The Führer did so immediately. It will mean a hard struggle, but we shall triumph in the end.

*Source*: as source A.

## evaluation

Hitler had clearly taken a monumental gamble in rejecting political office. Then, in the elections of November 1932, Nazi support fell significantly and the impression of invincibility which Goebbels had carefully built up was visibly dented. Unrest within the Nazi party began to grow. The party finances and Hitler's own financial circumstances were in dire straits. It seemed possible at this stage that in rejecting the post of Vice-Chancellor, Hitler could have made an error of the greatest magnitude, seriously overplaying his hand. Would Hitler ever achieve his goal? In understanding why Hitler was finally given political office we must look beyond the propaganda campaigns and the election booths and investigate the period of negotiation and intrigue which took place between August 1932 and January 1933 and which directly led to the Reich President changing his mind. At the same time a third major player now entered the political game: the army. Increasingly alarmed by the rise of revolutionary Marxism and the growing mayhem on the streets, the army leadership now looked anxiously for any solution that could effectively restore order in the shattered country. The possibility of a full-blown civil war between the NSDAP and the Communists, with the army and the police caught in between, was a scenario that the army could not welcome. Meanwhile the intrigues of General Kurt von Schleicher gathered pace, this time directed at von Papen. By the time von Papen fell victim to Schleicher's manoeuvring in the autumn of 1932, Hitler was attracting increasing support from the conservative establishment and powerful circles within the army, and von Papen's removal meant there was also an increased opportunity for Hitler to attract the support of some wealthy businessmen.

## 8.11 the period of intrigue

Few people can have presented as relentlessly optimistic and one-sided a perspective on the rise of the Nazi party as the party propagandist Josef Goebbels. Yet in the autumn of 1932 even Goebbels had reason to doubt whether the political master he so unconditionally adored would ever reach the position of Chancellor. Goebbels was entitled to be apprehensive. The party funds had been ploughed into the propaganda extravaganza of July 1932, leaving the finances for future elections in doubt. Hitler's decision to reject the position of Vice-Chancellor had attracted criticism from within the party and heightened the sense that factionalism existed, not just concerning this decision, but Hitler's leadership overall and the nature of the direction within the party. Hitler's policy of continued agitation and of steadfastly refusing to compromise was not in itself enough to break the logjam.

## 8.12 Schleicher as Chancellor

Events through the winter of 1932 played into Hitler's hands. General von Schleicher became Chancellor on 2 December 1932 but his ability to restrict the ambitions of Hitler and the Nazi party soon appeared limited. While Schleicher genuinely entertained the belief that he could encourage division within the Nazi party it soon became clear that he had seriously underestimated Hitler. Schleicher's tactics are reflected in the extract that follows.

**SOURCE A**

EXTRACT FROM THE MEMOIRS OF FRANZ VON PAPEN.

It was then (2 December 1932) Schleicher's turn. He said he had a plan which would absolve the President from taking his last drastic step (suspending the Reichstag). If he took over the government himself, he thought he could bring about a split in the National Socialist Party which would ensure a parliamentary majority in the present Reichstag. He then gave a detailed explanation of the differences of opinion within the Nazi movement which made it more likely that he would be able to attract the support or Gregor Strasser and about sixty members of the Reichstag. Strasser and one of two of his close supporters would be offered posts in the government, which would be based upon the support of the trade unions, the Social Democrats and the bourgeois parties. This would provide a majority which would make it possible to put through the economic and social programme of the Papen government.

*Source*: J. Noakes and G. Pridham (ed.), *Nazism 1919–1945: A Documentary Reader. Vol. 1: The Rise to Power* (1998).

**While Strasser was prepared to leave the party, as shown in the two extracts that follow, Hitler was easily able to quell any wider sense of dissatisfaction and the process merely served to emphasize the extent of his personal hold over the party.**

## SOURCE B

STRASSERS'S RESIGNATION SPEECH TO THE SENIOR GAULEITERS (THE PARTY'S REGIONAL INSPECTORS), 8 DECEMBER 1932.

The Führer has not been following a clear line of policy in his endeavour to achieve power. He is only clear about one thing – he wishes to become Reich Chancellor. He should, however, have become aware of the fact that he is being consistently refused this post by everybody and that in the foreseeable future there is no prospect of his attaining this goal. As a result of this situation, the movement is being put under considerable stress which is undermining its unity and may expose it to splits and disintegration.

*Source*: as source A.

## SOURCE C

HITLER REFUTES STRASSER'S CHARGES, SPEAKING TO THE SAME AUDIENCE.

Notes on Hitler's speech to the Gauleiter, 8 December 1932

1 . . . He spoke to you about the legal path to the conquest of power and declared that it was my duty in August to accept the office of Vice-Chancellor. Herr Strasser knows quite well that Herr von Papen and Herr von Schleicher are not National Socialists and therefore are not willing to follow National Socialist policies. Judging by the measures introduced by, and the results, of, the policy of Reich Chancellor von Papen, as Vice-Chancellor I would have had serious differences with him within the first week . . . I would have had to protest against policies . . . Here von Papen would have declared to me with a smile, 'Forgive me, Herr Hitler, but I am Chancellor and head of the Cabinet. If my political course and the measures which result from it do not suit you, I am not forcing you to stay. You can resign your office.'

2 The illegal path to the conquest of power is even more dangerous and more fatal. It cannot be said that I do not have the courage to carry out a coup by force and, if necessary, by a bloody revolution, I tried it once in Munich in 1923. Herr Strasser knows that; he was there. But what was the result and what would the result be now? Our formations are without weapons and . . . they would have no effect against the united action of the police and the Reichswehr which are armed with the most modern weapons. You surely do not believe that they would stand by.

*Source*: as source A.

## the endgame – an examination of source material concerning the backstairs intrigue

With Hitler's successful handling of the short-lived Strasser crisis behind him, attention now focused on the activities of those who operated in the highest circles of German political life. The election setback of November 1932 began to pale into insignificance as informal negotiations began between unelected but powerful figures from the worlds of finance, big business, the army and the political elite and key figures from the National Socialist party, represented most importantly by the go-between and political opportunist, Joachim von Ribbentrop.

**SOURCE A**

A CRUCIAL MEETING, 4 JANUARY 1933.

Kurt von Schroeder, evidence given at the Nuremberg Trial.

On 4 January 1933 Hitler, von Papen, Hess, Himmler and Keppler arrived at my house in Cologne. Hitler, von Papen and I went into my study where a two-hour discussion took place. . . . Papen went on to say that he thought it best to form a government in which conservative and nationalist elements that had supported him were represented together with the Nazis. He suggested that this new government should, if possible, be led by Hitler and himself together. Then Hitler made a long speech in which he said that, if he were elected Chancellor, Papen's followers could participate in his (Hitler's) Government as Ministers if they were willing to support his policy which was planning many alterations in the existing state of affairs. He outlined these alterations, including the removal of all Social Democrats, Communists and Jews from leading positions in Germany and the restoration of order in public life. Von Papen and Hitler reached agreement in principle. . . . The general desire of businessmen was to see a strong man come to power in Germany who would form a government that would stay in power for a long time.

*Source*: J. Noakes and G. Pridham (ed.), *Nazism 1919–1945: A Documentary Reader. Vol. 1: The Rise to Power* (1998).

**SOURCE B**

FROM PAPEN TO SCHLEICHER.

Otto Meisner, evidence given at the Nuremberg Trial.

When it became clear that Hitler was not willing to enter Schleicher's Cabinet and that Schleicher on his part was unable to split the National Socialist Party, as he had hoped to do with the help of Gregor Strasser, the policy for which Schleicher had been appointed Chancellor was shipwrecked. . . . So he now changed his mind and decided to fight against the Nazis – which meant that he now wanted to pursue the policy which he had sharply opposed when Papen had suggested it a few weeks before. Schleicher came to Hindenburg therefore with a demand for emergency powers as a prerequisite of action against the Nazis. . . . Hindenburg at once evinced grave doubts as to its constitutionality. . . . When Schleicher renewed his demand for emergency powers, Hindenburg declared that he was unable to give him such a blank cheque and must reserve to himself decisions on every individual case. Schleicher . . . said that under these circumstances he was unable to stay in office and tendered his resignation on 28 January.

Despite Papen's persuasions, Hindenburg was extremely hesitant, until the end of January, to make Hitler Chancellor. . . . Papen finally won him over to Hitler with the argument that the representatives of the other right-wing parties which would belong to the Government would restrict Hitler's freedom of action. . . . The President's son . . . Oskar von Hindenburg, was opposed to the Nazis up to the last moment. Oskar von Hindenburg was told that Hitler wanted to talk to him. . . . I was somewhat surprised at his accepting this suggestion and vanishing into another room for a talk which lasted quite a while – about an hour. What Hitler and Oskar von Hindenburg discussed during this talk I do not know . . . Hitler had succeeded in getting him under his spell.

*Source*: as source A.

## SOURCE C

GENERAL VON HAMMERSTEIN, ARMY COMMANDER-IN-CHIEF, FROM NOTES MADE IN 1935.

On the morning of 26 January I went to see Schleicher and asked him what was true in the rumours about a change in government. Schleicher confirmed that the Reich President would almost certainly withdraw his confidence either today or tomorrow, and that he would resign. . . . Hindenburg angrily forbade me to intervene in political matters, but then said, apparently to reassure me, 'that he had no intention of making the Austrian lance-corporal War Minister or Reich Chancellor' Hindenburg failed to understand my fear that the army might become involved or be misused in a fight between Papen-Hugenberg on the one hand and the National Socialists and the entire Left on the other. I departed with my fears increased, for Schleicher's dismissal was already settled. What was to follow was obviously completely unclear.

On 29 January a discussion took place in my office between Schleicher and myself. We were both convinced that only Hitler was possible as future Reich Chancellor. Any other choice would lead to a general strike, if not a civil war, and thus to a totally undesirable use of the army against the National Socialists as well as against the Left. We considered whether we knew of any other way to influence the situation to avoid this misfortune. . . . Finally I decided, in agreement with Schleicher, to seek a meeting with Hitler.

*Source*: as source A.

## SOURCE D

INTRIGUE BEARS FRUIT.

Notes taken by Ribbentrop's wife.
Wednesday, 18th January: In Dahlem at noon; Hitler, Röhm, Himmler, Papen.

Hitler insists on being Chancellor. Papen again considers this impossible. His influence with Hindenburg was not strong enough to effect this. Hitler makes no further arrangements for talks. Joachim tentatively suggests a meeting between Hitler and Hindenburg's son.

Sunday, 22nd January: Meeting at Dahlem at 10 pm. Papen arrives alone at nine o'clock. Present: Hitler, Frick, Goring, Krner, Meissner, young Hindenburg, Papen and Joachim. Hitler talks along to young Hindenburg for two hours, followed by Hitler-Papen talk. Papen will now press for Hitler as Chancellor, but tells Hitler that he will withdraw from these negotiations forthwith if Hitler has no confidence in him.

Monday, 23rd January: In the morning Papen saw Hindenburg, who refused everything. Joachim goes to Hitler to explain this. Long talks about the possibility of a Schacht Cabinet. Hitler rejects everything.

Friday, 27th January: Hitler back in Berlin. Long talk with him at Goring's flat. Hitler wants to leave Berlin forthwith. . . . New meeting with old Hindenburg arranged. Hitler declares that he has said all there is to say to the Field Marshal, and does not know what to add. Joachim persuades Hitler that this last attempt should be made, and that the situation is by no means hopeless.

*Source*: as source A.

**SOURCE E**

Notes taken by Ribbentrop.

In the evening I saw Papen and convinced him eventually that the only thing that made sense was Hitler's Chancellorship, and that he must do what he can to bring this about. . . . Papen is now absolutely certain that he must achieve Hitler's Chancellorship at all costs, and that he must abandon his belief that it is his duty to remain at Hindenburg's disposal. Saturday, 28th January: About 11 am I went to see Papen who received me with the question: 'Where is Hitler?' I told him that he had probably left, but could perhaps be contacted in Weimar. Papen said that he had to get back without delay, because the turning point had been reached; after a long talk with Hindenburg he, Papen, considered Hitler's Chancellorship possible. I went to see Goering immediately and heard that Hitler was still at the Kaiserhof. Goering telephoned him, Hitler will remain in Berlin. . . . Goering and I went to see Hitler. Long talk with Hitler alone explaining that a solution depended entirely on trust and that his Chancellorship did not now appear to be impossible . . .

Sunday, 29 January: Hitler declared that on the whole everything was clear. But there would have to be general elections and an Enabling Law. Papen saw Hindenburg immediately. I lunched with Hitler at the Kaiserhof. We discussed the elections. As Hindenburg does not want these, Hitler asked me to tell the President that these would be the last elections. In the afternoon Goring and I went to Papen. Papen declared that all obstacles are removed and that Hindenburg expects Hitler tomorrow at 11 a.m.

Monday 30 January: Hitler appointed Chancellor.

*Source*: as source A.

1 Produce bullet-point summaries of sources A–E.
2 What role appears to have been played in these meetings by:
  (a) Hitler?
  (b) Hindenburg?
  (c) Schleicher?
  (d) Hindenburg's son, Oskar?
  (e) von Papen?
3 What conclusions would you now reach about the reasons why Hitler was appointed Chancellor on 30 January 1933?

# the Third Reich, 1933–39

## 9.1  Hitler as Chancellor, January 1933

By 10.00 a.m. on the morning of 30 January 1933 a large crowd had gathered outside the gates of the Chancellery, the very centre of German political power. At approximately 11.45 a.m. the gates were opened and tension gave way to excitement. The crowd roared their approval as a car carrying the new Chancellor of Germany sped down the driveway and into the square. Standing in the back of the car to receive the crowd's good wishes was Adolf Hitler who, at the age of 43, had just become the sixteenth German Chancellor since 1918. Shaking with emotion and with tears in his eyes, Hitler swept into the Hotel Kaiserhof so that he could share his good news with his closest associates. President Hindenburg had appointed 'the Government of National Concentration' with Hitler as Chancellor, Wilhelm Frick as Minister of the Interior and the Reichstag President (Speaker) and Herman Goering as Minister without portfolio in charge of the Prussian Ministry of the Interior. The majority of the remaining cabinet members were conservatives, leaving the Nazis heavily outnumbered. Hitler told the leading Nazis that at his first Cabinet meeting that afternoon he would insist that the Reichstag be dissolved once again and that in March the German people be asked to vote in the third major election in nine months. Hitler's objective was to gain sufficient control of the Reichstag to render obsolete his earlier need to co-operate with the conservative parties.

That night the Nazis celebrated with a massive torchlight parade through the centre of Berlin. From 7.00 p.m. until after midnight, more than 25,000 of Hitler's most fervent supporters took part in a uniformed march through the Brandenburg Gate and past the Chancellery. In an illuminated window, Hitler stood with his arm outstretched towards his followers. The Nazi salutes, demonstrations, the uniforms and the flags which for so long had been the symbols of protest had in the space of one long day come to represent a new and fearsome authority. A few windows along from Hitler, President Hindenburg – 84 years old and one of the few representatives of continuity that Germany had left – tapped his cane in time to the music of the bands that marched past below. Earlier that day, he had given his consent to the dissolution of the Reichstag and the calling of a new election. The scene had been set for the most dramatic election campaign in Germany's short history. In the extract that follows Richard Bessel indicates the real nature of the change that had taken place:

> If the main thrust of Nazi policy during the 1930s was the drive to war, the domestic policies of the regime need to be viewed as subordinate to this end. For Hitler, the function of domestic politics, of propaganda and of the Nazi Party was to ensure that the German people would take up the historic task he was placing before them. Popular measures – putting Germans back to work, creating imposing propaganda spectacles, or promoting an extreme nationalist cultural agenda – were exploited to mobilize support for the regime and its warlike aims. For those who resisted the message there was ruthless suppression of dissent.[1]

Meanwhile General Ludendorff took the time to write to Hindenburg with these words of foreboding: 'You have delivered up our holy German Fatherland to one of the greatest demagogues of all time. I solemnly prophesy that this accursed man will cast our Reich into the abyss and bring our nation to inconceivable misery. Future generations will damn you in your grave for what you have done.'[2]

## 9.2 consolidation of power and the destruction of democracy, 1933–34

### biographical details of Paul von Hindenburg (1847–1934), German soldier and President

| | |
|---|---|
| 1866 | Fought at Königgrätz |
| 1870–71 | In Franco-Prussian War |
| 1903 | Became general |
| 1911 | Retired, but recalled at outbreak of First World War |
| 1914 | Won victory at Tannenberg with Ludendorff |
| 1916 | Became Chief of General Staff |
| 1918 | Organised withdrawal from Western Front |
| 1919 | Advised Kaiser to abdicate and arranged Armistice |
| 1925–32 | Elected and served as President of the Weimar Republic |
| 1932 | Defeated Hitler in presidential election and served his second term as President until his death in 1934 |
| 1933 | Appointed Hitler as Chancellor |
| August 1934 | Died |

While the old man might have wondered whether he would live to see another election, he cannot have imagined that the opportunity for the German people to vote freely for the party of their choice was about to come to an end. Over the next two months the Nazis mounted an election campaign which surpassed in its intensity even the frenzied efforts of July 1932. In a diary entry of January

1933 Goebbels anticipated a 'masterpiece of agitation'. This was launched by Hitler himself late in the evening of 1 February when, on the radio network, he read his inflammatory 'Proclamation to the German People'. In a vitriolic speech Hitler once again raised the spectre of Communism: 'Fourteen years of Marxism have ruined Germany; one year of Bolshevism could destroy her. The richest and fairest territories of the world would be turned into a smoking heap of ruins. Even the sufferings of the last decade and a half could not be compared to the misery of a Europe in which the red flag of destruction had been hoisted.'[3]

Hitler claimed that the objective of the election would be to 'revive in the nation the spirit of unity and co-operation'. It was now apparent that the Communist Party and the Socialists would be the target of a massive programme of intimidation. At the start of February the Reich press agency announced that Hitler would be keeping his humble apartment in Munich and that he would not be drawing the new salary he was entitled to as Chancellor. However, beneath the smokescreen of virtuous words, the Nazis' action towards their political opponents soon revealed that they were prepared to go to any lengths to ensure a massive victory in the forthcoming election. On 4 February the decree 'For the protection of the German people' was issued, allowing the government – on the vaguest of grounds – to prohibit political meetings and to ban the newspapers and publications of other political parties.

## the apparent limitations of Hitler's position

Ostensibly Hitler's opponents within the political elite began his chancellorship under the illusion that they had him in a corner. His inexperience of office, the fact that the cabinet contained far more conservatives than Nazis and the overwhelming scale of the domestic economic crisis he now had to contend with, all seemed to point to the fact that the realities of office would curb Hitler's aggressive instincts.

However, the key cabinet position besides that of Hitler was unquestionably Goering's, who as Commissary Prussian Minister of the Interior was placed in control of the police in Germany's biggest and most important state. The coalition partners were agreed on the need to wipe out Marxism for good. Conservative anxiety to smash the Left again played wholly into Hitler's hands by supporting the legal framework within which violent repression could take place. In mid-February Goering ordered the Prussian police to support the Nazi paramilitary forces and invited, with his full backing, the ready use of firearms to crush 'subversive organizations' which provided licence for an orgy of violence from storm troopers against Communists and Socialists. The burning down of the Reichstag on the night of 27 February 1933 now gave him the opportunity to weaken their position still further and significantly tighten his own hold on power.

## Goering and the Prussian police force

The Third Reich's elaborate apparatus of policing and repression was directed in the first place at hunting down and apprehending Nazism's enemies within

Germany. Organized opposition was ruthlessly swept aside in the first months of 1933, their leaders exiled or imprisoned. Within a week of Hitler's appointment as Chancellor, Goering had drawn up a list of police officers and government officials to be purged. On 11 February, auxiliary police were brought into the Rhineland area with instructions to back up the ordinary police in their campaign against left-wing subversive elements in the Ruhr cities. By the middle of February, key police chiefs had been ousted and replaced by high-ranking SA leaders. The brutal simplicity of the takeover was revealed in the astonishingly frank advice by Goering to his new 'police officers'. In their dealings with the Left the police were told to 'make free use of their weapons whenever necessary'. If they had still not appreciated what Goering had in mind, his subsequent instructions left no room for doubt: 'Every bullet that is now fired from the barrel of a police pistol is my bullet. If that is called murder, then I have committed murder, for I have ordered it all; I take the responsibility for it.'[4]

## the Reichstag fire

It was against this well-organized campaign of intimidation that the left-wing parties had to fight for their political survival. However, their prospects were sorely diminished when on the night of 27 February 1933 the Reichstag building was burned down. The swift manner in which the Nazis blamed and then punished the Communists for the fire has led many historians to assume that the fire was actually instigated by the Nazis to provide them with the excuse they desperately needed for moving against their arch-enemies.

**SOURCE A**

Goering and Goebbels were looking for some pretext to smash the Communist Party. After rejecting various plans – such as an attack on Hitler – they hit on the notion of setting fire to the Reichstag building. An underground passage linked Goering's Palace of the President of the Reichstag with the main building across the street. Through this a small group of S.A. men under the command of Karl Ernst, the leader of the Berlin S.A., entered the deserted building on the evening of the 27th and scattered a chemical preparation with a delayed-action effect over carpet, curtains and chairs. After doing this they made their way back to safety by the underground tunnel. As they were leaving, a half-crazed young Dutchman, who had been picked up by the S.A. after attempting to set fire to other buildings, and carefully groomed for the dupe, climbed into the Reichstag from the outside and proceeded to start fires at a number of points. By the time the police and the fire-brigades arrived the fire was out of control and rapidly engulfed the building.

Source: Alan Bullock, *Hitler: A Study in Tyranny* (1954).

**SOURCE B**

THE REVISIONIST VIEW.

Goering seems to have been utterly thunderstruck; he went at once to the burning building. His first thought was to save the tapestries and the library. He arrived at about 9.30 pm shortly after the main hall had gone up in flames and the fire had reached ten-alarm proportions. It cannot be inferred from Goering's behaviour that he welcomed the fire. He . . . spoke to Fire Chief Gempp, and inquired after Councillor Galle, the president of the Reichstag. Assistant Secretary Gravert, who was with him, inquired at once into the origin of the fire, learned of grounds for suspecting Ernst Torgler and Wilhelm Koenen (2 senior members of the KPD) and was convinced from that moment on that the Communists were behind the fire.

Goering later said that the moment he heard the word 'incendiary' the idea that the Communist Party was to blame had come to him spontaneously. But it seems more likely that the idea was first suggested by the information he obtained from Gravert.

Source: Hans Mommsen, *Aspects of the Third Reich* (1985).

**SOURCE C**

Rudolf Diels, Head of the Prussian political police.

When I pushed my way into the burning building with Schneider, we had to climb over the bulging hoses of the Berlin fire brigade, although as yet, there were few onlookers. A few officers of my department were already engaged in interrogating van der Lubbe. Naked from the waist upwards, smeared with dirt and sweating, he sat in front of them breathing heavily. He panted as if he had completed a tremendous task. There was a wild triumphant gleam in the burning eyes of his pale young face . . .

The voluntary confessions of Marinus van der Lubbe prevented me from thinking that an arsonist who was such an expert in his folly needed any helpers. Why should not a single match be enough to set fire to the cold yet inflammable splendour of the Chamber, the old upholstered furniture, the heavy curtains, and the bone-dry wooden panelling! But this specialist had used a whole knapsack full of inflammable material. He had been so active that he laid several dozen fires. With a firelighter, the 'Industrious Housewife', he had set the chamber aflame. Then he had rushed through the big corridors with his burning shirt which he brandished in his right hand like a torch to lay more fires under the old leather sofas. During this hectic activity he was overpowered by Reichstag officials.

*Source*: J. Noakes and G. Pridham (ed.), *Nazism 1919–1945: A Documentary Reader. Vol. 1: The Rise to Power* (1998).

Many historians now argue that the real importance of the Reichstag fire lies not so much in the continuing mystery of who started it but rather in the political use made of it by the Nazis. While the building was still smouldering, Hitler confronted a shocked and disorientated Hindenburg and persuaded him to authorize an emergency 'Decree for the Protection of the People and State'. This gave Hitler massive powers of repression and control, backed by the fact that he was able to claim that he had obtained these extra powers constitutionally. Richard Evans's perspective strips away some of the mystery of the event. He concludes:

A lone Dutch anarcho-syndicalist, Marinus van der Lubbe, burned down the Reichstag building in protest against the injustices of unemployment. Hitler and Göring persuaded a willing cabinet effectively to suppress the Communist Party. Four thousand Communists including virtually the entire party leadership were immediately arrested, beaten up, tortured and thrown into newly created concentration camps. . . . All of this was sanctioned by an emergency decree signed by Hindenburg the night after the fire suspending civil liberties. . . . Van der Lubbe's lone act was portrayed by Joseph Goebbels, soon to become Reich Propaganda Minister, as the result of a Communist conspiracy to stage an armed uprising.[5]

In the Reichstag elections on 5 March 1933, the Nazis won 288 seats compared with 196 in the November 1932 election. They had increased their percentage of the vote from 33.1 to 43.9. They had still failed to gain an absolute majority. However, events now moved with an inexorable force as one after another of Germany's democratic safeguards was brushed aside with shocking simplicity. The day after the March election, storm troopers rampaged along the Kurfurstendamm, a fashionable shopping street in Berlin, hunting down Jews and beating them up. Synagogues were ransacked, while all over Germany gangs of brownshirts burst into courthouses and intimidated Jewish judges and lawyers. The Nazi seizure of power in the Länder brought a drastic escalation of violence in the states which had not previously been under Nazi control. Tortures, beatings and murders of countless political opponents took place in hastily devised prisons and camps run by the SA. On 20 March the Munich Police President Himmler announced the establishment of the first concentration camp near Dachau.

With 81 Communist deputies either under arrest or on the run, the Nazis now held a majority in the Reichstag but the Enabling Act that Hitler now wanted to pass into law required a two-thirds majority. After personal contact with Hitler the Centre Party agreed to support the measure. It was ruled that protests against the act, in the form of abstaining by not turning up to vote, would not be allowed. On the afternoon of 23 March 1933, Hitler addressed the Reichstag, the chamber whose powers he was about to shackle. In a speech lasting for more than two hours he called for 'far-reaching moral renewal'. Ominously, he stated that the Judiciary would need to use 'elasticity of judgement' for the wider benefit of society. Towards the end, in assuring tones, Hitler said that the Reichstag was not under threat, and the rights of the Churches would not be reduced. In the early evening, the SPD leader Otto Wels made a courageous stand before the menacing ranks of the NSDAP members in the Reichstag. He defended the principles of humanity and justice while Hitler sat, scribbling notes. When Hitler returned to the rostrum to waves of applause he told the Reichstag that 'we appeal in this hour to the German Reichstag to grant us that which we could have taken anyway'. He reserved his most withering comments for the SPD, telling them that he did not want their support and that 'Germany will become free, but not through you.' With 411 votes in favour, and 94 brave votes of dissent from the SPD, and to the lasting shame of the Centre Party, the 'Act for the Removal of Distress from People and Reich' became law. This signified the destruction of parliamentary democracy and passed all legislative control from the Reichstag to the government. Despite attempts by some of the other parties to insert limiting provisions within the bill. the Reichstag had been reduced to a sounding board, or an applause mechanism, for Hitler's speeches.[6]

This was accompanied by a rapid decline in the significance of cabinet government as a restraint on Hitler. Initially, when Hitler first became Chancellor the cabinet had continued to meet regularly in order to pass draft decrees for forwarding to the President. From the end of March, however, it started to be bypassed by the Reich Chancellery and the individual Ministries. Increasingly, therefore, the cabinet met only to rubber-stamp previously decided legislation. Of the 17 cabinet Ministers in office in May 1934, however, a clear majority – 9 – were long-term members of the Nazi Party. It is clear that the original plan of impeding Hitler with a conservative cabinet had been easily swept aside and Hitler continued to take the initiative. It was announced that Hitler had granted the long-standing request of the labour and trade union movement to have a Day of National Labour, as a paid holiday, on 1 May 1933. Whilst Hitler's apparently generous gesture bolstered his image as the true guardian of the workers' interests, the union leaders returned to work on 2 May to find that their offices had been occupied and that they were under immediate arrest. In an instant, the independent union movement had been shackled, to be replaced by a further mouthpiece of the Third Reich, the German Labour Front (DAF).

The remaining independent political parties were the next to give way. While the Communist Party had been attacked after the Reichstag fire, the Socialists had campaigned against the Enabling Act and paid the price when they were suppressed on 22 June. The Centre Party dissolved itself on 5 July and a week later a new law declared that the only legal party in Germany was the NSDAP. Henceforth, any alternative political activity carried the penalty of three years' imprisonment.

## 9.3 the Röhm purge

On 6 July 1933 Hitler gathered leading Nazis together for a review of the first six months of the Nazi state. The Chancellor made it clear that as far as he was concerned revolution was not a permanent condition and the street violence of late spring had to be checked. Hitler was increasingly wary of the power that the excesses of the ever-expanding SA gave to its leader, Ernst Röhm. In addition, although Hitler had to a large extent succeeded in removing external domestic opposition by 1934, he still had to contend with powerful forces inside his own party which wanted to see him lead German society in a more radical, socialist direction. In the spring of 1934, powerful members of the party such as Gregor Strasser and Ernst Röhm repeatedly urged Hitler to reconsider the whole nature of his social policies. At the same time the army was still by no means under

Nazi control. Many of the leading generals shared an arrogant contempt for the Nazis. On a four-day cruise in the navy vessel *Deutschland* off Norway in mid-April, Hitler, Blomberg and top military officers seem to have reached an agreement that the time for the power of the SA to be curbed was drawing nearer. Meanwhile powerful Nazis like Goering and Himmler viewed Röhm with real concern. Each of these individuals was primarily concerned with the extension of his own power base.

By June 1934 it was clear that the ageing President von Hindenburg did not have long to live. If, as many anticipated, Hitler wished to then combine the offices of Chancellor and President he would need the full support of the army. His concern was that the army might persuade Hindenburg to nominate an alternative successor before he died. Hitler knew that the power of the SA was a big worry to the army, and realised that decisive action against Röhm would bring him greater support from the leading generals. Set against this was Hitler's personal sense of loyalty to Röhm, who had been at his side in the Munich Putsch. Throughout June, Hitler received warnings of imminent danger from enemies of Röhm, but he remained indecisive and uncertain.

Just before midnight on 28 June 1934, Hitler received a message of the utmost importance from Himmler in Berlin. Himmler convinced his leader that the Berlin SA had finalized its preparations to unseat the Führer in a desperate coup d'état. The SA, he told Hitler, would be ready to move by 4.00 p.m. and would begin the occupation of government buildings at 5.00 p.m. Hitler was unable to contain his rage, and his natural tendency to hesitate now gave way to furious action. At 2.00 a.m., still shaking with anger and agitation, he climbed aboard a three-engined aircraft with his closest companions and set off for Munich. When the plane touched down at Oberwiesenfeld airport dawn had just broken. Three fast cars were ready to take Hitler and his heavily armed entourage to the small spa town of Bad Wiessee. Hitler tersely informed a Reichswehr officer that he was going to 'pass severe judgement' on his former ally. Meanwhile Röhm slept on, oblivious to the events which he was alleged to have set in motion and which were soon to consume him.

**SOURCE A**

I drive up carefully to the hotel entrance as Hitler had ordered. Hitler jumps out of the car and after him Goebbels, Lutze and the adjutants. Right behind us another car stops with a squad of detectives which had been raised in Munich.

I run quickly up to the first floor where Hitler is just coming out of Röhm's bedroom. Two detectives come out of the room opposite . . .

Meanwhile, Röhm comes out of his room in a blue suit and with a cigar in the corner of his mouth. Hitler glares at him but says nothing. Two detectives take Röhm to the vestibule of the hotel where he throws himself into an armchair and orders coffee . . . I stay in the corridor a little to one side and a detective tells me about Röhm's arrest. 'Hitler entered Röhm's bedroom with a whip in his hand. Behind him were two detectives with pistols at the ready. He spat out the words "Röhm, you are under arrest." Röhm looked sleepily from his pillow: "Heil, my Führer." "You are under arrest," bawled Hitler for the second time, turned on his heel and left the room.' . . .

To my horror, a lorry full of heavily armed SA men rattles into the yard. Now there'll be some shooting, I think to myself. . . . At this moment Hitler goes up to him: 'Drive back to Munich immediately!' he tells the puzzled fellow. 'If you are stopped by SS on the way, you must let yourselves be disarmed without resistance.' . . . At last Röhm too is led from the hotel. He walks past Hitler with his head bowed, completely apathetic.

Source: J. Noakes and G. Pridham (ed.), *Nazism 1919–1945: A Documentary Reader.* Vol. 1: *The Rise to Power* (1998).

## SOURCE B

THE GOVERNOR OF STADELHEIM PRISON, MUNICH.

Two SS men asked at the reception desk to be taken to Röhm . . . . There they handed over a Browning to Röhm, who once again asked to speak to Hitler. They ordered him to shoot himself. If he did not comply, they would come back in ten minutes and kill him. . . . When the time was up, the two SS men re-entered the cell and found Röhm standing with his chest bared. Immediately one of them from the door shot him in the throat, and Röhm collapsed on the floor. Since he was still alive, he was killed with a shot point-blank through the temple.

Source: as source A.

## SOURCE C

DEFENCE MINISTER GENERAL VON BLOMBERG, JULY 1934.

The Führer with soldierly decision and exemplary courage has himself attacked and crushed the traitors and murderers. The Army, as the bearers of arms of the entire people, far removed from the conflicts of domestic politics, will show its gratitude through devotion and loyalty.

Source: as source A.

## SOURCE D

REICH PRESIDENT VON HINDENBURG, 2 JULY 1934.

I note from the reports I have received that through your decisive intervention and your courageous personal commitment you have nipped all the treasonable intrigues in the bud. You have saved the German nation from serious danger and for this I express to you my deeply felt gratitude and my sincere appreciation. 13

Source: as sourceA.

## SOURCE E

EXTRACT FROM THE MINUTES OF THE REICH CABINET MEETING, 3 JULY 1934.

At the meeting of the Reich Cabinet on Tuesday 3 July, the Reich Chancellor, Adolf Hitler, began by giving a detailed account of the origin and suppression of the high treason plot. The Reich Chancellor stressed that lightning action had been necessary, otherwise many thousands of people would have been in danger of being wiped out.

THE VERDICT OF A GERMAN HISTORIAN.

The smoothness with which the murders of 30 June were carried out is eloquent proof that no Röhm putsch was imminent. There was no resistance encountered anywhere, not even among the armed elite formations of the SA; many victims unsuspectingly surrendered of their own accord, having faith in their Führer and in the eventual clarification of an obvious mistake. The only shots fired were those of the executioners. . . . The number of victims, officially set at 77, is estimated to have been between 150 and 200.

*Source*: Karl Dietrich Bracher, *The German Dictatorship* (1971).

## analysis of the purge

Evans describes the victors of the 1934 blood purge as the army (*Reichswehr*) and the SS – which carried out the killing with the ruthless and ambitious head of its Security Office, Reinhard Heydrich, who was second only to Himmler in the SS playing a key role. He describes the impact of the purge on Hitler's standing as 'a propaganda coup par excellence', although he reveals that the atmosphere in Goering's office, where the Prussian Minister-President was side-by-side with Heydrich and Himmler, was one of 'blatant bloodthirstiness' and hideous vindictiveness'.[7] Amongst those targeted alongside Röhm were Nazi dissident Gregor Strasser and the former Chancellor, General Schleicher.

### QUESTION

To what extent do the sources presented here convince you that Hitler genuinely believed that Röhm presented a threat to his personal authority?

## the extension of power – the death of Hindenburg and the army oath of allegiance

With the SA removed, Hitler's next opportunity to extend his personal power base presented itself only a month later. On 2 August 1934 President Hindenburg died aged 85. His heart was still beating when it was announced that, from now on, the office of Reich President would be combined with that of Reich Chancellor and that both posts would be held by Adolf Hitler. Still grateful to Hitler for his action against the SA, the army accepted this extension of his authority without question. The degree to which Hitler had become the dictator of Germany was reflected in the oath of loyalty and unconditional obedience to Adolf Hitler, the Führer of the German nation and people, Supreme Commander of the Armed Forces, which all soldiers in the German army were now forced to take. Social scientists have drawn a useful distinction between the 'normative state', with traditional rules, procedures, and conventions and consisting of formal institutions such as the Reich Chancellery, and the 'prerogative state', an extra-legal system that derived its 'legality' entirely from the supra-legal authority of the leader. In the prerogative state, the murders committed on the 'Night of the Long Knives' were sanctioned by the leader's authority and so in fact were not illegal.

Hitler's political judgement seemed unerring. The oath of loyalty constituted an almost physical bond which no honourable soldier, particularly those in the officer corps, would contemplate compromising. Hitler's conquest of his main opponents and his consolidation of power among his own party were complete, but the support of the ordinary people towards to regime was not something he could afford to take for granted. However, the brutal reckoning with Röhm must have been in people's minds when they were asked to approve of Hitler's merging of the presidency and the chancellorship in a yes-or-no plebiscite campaign in the summer of 1934. The extract that follows indicates the extent of the intimidation that surrounded this vote, which resulted in the government announcing a 'Yes' vote of 89 per cent.

---

**background to the plebiscite campaign of August 1934**

1  Before the election. The verdict of a Social Democrat
   (a)  Hitler's portrait hanging from every window, every car, public loudspeakers to broadcast the speeches on the radio
   (b)  The moral pressure: those who said 'no' were branded as traitors, rogues, saboteurs of national reconstruction
2  During the voting
   (a)  The uniformed SA people and Party members in the polling stations created an atmosphere of terror in the polling room right from the start
   (b)  In many cases there were no polling booths at all, in others it was made virtually impossible to enter them. Either the booth was put in a far corner, or SA men barred the way to it or there were posters to put people off

(E.g. 'Every German Votes Publicly, Who Votes Otherwise?' or 'Only Traitors Go in Here')[8]

---

## 9.4 culture, the arts and propaganda

### propaganda

'The revolution we have made', declared Joseph Goebbels, on 15 November 1933, 'is a total one. It has encompassed every area of public life.'[9] Not 37 per cent of people, as Goebbels said on 25 March 1933, referring to the highest proportion of the vote the Nazis had ever succeeded in winning in a free

German election, but 100 per cent of the people must be behind them. It was to this end that Hitler had created a new Ministry of Popular Enlightenment and Propaganda on 13 March 1933 and put Goebbels himself into the Ministry, with a seat in the cabinet. Goebbels was perfectly equipped for the task, gifted with words and with a deep understanding of propaganda techniques. On 25 March, he defined the Ministry's task as the 'spiritual mobilization' of the German people. This included ceremonies and rituals such as the torchlit parades held to mark the appointment of Hitler as Reich Chancellor on 30 January 1933, the formal state opening of the Reichstag at Potsdam on 21 March 1933, the annual Nazi Party rally in Nuremberg every autumn, the 'Day of National Labour' on 1 May, and much more besides. The embedding of the Hitler cult in everyday life was nowhere more obvious than in the introduction of the German greeting – 'Heil Hitler' – to be used on all official correspondence by state employees from 13 July 1933. Borrowing on influences from the spectacle of the church, the Nazi movement used colour, dramatic lighting and elaborate choreography to bring a sense of drama and pageantry to the lives of ordinary people. It seems likely however, that the impact of such spectacles probably diminished over the course of time, as the realities of ordinary life seeped through the regime's picture of perfection.

## 9.5 sources : Josef Goebbels: a career in propaganda

**SOURCE A**

One way ordinary Germans could secretly express dissatisfaction with the Nazi regime was through jokes. Anti-Nazi humour was a low-level form of opposition. The Nazi leaders provided endless ammunition for jokes. Hitler jokes tended to stress his enormous power and brutality. Joseph Goebbels was the subject of a great many jokes, usually revolving around the fact that he did not live up to the promised image of the master race. Goebbels had many nicknames, most notably the 'Poison Dwarf'. Perhaps the major source of jokes was the repressive nature of the regime. It was claimed nobody would go to the dentist in Nazi Germany because they would never be able to open their mouths in front of a stranger.

*Source*: F. McDonough, *Hitler and Nazi Germany* (1999).

**SOURCE B**

EXTRACT FROM ALBERT SPEER'S FINAL STATEMENT AT THE NUREMBERG TRIALS IN 1946.

Hitler's dictatorship differed in one fundamental point from all its predecessors in history. His was the first dictatorship in the present period of modern technological development, a dictatorship that made complete use of all technical means for the domination of its own country.

Through technical devices like the radio and the loudspeaker, eighty million people were deprived of independent thought. It was possible thereby to subject them to the will of one man. As a result of this there arises the new type of individual who uncritically obeys orders.

## SOURCE C

Propaganda was the genius of National Socialism . . . Joseph Goebbels was the brain behind this manipulation of minds, 'the only really interesting man in the Third Reich besides Hitler'. One of the most astonishingly gifted propagandists of modern times, he stood head and shoulders above the bizarre mediocrity of the rest of the regime's top-ranking functionaries. He was one of the few real powers in the movement's leadership, not merely a figurehead drawn into the light of history 'in the wake of the victorious cause'. These two, Hitler and Goebbels, complemented each other in an almost unique manner. For Hitler's somber, complex-determined visions, his intuitive, ecstatic relationship with the masses, Goebbels found the techniques of persuasion, the rationalization, the slogans, myths and images. It was from Goebbels that der Führer, the term by which Hitler appeared as redeemer . . . and blessed saviour, received its visionary content . . . 'The essence of propaganda', he once remarked, 'consists in winning people over to an idea so sincerely, so vitally, that in the end they succumb to it utterly and can never again escape from it.'

*Source*: Joachim Fest, *The Face of the Third Reich* (1970).

## SOURCE D

Extract from Josef Goebbels's annual message to the German people, New Year's Eve, 1934.

My fellow German citizens!

My goal is not to add a bitter taste to the holiday's festive glass of cheer. I believe that every level and class of the German people has reason to celebrate today with confidence. And there is no reason to be moderate. We Germans over the last 20 years have had too much pain, sorrow, and disappointment to run the risk of overdoing our celebration . . .

But now we raise our hearts and see with satisfaction that a year of success is behind us, and that the blessing of heaven has fallen on the German people. Our whole hearts rejoice. It is a kind of joy that looks back with pride on what has been accomplished, and that gives strength for new plans and decisions. . . . We Germans have once more learned to love life in all its splendor. We affirm it and accept all its demands, even if they be hard and pitiless. National Socialism affirms life, it does not deny it. We draw from it the joyful strength that so wonderfully fills us in the last hours of the passing year. No one is left out. It fills the festive streets of the great cities and the lonely alleys and paths of our German villages. It fills huts and palaces, the rich and the poor. It fills the heart of the lonely wanderer who greets the new year in the snow-capped and towering mountains, or those who are part of the crowds on Berlin's Unter den Linden. It was a blessed year. The German people found themselves once more, and regained a hope that lets them look confidently into the coming year. What a difference from the New Year's Eve of a year ago. Then the Reich stood before the abyss. The people were torn by hatred and civil war. The parties and the government lacked the strength even to recognize the catastrophe, much less to deal with it. Collapse and desperation were rising wherever one looked, and the specter of Bolshevism was everywhere. But today? The Reich is once more strong and powerful, the people more united and firm than ever before, led by a strong hand who is dealing with the problems we face. . . . The flags of national renewal fly over the Reich, and a revolution of vast extent has captured the German people and given them back their true nature.

**SOURCE E**

EXTRACT FROM GOEBBELS'S SPEECH ON TOTAL WAR, FEBRUARY 1943.

I do not know how many millions of people are listening to me over the radio tonight, at home and at the front. I want to speak to all of you from the depths of my heart to the depths of yours. I believe that the entire German people has a passionate interest in what I have to say tonight. I will therefore speak with holy seriousness and openness, as the hour demands. The German people, raised, educated and disciplined by National Socialism, can bear the whole truth. It knows the gravity of the situation, and its leadership can therefore demand the necessary hard measures, yes even the hardest measures.
We Germans are armed against weakness and uncertainty. The blows and misfortunes of the war only give us additional strength, firm resolve, and a spiritual and fighting will to overcome all difficulties and obstacles with revolutionary élan.

Now is not the time to ask how it all happened. That can wait until later, when the German people and the whole world will learn the full truth about the misfortune of the past weeks, and its deep and fateful significance for the whole Eastern Front. It was not in vain. The future will make clear why. . . .
My task is to give you an unvarnished picture of the situation, and to draw the hard conclusions that will guide the actions of the German government, but also of the German people. . . . The nation is ready for anything. The Führer has commanded, and we will follow him. In this hour of national reflection and contemplation, we believe firmly and unshakably in victory. We see it before us, we need only reach for it. We must resolve to subordinate everything to it. That is the duty of the hour.

*Source*: J. Noakes (ed.), *Nazism 1919–1945: A Documentary Reader. Vol. 4: The German Home Front in World War II* (1998).

**QUESTION**

Using the material contained in each of these sources and your own knowledge explain how far you agree with the view that the Nazi regime relied on the propaganda efforts of Joseph Goebbels for its popular support.

## film, cinema and radio

The dynamic modernity of the Nazi movement was reflected in its enthusiasm for the use of film techniques to propagate the message. It was fortunate for Hitler that he was able to secure the services of an incredibly gifted young film director, Leni Riefenstahl, in turning the 1934 Nuremberg party rally into a film that remains technically impressive today. In *The Triumph of the Will*, released in March 1935, Hitler was portrayed as the man who had singlehandedly restored faith to a nation that had been crippled with self-doubt. A film described by Goebbels as a 'magnificent cinematic vision of the Führer'[10] was not followed by further films about Hitler himself, but state control of the cinema did grow exponentially. By 1936 the government was funding nearly three-quarters of all German feature films. Works abhorred by the regime, such as the cartoons of Walt Disney, were scarcely shown in Germany at all. The Nazis also extended their grasp to the production of wireless sets, paying large subsidies to manufacturers to make and sell cheap radios known as People's Receivers (*Volksempfanger*), available for 76 Reichsmarks or, in a smaller version, at only 35. By the middle of 1939 over 70 per cent of households in Germany owned a wireless. While people may have appreciated the material benefit this represented, we cannot know for certain what they came to think of the relentless message that poured constantly from their radio sets.

## theatre and the arts

A Theatre Law passed in 15 May 1934 brought all theatrical licensing under the direct control of the propaganda minister. The extent to which the attack on freedom of expression was sustained by the regime was shown in the events of 20 March 1939 when more than 5,000 works of art were piled up in the courtyard of the central fire station in Berlin and set alight. The bonfire bore a striking resemblance to the earlier book-burnings of 10 May 1933 that had consumed the works of Jewish, socialist and modernist writers on the public squares of Germany's university cities.

## architecture

The new public buildings of the Third Reich were designed on an extravagant scale. They were influenced by Hitler's own personal architectural and design schemes. He spent hours working with architects on grandiose plans, poring over models and building an elaborate vision of the German cities of the future. Anti-Semitism permeated all aspects of society, and in this context the Reich Chamber of Architects soon expelled Jewish practitioners from the profession. In Berlin, a huge new airport terminal was built at Tempelhof, with over 2,000 rooms. Once again, the regime's drive for modernity can be seen. Meanwhile, a rising member of Hitler's entourage, a gifted and driven talent, Albert Speer, designed the new Reich Chancellery.

Musical culture, both classical and popular, was of great importance to the German people. Control over classical concerts and operas was relatively easy, but the type of popular music that was played in dance-halls, nightclubs, hotel bars and similar venues, above all in Berlin, was far more difficult to control. Archive material from the files of the Gestapo show the frustration of the regime in its failure to entice young people away from the American swing and jazz music that Hitler personally despised.

## language

The influence of the regime on all aspects of cultural life was so pervasive that even the spoken and written word could not escape its sway. Words like 'brutal', 'ruthless' and 'uncompromising' all became words of praise instead of disapproval, while the notion of 'tolerance' was discredited. One of the most striking elements of the use of language within the regime was in the constant demand for verbal approval. This can be seen in the mass acclamation which the regime demanded on occasions such as Hitler's birthday, anniversaries of key events within the Reich, plebiscites and elections.

## 9.6 education and youth in Nazi Germany

Hitler's immediate need for acclamation and approval from all sectors of society, including young people, was of crucial importance in the collective psychology of the regime. In addition, the arrogance of those who held power in the Nazi state created a widely held assumption that the regime was likely to be in power for generations to come. Therefore it was not just the immediate imperatives of power but the need to assert authority for generations to come that motivated the Nazis to use education and the indoctrination of youth as a foundation stone for the regime. Finally, it is important to recall that one of the central purposes of the Nazi state was to instil militaristic values in all levels of society. This process was to take place through the elaborate organization of the Hitler youth, the purging of the teaching profession and the careful manipulation of the entire curriculum. This extract from a speech by Hitler illustrates the nature of his ideology for young people:

**SOURCE A**

HITLER'S SPEECH AT NUREMBERG, 14 SEPTEMBER 1935.

The ideal of manhood has not always been the same even for our own people. There were times which now seem to us very far off and almost incomprehensible, when the ideal of the young man was the chap who could hold his beer and was good for a drink. But now his day is past and we like to see not the man who can hold his drink, but the young man who can stand all weathers, the hardened young man. Because what matters is not how many glasses of beer he can drink, but how many blows he can stand; not how many nights he can stand on the spree, but how many kilometres he can march.

We no longer see in the boorish beer-drinker the ideal of the German people: we find it in men and girls who are sound to the core, and sturdy.

What we look for from our German youth is different from what people wanted in the past. In our eyes the German youth of the future must be slim and slender, swift as the greyhound, tough as leather, and hard as Krupp steel. We must educate a new type of man so that our people is not ruined by the symptoms of degeneracy of our day.

Source: J. Noakes and G. Pridham (ed.), *Nazism 1919–1945: A Documentary Reader.* *Vol. 2: State, Economy and Society 1933–39* (1995).

The weeks following the Nazi takeover saw a number of ad hoc measures by the various states to purge the profession of unreliable teachers, which then gave way to the introduction of the Law for the Re-establishment of a Professional Civil Service of 7 April 1933. This control mechanism was also applied to the curriculum itself, as shown in this extract on the teaching of history in secondary schools and the subsequent extract that illustrates how the ideas of the racial state permeated the classroom.

**SOURCE B**

GUIDELINES FOR THE TEACHING OF HISTORY ISSUED BY THE GERMAN CENTRAL INSTITUTE OF EDUCATION IN 1938.

The German nation in its essence and greatness, in its fateful struggle for internal and external identity is the subject of the teaching of history. It is based on the natural bond of the child with his nation and, by interpreting history as the fateful struggle for existence between the nations, has the particular task of educating young people to respect the great German past and to have faith in the mission and future of their own nation and to respect the right of existence of other nations. The teaching of history must bring the past alive for the young German in such a way that it enables him to understand the present, makes him feel the responsibility of every individual for the nation as a whole and gives him encouragement for his own political activity.

Source: as source A.

**SOURCE C**

EXTRACTS FROM GERMAN MATHEMATICS TEXTBOOKS.

(a) The construction of a lunatic asylum costs 6 million RM. How many houses at 15,000 RM each could have been built for that amount?

(b) To keep a mentally ill person costs approx 4 RM per day, a cripple 5.50 RM, a criminal 3.50 RM. Many civil servants receive only 4 RM per day . . . unskilled workers not even 2 RM per head for their families. (a) illustrate these figures with a curriculum – according to conservative estimates, there are 300,000 mentally ill, epileptics etc, in care. (b) How much do these people cost to keep in total, at a cost of 4 RM per head? (c) How many marriage loans at 1000 RM each . . . could be granted from this money?

(c)     A modern night bomber can carry 1,800 incendiaries. How long (in kilometres) is the path along which it can distribute these bombs if it drops a bomb every second at a speed of 250 km per hour? How far apart are the craters from one another? How many kilometres can 10 such planes set alight if they fly 50 metres apart from one another? How many fires are caused if ⅓ of the bombs hit their targets and of these ⅓ ignite?

*Source*: as source A.

## QUESTION

To what extent do the sources presented here suggest that Hitler's regime successfully achieved its objectives with regard to education and youth?

## 9.7  the role of women in Hitler's Germany

This extended extract from a speech made by Hitler in 1934 gives an immediate insight into the nature of Hitler's attitudes towards women and their place in the Nazi society.

### SOURCE A

EXTRACTS FROM SPEECH BY HITLER TO THE NATIONAL SOCIALIST WOMEN'S SECTION (NSF), 8 SEPTEMBER 1934.

The slogan 'Emancipation of women' was invented by Jewish intellectuals and its content was formed by the same spirit. In the really good times of German life the German woman had no need to emancipate herself. She possessed exactly what nature had necessarily given her to administer and preserve . . . If the man's world is said to be the State, his struggle, his readiness to devote his powers to the service of the community, then it may perhaps be said that the woman's is a smaller world. For her world is her husband, her family, her children and her home. But what would become of the greater world if there were no one to tend and care for the smaller one? . . . The sacrifices which the man makes in the struggle of his nation, the woman makes in the preservation of that nation in individual cases. What the man gives in courage on the battlefield, the woman gives in eternal self-sacrifice, in eternal pain and suffering. Every child that a woman brings into the world is a battle, a battle waged for the existence of her people . . .

So our women's movement is for us not something which inscribes on its banner as its programme the fight against men, but something which has as its programme the common fight together with men.

*Source*: J. Noakes and G. Pridham (ed.), *Nazism 1919–1945: A Documentary Reader. Vol. 2: State, Economy and Society 1933–39* (1995).

The raising of children was of crucial importance not just to Hitler's view of women and marriage but to to the whole nature and purpose of the Nazi state and its ideology. In the words of Burleigh and Wipperman: 'The main object of [Nazi] social policy remained the creation of a hierarchical racial new order. Everything else was subordinate to this goal.'[11] There was, as Gotz Aly has described it, a 'unity of economic, social, racial, and war policy'.[12] This is reflected in the document that follows, ostensibly illustrating the party's attitude towards marriage but also reflecting the importance to Hitler of reducing the level of male unemployment as an absolute priority.

## SOURCE B

From Section 5 of the Law for the Reduction of Unemployment of 1 June 1933.

The Reich encourages marriage in accordance with the following regulations. Marriage loans, section 1

1  People of German nationality who marry one another after this law has come into force can on application be granted a marriage loan of up to 1000 Reichsmarks. The application for the marriage loan can be made before marriage. . . . The conditions which must be fulfilled before the grant of a marriage loan are as follows:
    (a) That the future wife has spent at least six months in employment in Germany between 11 June 1931 and 31 May 1933.
    (b) That banns has been issued by the Registry Office and that the future wife gives up her job at the latest at the time of the wedding . . .
    (c) That the future wife pledges herself not to take up employment so long as her future husband receives an income (within the meaning of the Income Tax Law) of more than 125 Reichsmarks a month.

*Source*: as source A.

An indication of the extent to which race was at the forefront of party thinking and the pervasive nature of this policy is shown in the 'Ten Commandments for the Choice of a Spouse' (1934) listed here.

## SOURCE C

1  Remember that you are a German.
2  If you are genetically healthy you should not remain unmarried.
3  Keep your body pure.
4  You should keep your mind and spirit pure.
5  As a German choose only a spouse of the same or Nordic blood.
6  In choosing a spouse ask about his ancestors.
7  Health is also a precondition for physical beauty.
8  Marry only for love.
9  Don't look for a playmate but for a companion for marriage.
10  You should want to have as many children as possible.

4 incentives for women to have more children
May 1939: The Mother's Cross
Gold: for those with 8 children.
Silver: for those with 6 children.
Bronze: for those with 4 children.

*Source*: as source A.

The state was concerned not just with the numbers of children being brought into the world but, more disturbingly, with their health.

**SOURCE D**

POPULATION CONTROL: THE LAW FOR THE PREVENTION OF HEREDITARILY DISEASED OFFSPRING, ISSUED ON 14 JULY 1933.

1) Anyone who has a hereditary illness can be rendered sterile by a surgical operation if, according to the experience of medical science, there is a strong probability that his/her offspring will suffer from serious hereditary defects of a physical or mental nature.
2) Anyone is hereditarily ill within the meaning of this law who suffers from one of the following illnesses:

(a) Congenital feeble mindedness  (e) Huntington's chorea
(b) Schizophrenia  (f) Hereditary blindness
(c) Manic depression  (g) Hereditary deafness
(d) Hereditary epilepsy  (h) Serious physical deformities

*Source*: as source A.

**QUESTIONS**

1 To what extent do the Nazi regime's claims to modernity conflict with the objectives reflected in the sources presented here?
2 How far did the Nazis successfully implement their policies with regard to the role of women in German society?

## 9.8 the Nazi economy and popular support for the regime

When a journalist asked Hitler to outline his objectives for the German people he replied: 'I have the ambition to make the German people rich and Germany beautiful. I want to see the living standard of the individual raised.' Beyond the rhetoric, Hitler's real ambitions involved a much more perilous route for the German people than the pursuit of domestic happiness. In Hitler's eyes the domestic economy functioned purely to ensure that the German people would have the means to take up the historic task when it was presented to them. When Hitler came to power, the main focus of public concern was the eviscerated state of the economy. Hitler tackled this crisis with what Klaus-Jurgen Müller called 'gigantic rearmament',[13] a process so powerful that it ultimately led to a dangerously overheated economy that by 1937 faced a crisis potentially as serious as the one he had inherited.

It is important to recall that in strictly economic terms, Hitler did not have a difficult act to follow. Hitler's ability to present himself as the Messiah performing an 'economic miracle' was made easier by the fact that for many Germans the last, desperate years of the Weimar period were used as a reference point, rather than the relatively prosperous period of 1924–28. In the death throes of the Weimar Republic a once-successful nation had collapsed into a period of mass unemployment, food shortages, poverty and bitter street battles. In the groundbreaking election campaigns of 1932 Hitler promised an immediate reduction in unemployment, bread for the masses, the restoration of law and order, urgent attention to the plight of the peasants and the embattled farmers, the curtailing of the trade unions and the moral recovery of the nation.

While unemployment did rapidly decline, many other aspects of the economic situation remained difficult, prompting a worsening mood in the population at large. In mid-August 1935 Goebbels noted in his diary: 'Führer gives an overview of the political situation. Sees a decline.' A report on price and wage levels prepared for Hitler in autumn 1935 revealed that almost 50 per cent of the German workforce were earning gross wages of 18 Reichsmarks or less per week, a figure placing them significantly beneath the poverty line. Meanwhile, in the countryside, acute shortages of domestic fodder and falling livestock herds led to serious food shortages. Stocks of fats and eggs had been almost entirely used up before the end of 1935. The insatiable demands of the armaments industry meant that funds could not easily be diverted to resolve these problems. Hitler's ringing words about economic renewal may have sounded hollow when, two year's into his chancellorship, the shelves in so many food shops were empty. In the largest cities food queues became part of the daily routine and staple elements of the diet such as butter, eggs and meat became scarce and expensive. Nowhere was the 'food crisis' more acute than in the working-class districts. Police reports in the capital in 1935 drew an alarming picture of popular discontent. Such was the tension surrounding sales of butter that these events had to be presided over by the police. As 1936 began, police updates revealed high levels of negativity towards the State with regard to its failure to provide sufficient supplies of basic foods.

An alternative analysis of the situation in 1937 is worth considering at this point, contending that it could appear that Hitler achieved his objectives. As economic historian Adam Tooze states: 'In 1937, at the Paris world's fair, the German pavilion was one of the star attractions. In its fifth year, Hitler's regime could present itself as the model dictatorship. Unemployment had fallen to negligible levels. The economy was booming. Life for millions of German households was returning to something like normal.'[14] This interpretation seems to be borne out by the remarkable decrease in unemployment shown in table 9.1.

table **9.1  unemployment in Germany, 1933–39**

| year | unemployment |
|------|--------------|
| 1933 | 6,013,612 |
| 1934 | 3,772,792 |
| 1935 | 2,975,544 |
| 1936 | 2,250,499 |
| 1937 | 1,853,460 |
| 1938 | 1,051,700 |
| 1939 | 301,900 |

*Note:* statistics as in January in each year.

For many Germans, Hitler was directly responsible for the economic recovery and was seen as a moderate figure, curbing the instincts of his more radical followers. This carefully cultivated image was remarkably durable throughout the pre-war period. The perspective of a socialist writing in 1936 is valuable in this context: 'Hitler is still outside the line of fire of criticism but the messianic belief in him has more or less died out, whereas for example Goebbels is almost universally despised.'[15]

Hitler promised a classless *Volksgemeinschaft* (people's community) with the old social differences put to one side under the unifying message of 'Ein Reich, Ein Volk, Ein Führer' ('One Country, One People, One Leader). With this aim in mind, the 'Winter Help' programme involved wealthier people collecting money and making donations to provide food and assistance for the unemployed, while the 'one-pot meal' was aimed at families who could manage with simpler meals once a week, with the money that was saved being passed to the poor. These high-profile schemes were faithfully relayed to the people through cinema newsreels, which invariably showed leading members of the Nazi hierarchy collecting charity money or caring for the less well-off.

The relentless propaganda campaign was also played out amongst the workforce. The party placed immense importance on the symbolism of phrases such as 'the honour of labour', 'German quality work' and 'a factory community' in the industrial workplace and 'blood and soil' propaganda in the rural areas. The German Labour Front (DAF), under the leadership of Robert Ley, claimed to replace the 'class conflict' of the trade unions with a new, cohesive movement celebrating the 'dignity of labour'. Hitler asserted that 'there is no dishonour in menial labour' and stressed the value to the German community of workers, farmers and peasants. The emphasis on traditional values did not stop the regime from emphasizing its modernity. Large-scale prestige projects such as the construction of a national autobahn system, the mass production of the Volkswagen car (VW) and the production of cheap transistor radios (VE) provided further employment opportunities and made the regime look innovative and dynamic. Tooze puts these products into perspective with this analysis: 'The Volksempfaenger (VE) and the Volkswagen were both desirable consumer goods and attractive symbols of modernity. But they were strictly items of discretionary expenditure. They impacted only marginally on the day-to-day material preoccupations of the vast majority of Germans. These centred around food, clothing and housing.'[16]

Hitler was acutely sensitive to the impact any deterioration in the economic position could have on his own relationship with the German people. When steep price increases in butter, meat and bread in 1933–34 roused widespread resentment, an agitated Hitler reminded his cabinet in the sharpest terms that he had promised the workers that he would not tolerate price increases. He would be accused of breaking his word if he did not take action against price increases and 'revolutionary conditions' among the people would be the consequence. In 1939 Hitler instructed Albert Speer that buildings to be constructed in Berlin's Adolf Hitler Platz must be equipped with bulletproof shutters and steel doors in the event that riots ensued following the implementation of unpopular measures that he might have to take in the future.

## rearmament

Some historians have claimed that the popular reaction towards the military build up was fairly ambivalent. However, the type of everyday grumbling that accompanied any perceived focus on 'guns rather than butter' did not threaten the regime in any serious way, given the efficiency of the police apparatus in curbing popular protest or dissent. Tooze offers a radical alternative with this thought:

> Is it really right to see rearmament simply as a drag on the standard of living, as one more obstacle to the realization of dreams of mass-consumption? Or might it in fact be more appropriate to reverse this train of logic and to think of rearmament as a particular form of collective mass-consumption . . . ? From an economic point of view again, the reintroduction of conscription in 1935 amounted to an enormous collective holiday for millions of young men, who were fed and clothed at public expense whilst not engaged in productive labour. It is hard to deny, furthermore, that there is a degree of parallelism between the various mass youth organizations of the Nazi party, the organized collective activity of the military and the organized mass leisure activities of the KdF (Kraft durch Freude) . . . there can be very little doubt that rearmament in the 1930s was as much a popular spectacle as it was a drain on the German standard of living, a form in other words of spectacular public consumption . . . remarkable evidence collected by labour historians demonstrates the passionate identification that many German workers in the 1930s clearly felt with the weapons they were producing. . . . They were assertions of national strength, the common property of the German nation, to be handled by the pick of German manhood.'[17]

**SOURCE A**

A BIOGRAPHICAL ACCOUNT.

Hermann Goering has emerged from the bleak history of the Third Reich as a corrupt rather than an evil figure. . . . His greed . . . and incompetence contrast with the ascetic fanaticism of the other leading Nazi politicians. . . . He remains the political gangster; . . .

Yet this image of Goering, the cheerful if vicious booty-hunter, could not be further from the truth. While . . . Goering was flamboyant and conceited, and equally true that he profited unscrupulously and ruthlessly from the plundering of Europe's great museums and households, these are not what make him historically important. For most of the. . . . Third Reich, he was second only to Hitler in the Nazi movement and the state. He shared Hitler's ambitions and played a crucial role in the attempt to fulfil them. He was compelled to work closely with the . . . reality of German politics and strategy, thus forming an important bridge between Hitler and the wider political world of the Third Reich. . . . His contemporaries took him seriously enough. His brutality and lack of scruple earned for him the nickname 'der Eiserne', the 'Iron Man' . . .

He worked from a deep conviction that the course on which Hitler and Germany had embarked was the right one. . . . Goering's most important contribution came from his role in the economy and the waging of war. Goering was permitted a degree of autonomy in his leadership of the air force and in his capacity as overlord of the German economy between 1937 and 1942 enjoyed by few if any of Hitler's other subordinates. . . . During the period between 1936 and 1942 Goering not only controlled the Luftwaffe but intervened extensively in strategic and military matters as a whole. In the economy he gradually extended his power and authority . . . to embrace the whole structure of economic policy-making. He was charged by Hitler with the task of preparing the Germany economy for the Nazi's imperial ambitions. . . . Once war had broken out Goering continued to consolidate his authority in economic affairs while at the same time accepting Hitler's commission to organize the creation of the economy of the New Order in Europe . . .

The central role played by Goering during this period in the reorientation of the economy is worth emphasizing because Goering has often been characterized as the moderate in the Nazi party, a friend to big business and an opponent of radical change. . . . What all his many activities did amount to was the largest political and administrative empire controlled directly by any of Hitler's paladins.'

*Source*: R. J. Overy, *Goering: The Iron Man* (1984).

Extract from the memorandum for the Four-Year Plan.

The nation does not live for the economy, for economic leaders, or for economic or financial theories; on the contrary, it is finance and the economy, economic leaders and theories, which all owe unqualified service in this struggle for the self-assertion of our nation. Germany's economic situation is, however, in the briefest outline as follows:

> We are overpopulated and cannot feed ourselves from our own resources . . . Despite the difficult food situation, the most important task of our economic policy is to see to it that all Germans are incorporated into the economic process, and so the normal prerequisites for normal consumption are created. . . . The yield of our agricultural production can undergo no further substantial increase. It is equally impossible for us at present to manufacture artificially certain raw materials. . . . There is, however, no point in endless repetition of the fact that we lack foodstuffs and raw materials; what matters is the taking of those measures which can bring about a final solution for the future . . .

The final solution lies in extending our living space, that is to say, extending the sources of raw materials and foodstuffs of our people. It is the task of the political leadership one day to solve this problem. . . . It is, however, impossible to use foreign exchange allocated for the purchase of raw materials to import foodstuffs without inflicting a heavy and perhaps even fatal blow on the rest. But above all it is absolutely impossible to do this at the expense of national rearmament . . . war makes possible the mobilization of even the last remaining supplies of metal. For then it becomes not an economic problem, but solely a question of will . . .

In short, I consider it necessary that now, with iron determination, a 100 per cent self-sufficiency should be attained in every sphere where it is feasible, and that not only should the national requirements in these most essential raw materials be made independent of other countries, but we should also thus save the foreign exchange which in peacetime we need for our imports of foodstuffs. . . . Nearly four precious years have gone by. . . . There has been time enough in four years to find out what we cannot do. Now we have to carry out what we can do.

I thus set the following tasks;

    I.   The German armed forces must be operational within four years.
    II.  The German economy must be fit for war within four years.

Adolf Hitler, August 1936

*Source*: J. Noakes and G. Pridham (ed.), *Nazism 1919–1945: A Documentary Reader: Vol. 2: State, Economy and Society 1933–39* (1995).

GOERING READS OUT HITLER'S MEMORANDUM TO THE CABINET, 4 SEPTEMBER 1936.

The Colonel-General reads the memorandum of the Führer.

The Colonel-General is responsible for the execution of the tasks outlined in the memorandum. . . . Two basic principles:

1. We must strive with the greatest energy for autarky in all those spheres in which it is technically possible;
2. We have to tide over with foreign exchange all cases where it seems necessary for armaments and food.

All measures must be taken as if we were actually at the stage of imminent mobilization.

The execution of the order of the Führer is an absolute command.

*Source*: as source B.

DECREE ON THE EXECUTION OF THE FOUR YEAR PLAN, 18 OCTOBER 1936.

The realization of the new Four-Year Plan as proclaimed by me at the Party Congress of honour requires the uniform direction of all the powers of the German nation and the rigid consolidation of all pertinent authorities within Party and State.

I assign the execution of the Four-Year Plan to Minister-President General Göring.

Minister-President General Göring will take all the necessary measures for the fulfillment of the task given him, and in this respect he has authority to issue legal decrees and general administrative regulations. He is authorized to hear and to issue instructions to all authorities, including the Supreme Authorities of the Reich, and all agencies of the Party, its formations and affiliated organizations.

Adolf Hitler, October 1936

*Source*: as source B.

In the end, everything hung on Hitler. And Hitler clearly appreciated the importance of the moment. He was not in the habit of drafting policy statements and did so only at decisive moments in the history of his regime. The memorandum of August–September 1936 is remembered above all as an economic policy statement. Indeed, it is universally referred to as the 'Four Year Plan memorandum', providing Goering with the warrant for his new economic programme. But Hitler's statement has as much to say about grand strategy and armaments as it does about economics. . . . What was at stake was the future of the Third Reich . . .

Goering was given Hitler's formal authorization as general plenipotentiary for the Four Year Plan. . . . Goering was now established as the second man in the Reich, not only as head of the Luftwaffe and the entire Prussian administration, but also as the new supremo of economic policy.'

*Source*: Adam Tooze, *The Wages of Destruction: The Making and Breaking of the Nazi Economy* (2006).

Using the information in each of the sources and your own knowledge, explain the importance of Goering's contribution to the Nazi state.

## 9.10 law and order

One of the key platforms for the Nazi electoral machine was the theme of law and order and the accompanying call for a return to traditional values. The Weimar Republic was depicted as lawless and decadent while the Nazis habitually accused the Weimar prison service of being soft on criminals, providing inmates with ample food and even entertainment. Even after 1933, the Nazis remained dissatisfied with the role of the judiciary and the courts in dealing with sentencing. Reinhard Heydrich, second only to Himmler in the SS hierarchy, complained that the regular courts were continuing to pass sentences on 'enemies of the state' that were 'too low according to the normal popular feeling'.[18] In the tumultuous period of spring 1933 the change of attitude towards those convicted of crimes soon made itself felt. Whereas prison conditions had in fact been cramped and unpleasant during the Weimar period, this was replaced by a new regime of unparalleled violence. Those arrested in the first months of Nazi rule faced persistent beatings, whippings, deliberate attacks by prison dogs and even in some cases outright murder. New legislation, sweeping police powers and indiscriminate arrests meant that the population in all types of state prisons increased rapidly throughout 1933, until it reached a peak of 122,000 at the end of February 1937, compared to only 69,000 in 1927. Many of those imprisoned were accused of offences with a political or ideological slant and branded 'public enemies'. Approximately seventy concentration camps dealing mainly with left-wing politicians were set up in 1933. This wave of arrests and injustice subsided somewhat by 1934, although this did not prevent a centralization of control of such camps at the hands of Himmler and the SS, a process that accelerated after the bloody purge of June 1934. Ominous signs of future atrocities were reflected in a fresh wave of arrests in 1936 coordinated by Heydrich and aimed at beggars, tramps and travellers.

The introduction through the winter of 1937–38 of a system where every inmate had to wear an inverted triangle on the left breast of their striped prison uniform – black for an asocial, green for a professional criminal, blue for a returning Jewish emigrant, red for a political offender, violet for a Jehovah's Witness, pink for a homosexual – was also a sign of what was to come. Despite these disturbing developments there is ample evidence that Hitler was associated in the public mind with a general improvement in law and order, public safety and the treatment of criminals.

## 9.11 organized religion

### the Protestant Church

The Protestant Church and the Nazi regime shared some common ideological territory with their emphasis on anti-Marxism and support for authoritarianism. However, the Nazis abhorred the confessional division of Germany and in an obvious parallel to their policy of coordination in secular areas of politics, culture and society, many of them wanted a single national religion with a single national Church. For nationalist Protestants the enemy was Marxism. The Nazis capitalized on this. In 1933 they organized massive celebrations for the 450th anniversary of Martin Luther's birth, reworking his memory to convert him into a precursor of themselves. Pseudo-restorationist events, such as the Day of Potsdam in March 1993, deliberately held in the garrison church in order to underline the symbiosis of Protestant religion and Prussian tradition, exerted a strong influence on many Protestants. It was not surprising that there were serious moves to Nazify the Evangelical Church in 1933. Hitler seems to have had the ambition of converting it into a new kind of national Church and eventually winning over the mass of Catholics to the Nazi cause as well. The key role was to be played here by the 'German Christians', a pressure group organized by Nazi supporters among the clergy in May 1932. These moves brought to dominance Protestants whose declared aim since well before the Nazi seizure of power had been to oppose the 'Jewish mission in Germany'. On 13 November 1933, to mark their triumph within the Protestant Church, 20,000 German Christians assembled at the Sports Palace in Berlin demanded the sacking of all pastors who had not yet declared in favour of the new regime. Oppositional pastors soon began to organize in groups. Among them was Martin Niemoller. In September 1933, he set up the Pastors' Emergency League. Led by Bonhoeffer and Niemoller, the Emergency League won the allegiance of nearly 6,000 pastors by the end of 1933. Yet the Confessing Church never became a general centre of opposition. Niemoller's trial was a fiasco, and he was acquitted of all serious charges. Niemoller himself said that he was far from being a political opponent of the Nazis. He was immediately released. However, when Niemoller was freed on 2 March 1938, he found the Gestapo waiting for him at the prison gates. Hitler had personally ordered him to be rearrested. Niemoller was placed in solitary confinement in Sachsenhausen concentration camp. He came to regret the compromises he had made with the regime, as he said in this now famous lament:

> First they took the Communists, but I was not a Communist, so I said nothing. Then they took the Social Democrats, but I was not a Social Democrat, so I did nothing. Then it was the trade unionists' turn, but I was not a trade unionist. And then they took the Jews, but I was not a Jew, so I did little. Then when they came to take me, there was no one left who could have stood up for me.[19]

Despite Niemoller's despair, the Christian churches retained some independence and attempts to 'co-ordinate' the Protestant Church were eventually abandoned.

## the Catholic Church

As the political parties collapsed in the spring and early summer of 1933 it was the Catholic Centre Party that stood firm for the longest. By the end of June the struggle was almost over as the Centre Party was obliged to relinquish its links with the clergy since the Vatican, in its Concordat negotiations, had agreed that Catholic clergy must take no further part in political activities. The Catholic parties, the last independent political organizations in the whole of Germany, dissolved themselves. This was followed by a formal announcement on 14 July 1933 that the NSDAP was now the only legal political party in Germany. Despite this apparent lack of resistance the Nazis never attempted to destroy the organizational framework of the Catholic Church. The Nazis could not dissolve the institutional hold over the Catholic population inculcated by its youth groups, schools, festivals and traditions. During the period of Hitler's rise to power, relations between the Catholic Church and the Nazi Party were rather mixed. Reservations about the nature of Nazism expressed from the Catholic pulpit were numerous. Despite its Bavarian origins, the Party's bastions of support even in its early years had lain mainly in the Protestant stretches of northern Bavaria rather than in the overwhelmingly Catholic south. The Nazi vote remained low in Catholic areas, in contrast to the immense support forthcoming in Protestant regions. It was not until the election of March 1933 that the Nazis made truly significant inroads into the Catholic vote. This indication of coming to terms with Hitler may have influenced the Catholic bishops, following Hitler's promises to uphold the rights of the Catholic Church, to offer an endorsement to the new regime. In spite of the Concordat with the Papacy, ratified in summer 1933, it soon became clear that the fears about the threat to organized religion from Nazi ideology had considerable justification. The 'Church struggle', the campaign within the Church against the Nazis, reached its peak in 1936–37 and flared up again in 1941, confirming that the Catholic subculture would always be a relatively difficult area for the Nazis to penetrate.

## 9.12 sources : Church and State in Nazi Germany

SOURCE A

EXTRACT FROM GAULEITER REPORTS FOR JUNE 1943.

The war with all its sorrow and anguish has driven some families back into the arms of the Catholic Church.

The districts report that the churches of both confessional orientations are engaging in exceptionally heavy activity. In comparison to the party; the church today still has much manpower at its disposal.

In their weekly reports the party regional organizations have repeatedly emphasized that the churches of both confessions – but especially the Catholic Church – are in today's fateful struggle one of the main pillars of negative influence upon public morale.

## SOURCE B

The Gestapo report of December 1935 was even gloomier. Protestants were secretly circulating anti-Nazi writing. The Catholic Church was systematically and ceaselessly trying to make its followers anti-Nazi. The lower classes were ripe for recruitment by the workers underground. People were still shopping in Jewish stores. Former Conservatives were disgusted with the party. Thus there were many elements dissatisfied with the Third Reich in 1935, for almost as many different reasons as there were identifiable groups. And that is one of the major reasons disaffection was not likely to produce any organized opposition or cohesive action against the NSDAP.

*Source*: R. S. Allen, *The Nazi Seizure of Power* (1968).

## SOURCE C

THE CONCEPT OF POLITICAL RELIGION.

Neither Hitler nor Mussolini dispensed entirely with God as a source of ultimate validation for his political mission. However, political religions were emphatically 'this-worldly', partly to distinguish them from a supposedly obsolescent Christianity, whose values they sought to replace, whatever their tactical accommodations with the Churches. Nor did they function like religions, unless one equates the enthusiasm they encouraged with 'worshipping' a football team. Rather, they caricatured fundamental patterns of religious belief, in modern societies where sacralised collectivities, such as class, nation or race, had already supplanted God as objects of mass enthusiasm or veneration. The united nation, purged of all racial or political contaminants, and bereft of any external moral reference points, became a congregation of the faithful, with new 'leaders' who spoke with an emotional power . . .

Hitler was concerned that a full-blown religion might function independently of him , the sole source of all doctrinal authority, and that it might provoke the Christian churches to abandon support for a regime which, incredibly enough, they often believed was restoring authority and morality after the drift of the Weimar Republic. . . . But Hitler assimilated biological notions of degeneration and purification to religious narratives of perdition and redemption. . . . A mutant, racialised Christianity, divested of unGerman 'Jewish' elements, and purged of humanitarian sentimentality. . . . In this sense, Nazism was neither simply science run riot, however, much this definition suits critics of modern genetics, nor bastardised Christianity, however much this suits those who see

Nazism simply as the outgrowth of Christian anti-Semitism. It was a creative synthesis of both.

*Source*: Michael Burleigh, *The Third Reich: A New History* (2000).

## QUESTIONS

1 How significant was the role of organized religion in the Nazi state?
2 To what degree did organized religion present a limit to the extent of Hitler's personal authority?

## 9.13 the Nazi euthanasia programme

Although Hitler's publicly stated task was to 'defend the Nazi racial community', even those who reflected on the content of speeches such as this one from 1929 in which he complained that 'a sense of charity ensures that even cretins are able to procreate'[20] may have failed to anticipate the grim extent of Hitler's personal commitment to this ideological extreme. An indication that the Nazis would honour their commitment to the realization of a racial state came in July 1933 with the passage of the Sterilization Law, which introduced compulsory sterilization for so-called 'inferiors', that is, those who were 'mentally handicapped'.

Six years later, on the eve of war, Hitler gave personal authorization to the murder of children in a manner that was indicative of the haphazard nature of his personal rule when the KDF (Chancellery of the Führer) authorized the euthanasia of a severely handicapped child. This was in response to a parental request rather than through a traditional legislative channel. The murder took place in a Leipzig hospital in July 1939 and was followed by a systematic programme of child euthanasia, involving at least 5,200 murders, carried out at clinics such as the one at Egelfing-Haar near Munich. Great care was taken for this secret programme not to be associated with Hitler himself. Meanwhile, an order from Hitler issued in June–July 1939 instructed a senior medical official, Dr Conti, to organize a top-secret euthanasia programme for adults. This became known as T4, based on the postal address in Berlin of Department II of the Führer's Chancellery, which was at the centre of the euthanasia programme. In October 1939, on personal notepaper from Hitler's office, Hitler charged a medical team with 'responsibility to extend the powers of specific doctors in such a way that, after the most careful assessment of their condition, those suffering from illnesses deemed to be incurable may be granted a mercy death'.[21] This programme, with no basis in legislation or the law, resulted in the deaths of many thousands of people until it was interrupted in 1941. It is interesting to briefly examine the circumstances in which the programme was halted. During that year several members of the Church protested from the pulpit. Hitler was not prepared to face a critical association with this policy and he personally ordered it to be brought to an immediate conclusion. By this time, many thousands had died in special institutions, murdered with the use of gas. In the words of Peter Longerich: '"Euthanasia", or the programme of systematically murdering the inhabitants of institutions, displays remarkable parallels to the systematic murder of the European Jews from 1941/42 onwards. It is possible to see in the "euthanasia" programme a trial run, in the course of which the regime was collecting significant experience for the Endlosung or "final solution" that was to come.'[22]

## 9.14 consent and opposition

A superficial examination of a Nazi newsreel of 1935 or 1936 would indicate that when Hitler began to visibly reverse the economic ruination that had afflicted Germany since 1929, he started to occupy a place reserved for very few political leaders of the modern age. The news coverage would show a politician at the height of his considerable powers communicating through a surge of frenzied excitement and adrenalin with a people who responded as though they were in the presence of a mystical saviour. The carefully choreographed images, the impressive scale and grandeur and the impassioned oratory reached an audience who were shown to respond with genuine love and gratitude. The grateful middle classes, women in traditional costume, children incredulous at the sight of the Führer, young men reacting to a politician in a way that had seldom been seen, all of them seemed to have a uniquely emotional relationship with their political leader. Of course, the same piece of footage in the hands of a dispassionate historian could be looked at very differently. An alternative perspective would note the lies being told, the manipulation of the truth, the shameless and ruthless use of scapegoats such as the Jews, and perhaps most of all, the fact that any view other than the one presented by Hitler was now effectively illegal. So for every person shown smiling and waving, arm outstretched in the Hitler salute, there could be another citizen who had decided to keep their views secret. This raises a difficult issue for those examining the balance in the Third Reich between cooperation and consent and opposition and dissent. In a sense, it is the people missing from the newsreel that could tell us so much. In examining this area two concepts contained in the work of recent interpretations of this period are of particular importance.

### 'working along the lines the Führer would wish'

In constructing his immense, two-volume biographical study of Hitler, Professor Ian Kershaw came across a relatively routine document that helped to shed considerable light on the way in which those charged with implementing Hitler's wishes carried out their duties. A prominent Nazi declared in 1934 that in the Third Reich it was 'the duty of everybody to try to work towards the Führer along the lines he would wish'.[23] Fanatical followers of Hitler took this literally. In the case of the Third Reich, this could be taken to indicate that not only Hitler and the Nazi Party, but also the traditional power elites – able through the entente with Nazism to refurbish in some measure their own power base – profited from the loss of power of democratic institutions.

Professor Kershaw also offers a further concept that can help to develop our understanding of the nature of Hitler's personal rule through the work of the noted sociologist, Max Weber.

## 'charismatic rule'

Ian Kershaw states:

> A key to an understanding of the gradual expansion of Hitler's power can be found in a concept of Max Weber: that of 'charismatic rule'.[24] Charismatic authority' is founded upon the perceptions – by a 'following' of believers – of heroism, greatness, and a 'mission' in a proclaimed 'leader'. 'Charismatic rule' is inherently unstable. It tends to arise in crisis conditions. It seems clear that this form of rule in a modern state system could only be the product of the most severe crisis conditions imaginable.
>
> The 'charismatic community' comprised in the first instance those closest to the Hitler – the immediate 'following' among the Nazi leadership elite. Further crucial bearers and exploiters of Hitler's 'charisma' were the leaders and functionaries of those organisations – the most important of which was the SS – which owed their own existence and expansion of power to their close attachment to the Führer. Beyond them was the mass of 'Hitler believers' in the population at large, whose adulation provided Hitler with a platform of popularity which greatly strengthened his position of power.

## terror and repression

Terror and repression were highly selective in their application. Workers associated with left-wing parties were thrown into concentration camps in their thousands, especially during the initial onslaught of the new regime. Industrialists, landowners and bankers were left untouched. Police harassment was far more prevalent in working-class than middle-class areas of big cities. There was no assault on the farming and small property-holding population of the countryside. There was no army purge other than the actions connected with the removal of Blomberg and Fritsch in 1938 and the vengeful acts against those involved in the 1944 bomb plot. Generally, then, repression was aimed at the powerless and unpopular sections of society. Nor was repression a constant over time. After the early 'settling of scores' as tens of thousands of the political enemies of the Nazis were subjected to the frenzied retaliation of the Nazi hordes, there was a decline for some years in the levels of repression, reflected in the drop in the number of cases brought before the newly instituted 'special courts' and in the falling numbers of inmates in concentration camps. The numbers stated to rise again in the two years leading up to the outbreak of the war. The beginning of the war was accompanied by an extended range of offences and draconian punishment against anyone seeming to undermine or threaten the war effort. But the worst of the repression within Germany was now borne above all by racial 'undesirables' – especially Jews.

## consensus and coordination

The coercive force which lay behind Hitler's power is inseparable from the consensus in broad swathes of German society with much of what was happening in Hitler's name. Coercion and consent were two sides of the same coin – twin props of Hitler's power. In Germany, organizational forms of political opposition were destroyed within six months. The only major societal institutions other than the army which had not been 'coordinated' (or Nazified) – the Christian churches – had been pushed on to the defensive, adopting reactive and inward-looking stances in which political compromise went hand in hand with a tenacious struggle to fend off Nazi inroads where church practices and institutions were concerned. By mid-1934 a perceptive report from the exiled social democratic organization was pointing out that 'the weakness of the opposition is the strength of the regime'. Nazi opponents were ideologically and organizationally weak. Tortures, beatings and murders of countless political opponents took place in hastily devised prisons and camps run by the SA. On 20 March the Munich Police President Himmler announced the establishment of the first concentration camp near Dachau.

## the Gestapo

Recent research has called into question the notion of an all-powerful, ever-present, ruthlessly efficient Gestapo. In particular, two German historians, Klaus-Michael Mallmann and Gerhard Paul,[25] have shown that the Gestapo was not a 'thoroughly rationalized mechanism of repression . . . keeping the entire population under close surveillance' and that 'in quantitative terms alone, the Gestapo at the local level was hardly an imposing detective organisation, but much rather an under-staffed agency'. They cite the example of Düsseldorf, where, in 1937, the Gestapo district office of just 271 agents was responsible for a huge area containing 4 million people. The authors also point out that the problem of under-staffing became even more acute when the war broke out in 1939. Nazi terror was nowhere more apparent than in the emerging power and fearsome reputation of the Gestapo, and the organization attained an almost mythical status. The reality was very different. The Gestapo was relatively small, relying to a considerable extent on information and intelligence from the public. Some elements of denunciation were political. For example, people could be reported for telling a political joke that was at the expense of the regime. In addition, however, neighbours denounced noisy or unruly people living in the same building. Evans describes how every group of houses had a 'block warden', the popular name for a variety of officials on the lowest rung of the Nazi hierarchy whose task it was to ensure that everybody hung out bunting and Nazi flags on special occasions and went along to Nazi rallies and parades. The Gestapo was only one part of a much wider net of surveillance, terror and persecution, the criminal police, the prison service, the social services and employment offices, the medical profession, health centre and hospitals, the Hitler Youth, the block wardens and even apparently politically neutral organizations like tax offices, the railway and the post office added to the sense that this was a society under surveillance.

## organized opposition

| group | origins and nature | dates of activity | outcome |
|---|---|---|---|
| the Red Orchestra | A left-wing opposition movement formed by a young Luftwaffe pilot named Harro Schulze-Boysen. He joined forces with Arvid and Mildred Harnach. The organization was named the Rote Kapelle by the Gestapo | Boysen became a member of the Young German Order in 1932 but he was arrested in 1933. Upon his release he resumed his opposition activities and passed information to the Russians during the war | Boysen and other members of the Red Orchestra were arrested in 1942. Boysen was executed on 22 December 1942, with his wife, Libertas |
| swing groups | Formed amongst young people interested in American swing music. The movement spread across dance halls. The casual lifestyle of these youth groups constituted a low-level resistance to the Nazi state | Emerged towards the end of the 1930s and continued into the war | Gestapo reports suggest that concerns about 'decadent youths' lasted into the war years. Clearly many young people were not prepared to be regimented |
| Eidelweiss Pirates | Young people, mainly in urban areas, wearing badges portraying an eidelweiss (a small, white alpine plant) and distinctive clothes. This represented an alternative culture to | These groups developed in several cities in Western Germany in the late 1930s | These groups flourished during the war years and attracted adverse comment from Hitler Youth groups. Although some of the ringleaders were arrested and |

| | | | |
|---|---|---|---|
| | those alienated by the regimented nature of the Hitler Youth | | imprisoned, the Nazis were unable to subdue this aspect of youth culture |
| opposition within the military | These groups formed the most serious direct threat to Hitler. A conservative group formed around the former mayor of Leipzig, Carl Goerdeler, and Ludwig Beck, who resigned as army Chief of Staff in 1938 | This opposition stemmed from the conservative elite who had originally given their support to Hitler but who became increasingly concerned with his radical foreign and racial policies. Goerdeler was selected by the civilian–military resistance to replace Hitler as Chancellor if he could be removed | Following the failure of the July Plot, Goerdeler was arrested on 12 August 1944 after an extensive search. He was sentenced to death in September and executed on 2 February 1945 |
| the Kreisau Circle | Established by Count Helmuth James von Moltke, the group had a Christian and socialist philosophy | Secret meetings at Moltke's Kreisau estate began in 1940 | Moltke was arrested in 1944 and executed in 1945 |

### individual resistance to Hitler

| | |
|---|---|
| Hans and Sophie Scholl | Based at Munich University, these two students set up the White Rose resistance group. Gradually becoming more daring, they left out leaflets condemning the Nazi dictatorship and urging German youth to express their views. They were arrested and executed in February 1943. On the day of their execution, students at the university demonstrated their loyalty to Hitler. |
| Johan Elser | A member of the League of Red Front-Line Fighters, he decided to carry out a direct attempt on Hitler's life. On 8 November 1938 an explosive device killed eight people at a beer hall in Munich where Hitler had been speaking. He |

| | |
|---|---|
| | had already left the hall when the device went off. Elser was quickly arrested but was not murdered until 1945 |
| 'Beppo' Romer | A former Friekorps leader, he rallied together revolutionary militants from both the left and the right. Between 1942 and 1943 nearly 150 members of his group were tried and executed |
| Count Helmuth James von Moltke | A lawyer by training, he served in the Supreme Command of the Armed Forces when war broke out but had already formed a deep sense of abhorrence of the regime. From 1940 he began to convene secret opposition meetings at his Kreisau estate in Silesia. His links with other resistance groups led to his arrest on 9 January 1944. He was found guilty by the People's Court and executed in Plotzensee prison on 23 January 1945 |
| Dietrich Bonhoeffer | A Protestant theologian and Doctor of Philosophy, his profound personal convictions led in 1940 to him being banned from lecturing and publishing. He now moved from religious towards political resistance. He became a member of the German Resistance Movement but was arrested by the Gestapo on 5 April 1943. He was murdered in Flossenburg in April 1945 |

## the opposition parties

*The Social Democrats*

A small number of radical Social Democrats gathered since 1929 in a group that called itself New Beginning. Although some members, like the future historian Francis Carsten, tried to continue, waves of arrests by the Gestapo soon crippled the remnants of the movement

*The Communist Party (KPD)*

The reconstituted German Communist Party could do little more than its Social Democrat counterpart. There were a few isolated instances of sabotage and a handful of Communists tried to obtain military information. They held secret meetings, distributed illicit imported political propaganda, collected membership dues and produced and circulated crude mimeographed flysheets and newsletters. The newspaper *The Red Flag*, for instance, was edited in exile. The local organisers and many of the rank and file of the Communist resistance had spent too long fighting the Social Democrats to abandon their hatred now. Through careful information gathering, house searches, ruthless interrogation and torture of suspects and the use of spies and informants, the Gestapo had succeeded in destroying the organized resistance of the Communist Party by the end of 1934

From an early stage the regime turned to plebiscitary consultation of the masses as in the 'yes-or-no' vote held on 19 August 1934 to set the seal of popular approval on Hitler's personal appointment as Head of State. The polling booths had been removed, access to them was barred by brownshirts, or they were labelled 'Only traitors enter here'. Four years later, the regime had perfected its techniques of electoral terror and manipulation to the extent that it achieved a 'yes' vote of more than 99 per cent in the April 1938 plebiscite on the union with Austria, which was coupled with a personal vote of confidence in Hitler and his actions to date. People who refused to vote, or threatened to vote 'no' were beaten up, forced to parade through the streets with a placard round their neck or consigned unceremoniously to lunatic asylums.

For most Germans, Nazi terror rapidly evolved from a reality, as it was in the near-universal violence of the first half of 1933, into a threat that was seldom translated into action. By the end of 1935 organized opposition had been completely crushed. The 'Night of the Long Knives' was also a lesson to dissenters within the Nazi movement. But from 1936 onwards, overt terror was directed increasingly against relatively small minorities such as persistent or committed Communists and Social Democrats, the asocial and work-shy, petty criminals, Jews and homosexuals. For the vast majority threat of arrest, imprisonment and concentration camp receded into the background. More general still were measures such as the Law on Malicious Gossip, which clamped down on the most trivial expressions of dissent and put people who told jokes about Hitler and Goering in prison.

## 9.15 sources: how popular was Hitler as the leader of Germany?

### SOURCE A

FROM AN OFFICIAL ACCOUNT OF THE MAKING OF A WEEKLY NEWSREEL, ON THE FÜHRER'S BIRTHDAY, 1939.

The Führer's fiftieth birthday. Berlin puts on its finery, makes the last preparations for this twentieth of April 1939, which is to become a unique day of thanks giving. The Filmwochenschau has a specific assignment in this . . . it must create an historic document for the future, to capture in pictures the greatness of this day. . . . Under a bright shining sky the birthday itself begins. Cheerful marching tunes resound . . . Hitler receives the homage. . . . A gigantic crowd in front of the Reich Chancellor swells in a song of jubilation for Hitler. Now Hitler appears on the balcony before the crowd, which breaks out into a repeated ovation.

Source: J. Noakes and G. Pridham (ed.), *Nazism 1919–1945: A Documentary Reader: Vol. 2: State, Economy and Society 1933–39* (1995).

THE VERDICT OF AN HISTORIAN.

Although the regime deployed a formidable apparatus of terror, it is clear that it was also based on a large measure of consent from broad sections of the population. The fact that Hitler was associated with the solving of the unemployment problem and with the restoration of Germany's position as a European power appeared to many to confirm the message of Goebbel's propaganda . . .

A crucial element in popular consent to the regime was the fact that Nazism embodied, albeit in an extreme form, many of the basic attitudes of a very large section of the German people. .-. . Such people approved of the regime's hostility towards unpopular minorities, not just Jews but also gypsies, and of its harsh attitude towards deviant groups – homosexuals, tramps, habitual criminals, the so-called asocials and 'workshy'. They welcomed the fact that such people were now being locked up in concentration camps.

*Source*: as source A.

**SOURCE C**

FROM A REPORT OF THE SOPADE, THE GERMAN SPD PARTY IN EXILE, 1938.

Among industrial workers there are many who do not give a damn about the successes of the Hitler system and have only scorn and contempt for the whole show. Others, however, say 'Well, there are a lot of things Adolf does not know about.' But one is never quite sure with them whether they mean it seriously or only want to protect their backs. Naturally, there are many who have become unpolitical. The further one goes down into the poorer sections the more opposition there is. But even now – although they know there is a labour shortage – they are all scared of losing their jobs. The years of unemployment have not been forgotten.

Those who are still Nazis in this factory are subdued. One has the feeling that many of them stay in the Party to get an easier life. If discussions occur they usually give in or do not get involved.

**SOURCE D**

The shift in the mood of the population, the dropping morale which began to be felt throughout Germany in 1939, was evident in the necessity to organise cheering crowds where two years earlier Hitler had been able to count on spontaneity. What is more, he himself had moved away from the admiring masses. He tended to be angry and impatient more often than in the past, when as still occasionally happened, a crowd on Wilhelmsplatz began clamouring for him to appear. Two years before, he would have stepped out on the historic balcony. Now he sometimes snapped at his adjutants when they came to him with a request that he show himself, 'stop bothering me with that'.

*Source*: Albert Speer, *Inside the Third Reich* (2005).

To most observers, both internal and external, after four years in power the Hitler regime looked stable, strong and successful. Hitler's own position was untouchable. The image of the great statesman and national leader of genius, manufactured by propaganda, matched the sentiment and expectations of much of the population. The internal rebuilding of the country and the national triumphs in foreign policy, all attributed to his genius, had made him the most popular political leader of any nation in Europe. Most ordinary Germans – like most ordinary people anywhere most times – looked forward to peace and prosperity. Hitler appeared to have established the basis of these.

*Source*: Ian Kershaw, *Hitler 1936–1945* (2000).

The longer the regime lasted, the less people believed its slogans about the new solidarity of the 'works community' and the 'national community'. Workers' disapproval and criticism related primarily to practical everyday matters, and to the social achievements and failures of the regime. The personal figure of Hitler, as SOPADE reports confirm, was largely exempt from criticism. When analysing the popular mood in general, the fact that people's high regard for the figure of the 'Leader' was unaffected by the general 'grumbling' can be taken as an indication of a certain basic consent to the regime, or at least of a passive adjustment to a situation which could not be changed.

The less the Volksgemeinschaft propaganda matched the everyday reality of workers' lives, the greater became the mockery, and even contempt, directed by workers at the relatively small number of their fellows who paraded their zeal in the Nazi organisations or tried to contrive their own personal advancement at the expense of their colleagues. Miners in the Ruhr divided the wearers of brown shirts into 'poor sods' and 'brutal sods'.

*Source*: D. J. K. Peukert, *Inside Nazi Germany: Conformity, Opposition and Racism in Everyday Life* (1989).

Frustration and disappointment with the realities of everyday life under National Socialism led ordinary Germans to grumble and complain, but seldom to engage in behaviour that can be appropriately termed 'resistance'. Why? Organised terror played a central role. But the most important mechanism promoting unity and social integration in Nazi Germany was Hitler's charismatic leadership. The 'Hitler myth' secured the loyalty to the regime even of those who opposed the Nazi movement.

*Source*: Ian Kershaw, *The Hitler Myth: Image and Reality* (1994).

## QUESTIONS

1 What difficulties are faced by an historian in attempting to assess the popularity of the Nazis?

2 Can you find any genuine evidence here either of Hitler's personal popularity or of successful party policies which may have won popularity for the Nazis?

## 9.16 sources: Hitler's personal role in the Third Reich

**SOURCE A**

Locating Hitler's role and function within the Nazi system of rule is less straightforward than initially it may seem. Indeed, it has become a central problem of interpretation in a debate between leading historians of the Third Reich. . . . Above all, the moral issue – the feeling that the evil of the central figure of the Third Reich is not being adequately portrayed, that Hitler was underestimated by contemporaries and is now being trivialized by some historians – lies at the root of the conflict and determines the character of the debate.

*Source*: Ian Kershaw, *The Nazi Dictatorship: Problems and Perspectives of Interpretation* (1985).

**SOURCE B**

It might be argued that Hitler was 'weak' in the sense that he regularly shirked making decisions, and was compelled to do so in order to protect his own image and prestige, dependent upon the Führer remaining outside factional policies and unassociated with mistakes or unpopular decisions. This would mean that the chaotic centrifugal tendencies in the Third Reich were 'structurally' conditioned and not simply or mainly a consequence of Hitler's ideological or personal predilections, or of a Machiavellian 'divide and rule' strategy.

*Source*: as source A.

**SOURCE C**

The point cannot be stressed too strongly, Hitler was master in the Third Reich.

*Source*: N. Rich, *Hitler's War Aims* (1980).

**SOURCE D**

Unwilling to take decisions, frequently uncertain, exclusively concerned with upholding his personal prestige and personal authority, influenced in the strongest fashion by his current entourage, in some respects a weak dictator.

*Source*: H. Mommsen, *National Socialism: Continuity and Change* (1979).

**SOURCE E**

There is, in fact, abundant evidence that the smack of firm government was conspicuously absent from the chancellery. . . . For the first year or so, as long as Hindenburg was alive, Hitler conformed to the irksome restriction of regular office hours. Very soon after the old man's death the pattern of decision-making at the level of Führer and Chancellor became disorderly and somewhat haphazard as the business of state started to revolve around the erratic personal habits of the dictator. . . . If lucky enough to catch the Führer, callers often had to conduct business either walking alongside him on his way to lunch, or buttonhole him in some corner where he was surrounded by members of his immediate entourage. Pressed for decisions on matters which the suitors thought urgent, Hitler often displayed a marked aversion to clear concise orders . . . he took refuge behind open-ended generalities or even evaded a decision completely.

*Source*: William Carr, *Hitler: A Study in Personality and Politics* (1978).

## SOURCE F

We can begin by accepting unequivocally the unique place of Hitler in the course of German history between 1933 and 1945.Would a terroristic police state under Himmler and the SS have been erected without Hitler as head of government? Would Germany have been engaged in general war by the end of the 1930s under a different form of authoritarian regime? Would discrimination against Jews have culminated in genocide under a different head of state? In each case, it seems highly improbable. Hitler, one can then suggest at the outset, was crucial to these developments.

*Source*: Ian Kershaw, *Hitler: Profiles in Power* (1991).

## ESSAY QUESTION

Hitler: master of the Third Reich or weak dictator? Use the views of the historians shown here to explain which interpretation you feel is most accurate.

# anti-semitism, 1933–39

## 10.1 the context of the Jewish people in German society and the impact of 1933

When Hitler became Chancellor on 30 January 1933 the Jewish population of Germany stood at approximately 525,000, which amounted to 0.7 per cent of the total. This community played a rich and important role in the cultural, academic, economic and sporting life of the nation. Yet within six years the Jewish people had been pushed to the edge of the abyss. Jewish financial assets calculated at approximately twelve billion Reichsmarks in 1933 had been halved by the start of 1938. By 1939 approximately 75 per cent of Jewish-owned businesses had closed down. More than 400 laws specifically designed to isolate and humiliate German Jews were enacted between 1933 and 1939. The rich contribution of Jews to German cultural life and scientific discourse was systematically removed. Within the first five years of Nazi rule almost 130,000 Jews had emigrated from Germany. In 1939 a further 78,000 Jews left Germany. Those who remained were completely isolated. In the same period the remainder of the German population was subjected to an intensive propaganda campaign which further diminished the standing of Jews in German society. Vicious attacks on the Jews were waged by the government's formidable propaganda machine. Virulent publications such as *Der Angriff* and the feverish activities of extremists such as Julius Streicher intensified the anti-Semitic climate, but may well have offended and disturbed those with more moderate sensibilities. It is likely that the regime's simultaneous emphasis on moral regeneration and a return to traditional values which was designed to highlight the superiority of German culture was more significant in capturing the hearts and minds of middle-class Germans than radical anti-Semitism. The propaganda drive was maintained in the workplace, where great emphasis was placed on notions of 'German quality work', 'the honour of labour' and a 'factory community'. In the wider community the German historian Detlev Peukert has shown that there was broad support for the strong imposition of law and order, creating a climate in which bicycles could be left unattended and the 'work-shy' were made to work.[1] Yet this was also a climate that isolated the Jews and a culture in which the Jewish people could no longer expect protection from the police and the state.

More broadly, the emphasis on inclusion in the *Volksgemeinschaft* (National Community) can only have increased the growing sense of isolation felt by the Jewish community. In the words of Norbert Frei, 'People experienced the breakneck speed of the economic and foreign resurgence of Germany as a sort of frenzy ... with astonishing rapidity, many identified themselves with the social will to construct a *Volksgemeinschaft* that kept any thoughtful or critical stance at arm's length.'[2]

These movements served to condition the minds and behaviour of large sections of the community. It could be argued that a simultaneous psychological effect was a reduction in the likelihood of any type of opposition to the mounting isolation of the Jews. Recent research has revealed very little active resistance to the government's anti-Semitic programme and has identified a pattern of 'passive complicity'. Dissent, where it occurred, was on a minor scale and tended to focus on pragmatic economic concerns or to stem from religious-ideological objections. As the general climate of support for, or acceptance of the government's policies developed (later boosted further by foreign policy successes) and Hitler's charismatic rule became more pronounced, those within the regime who wanted to harm the Jews would have appreciated the mounting possibilities for a radicalization of their policies.

## 10.2 intentionalists and functionalists

Historians have been divided on central issues concerning Hitler's policies towards the Jews. Some historians – a group which for a time came to be labelled as intentionalists – have argued that Hitler always intended to take action against the Jews at the earliest possible opportunity. They see a fairly straight and unswerving line connecting Hitler's formative anti-Semitic period in Vienna (a period which is now subject to renewed scrutiny), his desire for revenge when he was traumatized in a gas attack in 1918 and the details of his anti-Semitic philosophy in *Mein Kampf*. This continuity was maintained through the systematic anti-Jewish legislation of 1933–39, the atrocities perpetrated in Poland from September 1939 and the inhumanity of the Holocaust in Eastern Europe following the invasion of the Soviet Union in 1941. In this scenario, Hitler was at the centre, dictating the timing of the systematic campaign against the Jews, approving the finer detail of concerted legislation and personally authorizing the unthinkable when the time was right. Amongst his followers Hitler tended to present himself as a visionary of unswerving conviction. This characteristic seemed to support the notion prevalent in initial studies that Hitler had led his followers in implementing a 'master plan' against European Jewry. This moved inexorably from the campaign against Jewish business and culture in the first months of 1933 to the wartime catastrophe in the death camps of Poland. The enormity of the Holocaust led many to believe that the attempted destruction of the Jewish race had been carefully planned and systematically executed.

More recently, however, historians have moved a considerable distance from this position. A group of historians who were termed functionalists saw the evolution of Hitler's anti-Semitic policy as relatively haphazard. They argued that when Hitler became Chancellor he did not yet have a clear plan as to what to do about the Jews. Hitler's personal indecision, the diverse factions within the party, the constraints of public opinion and pressing economic concerns all went against the notion of a clear plan being carried out based on clarity of direction and firm policy decisions.

## 10.3  Hitler's anti-Semitism

Ian Kershaw states that Hitler's personal desire to destroy the Jews was his central political idea after 1919.[3] Hatred of the Jews became his obsession, a driving force that he found difficult to suppress. Hitler's racial views were fixed but the route to implementing his policy was 'uncharted'. In the early stages of his political career, when Hitler sensed that his evolving ideology was supported by external social tendencies of anti-Semitism, racism, fervent anti-Marxism, eugenics and pseudo-scientific-biological theory, he was willing to express his hatred of the Jews in the most extreme language. Detailed analysis of Hitler's speeches from 1927 to 1931 reveals that at a critical time in the development of the National Socialist party he remained willing to exploit racial issues on a regular basis. However, when Hitler became Chancellor the constraints he faced were substantial and Hitler was capable in this context of restraining his inner hatred of the Jews for the time being.

Although Hitler's own degree of anti-Semitism is not in doubt, there is still a considerable range of opinion as to the precise nature of his role in leading this aspect of government policy in the period 1933–39. Clearly, Hitler's assumption of power marked a critical turning point in the position of the Jews. Kershaw notes that Hitler's appointment as Chancellor led directly to the 'astonishingly swift jettisoning of constraints on inhumane behaviour whose path ended in Auschwitz'.[4] Definitive judgements on the personal role of Hitler in the development of anti-Semitic policies remain difficult, but the idea of a straight line between 1933 and 1945 has been significantly undermined.

In the words of Saul Friedlander: 'The anti-Jewish policies of the thirties must be understood in their context, and even Hitler's murderous rage and his scanning of the political horizon for the most extreme options do not suggest the existence of any plans for total extermination in the years prior to the German invasion of the Soviet Union. But at the same time, no historian can forget the end of the road.'[5]

## 10.4  Hitler in power, 1933

It is clear that Hitler's appointment to high office by no means placed him in the position of being an outright dictator. As a consequence of this political reality Hitler refrained from expressing his obsession with the Jewish race in any major public statement during 1933. Perhaps, in the words of his biographer Joachim Fest, Hitler was 'displaying his capacity for restraint'.[6] When Hitler became Chancellor in January 1933 there seems to have been no immediate sense of panic or urgency among the majority of the 525,000 Jews in Germany. However, the political landscape was rapidly changing and in the aftermath of the Reichstag Fire and Hitler's further success in the election of March 1933 a series of violent anti-Semitic incidents took place across the country. At this stage the initiative appeared to stem largely from below. Radical elements within the Nazi Party were very willing to take physical action against the Jews. In Bavaria, a Jewish man was abducted and killed. In Breslau Jewish lawyers and judges were beaten. In Cologne, Jews were now banned from using municipal sports facilities. Concerted pressure was exerted to restrict the contribution of Jews in the cultural domain. In Dresden, the prestigious Opera House dismissed its musical director on the grounds that he had too many Jewish contacts.

These events took place without public comment from Hitler. At this critical stage in his political development he was able to appear as a man of moderation, holding back the more radical elements within his own party. Not for the last time Hitler was, to some extent, torn between his own seething hatred of the Jews and desire for radical action on the one hand, and the need for tactical restraint on the other. Certainly at this stage opportunities for further measures seemed limited and the constraints faced by Hitler were substantial. Internal priorities, the fact that economic recovery was all-important, conservative officials in key posts, the sensitivities of diplomatic relations, all served to limit Hitler's freedom for manoeuvre. Hitler now demonstrated his willingness to avoid or tone down public attacks on Jews purely for tactical reasons. Hitler was helped in this stance by the fact that ordinary people perpetrated so many of the early anti-Semitic actions.

## 10.5 the boycott of Jewish shops, 1 April 1933

There is clear evidence to suggest that Hitler's surprisingly restrained approach towards the Jews caused some disquiet amongst the more radical element within the party. Towards the end of March 1933 the party press was calling for a boycott of Jewish shops, doctors and lawyers. Closer analysis of this initiative has revealed the role of radical factions within the SA and influential individuals such as party propagandist Josef Goebbels, the jurist Roland Freisler and the virulent anti-Semite Julius Streicher. It is possible that these disparate forces urged a somewhat hesitant Hitler to begin to implement the type of radical measures he had spoken so freely about in his pre-Chancellery days. An alternative perspective would be that a cautious Hitler preferred an institutionalized approach to the Jews to the spontaneity which had gone before and which was in danger of getting out of control. At any rate, on March 29 Hitler informed his cabinet of the impending boycott and said that he himself had called for it. However, the nationwide boycott of 1 April was called off after one day in the face of a generally apathetic public reaction and even some expressions of loyalty towards Jewish businesses. Hitler now recognized that the boycott was incompatible with the more pressing need for economic recovery. Consequently on 7 July Rudolf Hess informed his colleagues that further boycotts of Jewish department stores would not be allowed. A week later, at a cabinet-level meeting, and with Hitler present, it was agreed that contracts would not be automatically withheld from Jewish firms. However, on the same day in July an ominous sign of what was to come was signalled by the adoption of the Law for the Prevention of Genetically Diseased Offspring. The eugenic ideology which underpinned this measure was of direct relevance to the future position of the Jews.

Meanwhile, despite the setback of 1 April the momentum against the Jews was sustained in other areas. It is interesting to note that the initiative in these cases seems to have stemmed from the ranks of officialdom. Ian Kershaw has given considerable importance to the notion that during this period many Germans found motivation from the idea that they were 'working towards the Führer along the lines he would wish'.[7] Perhaps it was this type of thinking that was involved in the initiatives which developed in the spring of 1933.

Within a week of the failed boycott, the Law for the Restoration of the Professional Civil Service based on detailed legislation drawn up by Wilhelm Frick excluded Jews and other political opponents from that area of public life. Against a backdrop of violent attacks against Jewish judges, lawyers and jurists, Hitler also agreed to a decree which restricted Jews from practising law. In this case the initiative appeared to stem from the state secretary at the Ministry of Justice. Before the month was out a 'Law Against the Overcrowding of German Schools' restricted the number of Jewish students allowed to enter German schools. The sheer scale and breadth of legislation is reflected in the fact that further measures were also passed restricting Jewish involvement in areas such as agriculture, the press and academic life.

The extent to which the climate was changing was reflected on 10 May when 20,000 books by 'degenerate' authors were thrown on a bonfire in front of the Opera House in Berlin. The sight of university students enthusiastically burning books was just one disturbing aspect of this spectacle. It is important to note, as Martin Gilbert points out, that 'the burning of books and the killing of individuals went on side by side . . . in the last two weeks of May, four Jews were murdered'.[8]

## 10.6 the nature of the racial society

Writing in 1978, William Carr compared the Nazi state to a 'feudal society, where vassals great and small struggled endlessly with each other and with their overlords to establish themselves as the king's chief adviser. The administrative structure of Nazi Germany formed a complex mosaic of party and state agencies with ill-defined and overlapping jurisdictions, sometimes complementing each other, more often mutually antagonistic.'[9] While this analogy remains helpful,

Saul Friedlander argues that this bureaucratic emphasis has been taken too far. He states that 'Nazism was not driven by the chaotic clash of competing bureaucratic and party fiefdoms.'[10] Friedlander contends that this focus on the somewhat chaotic administrative structure can obscure the all-important fact that 'in all its major decisions the regime depended on Hitler. Especially with regard to the Jews, Hitler was driven by ideological obsessions that were anything but the calculated devices of a demagogue; that is, he carried a very specific brand of racial anti-Semitism to its most extreme and racial limits.'[11] Friedlander portrays Hitler's ideological viewpoint as 'redemptive anti-Semitism'. He sees Hitler as a leader brimming with 'murderous rage' and with an 'idealistic goal'.[12]

With this in mind, it could be argued that administrative structures counted for a lot less than the driving force of Hitler's personal obsession. The fact remains that by the autumn of 1933 the position of the Jews had already deteriorated to a significant extent. The role of ordinary people in creating a climate of intolerance is reflected in the fact that signs now began to appear across the country in towns, villages and at public amenities saying 'Jews are not welcome here'. In some cases the names of Jewish soldiers who had served for Germany in the First World War were now ostentatiously removed from war memorials. This type of 'visual instruction' was of immense symbolic and psychological importance in conditioning people for what was to follow. With measures of this type in mind it is worth considering the words of Avraham Barkai, who has written that 'without the prior depravation, ostracism and institutionalized plunder of the German Jews – in full view and with the increasing approval and complicity of millions of Germans – the Final Solution would not have been possible'.[13]

Further legislation in 1934 included a ban on Jewish actors performing on stage in March, Jewish students being forbidden from taking law examinations in July and a ban on the public sale of Jewish newspapers in October. Nevertheless, the period between the end of 1933 and the spring of 1935 saw a relative lull in the intensity of anti-Semitic measures. A sign that this was a purely temporary respite came with a dramatic extension of anti-Semitic legislation in the summer of 1935.

## 10.7 the Nuremberg Laws, 1935

Although Hitler's personal power was significantly greater by 1935 than when he had first entered the Chancellery he remained, in some respects, a cautious figure still subject to a range of awkward constraints. One difficulty for him was the incompatibility of the all-important need for economic recovery with a fresh outbreak of anti-Jewish outrages. He was acutely aware, for example, that ugly scenes of anti-Jewish violence on the streets of Munich in May 1935 and in Berlin in July had disturbed rather than impressed many onlookers both at home and overseas. It was plain to see that while violent outbursts pleased the party radicals they were not welcomed by the general public who, above all, had supported Hitler's promises of a stable economy and a return to law and order. The potential for damaging Germany's image and commerce abroad was obvious. While Goebbels, more than anyone else in Hitler's immediate entourage, was urging the Führer to take further action against the Jews, Hitler remained conscious of the delicate nature of the economic recovery and was reluctant to damage the contribution made by Jewish firms to important export markets. Essentially, Hitler's leadership at this time corresponded to the context described by Friedlander of a tension between 'the revolutionary-charismatic impulse of Nazism and the authoritarian conservative tendencies of the pre-1933 German state'.[14] This was the background against which the Nuremberg Laws were unveiled.

On the face of it, Hitler's personal initiative in the production of the notorious anti-Semitic legislation known as the Nuremberg Laws was clear-cut. In the middle of the massive party rally in September 1935, without consulting anyone else, he ordered Bernhard Losener – a civil servant in the Ministry of the Interior – to come to Nuremberg and receive his orders. The urgent brief was to draw up a new package of anti-Semitic laws in time for Hitler to present them for ratification at a specially convened Reichstag session on the last day of the party rally on 15 September. Four draft laws were presented to Hitler who, still anxious to present himself as a moderate, opted for the least severe one. The hasty and haphazard manner in which the legislation was being produced is indicated by the fact that the finishing touches to the legislation were drawn up on the back of a menu at 2.00 a.m. on the morning of 15 September. Later that morning Hitler took a pencil to the draft Law for the Protection of German Blood and struck out the moderating clause 'This law is only valid for full Jews'. As usual, Hitler's ability to present himself as a man of moderation while satisfying his gut feelings of anti-Semitism was remarkable.

It is important to recognize that many other factors played a part in these developments and Hitler's personal role should be placed in context. For example, there is no doubt that the party rank and file were desperate for Hitler to resume the initiative against the Jews. Secondly, other individuals like Goebbels and Wagner were pressing for action. Crucially, Hitler was determined to stave off pressure for a 'Jew-free economy', but realized that this would make him vulnerable to criticism; he was therefore eager to present his racial laws as an acceptable and less damaging initiative. Hitler had got what he wanted and boosted his own position with the party faithful.

American historian Eric Johnson states that the new laws 'greatly increased the Jews' legal vulnerability and social isolation. . . . The increased bureaucratization of Jewish affairs enabled the Nazi regime to press ahead with the persecution of Jews with more discretion as well as with more precision.'[15] The apparently hasty manner in which the legislation was drawn up has meant that debate remains as to whether the Nuremberg Laws were the product of a coherent plan or a haphazard decision. Were the laws the result of an impulsive attempt by Hitler to placate radicals within the party? Perhaps a further factor may have been Hitler's desire to provide his adoring followers at the Nuremberg rally with an element of legislative substance and an assurance that the radical instincts of old had not been completely extinguished by the responsibilities of high office. Was Hitler's intervention purely designed to make life more difficult for the Jews, or was it a desire for compromise aimed at showing the party that anti-Jewish measures would be taken when the time was right? At any rate, on 15 September Hitler recommended three new laws to the Reichstag. It was the first time since he had become Chancellor that he had devoted a major address to the 'Jewish Question'.

It is now clear that as early as July 1933 a committee in the Ministry of the Interior had been instructed to begin drafting proposals for legislation to exclude the Jews from full citizenship rights. However, it seems that the new wave of anti-Semitic action from below which marked the summer of 1935 prompted Hitler to act 'legally' against the Jews as a way of defusing the situation on the streets of some of Germany's most important cities.

## 10.8  the Berlin Olympics of 1936

The extensive Nazi preparations for the Winter Olympics at Garmisch-Partenkirchen in February 1936 and the Olympic Games staged in Berlin in August 1936 illustrate Hitler's capacity for self-control. The need to present a positive image and the sensitivities of foreign policy meant that the regime was unable to risk the adverse publicity which anti-Semitic scenes would attract. Hitler personally ordered the removal of the anti-Jewish signs that had been placed at the entrance to so many towns and villages. The games were a great success in political and propaganda terms and also on the track and field, where German athletes won more medals than any other country. This reinforcement of German superiority was noted by the Jewish academic Victor Klemperer, who observed in his diary how 'It's incessantly drummed into the people and foreigners that here you can see the revival, the blossoming, the new spirit . . . of the Third Reich lovingly embracing the whole world.'[16] In the words of Deborah E. Lipstadt, 'Tourists and visiting reporters – there were over 1,500 of the latter at the Games – were so impressed by what they saw that many dismissed the stories of brutalities as exaggerated.'[17]

## 10.9  autumn 1936 to autumn 1938

The two-year period following the Olympic Games has often been depicted as a time when the momentum against the Jews slowed down until the sudden, disturbing eruption of the 'Night of Broken Glass' of November 1938. With Hitler's attention drawn increasingly to matters of foreign policy, key government posts still, for a time, in the hands of men with a conservative disposition and with lack of overt action against the Jews, it has been assumed that this was a period of relative respite for the Jews. However, it may be more accurate to see this period as a time when Hitler's key ideological principles in foreign policy and anti-Semitism came to overlap more closely than ever before.

Ultimately, it was precisely Hitler's preoccupation with foreign policy which would provide the context for genocide. As Goering stated at a meeting in the Air Ministry on 12 November 1938, 'If the German Reich comes into foreign-political conflict in the foreseeable future, it can be taken for granted that we in Germany will think in the first instance of bringing about a great showdown with the Jews.'[18]

As Ian Kershaw explains: 'For Hitler . . . the connection between the war he knew was coming and the destruction of Europe's Jews was beginning to take concrete shape.'[19] While the darkening international scene was disturbing in itself, recent findings have indicated that, far from being distracted, the appropriate authorities remained focused on exploiting opportunities for persecuting the Jews. In his recent book, *Nazi Terror, The Gestapo, Jews and Ordinary Germans*, Eric Johnson contends that action against the Jews in the period 1936–38 may have been less high-profile than between 1933 and 1935 but was nevertheless intense. He states:

> If there was something of a lull in outwardly extremist acts against the Jews after the passage of Nuremberg Laws in the fall of 1935, it did not mean that Germany had returned to its senses. . . . The persecution of the Jews was merely carried on more quietly in the next few years. . . . Evidence from the . . . Gestapo case files, in fact, suggests that the pace of persecution picked up. . . . The civilian population became more active in their initiation, perhaps suggesting that there was no real decline in popular anti-Semitic sentiment as some have maintained.[20]

Saul Friedlander also supports the notion that this period was very damaging for the Jews. He observes that 'the liquidation of the Jewish economic life in Nazi Germany had started at an accelerated pace in 1936, and by late 1937, with the elimination of all conservative influence, the enforced Aryanization drive had become the main thrust of the anti-Jewish policies, mainly in order to compel the Jews to emigrate'.[21] The staging in November 1937 of 'The Eternal Jew', a massive anti-Semitic exhibition at the Deutsches Museum in Munich, adds further weight to the argument that this period was not in real sense a lull in the campaign against the German Jews.

A further factor in a hastening the deteriorating situation came with the Anschluss of March 1938. The persecution of Jews in Austria in general and in Vienna in particular plumbed new depths and was more open and vicious than anything that had happened in Germany. This 'Austrian model' may have encouraged the Nazi hierarchy to take more drastic measures against the Jews in the future. In fact, 1938 had seen several serious acts of anti-Semitic violence in Germany long before the disturbing events of November. Incidents of street violence in the spring were followed by an arson attack on a synagogue in Munich in June and a similar incident in Nuremberg in August.

Meanwhile, German historians Klaus-Michael Mallman and Gerhard Paul have explored a further interesting avenue of research in this area. Their work on Gestapo archives has led them to question the 'omniscient, omnipotent, omnipresent' nature of the secret police. They claim that the 'aura of a perfectly operating secret police was preeminently an image created by means of propaganda … thereby furnishing the Gestapo with the aura of the most extreme criminological efficiency, which constituted a not insignificant part of its effectiveness, even though it was fictional'.[22]

## 10.10 Reichskristallnacht, 9–10 November 1938

The awful scenario envisaged by Hitler in his virulent comments of 1935 came near to fruition in the winter of 1938 when the position of the Jews deteriorated dramatically. Closer examination of the circumstances does not reveal a picture of a carefully controlled programme instigated by Hitler. Indeed, in the autumn of 1938 he was completely preoccupied with problems of foreign policy and went to the trouble of reminding the party that further anti-Semitic initiative would be unwelcome. However, a series of chance factors came together so that the plight of the Jews worsened in spite of the Führer's intentions.

In the autumn of 1938, Josef Goebbels – party propaganda chief and virulent anti-Semite – was desperate to restore his position of favour with the Führer. Hitler had made it clear that he thoroughly disapproved of Goebbels's well-publicised affair with a famous actress. The chance Goebbels was waiting for presented itself when a German diplomat in Paris was murdered by a Jewish youth. Goebbels ensured that the party press gave massive coverage to the 'Jewish outrage' and waited for Hitler's enthusiastic response. In a major speech the next day, Hitler did not even mention the incident. Goebbels dashed to Munich and urged Hitler to give his seal of approval to a 'spontaneous' reprisal. Hitler told Goebbels that 'the SA should be allowed its last fling' and the awful reprisals began.

In 24 hours of frenzied street violence, 91 Jews were murdered and more than 30,000 arrested and sent to camps. In his monumental study of the Holocaust, Martin Gilbert paints a frightening picture of the scene in Leipzig on the night of 9–10 November 1938. According to the US consul in Leipzig David H. Burffurn:

> The Nazis practised 'tactics which approached the ghoulish', uprooting tombstones and violating graves. . . . Having demolished dwellings and hurled most of the effects to the streets, the insatiably sadistic perpetrators threw many of the trembling inmates into a small stream that flows through the Zoological Park, commanding horrified spectators to spit at them, defile them with mud and jeer at their plight.

Another observer, Dr Arthur Flehinger,

> recalls that all Jewish men in the town were marched through the streets to the synagogue. Once inside, they were confronted by exuberant Nazi officers and SS men. Dr Flehinger himself was ordered

to read out passages from *Mein Kampf* to his fellow Jews. 'I read the passage . . . so quietly that the SS men posted behind me repeatedly hit me in the neck . . . after these readings there was a pause. Those Jews who wanted to relieve themselves were forced to do so against the synagogue walls, not in the toilets, and they were physically abused while doing so.'[23]

The initiative now passed to Goering who, with his combined responsibilities for the economy and rearmament, saw the opportunity to exploit the latent wealth of the Jewish community. On 12 November he issued the following decree:

All damage which was inflicted on Jewish businesses and dwellings on 9 and 10 November 1938 as a result of the national indignation about the rabble-rousing propaganda of international Jewry against National Socialist Germany must at once be repaired by the Jewish proprietors or Jewish traders. . . . The hostile attitude of the Jews towards the German people and Reich which does not shrink even from cowardly murders, demands decisive resistance and heavy reparation. . . . The Jews of German nationality are required communally to pay a contribution of RM 1 billion to the German Reich.[24]

In the wake of Reichkristallnacht it was made illegal for Jews to attend German schools and universities, and they were even excluded from cinemas, theatres and swimming pools. Having resisted the campaign for a 'Jew-free economy' for so long, Hitler had become an enthusiastic onlooker at the initiatives initially of Goebbels and subsequently Goering. The brutal pogrom known as Reichskristallnacht, 'the night of broken glass', represents, in the words of Kershaw, a 'night of horror, a retreat in a modern state to the savagery of bygone ages'.[25] On a national scale this event amounted to what writer Peter Loewenberg calls 'a public degradation ritual'.[26] The actual events of the night of broken glass remain open to further detailed regional investigation. There is still no completely reliable record of how many Jews were murdered between 9–10 November and in the immediate aftermath. It is not even entirely clear exactly how much property was destroyed. Recent research by Professor Meier Schwarz suggests that more than a thousand synagogues were destroyed and at least four hundred German Jews died.[27] Approximately 7,000 Jewish shops were destroyed. Kershaw estimates that around 30,000 Jews were rounded up and incarcerated in the immediate aftermath of the November pogrom.[28]

The immediate origins of the pogrom are well documented. On 7 November 1938, Ernst vom Rath, a German diplomat based at the embassy in Paris, was fatally wounded by Hershel Grynszpan, a 17-year-old Jew. The machinations within the Nazi hierarchy which followed illustrate the bitter tensions and rivalries which permeated the leadership that orbited Hitler. The diplomat's death two days after the shooting was immediately identified by Josef Goebbels as an ideal opportunity for him to personally take the initiative in whipping up anti-Semitism to new heights. Goebbels was saturated with ambition and felt that he could rejuvenate his own personal standing with Hitler by leading a popular atrocity against the Jews. It was of immense importance to Goebbels that he was able to obtain personal approval from Hitler for the Jews to 'feel the anger of the people'. Goebbels was acutely aware that other leading Nazis, most notably Goering, would resent his initiative and challenge his actions on the grounds that they would cause considerable economic damage. Similarly, Himmler and Heydrich, at the summit of the SS hierarchy, only learnt of the pogrom after it had begun. They criticized Goebbels's initiative on the grounds that it would adversely affect their emigration plans.

Undoubtedly a desire to damage Goebbels was also a factor in what, at times, resembled a court intrigue. It is clear that Hitler was careful to avoid direct personal involvement in this brutal pogrom. Kershaw notes that 'Hitler took care to remain equivocal. He did not praise Goebbels, or what had happened. But nor did he openly, even to his close circle, let alone in public, condemn him outright or categorically dissociate himself from the unpopular Propaganda Minister.'[29] Those who disapproved of the November events were able to blame Goebbels rather than Hitler for the violence and destruction which had been visited upon the Jewish people.

Most historians now believe that the escalation marked by the events of November 1938 had been coming for some time. Key changes in personnel in the period 1937–38 were of major importance. In particular the removal of conservatives such as Blomberg, Fritsch and Neurath from the army and the Foreign Office made it easier for Hitler and his key advisers to take more radical steps than ever before. A key change came with the dismissal of Hjalmar Schacht as Reich Minister of Economics in November 1937. This paved the way for Goering to come to the fore. Goering's powerful position was based on a combination of close proximity to Hitler, disdain for the constraints of foreign opinions, radical anti-Semitism and enormous influence on the preparation of the economy for war. It may well be that Goering's awareness of the value of Jewish assets was a further factor in the increasingly bleak scenario which the Jews now faced. It is interesting to note that Goering had no role in the Reichskristallnacht itself but was then able, in the words of William Carr, to 'forget his objections and take the lead in plundering the Jews'.[30] Amid a range of fresh legislation came the vindictive measure of forcing the Jewish community to bear the cost of repairs with a collective payment of 1,000 million marks to be paid to the German Reich. It appears that Goering consulted Hitler closely on the details of new legislation and that together they presided over the liquidation of Jewish business assets, the surrendering of all shares and gold and silver belongings. Combined with further legislation excluding all Jews from schools, universities, cinemas, sports stadia and theatres, the isolation of the Jewish community was now virtually complete.

| | |
|---|---|
| 30 January | Within weeks of Hitler becoming Chancellor a number of Jewish artists and intellectuals take the decision to leave Germany. The scientist Albert Einstein, who is visiting the USA at the time, decides never to return to Germany. Within six years, a century of equal opportunities and integration will be eliminated. Other groups subjected to persecution will include the gypsies (Roma), political dissidents, homosexuals, the handicapped and Jehovah's Witnesses. |
| March | A series of violent anti-Jewish incidents occur across the country in the wake of the March elections. Many of these initiatives appear to stem from the radical elements within the Nazi movement. The SA seizes dozens of Jews in Berlin and they are taken to concentration camps. In Breslau, Jewish lawyers and judges are beaten. In Bavaria a Jewish man is taken from his house and killed. Other initiatives are more bureaucratic. In Cologne Jews are banned from using municipal sports facilities. Hitler offers no public comment. The interpretation of many Germans is that Hitler is trying to hold back many of the extremists within his own party. |
| 20 March | The first concentration camp opens at Dachau, near Munich. Its initial purpose is to house arrested communists and other left-wing opponents of the Nazi regime. In the future it will be used to detain and ultimately murder Jews. |
| 28 March | The Nazi press agitates for a boycott of Jewish shops, doctors and lawyers. Historians have identified various radical groups (such as sections of the SA) and certain individuals (such as Goebbels, the jurist Roland Freisler and the virulently anti-Semitic Julius Streicher, a leading Nazi based in Nuremberg) who are at the centre of this and subsequent initiatives. Their interpretation has been that Hitler was now facing other imperatives and that radicals within the movement had to agitate for the anti-Semitic measures which Hitler had promised in his earlier speeches. Some elements in the party speak privately of Hitler having come to terms with the establishment having lost the violent edge of his pre-Chancellery days. However, on 29 March Hitler informs his cabinet of the boycott and tells them that he himself had called for it. He terms the boycott 'spontaneous popular violence'. Goebbels's diary entries for the end of March reveal his excitement and show him consulting with Hitler on the timing and duration of the boycott. |
| 1 April | A nationwide boycott of Jewish shops is abandoned after one day. The general public reaction is one of indifference. It |

becomes apparent that the boycott is incompatible with the stated priority of economic recovery. It soon becomes clear to Hitler and his colleagues that further boycotts can only damage the fragile German economy. However, over the next few months many top firms part company with Jewish members at boardroom level. Meanwhile a number of eminent Jewish musicians leave the country. The new president of the Prussian Theatre Commission calls them 'Jewish artistic bankrupters'. The Dresden Opera House dismisses its musical director on the grounds that he has too many Jewish contacts. It is the Jewish contribution to culture which is first to be seriously restricted by the new regime.

| | |
|---|---|
| 7 April | The Law for the Restoration of the Professional Civil Service excludes Jews and other political opponents. The detailed legislation is drawn up by Wilhelm Frick. Meanwhile widespread outbreaks of violence against Jewish judges, lawyers and jurists lead Hitler to agree to a decree restricting Jews from practising the law. This time the initiative stems from the state secretary at the Ministry of Justice. Hitler appears to be reacting to initiatives which in turn stemmed from localized attacks against the Jews. At the same time Hitler personally defers action against Jewish physicians partly because he recognizes that action in this area will affect German patients. |
| 25 April | The Law against the Overcrowding of German Schools restricts the numbers of Jewish students allowed to enter German schools. Meanwhile action is taken to exclude Jewish professors and academics from university faculties. |
| 10 May | Goebbels is at the centre of a campaign which leads to over 20,000 books by Jews and left-wing writers being thrown onto bonfires in Berlin. Goebbels addresses a large crowd outside the Kroll Opera House in which he condemns Jewish culture. Similar events are staged in every other large German city. |
| 7 July | Hess informs his colleagues that further boycotts of Jewish department stores will not be permitted. Hitler's commitment to economic recovery and his acute sense of his own image with the German people make him extremely wary of jeopardizing his own popularity. One interpretation sees Hitler as holding back the violent radicals in his movement who are itching for action against the Jews. |
| 14 July | At a cabinet meeting, with Hitler present, it is decided not to withhold contracts from Jewish firms. Hitler's priority is to deliver to the German people the economic recovery which he has promised. On the same day the Law for the Prevention of Genetically Diseased Offspring is adopted. This makes it |

possible to sterilize anyone suffering from hereditary diseases. The eugenic rationale behind such measures is of relevance to the Jews. By the end of July, over 26,000 Germans, including a large number of Jews, have been arrested and taken to concentration camps. In August a small number of Jews are killed.

September    Jews are banned from owning farms or practising agriculture.

4 October    Jews are banned from holding the post of newspaper editor. Meanwhile a new set of disciplinary procedures are implemented at Dachau, including the ruling that from now on 'agitators are to be hanged'. By the end of the month thousands of placards have appeared across the country in towns, villages and various public places, saying 'Jews are not welcome here'. In some areas the names of Jewish soldiers are removed from war memorials.

December    By the end of the year 36 Jews have been murdered, a further 6 killed in 'mob outrages' and 3 others killed attempting escape. More than 35,000 Jews have fled the country.

**QUESTION**

Here are two interpretations of the anti-Semitic programme of 1933. (a) A Hitler-centred programme. (b) A programme restrained by Hitler. Using the material provided here and your own further reading, explain which you feel is most accurate.

## 10.12 1935–39: a detailed chronology

The chronology which follows illustrates how the position of the Jews steadily deteriorated from 1935 onwards. Read the outline of events and decide whether this constituted a clear, preconceived programme.

*1935*

21 May    The Military Service Act makes 'Aryan descent' a prerequisite for military service.

summer    Josef Goebbels, the most outspokenly anti-Semitic of Hitler's senior colleagues, pushes for fresh initiatives against the Jews.

September    During the Nuremberg rally, Hitler, without consulting colleagues, instructs Bernhard Losener, a civil servant, to immediately draft new laws to prohibit sexual relations between Jews and Gentiles.

15 September    Promulgation of the 'Nuremberg Laws' forbidding Jews the status of Reich citizenship. Marriage and sexual

| | relations between Jews and non-Jews are outlawed through the 'Law for the Protection of German Blood and German Honour'. |
|---|---|
| *1936* | |
| summer | Anti-Semitic propaganda is repressed for the duration of the Olympic Games in Berlin. |
| *1937* | |
| | On at least three occasions Hitler personally defers new anti-Semitic measures because of technical or legal objections. |
| 14 March | Pope Pius X1 criticizes Nazi racial policy in his encyclical statement 'with burning concern'. |
| *1938* | |
| 12 March | German troops march into Austria (anti-Semitism). |
| 9 June | Munich's largest synagogue is pulled down. |
| 25 July | New restrictions are imposed on Jewish doctors. |
| 10 August | Nuremberg's synagogue is destroyed. |
| 17 August | All Jews in Germany are obliged to add the forenames 'Sara' or 'Israel' to their name. |
| 27 September | Jewish lawyers are forbidden to practise. |
| 28 October | Deportation of 17,000 Jews of Polish nationality to Poland. |
| 7 November | A young Jew, Herschel Grynszpan, shoots and fatally wounds Ernst vom Roth, a German official, at the Paris embassy. |
| 9–10 November | Reichkristallnacht – 'the Night of Broken Glass'. A pogrom on a national scale results in the murder of 91 Jews, the burning of 191 synagogues and the ransacking of more than 7,000 Jewish shops. Around 30,000 Jews are arrested and imprisoned. The pogrom is not marked by any particular policy decision or decisive meeting. However, in the words of historian Daniel Goldhagen, 'the nationwide pogrom . . . was an event of enormous significance. The Germans' measures taken until then had not succeeded in completely removing the Jews from their country, so it was time to become more severe, to send an unmistakable message and warning; Leave, or else.'[31] |
| *1939* | |
| 30 January | On the sixth anniversary of his coming to power Hitler delivers a venomous speech to the Reichstag predicting the future annihilation of the Jewish race. |
| 14–15 March | German troops occupy Czechoslovakia. |

| | |
|---|---|
| 1 September | Germany invades Poland. Special SS units accompany the regular troops. They display great brutality towards the Polish Jews but killings are generally confined to the leaders of the Jewish community. |
| 6 October | Conquest of Poland complete. |
| 12–17 October | Jews deported from Austria and Czechoslovakia to Poland. |
| 18 November | Through his military adjutant, Hitler dismisses concerns amongst sections of the army leadership about the violence of the anti-Jewish policy as 'childish'. |
| 23 November | Polish Jews are obliged to wear the yellow Star of David. |
| December | Officials planning Poland's future discuss the destruction of Jewish 'sub-humanity' living in the ghettos. |

## ESSAY QUESTIONS

1 Why did the position of European Jewry deteriorate so markedly between 1935 and 1942?

2 To what extent was the worsening situation of the Jews due to the personal intervention of Adolf Hitler?

3 'The Reichkristallnacht of November 1938 was the turning point for the Jews' – how far would you agree with this?

# the origins of the Second World War

## 11.1  overview: the origins of the Second World War

### Hitler's war?

In his excellent study *Hitler: Profiles in Power*, Ian Kershaw briefly imagines a Third Reich without Hitler and poses the following important questions:

> Would a terroristic police state under Himmler and the SS have been erected without Hitler as head of government? Would Germany have been engaged in general war by the end of the 1930s under a different form of authoritarian regime? Would discrimination against Jews have culminated in genocide under a different head of state? In each case, it seems highly improbable. Hitler, one can then suggest at the outset, was crucial to these developments.[1]

Like other historians who have recently re-examined Hitler's ideology, Kershaw has concluded that certain key principles were in fact of the utmost importance to Hitler. These ideas – anti-Marxism, anti-Semitism and a desire for *Lebensraum* (living space) in the east – were not merely paraded at torchlit rallies and on election posters for political convenience but were the foundation stones for the drive to war that Hitler created. Although Hitler was as opportunistic a politician as it was possible to be, it is now clear that he was also firmly and irrevocably committed to certain key ideas.

As Kershaw states:

> It was for long thought after the collapse of the Third Reich that Hitler's message consisted of no more than the empty phrases of the power-thirsty demagogue, that the man behind the message was as devoid of genuine ideas as were the classical tyrants of old. It is now understood that behind the vague missionary appeal lay a set of interrelated ideas – however repulsive and irrational – which congealed by the mid-1920s into a cohesive ideology. . . . Though he was often indecisive about precise political actions, Hitler never wavered about the certainty of

his ideas. . . . The essence of Hitler's personal world-view comprised a belief in history as racial struggle, radical anti-Semitism, a conviction that Germany's future could be secured only through conquest of *Lebensraum* ('living space') at the expense of Russia, and the uniting of all these strands in the notion of a life-or-death fight to the finish with Marxism – most concretely embodied in the 'Jewish Bolshevism' of the Soviet Union.[2]

These were the ideas that took Hitler and Germany from peace to war and from a form of economic recovery to a situation of complete ruination. The culmination of this fierce ideological commitment came on 1 May 1945 when Hamburg Radio interrupted its broadcast of Bruckner's Seventh Symphony with the announcement that Adolf Hitler, 'fighting to the last breath against Bolshevism, fell for Germany this afternoon in its operational headquarters in the Reich Chancellery'. Hitler had proclaimed that the Third Reich would endure for 1,000 years, but after just 12 years as leader, and 6 years of brutal conflict, his creation lay defeated, symbolized by the smouldering ruins of the capital city, Berlin. The 'thousand-year Reich' dreamt of by Hitler had ended with the charred remains of its creator after only 12 years. Hitler's war was over. How did it begin? Hitler's foreign policy has remained one of the most controversial aspects of the Third Reich's history. The historical significance of the foreign policy conducted by Germany from 1933 to 1939 is clearly immense. Europe and the wider world were plunged into a war unparalleled in its scale and brutality. Between September 1939 and August 1945 at least 56 million people were killed. Recent research has indicated that the scale of the suffering may have been even greater. Historians remain divided on the central issue: to what extent was German foreign policy instigated and controlled by one man – Adolf Hitler?

At first the answer seemed all too obvious. At the Nuremberg Trials (1945–46) of the Nazi war criminals, almost every testimony referred to the hypnotic grip which Hitler had exerted over his followers; to the extent that they had blindly followed him in provoking the Second World War and annihilating the Jewish race in Europe. This was not enough to save them. The Nazi leadership was finally wiped out by a combination of the hangman's noose, suicides and massive prison sentences. Yet the public felt that the real villain of the piece was the man who could now never be brought to trial. In a curious way, Hitler still dominated the proceedings at Nuremberg.

In turn, he has continued to dominate the thoughts of historians of the Third Reich. For many years the verdict that Hitler was solely responsible for the Second World War remained completely unchallenged. Ironically, it was at the Nuremberg Trials that there was just a hint that this outlook was not perfectly valid. With Hitler dead, Hermann Goering was the leading Nazi who remained. At the Nuremberg Trials, Goering seemed to relish being in this position and made no attempt to evade responsibility. On the contrary, he emphasized that he was proud of the key role he had played in foreign affairs: 'I was responsible for the rearmament, the training and the morale of the Luftwaffe. Not so much the Führer as I, personally bear the full and entire responsibility for everything that happened.'[3] More specifically, Goering claimed that it was he who had engineered the German annexation of Austria in March 1938, 'fulfilling an old, old longing of the German people to become a unified Reich'.[4]

Goering claimed that important military leaders such as General Keitel had exerted little influence on the decision-making process because they 'came between the millstones of stronger personalities'.[5] According to Goering, the attitude of the German General Staff to Hitler was reticent and timid. The Reich Cabinet hardly met after 1937 because 'The Führer did not think much of Cabinet meetings.' Goering's conclusion was that 'at best, only the Führer and I could have conspired.'[6] Most observers were unconvinced by this testimony and attributed it more to personal vanity than to actual fact.

Yet Goering had provided his last clues to the mystery of how the Third Reich was governed. Sentenced to death by the Nuremberg Tribunal for his part in the Nazi war crimes, he chose suicide rather than the hangman's noose, taking his own life on the evening of 15 October 1946: in committing suicide Goering had followed Hitler's example for the last time. Who made the decisions when they were both alive?

## 11.2 sources: Hitler's ideology and German foreign policy

**SOURCE A**

We National Socialists must hold unflinchingly to our aim in foreign policy, namely to secure for the German people the land and soil to which they are entitled on this earth. . . . Much as all of us today recognise the necessity of a reckoning with France, it would remain ineffectual in the long run if this represented the whole of our aim in foreign policy. It can and will achieve meaning only if it offers the rear cover for an enlargement of our people's living space in Europe. For it is not in colonial acquisition that we must see the solution of this problem, but exclusively in the acquisition of a territory for settlement.

And so we National Socialists consciously draw a line beneath the foreign policy tendency of our pre-war period. We stop the endless German movement to the south and west, and turn our gaze towards the land in the east. At long last we break off the colonial and commercial policy of the pre-war period and shift to the soil policy of the future. If we speak of soil in Europe today, we can primarily have in mind only Russia and her vassal border states.

*Source*: Adolf Hitler, *Mein Kampf* (1925, trans.1939).

**SOURCE B**

Was Lebensraum Hitler's sole idea or indeed the one which dominated his mind? To judge from Mein Kampf, he was obsessed by anti-Semitism, which occupies most of the book. Lebensraum gets only seven of the seven hundred pages. Then and thereafter it was thrown in as a final rationalisation, a sort of 'pie in the sky' to justify what Hitler was supposed to be up to. Perhaps the difference between me and the believers in Hitler's constant plan for Lebensraum is over words. By 'plan' I understand something which is prepared and worked out in detail. They seem to take 'plan' as a pious . . . wish.'

*Source*: A. J. P. Taylor, *The Origins of the Second World War* (1961).

## SOURCE C

The policy in *Mein Kampf* . . . has little connection with the actual policy followed by Hitler in the 1930s. It is a character statement, a creed of violence; but it is only a guide book to Hitler's diplomacy in 1933 to 1939 by way of a very long stretch of imagination.

*Source*: H. W. Koch, *Hitler and the Origins of the Second World War* (1971).

## SOURCE D

Hitler disliked putting pen to paper; he wrote few letters, made no marginal notes on official documents and kept no diary. For these reasons his first book, *Mein Kampf*, published in 1925, has assumed considerable significance for those who seek to understand the mind of this enigmatic man. The book was an attempt by Hitler to establish himself as the dominant theorist as well as the best speaker in the party. For the most part it reveals his obsession with questions of race in general and anti-Semitism in particular. Hitler linked his anti-Semitism – in which he fervently believed – to questions of foreign policy, in which he advocated German expansion to the east.

*Source*: John Traynor, *Europe 1890–1990* (1991).

## SOURCE E

Was Hitler really just a more violent Mr Micawber sitting in Berlin and waiting for something to turn up: Something which, thanks to historic necessity, he could then turn to advantage? Certainly Hitler himself did not think so. He regarded himself as a thinker, a practical philosopher. .-. . And since he published a blueprint of the policy which he carried out, ought we not at least to look at this blueprint?

*Source*: H. R. Trevor-Roper, in *The Origins of the Second World War*, ed. E. M. Robertson (1971).

## SOURCE F

Nazism was inseparable from war. As a political movement, German National Socialism grew and triumphed in a country deeply scarred by the experience of and defeat in the First World War. Its leader had found meaning for his own life in war, which he described as 'the most memorable period of my life' compared with which 'all the past fell away into oblivion'. As a political ideology, Nazism revolved around war and struggle: to fight was at once the main purpose of a nation and the measure of the health of a 'race'. The ideology of Nazism was an ideology of war, which regarded peace merely as preparation for war.

*Source*: Richard Bessel, *Nazism and War* (2004).

With reference to each of the sources and your own knowledge, explain the significance of Hitler's personal ideology in the development of his foreign policy objectives.

## 11.3 Italy and Mussolini

Italy's invasion of Abyssinia (1935) had many short-term repercussions, all of them seemingly favourable to Hitler. The clear failure of the League of Nations to take effective sanctions against the aggressor state delivered a mortal blow to the democracies' chief instrument for keeping the peace. Despite their ideological affinities, Italy's opposition to Anschluss had kept the two dictators apart during the early years of Hitler's rule. However, Dolfuss, Chancellor of Austria since May 1932, was determined to stamp out the Nazi movement in his country. Political assemblies and parades were forbidden and, on 19 June 1933, the Nazi party in Austria was declared illegal.

In normal times these measures might have been successful, but in Hitler Dolfuss faced an exceptionally formidable opponent. In retaliation, Hitler announced in May that all German tourists visiting Austria would have to pay a 1,000-mark fee. The action inflicted a crippling blow on the Austrian tourist industry, a major source of government revenue. Within months the Austrian Nazis were planning the violent overthrow of the Austrian government. There is every reason to believe that Hitler knew details of these plans and gave the go-ahead to the conspirators. On 25 July 1934 the Nazis seized the Austrian chancellery and murdered Dolfuss.

This putsch was quickly suppressed by Austrian forces and President Miklas called upon Kurt von Schuschnigg to form a new government. Although the German Nazi Party denied any knowledge of the assassination plot, the murder of Dolfuss was a damaging blow to Hitler's reputation abroad. It also prompted Mussolini to mobilize his troops, ready to come to Austria's defence if the assassination were followed by an invasion attempt. Hitler was forced to rethink his tactics, and it was clear that a change in Italy's attitude was needed before Germany could act.

The crucial shift in the international situation came with Italy's invasion of Abyssinia in October 1935. Ostracized by the rest of Europe, Mussolini increasingly came to look upon Hitler as his natural ally. In February 1936 Mussolini told the German ambassador to Italy: 'It would now be possible to achieve a fundamental improvement in German–Italian relations and to dispose of the only dispute, namely, the Austrian problem.'[7] In the winter of 1936, with Italy at last feeling the pinch of economic sanctions, Mussolini informed Berlin that he was not opposed to Austria becoming 'a German satellite'.

*1934*
- - - - - - - - - - - - - - - - - - - - - - - - - - - -

Italian troops mobilize at the Brenner Pass to deter a potential German move against Austria

*1935*
- - - - - - - - - - - - - - - - - - - - - - - - - - - -

Meeting at Stresa, Britain, France and Italy condemn Germany's rearmament programme and express their desire to maintain Austrian independence

October | Italy's invasion of Abyssinia condemned by the European powers and drives an increasingly ostracized Mussolini towards Germany

*1937*
- - - - - - - - - - - - - - - - - - - - - - - - - - - -

November | Rome–Berlin Axis

*1938*
- - - - - - - - - - - - - - - - - - - - - - - - - - - -

March | Italy stands by as Germany invades Austria

May | As Hitler prepares for military action against Czechoslovakia, a visit to Italy makes it clear that Italy will not stand in the way of German expansion in Central Europe

September | Mussolini supports the Munich Conference to avoid a general European war

*1939*
- - - - - - - - - - - - - - - - - - - - - - - - - - - -

May | The Pact of Steel – formal alliance between Italy and Germany

## 11.4 relations with the armed forces, the issue of rearmament and the notion of continuity between Hitler and previous chancellors

Hitler entered the Chancellery in January 1933 with an immense degree of self-belief but also an acute sense of the limitations of his own position. Domestically, the dire economic situation, with its accompanying mass unemployment, created its own imperative. On the international stage, Hitler's room for manoeuvre was also limited both diplomatically and within his own government. The Reich President von Hindenburg had insisted that the conservative diplomat von Neurath should stay on as Foreign Minister while the army general, von Blomberg, would serve as new Reich Defence Minister. Hitler had to quickly come to terms with this situation, and as he sought to consolidate his relatively delicate power base he was in no doubt as to the importance of his own political relationship with the army leadership. He viewed the generals with a mixture of contempt, awe and respect. He was irritated by their aristocratic pretensions and was somewhat inhibited by his sense of his own social standing, but he had to be sure of the army's support. It was to Hitler's advantage that by 1933 the leadership in the army (*Reichswehr*) had concluded that the Weimar Republic had been unable to provide the rearmament programme they desired. It is sometimes supposed that rearmament was not a feature of German foreign policy until Hitler took power. The reality is that as early as 1926, the Reich

Defence Ministry had begun to investigate secret plans for rearmament. In 1928 a rearmament programme was initiated which called for a field army of 16 divisions to be achieved by 1932. This was superseded in 1932 by a second rearmament package which proposed a field army of 300,000 men by 1938. General von Schleicher, at this point the new Defence Minister and a future chancellor, took up the rearmament drive in a particularly vigorous way. In December 1933, the Defence Ministry put though a new plan which envisaged a peacetime army of 21 divisions (300,000) men and a field army of 63 divisions, based on the introduction of a conscription programme at the earliest opportunity. It is important to note that the rearmament initiative seemed to stem from the Defence Ministry rather than from Hitler himself. While the fact that the new Chancellor shared the army's rearmament goals seemed to bode well for relations between the novice Chancellor and the established army leadership, it would be wrong to assume that a strong relationship was guaranteed. The most significant barrier between Hitler and a strong working relationship with the army leaders was the existence of the SA, Hitler's paramilitary organization that, by the summer of 1933, contained two million men, compared to the professional army with only just over 100,000 men. With this threat to the army's independence prompting one senior figure to refer to the SA as 'our most dangerous enemy', it was clear that the relationship between Hitler and the generals was by no means guaranteed. So, when the new Minister of Defence, General von Blomberg, extended an invitation to the new Chancellor to address local commanders, he accepted straight away. In an after-dinner speech, behind closed doors on 4 February 1933, Hitler made it clear that he had maintained his radical outlook: 'How should political power be used when it has been gained? That is impossible to say yet. Perhaps fighting for new export possibilities, perhaps – and probably better – the conquest of new living space in the east and its ruthless Germanisation.'[8]

The stage had been set for 'the profound irrationality of Hitler's project' to begin. In the words of Adam Tooze: 'Hitler's regime after 1933 undertook a truly remarkable campaign of economic mobilization. The armaments programme of the Third Reich was the largest transfer of resources ever undertaken by a capitalist state in peacetime.'[9] While some generals were disturbed by the radical tone of Hitler's speech, most took encouragement from his firm commitment to rearm on a massive scale, reintroduce conscription and restore the military to their old, privileged position. Hitler left the building pleased with his reception and optimistic that he could work with the generals to rebuild the German armed forces.

While the events of 3 February had prepared the armed forces for the rearmament programme to come, a meeting at Goering's private villa a fortnight later may have marked the occasion when German business was formally invited to support Hitler's project. Speeches by the Chancellor and by Goering left the business leaders in no doubt that Hitler was willing to go to any lengths to crush the left and bring an end to parliamentary democracy and that, in return, they would be expected to provide a formidable injection of cash to shore up Nazi party funds in the first instance and to be a down payment for what was to come. Buoyed by the support of business he had been pledged, Hitler now decided that rearmament was to proceed on the basis of a plan drawn up by the previous chancellor, Schleicher, illustrating the fact that in many aspects of German foreign policy there is a clear sense of continuity between Hitler and the final chancellors of the Weimar period. This so-called immediate programme incorporated two four-year plans; the first designed to provide relief for farmers, the second to reduce unemployment. Where Hitler's programme departed from Schleicher's was in its greater emphasis on military projects. A typical multi-purpose measure was the *Reichsautobahnen* programme, which employed thousands of young men on the construction of 7,000 kilometres of new roads over six years. Not only did this have a major impact on unemployment, it also made an important contribution to the Nazis' military preparations.

## the German armed forces and the Treaty of Versailles

The strict limitations imposed by the Treaty of Versailles on Germany's armed forces were clear for all to see. Germany was allowed a token professional army of 100,000 men but was expressly forbidden to manufacture tanks, military aircraft or submarines. At the start of 1933 the Reichswehr consisted of a mere ten divisions. With Russian help, Germany had carried out a little rearmament since 1920 but her military position in 1933 was extremely weak. Germany possessed only about 80 aircraft and 450 trained flying personnel. The pilots who would one day form the German Luftwaffe practised on gliders belonging to the euphemistically named League of Air Sports. More significantly, the regulations limiting the size of the German army were flagrantly ignored; it trebled between 1933 and 1935. Any foreign diplomat could have seen what was going on, but the reaction of Britain and France was invariably one of anxiety rather than anger. On 9 March 1935 Goering revealed the existence of a German air force in an interview with the *Daily Mail*. Aircraft production assumed central importance in the industrial composition of the Third Reich. In the year before Hitler became Chancellor the German aircraft industry employed just over 3,000 people with the capacity to produce no more than a hundred aircraft per year. Within a decade the Nazis had created a multi-billion Reichsmark aircraft and aero-engine industry, employing more than 250,000 and producing over 10,000 advanced combat aircraft per year.

The news of an emerging German air force caused so little surprise that Britain and France did not even take the trouble to register a formal protest. One week later Germany announced that it has conscripted a peacetime army of 500,000. The casual manner in which the Nazis ignored the terms of the Versailles Treaty might have been taken by Britain as a sound indication of Hitler's unreliability. Instead, Germany's rearmament was excused by many as an understandable security measure. To some observers it seemed preferable to negotiate and bargain with the dynamic new regime rather than to confront

Hitler and run the risk of some fresh conflict. In addition, any agreement reached with Hitler might, it was argued, rein in the extent of his ambition. With all of this in mind, Britain concluded the Anglo-German Naval Pact of 1935. This convention, signed in June 1935, formally annulled the naval terms of the Versailles Treaty and allowed Germany to construct a navy equivalent to 35 per cent of the size of the British fleet. The manner in which the Anglo-German Naval Pact of 1935 was reached reflects the rather unconventional manner in which Nazi diplomacy operated. The agreement was drawn up with the British government through the hard bargaining of Joachim von Ribbentrop. In the spring of 1935 he had set up the Dienstelle Ribbentrop, an agency which soon became a rival to the more orthodox German Foreign Office. The successful conclusion of the Naval Pact – the first major agreement between the Nazis and a democracy – was a major coup for Ribbentrop and served to undermine the authority of the conservative old guard in Germany's Foreign Office.

By 1936 the increasingly anarchic structure of Germany's foreign policy administration was complemented by an economy which, though outwardly successful, was becoming dangerously imbalanced. The large-scale rearmament which Hitler desired could not be financed out of the budget (he had inherited a deficit for 1932 of RM 900 million). Hitler's appointment of Hjalmar Schacht as president of the Reichsbank in March 1933 marked a significant turning point in the way armaments were funded.

Schacht's major innovation was the Mefo bill. This acted as a form of short-term credit for up to five years. The idea was that industry would produce armaments for the government on a massive scale but payment would be deferred for five years on the basis of 4 per cent interest. Unfortunately for Schacht, when the time came for the bills to be redeemed his influence with the Führer was clearly on the wane. Hitler combined a marked reluctance to honour his old debts with a strong desire to open some new ones. An acceleration in the pace of rearmament in 1936, masterminded by Goering through a four-year plan, only increased the imbalance in the economy. It became clear by 1937 that Germany was moving towards a serious internal crisis. The sense of urgency which Hitler invariably brought to foreign policy stemmed from his awareness that the so-called Nazi economic miracle of 1933–36 was coming to an end. In the words of Klaus-Jurgen Müller, 'the borderline between defensive rearmament and offensive armament had been crossed. Military policy had developed a dynamic which threatened soon to get out of control.'[10] As Richard Bessel states:

> as a result of this gigantic rearmament, pressures were building up
> throughout the economy. The achievement of full employment in an
> overheated economy brought with it dangerous inflationary pressures,
> as labour became scarce. . . . Instead of integration into the world
> economy, Hitler sought autarky; instead of moderation in armaments
> spending in order to maintain sound government finances and to
> husband foreign exchange, Hitler ordered massive rearmament.'[11]

As early as the spring of 1936 the process of rearmament had gone far enough for Hitler to try his hand at tampering with the hated Versailles system.

## 11.5 the reoccupation of the Rhineland, March 1936

In the summer of 1935, French secret agents in Berlin reported back to Paris with alarming intelligence reports that Hitler had instructed his generals to prepare for the military reoccupation of the Rhineland. It would be Germany's most daring foreign policy move so far. The momentum of the German rearmament programme coincided with a highly favourable international situation. Italy's occupation of Ethiopia in 1935 meant that Mussolini faced international criticism from the League of Nations. However, the attempt to isolate Mussolini only served to push him towards the welcoming arms of Hitler. Hitler's behaviour over the next crucial month followed a pattern which was to be repeated during subsequent critical stages of foreign policy later in his career. Cautious and thorough diplomatic preparation was followed by astute and opportunistic exploitation of chances as they arose, a period of last-minute doubt and hesitation culminating in a period of ruthless and decisive action. In February 1936 Hitler consulted his military advisers about the Rhineland. They urged caution. This did not satisfy Hitler, who argued that: 'Passivity was, in the long run, no policy. . . . Attack in this case . . . was the better strategy.'[12] At the eleventh hour Hitler wavered and a postponement was considered but then rejected. The troops moved back into the Rhineland at dawn on 7 March 1936. Although the French reports had portrayed an overwhelming German force, the reality was less convincing. This consisted of 19 battalions of infantry with a total strength of 22,000, supported by 13 artillery groups and 54 single-seater planes.

The day after the occupation, a clear violation of the terms of Versailles, French military leaders came together to determine their response. Present at the meeting were generals representing the army, navy and air force. When Admiral Durand-Viel asked the military, 'Are you prepared to drive the Germans out of the zone?' he received the following reply from General Gamelin: 'By the fact of our entry into the zone, war would be unleashed. Such action would thus require general mobilisation. .-. . We can only enter the Rhineland zone . . . at the same time as the guarantor powers of Locarno (England and Italy). British and Italian contingents must be with us.' Admiral Durand-Viel then informed the meeting, 'At the moment England could give us nothing but moral support.'[13]

An American journalist, William Shirer, was in Germany at the time of the reoccupation. In his diary he vividly described the atmosphere in the Reichstag:

> March 7 1936: The Reichstag, more tense than I have ever felt it, began
> promptly at noon . . . Hitler began with a long harangue about the
> injustice of the Versailles Treaty and the peacefulness of Germans. Then
> . . . 'In the interests of the primitive rights of its people to the security
> of their defence, the German government has re-established, as from
> today, the absolute and unrestricted sovereignty of the Reich in the

de-militarised zone . . . First we swear to yield to no force whatever in restoration of the honour of our people. . . . Secondly, we pledge that now, more than ever, we shall strive for an understanding between the European peoples. . . . We have no territorial demands to make in Europe . . . Germany will never break the peace.'

March 8 1936: Hitler has got away with it, France is not marching. . . . No wonder the faces of Hitler and Goering and Blomberg . . . were all smiles this noon. . . . Oh the stupidity (or is it a paralysis?) of the French. I learned today on absolute authority that the German troops who marched into the de-militarised zone of the Rhineland yesterday had strict orders to beat a hasty retreat if the French army opposed them in any way.[14]

The successful reoccupation of the Rhineland provided a massive boost to Hitler's own position. Crucially, Germany's western frontier was now heavily fortified, giving Hitler much more freedom to act in the east. The only cloud on the horizon at the end of 1937 was the economic situation. This was a major turning point in fuelling Hitler's sense of his own destiny. It also reflected the fact that his most trusted adviser on foreign policy was the Nazi go-between von Ribbentrop, rather than von Neurath, the conservative Foreign Minister. For the Nazi path to war, the importance of the remilitarization of the Rhineland can hardly be overestimated. It was, as Michael Geyer has noted, 'the hinge on which all further steps of rearmament and operational planning depended'.[15]

Further analysis of this pivotal event is provided by Zachary Shore in his work, *What Hitler Knew: The Battle for Information in Nazi Foreign Policy*:

To march troops into the Rhineland before German rearmament had reached parity with France's was almost unanimously considered too risky. One man, however, the German foreign minister, Neurath, consistently urged the chancellor onward. In doing so, he took a considerable risk with his own political career.

Neurath's assurances were based not merely on his own political instincts but on reliable intelligence on French political and military leaders. . . . As the Rhine crisis mounted in 1935, Neurath found himself still besieged by the intrusive Ribbentrop. Ribbentrop attempted to wheedle his way into Neurath's domain by planting one of his personal representatives – or spies – at the foreign minister's daily top-level meetings. . . . Within this climate of perpetual infighting and internecine territorial rivalries between the Foreign Ministry and Party interlopers, Neurath felt compelled to tighten his control over the information flow to Hitler. It was an unstable environment that only worsened as the Rhineland crisis mounted . . . Others have asserted that Hitler's risk in the Rhineland was prompted by his need to fuel domestic support for the regime and to distract attention from unpopular issues such as the church conflict and growing food shortages. . . . But remilitarization had no guarantee of success. If Germany were forced to withdraw from the zone, domestic support for the Party would have dropped even further. Domestic concerns would have to have been paramount to warrant such a risk. Without reliable information on French intentions, remilitarization had to be a gamble . . .

As for Hitler, his risk in the Rhineland proved a public relations coup. His popularity soared among the German people. . . . Neurath's behaviour in the months preceding the Rhineland crisis demonstrates that decision making in Hitler's Reich suffered not only from chaotic information flow but from a tendency towards risk fostered by the frenetic system that Hitler, himself, created.[16]

## 11.6 the Spanish Civil War, 1936–39

The Spanish Civil War began in July 1936 when a group of right-wing army officers under the leadership of General Franco rebelled against the left-wing coalition of the government of the republic. Although the German Foreign Office initially intended to keep out of the conflict, Nazi party agencies recognized the economic opportunities of selling war materials to Franco's rebels, and perhaps the subsequent acquisition of Spanish raw materials. Hitler's focus was almost certainly more ideological, seeing events in Spain as one further landmark in the great struggle between the left and the right, with Italy, following the events of 1935 moving ever closer to Germany's side and with the Russians offering support to the Republicans. With economic and ideological forces in mind it did not take long for Hitler's support for Franco to be forthcoming. The events of the Spanish Civil War had a significant impact not just on the deteriorating international situation in general, but by providing a further outlet for the rapid development of the German military machine, acting as a limited-scale dress rehearsal for what was to come.

Adam Tooze provides a helpful overview of this event:

> In July 1936, right-wing officers launched their rebellion against the newly elected Popular Front government of Spain. Within weeks, the country was engulfed in a bloody civil war. . . . Hitler backed Mussolini in Africa and exploited the existing Anglo-French distraction to send German troops into the Rhineland, in a flagrant breach of the Treaty of Versailles. In the summer of 1936, Luftwaffe Ju 52 transports ferried Franco and his rebel troops to the Spanish mainland from Morocco. A few months later, the Luftwaffe's Condor legion went into action over Madrid.[17]

The Spanish Civil War moved Italy and Germany closer together than ever before and added to the sense of foreboding felt by those who desired peace.

## 11.7 the Hossbach conference, 1937

The successful and unopposed reoccupation of the Rhineland in 1936 provided a massive boost to Hitler's personal position and added to his sense that he was moving towards his own date with destiny. Strategically, the move into the

Rhineland meant that Germany was in a much less vulnerable position in the west and could now turn its gaze towards the east. Yet by the autumn of 1937 Hitler's perspective of events may have been rather mixed. In one sense his personal prestige was now immense. Unchallenged at home, feared by many abroad, with rearmament running at a massive level and prestige events such as the reoccupation of the Rhineland and the successful summer and winter Olympic games recently behind him, his own power base was probably at an all-time high. Yet at the same time events may have been compelling Hitler to feel increasingly driven to war. A personal sense of urgency was increasingly preoccupying Hitler, whose ill health in general and concerns about cancer in particular prompted him to believe that he might not have long to live. To make matters worse it is now clear that Hitler's advisers were in no doubt that the economic situation was increasingly fraught. The recovery of 1933–36 was giving way to a sharp recession in 1937, with prospects beyond the winter looking gloomier still. Hitler's antennae for his own political standing were acute and he had no capacity for tolerating bad news or for risking any diminution of his personal standing. Successful military action could render irrelevant any potential unease about domestic problems, or questions as to the firmness and dynamism of Hitler's personal leadership. Meanwhile, the rapid development of the Russian military machine under Stalin's five-year plan and the rearmament programmes of other nations only added to the sense of time running out. Above all, it may be that Hitler's drive for war stemmed most of all from his ideological convictions. It could be argued that the domestic events of 1933–37 were merely providing the groundwork for what was to come. With this in mind we will now examine in detail an important meeting that took place in the late afternoon and early evening of 5 November 1937. At the Nuremberg War Trials the meeting which Colonel Hossbach diligently recorded assumed enormous significance. The British prosecuting counsel referred to 'the plot ... divulged at the Hossbach meeting', while his American counterpart claimed that, 'as early as 5 November 1937 the plan to attack had begun to take definiteness as to time and victim'.[18] Richard Bessel is one of several historians who have stated that at this meeting Hitler 'explicitly presented his programme for war'. Present with Hitler at the meeting were War Minister von Blomberg, Werner von Fritsch for the army, Erich Rader for the navy and Hermann Goering for the air force – and Foreign Minister von Neurath, as well as Colonel Friedrich Hossbach, who recorded the notes.[19] Given the fact that within weeks of the meeting, the army had worked out a strategic plan for an offensive against Czechoslovakia, it is clearly worth examining the nature of the meeting in some detail.

SOURCE A

EXTRACTS FROM THE MINUTES OF THE CONFERENCE IN THE REICH CHANCELLERY, BERLIN, 5 NOVEMBER, 1937.

From 4:15 to 8:30 pm.
The Führer began by stating that the subject of the present conference was of such importance that its discussion would, in other countries, be a matter for

a full Cabinet meeting, but he, the Führer, had rejected the idea of making it a subject of discussion before the wider circle of the Reich Cabinet just because of the importance of the matter. His exposition to follow was the fruit of thorough deliberation and the experiences of his four-and-a-half years of power. He wished to explain . . . his basic ideas concerning the opportunities for the development of our position in the field of foreign affairs and its requirements, and he asked, in the interest of a long-term German policy, that his exposition be regarded, in the event of his death, as his last will and testament.

The Führer continued:
The aim of Geman policy was to make secure and to preserve the racial community [Volksmasse] and to enlarge it. It was therefore a question of space.

The German racial community comprised over 85 million people and, by reason of their number and the narrow limits of habitable space in Europe, it constituted a tightly packed racial core . . .

The Führer continued:
The aim of German policy was to make secure and to preserve the racial community and to enlarge it. . . . There remain still to be answered the questions 'when' and 'how'.

Case 1: Period 1943–45
After this date only a change for the worse, from our point of view, could be expected.

The equipment of the army, navy, and Luftwaffe, as well as the formation of the officer corps, was nearly completed. Equipment and armament were modern; in further delay there lay the danger of their obsolescence . . .

If the Führer was still living, it was his unalterable resolve to solve Germany's problem of space at the latest by 1943–45. The necessity for action before 1943–45 would arise in cases 2 and 3.

Case 2
If internal strife in France should develop into such a domestic crisis as to absorb the French Army completely . . . then the time for action against the Czechs had come.

Case 3
If France is so embroiled by a war with another state that she cannot 'proceed' against Germany.

Our first objective, in the event of our being embroiled in war, must be to overthrow Czechoslovakia and Austria simultaneously.

The second part of the conference was concerned with concrete questions of armament.

Certified correct.
Colonel (General Staff) Hossbach.

Source: J. Noakes and G. Pridham (ed.), Nazism 1919–1945: A Documentary Reader. Vol. 3: Foreign Policy, War and Racial Extermination (1988).

While few historians would completely support the interpretation offered at Nuremberg, historians remain divided on the significance of the Hossbach meeting. The position of two leading historians is set out below. Which view do you find the more convincing?

SOURCE A

THE TAYLOR THESIS.

Who first raised the storm and launched the march of events? The accepted answer is clear: it was Hitler. The moment of his doing so is also accepted: it was on 5 November 1937. We have a record of the statements which he made that day. It is called 'the Hossbach memorandum', after the man who made it. This record is supposed to reveal Hitler's plans. Much play was made with it at Nuremberg: perhaps we shall find in it the explanation of the Second World War; or perhaps we shall find only the source of a legend.

Hitler's exposition was in large part day-dreaming, unrelated to what followed in real life. Even if seriously meant, it was not a call to action, at any rate not to the action of a great war.

Why then did Hitler hold this conference? this question was not asked at Nuremberg; it has not been asked by historians. . . . The conference of 5 November 1937 was a curious gathering: only Goering was a Nazi. The others were old-style Conservatives . . . dismissed from their posts within 3 months. Hitler knew that all except Goering were his opponents; and he did not trust Goering much. Why did he reveal his inmost thoughts to men whom he distrusted and whom he was shortly to discharge? This question has an easy answer: He did not reveal his inmost thoughts. The conference was a manoeuvre in domestic affairs.

. . . The second part of the conference was concerned with questions of armament. This no doubt was why it had been called.

*Source*: A. J. P. Taylor, *The Origins of the Second World War* (1961).

SOURCE B

AN ALTERNATIVE VIEW.

The document is not a full and accurate record of the 5 November meeting. It is not the original record . . . but a copy of a copy . . . moreover, the conference was not called to discuss foreign policy but to decide on priorities in the allocation of armaments between the three armed services. This said, there is no reason why the memorandum should not be accepted as a guide to Hitler's ideas on foreign policy.

The Hossbach Memorandum confirms the continuity of Hitler's thinking: the primacy of force in world politics, conquest of living space in the east, anti-Bolshevism, hostility to France. Hitler's warlike intentions were now explicit.

Source: Anthony P. Adamthwaite, *The Making of the Second World War* (1977).

1 What aims in foreign policy does Hitler describe in this document?
2 Compare these aims with those described earlier in *Mein Kampf*. Do Hitler's aims appear to have changed or have they remained constant?
3 Hitler showed no interest in retaining Hossbach's record of this meeting. Can you draw any conclusions from this?
4 Try to summarize, in point form
  (a) Taylor's argument;
  (b) Adamthwaite's argument.
5 On which aspects of the meeting are the sources in agreement? Do they just agree on matters of fact – such as who was present – or is there also agreement on questions of interpretation – such as why the meeting was held?
6 In what ways do the two sources disagree?
7 What are your own conclusions about the significance of the meeting?

## 11.8 the Blomberg–Fritsch Crisis

While Hitler may have wanted to instil in foreign policy his own personal sense of urgency, it was precisely the pace of events which was beginning to cause unease in sections of the military leadership and Foreign Office. At the meeting on 5 November, Hitler's lengthy monologue had prompted animated interventions from War Minster von Blomberg and Werner Fritsch, the head of the army. It is surely likely, that as these key players left the meeting and headed into the November night, they had barely concealed their deep unease as to the direction and pace of the events that Hitler was now driving forward. A clear indication of the radicalization of Hitler's foreign policy came with key changes in senior personnel in the spring of 1938. Those who had urged caution or expressed dissent were now surgically removed. In the Foreign Office von Neurath gave way to the more ideologically reliable von Ribbentrop. In the senior echelon of the army Blomberg and von Fritsch were removed. Ominously, Hitler appointed himself as Supreme Commander of the German Army, another sign that any restraints he may have faced in 1937 were now being brushed aside.

Despite Hitler's rising dissatisfaction with the timidity of some of his more conservative military leaders it is not possible to confirm that the 'Blomberg–Fritsch crisis' of January–February 1938 was a premeditated move on Hitler's part. The course of events began when Blomberg, with the Führer's blessing and permission, married on 12 January 1938, with Hitler and Goering acting as high-profile chief witnesses. Within less than a fortnight the problematic 'past' of Blomberg's bride began to emerge. Meanwhile, an old scandal concerning Werner Fritsch, the supreme commander of the army, had been resurrected by the Gestapo. The story of his homosexual activities had first come to the fore some two years earlier, but Hitler had then refused to act upon the rumours and had remained loyal to the general. Goering, who had looked with some envy at Blomberg's position, and Himmler, who was always willing to discomfit the Wehrmacht, given his own hopes for an armed SS, now exploited Hitler's embarrassment over Blomberg to bring down Fritsch as well. Most historians feel that despite some of the objections raised at the Hossbach conference, Hitler had not been planning substantial personnel changes in the military leadership. It seems that when Hitler expressed surprise and anxiety over the affair that his reaction was genuine, leading Goebbels to see it as the most serious crisis since the blood purge of 1934. However, Hitler's combination of opportunism and ruthlessness enabled him to execute a bloodless purge of the old-guard national-conservative power elite. Blomberg's office of War Minster was abolished. Hitler himself took over as commander-in-chief of the armed forces, appointing the pliant General Wilhelm Keitel as head of the newly established supreme command of the Wehrmacht. Evans contends that, following the Reichstag fire and the Röhm crisis, the Blomberg–Fritsch affair was the third great milestone on the way to the Führer's absolutist power. As has been rightly said, it amounted practically to a coup d'état against the remnants of the old order. From early 1938 onwards, Hitler was increasingly surrounded by his own sort: adventurers, hard-liners, all-or-nothing gamblers, ideologues. And with the establishment of Führer absolutism, embodying a course whose unstoppable momentum was carrying Hitler, too, along with it, the grandiose 'vision' – whatever the risks – inevitably came increasingly to replace any lingering semblance of policy-making aimed at limited, 'rational' objectives. With the coup of February 1938, Hitler's supremacy over the one institution of state which could still topple him – the armed forces – was firmly established. There were no institutional constraints on his exercise of power; no decision of any significance could be taken without his approval; no organization presented an oppositional threat. Opposition was, of course, not eliminated. But it could take no organizational form, which was a danger to Hitler. The possibilities of an internal strike against Hitler were confined to the activities of small conspiratorial groups within the army or to the isolated actions of persons unattached to any grouping or organization (such as the remarkable solo attempt on Hitler's life in the Munich Bürgerbräukeller in 1939 by the Swabian joiner Georg Elser).

## 11.9  the Anschluss with Austria, 1938

Hitler's desire to bring about the union of Germany with Austria marked a crossover between his general commitment to dismantling the Treaty of Versailles and his personal agenda based on his own background and upbringing as an Austrian citizen. Anschluss – the political union of Germany and Austria – was forbidden under article 80 of the Versailles Treaty. As an Austrian by birth, it is perhaps not surprising to note that on the very first page of *Mein Kampf*, Hitler declared that Anschluss was 'a task to be furthered with every means'. Despite this, recent interpretations have indicated that Hitler did not necessarily take the initiative as the crisis over Austria unfolded. Goering played a key role, motivated by the prospect of seizing Austrian economic assets. In addition, analysis of the nature of the military incursion into Austria demonstrates quite clearly that this was a piece of improvisation rather than a carefully planned military operation.

Within Austria there was a flourishing and aggressive Nazi movement determined to promote Anschluss and disrupt the democratic government. In the winter of 1937, the Austrian chancellor, Kurt von Schuschnigg, came under increasing pressure to find some sort of agreement with Hitler. It was with this in mind that he made his fateful decision to accept an invitation to meet Hitler. On 12 February 1938 Schuschnigg made the short car journey to the Führer's picturesque mountain retreat at Berchtesgaden close to the Austrian border. It was not a meeting which Schuschnigg was likely to forget, and his account is generally regarded by historians as a reliable piece of evidence.

Hitler was waiting on the steps at the Berghof, and invited the Austrian chancellor into his study for a private conversation before lunch. Schuschnigg's polite remarks about the beautiful view from the window were swept aside as Hitler launched into a vitriolic attack on Austrian policy. 'The whole history of Austria is just one uninterrupted act of high treason. . . . And I can tell you here and now, Herr Schuschnigg, that I am absolutely determined to make an end of all this.'

Hitler let Schuschnigg know of his fury that Austria had begun to conduct defence works on the border. 'Listen. You don't really think that you can move a single stone in Austria without my hearing about it the very next day, do you? You don't seriously believe that you can stop me or even delay me for half an hour, do you?'

Finally, the Austrian chancellor was told that unless he gave his agreement to a package of changes proposed by Hitler, the Germans would have no alternative but to use force. 'Think it over, Herr Schuschnigg, think it over well. I can only wait until this afternoon. If I tell you that, you will do well to take my words literally. I don't believe in bluffing. All my past is proof of that.'[20]

## Hitler's demands to Schuschnigg

- The Austrian government was to recognize that National Socialism was perfectly compatible with loyalty to Austria
- Seyss-Inquart, a known Nazi sympathiser, was to be appointed Minister of the interior with control of the police
- An amnesty for all imprisoned Nazis was to be proclaimed within three days.
- Nazi officials who had been dismissed to be reinstated in their posts

Schuschnigg desperately tried to secure changes in the draft but Hitler refused to budge. Eventually Schuschnigg told Hitler that he was willing personally to accept the terms but there was no guarantee that these changes would be ratified by the Austrian government under a free constitution. Hitler threw open the door, ushering Schuschnigg out and shouting for General Keitel, the

Chief of the German High Command. Von Papen later described what Hitler was up to: 'Hitler could be heard shouting behind the open door: "Where is General Keitel? Tell him to come here at once." Keitel told us later that when he presented himself and asked for orders, Hitler grinned and said: "There are no orders. I just wanted you here."' Now Hitler told Schuschnigg that 'I have decided to change my mind for the first time in my life. But I warn you – this is your very last chance. I have given you three more days before the Agreement goes into effect.'[21]

The agreement seemed to have secured for Hitler the close co-ordination of Austria's foreign policy and economic development with that of Nazi Germany. It was now that the initiative passed briefly into the hands of Schuschnigg. On 9 March he announced his plan to hold a referendum for his fellow countrymen to express their support for 'a free and German, independent and social, Christian and united Austria'. It was a brave move, but Schuschnigg's stand against Hitler collapsed in the absence of any signs of support, either from within his own cabinet or from interested parties like Italy and Britain. On 11 March Schuschnigg announced that Austria would give in without a struggle. No plebiscite would be held and Seyss-Inquart would take over as Chancellor.

The next day, German soldiers entered Austria. Signs that the operation was hastily improvised rather than planned were everywhere. Panzer tanks had to refuel at petrol stations along the road to Vienna, and tank drivers had to use tourist maps to plan their route. Only after Hitler himself received a rapturous reception in his home town of Linz did he turn his initial plan of assimilation into a full-scale invasion.

## 11.10 Neville Chamberlain, the policy of appeasement and the fate of Czechoslovakia

### key events: 1938

| | |
|---|---|
| 28 March | Hitler encourages German minority in Czechoslovakia to agitate for the break-up of the state |
| 24 April | Germans in Sudetenland demand complete autonomy |
| 29 April | Britain reluctantly supports France in diplomatic action in defence of the Czech government |
| 9 May | Russia promises to help Czechoslovakia in the event of a German invasion if Poland and Romania will allow the passage of Russian troops. This is refused by both nations |
| 21 May | Czechoslovakia moves to partial mobilization in response to German troop movements on her border |
| 22 May | Britain warns Germany of dangers of military action but tells France that she does not favour military action herself |
| 12 August | Germany begins to mobilize |

| | |
|---|---|
| 11 September | Poland and Romania again refuse to allow the passage of Russian troops to help Czechoslovakia |
| 15 September | In their first meeting, at Berchtesgaden, Hitler tells Chamberlain of his determination to annex the Sudetenland on the grounds of self-determination |
| 18 September | Britain and France agree to persuade the Czechs to hand over territory to Germany in areas where over half the population is German. The Czechs at first reject this proposal but then agree to it |
| 22 September | In the second meeting between Hitler and Chamberlain, at Bad Godesberg, Hitler demands immediate occupation of the Sudetenland and names the date of the invasion as 28 September |
| 29 September | Hitler suspends the invasion pending the Munich Conference at which Chamberlain, Daladier, Mussolini and Hitler agree to the transfer of the Sudetenland to Germany, while guaranteeing the remaining Czech frontiers. The Russians are not invited to take part in the conference |

The British Foreign Secretary Lord Halifax had hardly taken office when Hitler annexed Austria on 12 March 1938. That evening a press photographer asked for a smile from War Minister Hore-Belisha as he left 10 Downing Street.

'Why should I smile?' he answered. Like many others, the minister feared that having consumed Austria, Germany would now hunger for Czechoslovakia. This pessimistic mood pervaded the whole cabinet. Such was the sense of gloom that before the year was out gas masks were issued to the entire population (except for babies) while the Home Office posted to every house in the country a handbook on protection against air raids.[22]

As anxiety mounted during the tense summer of 1938 Prime Minister Neville Chamberlain's sense of personal mission and his desire to appease Hitler had never been greater. In September he proposed to leave for Germany at once to talk with Hitler. It set in motion a dramatic trilogy – three visits by Chamberlain to Hitler over the course of two weeks – which came to symbolize the cause of appeasement. The first flight to Munich, in September 1938 was arranged in great haste and signified the most important mission of Chamberlain's life. Accompanied by a few trusted diplomats but without any other government minister, he was entering Hitler's lair. The man regarded as one of the most capable politicians of his generation had placed his reputation on the line. The stakes could not have been higher; the whole future of Europe was at risk. The potential prize was lasting European peace. By the end of the month Chamberlain's reputation had reached new heights. When he returned from the last of his three dramatic meetings with Adolf Hitler he was greeted as the man who had averted the threat to world peace. Acclaimed by the press, the public and fellow politicians, it seemed that Chamberlain would go down in history as one of the greatest British leaders of all time. Yet within a year Europe was at war, leaving Chamberlain to lament: 'Everything that I have worked for, everything that I have hoped for, everything that I have believed in during my public life, has crashed into ruins.'[23]

## the personality of Neville Chamberlain

When Neville Chamberlain became the British Prime Minister in May 1937 his reputation could hardly have been higher. He was a highly capable and extremely hard-working statesman, a tough, decisive leader who acted on the basis of firm conviction and inner strength. He did not like to be contradicted, dismissed those cabinet colleagues who disagreed with him as 'weaker brethren' and could be scathing when people blocked his path. As Chancellor of the Exchequer in the Baldwin cabinet (1932–37), he had become the dominant figure not just in financial matters but also with regard to foreign affairs. In January 1936 he noted in private that 'Defence policy' has been guided by me. ... When I am silent everyone else is also.'[24] Chamberlain believed that defence and economic strength were closely connected. In 1934 he placed himself at the centre of the British government's decision to spend increasingly large amounts on rearmament and linked the need for military preparations directly to the threat from Germany. By the time Neville Chamberlain became the British Prime Minister in May 1937, Hitler's demands for the resolution of Germany's international grievances were becoming increasingly aggressive. Hitler focused much of his attention upon the Treaty of Versailles (1919), which created specific German grievances over Austria, Czechoslovakia and Poland.

Chamberlain's name was directly linked to the controversial policy of appeasement, an attempt to deal with German grievances in a peaceful way. For a long time the prevailing view was that Neville Chamberlain and his weak-willed policy of appeasement played into Hitler's hands. Many historians argued that Chamberlain was a well-meaning but naïve statesman who was taken in by Hitler's empty promises. In the words of Cabinet Minister Duff Cooper's resignation speech: 'The Prime Minister has believed in addressing Herr Hitler through the language of sweet reasonableness. I have believed that he was more open to the language of the mailed fist.'[25]

More recently, however, historians have generally been more sympathetic towards Chamberlain. In particular, they have begun to appreciate that Chamberlain had to face a number of difficulties in dealing with a dictator like Hitler. A brief glimpse at the table that follows illustrates the point. Whoever was charged with conducting British foreign policy had to contend not just with the rise of aggressive and adventurous regimes in Italy under Mussolini and Germany under Hitler but also a similarly ideologically driven overseas policy in the Far East, where Japan had entered a period referred to by historians as the 'dark valley'.

Public opinion was clear in one respect. For all of those who had clear memories of the slaughter of 1914–18 there was no desire whatsoever to see a repeat. Phrases like 'a war to end all wars' and 'never again' summed up the sense that few people had the appetite for further conflict. Conversely there was a widespread desire for peace.

In a sense there was still a real sense of mourning for the 'lost generation' who had made the ultimate sacrifice in the First World War. Chamberlain himself had lost close friends and relatives in the war and came to regard armed conflict between nations as abhorrent. Beyond Chamberlain's moral condemnation of the futility of war, he was also keenly aware that money spent on armaments took away finance from public projects such as housing and schools. Therefore in September 1938 with war over Czechoslovakia seeming ever more likely, Chamberlain took the unprecedented step of taking his arguments for peace directly to Hitler. On Tuesday 13 September, with the annual National Socialist rally at Nuremberg fast approaching, Chamberlain decided to take matters into his own hands. Chamberlain wrote a short personal note to Hitler which prompted an invitation from Hitler to meet at the Führer's mountain retreat in Berchtesgaden.

**SOURCE**

CYPHER TELEGRAM TO SIR N. HENDERSON (BERLIN).

Foreign Office, September 13th 1938

*Most Immediate.*
You should ensure through Ribbentrop the delivery at the earliest possible moment of the following message to Herr Hitler as personal message to him from Prime Minister;-

'In view of increasingly critical situation I propose to come over at once to see you with a view to trying to find peaceful solution. I propose to come across by air and am ready to start tomorrow.

Please indicate earliest time at which you can see me and suggest place of meeting. Should be grateful for very early reply'.

NEVILLE CHAMBERLAIN

For your information. Our intention is to make no public reference to the above until the Chancellor has had opportunity of sending reply which we hope we may have at earliest possible moment. Repeated to Prague

*Source*: Public Records Office, London.

On the next day, Wednesday 14 September, Chamberlain informed the Cabinet meeting for the first time of his bold plan to meet Hitler.

## the first visit: Berchtesgaden

On Thursday 15 September, the Prime Minister flew to Munich, with Horace Wilson and Strang from the Foreign Office. From Munich, they travelled through the Bavarian countryside by special train to Berchtesgaden and then on by car to Hitler's Alpine retreat in Obersalzberg. The atmosphere at the first meeting between the two leaders has been described by American historian William Rock as 'proper but strained'.[26] Hitler spoke firmly but politely and insisted on the transfer of the Sudetenland to Germany. Chamberlain stated that while he personally was prepared to accept this solution he would first have to consult his cabinet colleagues and then return to Germany. Hitler showed some impatience, but agreed to this, although he was not prepared to discuss the wider issue of peace until the Czechoslovak issue was resolved.

## the second visit: Bad Godesberg

Within a week, Chamberlain was back in Germany, arriving in scenic Godesberg on the Rhine, ready to do business with Hitler and bring the Czech crisis to an end. The Prime Minister was stunned to encounter an aggressive and petulant Führer who now demanded the immediate German military occupation of the Sudetenland. Thirty-six hours of tense bargaining followed but Hitler's only concession was to defer the timetable for military occupation by a few days. With Hitler grumbling that Chamberlain was the first man to whom he had ever made such concessions, the Prime Minister returned to London. He was not the first politician to find a meeting with Hitler both bewildering and depressing.

Broadcasting to the nation on the night of 27 September, the Prime Minister announced his readiness 'to pay even a third visit to Germany' given the 'horrible, fantastic, incredible fact that Britain was preparing for war because of a quarrel in a far-away country between people of whom we know nothing'.[27]

## the third visit: Munich

The conference in Munich on 29 September 1938 was virtually a non-event since the details were cut and dried before the leading statesmen arrived. The Agreement, signed on 30 September, provided for German occupation of the

Sudetenland in ten days from 1 October, with an international commission from Britain, France, Germany, Italy and Czechoslovakia to supervise the operation. The conference at Munich stripped Czechoslovakia of her fortified frontier areas. The Czechoslovakian state was broken down into its federal components – Czechia, Slovakia and a smaller area known as Ruthenia (Carpatho-Ukraine).[28]

The emotional sense of relief shown by the general public in Germany and Great Britain disguised the fact that once again Hitler had got his way. The Czechs, their country dismembered and left wide open to subsequent German aggression, were not even invited to the conference and would never trust the Allies again.

## Chamberlain and the 'piece of paper'

Before he left Munich, and acting entirely on his own initiative, Chamberlain sought out Hitler at his apartment. He asked Hitler to sign a short declaration drawn up by Chamberlain himself, which expressed the two statesmen's determination to continue to strive to resolve their differences through consultation and negotiation. It was the slip of paper bearing this declaration that Chamberlain waved in the air when he arrived back in London. He was given a hero's reception by a relieved public. Chamberlain was convinced that he had pacified Hitler and that war had been avoided. Yet on 21 October, Hitler gave instructions to his armed forces to prepare 'to smash the remainder of the Czech state, should it pursue an anti-German policy'.[29] Chamberlain's hopes of peace would not survive the winter.

On 27 September an evening parade through Berlin intended to be a major demonstration of military resolve became more like a demonstration for peace. Hitler was said to have been infuriated by the fact that Chamberlain was given such a warm reception and this led Hitler to conclude that the German people lacked the martial spirit he desired.

When Chamberlain flew back to Hendon airport near London, he read out the document Hitler had signed before the assembled crowd and journalists:

> We, the German Führer and Chancellor, and the British Prime
> Minister, have had a further meeting today, and are agreed in
> recognizing that the question of Anglo-German relations is of the first
> importance for the two countries and Europe. We regard the agreement
> signed last night and the Anglo-German Naval Agreement as symbolic
> of the desire of our two peoples never to go to war with one another
> again. We are resolved that the method of consultation shall be the
> method adopted to deal with any other question which may concern
> our two countries and we are determined to continue our efforts to
> remove possible sources of differences, and thus to contribute to ensure
> the peace of Europe'.[30]

Chamberlain seemed to be at the height of his powers and quoted Shakespeare saying that he had 'plucked the flower safety from the nettle danger'.[31]

**SOURCE A**

Neville Chamberlain.

Do not let us . . . be deflected from our course. Let us remember that the desire of all peoples of the world still remains concentrated on the hopes of peace. . . . Though we may have to suffer checks and disappointments from time to time, the object that we have in mind is of too great significance to the happiness of mankind for us lightly to give it up or set it on one side.

*Source*: William R. Rock, *British Appeasement in the 1930s* (1977).

**SOURCE B**

François Poncet, French Ambassador in Berlin.

The fact that the head of the greatest empire in the world should have asked for an audience of the Chancellor of the Reich and agreed to go in person, not even to the German capital, but as far as Berchtesgaden, is considered by Hitler himself, his entourage and by German opinion as an immense success

*Source*: R. A. C. Parker, *Chamberlain and Appeasement: British Policy and the Coming of the Second World War* (1993).

**SOURCE C**

It is of course nonsense to depict him as ignorant of European politics. . . . Nor was Neville Chamberlain in any way attracted by Nazism or beguiled by Hitler himself, though he rashly once gave reason to believe that he was when he referred publicly to Hitler having pledged his word. He had been at the centre of the British rearmament effort since its inception in 1934 and had urged and pressed it forward, expressly relating it to the threat from Germany. . . . There is abundant evidence to show he doubted and distrusted Hitler's sincerity at every turn. . . . The sense that a new war was inevitable had its hold over him, as it had over virtually everyone in Britain. But he found it abhorrent, and fought against it.

*Source*: Donald Cameron Watt, *How War Came: The Immediate Origins of the Second World War 1938–39* (1989).

**SOURCE D**

Recent writing has had little patience with the simple stereotypes which once dominated the field. Chamberlain was not an ignorant meddler in matters which he had no experience. When he became Prime Minister he seemed at the time to be the only man for the job. Churchill praised him fulsomely when seconding his nomination for the Conservative Party leadership. Neville was efficient and energetic. He would bring to the Cabinet a sense of leadership which most of its members welcomed, in contrast to Baldwin's relaxed style. . . . Ultimately, it was Chamberlain's behaviour during these dramatic weeks in September 1938 that was to give the entire strategy of appeasement a bad name. Whatever his initial intentions, it has generally been thought that the Prime Minister's zeal for an agreement was humiliating. He allowed himself to be outplayed by Hitler at almost every point. That has been the predominant verdict of posterity. . . .

He did not grasp the dynamics of Hitler's regime and did not display a deep understanding of the aims, beliefs and practices of National Socialism. He had many admirable qualities but a profound imaginative insight into the mind of Germany during these years was not among them.

*Source*: Keith Robbins, *Appeasement* (1988).

Neville Chamberlain, writing shortly after the meeting with Hitler at Berchtesgaden.

Hitler played on Chamberlain's vanity. 'H.W. heard from various people who were with Hitler after my interview that he had been very favourably impressed. I have had a conversation with a man, he said, and one with whom I grasped the essentials. In short, I had established a certain confidence, which was my aim, and in spite of the hardness and ruthlessness I thought I saw in his face I got the impression that here was a man who could be relied upon when he had given his word.

*Source*: R. A. C. Parker, *Chamberlain and Appeasement: British Policy and the Coming of the Second World War* (1993).

Extract from Chamberlain's statement to the House of Commons, 28 September 1938.

We, the German Führer and Chancellor, and the British Prime Minister, have had a further meeting today, and are agreed in recognizing that the question of Anglo-German relations is of the first importance for the two countries and Europe.

We regard the agreement signed last night and the Anglo-German Naval Agreement as symbolic of the desire of our two peoples never to go to war with one another again. **We are resolved that the method of consultation shall be the method adopted to deal with any other questions which may concern our two countries and we are determined to continue our efforts to remove possible sources of differences, and thus to contribute to ensure the peace of Europe.**

*Source*: Donald Cameron Watt, *How War Came: The Immediate Origins of the Second World War 1938–39* (1989).

Extract from Hitler's military directive, May 1938.

Top secret, Military
Berlin, May 30 1938
It is my unalterable decision to smash Czechoslovakia by military action in the near future.

*Source*: J. Noakes and G. Pridham (ed.), *Nazism 1919–1945: A Documentary Reader. Vol. 3: Foreign Policy, War and Racial Extermination* (1995).

To what extent would you agree that the policy of appeasement was misguided and naïve from start to finish?

## 11.11 the crisis over Czechoslovakia

Hitler came away from the Munich conference with a sense of anger and frustration rather than any satisfaction at being handed the Sudetenland without any bloodshed. Despite Chamberlain's warm words of peace, Hitler immediately made clear to his generals that he must be able to smash Czechoslovakia should her policy become hostile to Germany, as this extract from Hitler's military directive of 21 October 1938 makes clear:

> The Wehrmacht must at all times be prepared for the following eventualities:
>
> 1 securing the frontiers of the German Reich and protection against surprise air attacks;
> 2 liquidation of the remainder of the Czech State;
> 3 the occupation of Memelland . . .
>
> 2   Liquidation of the Remainder of the Czech State
>
> It must be possible to smash at any time the remainder of the Czech state should it pursue an anti-German policy.[32]

While military preparations ensued, the degree of autonomy which the Munich agreement gave to the Slovaks allowed Hitler to encourage further demands from the Slovak separatists and exert remorseless pressure on the increasingly vulnerable Czech state. Apart from its substantial German minority, Czechoslovakia also contained large numbers of Slovaks and smaller numbers of Hungarians and Poles. At the start of 1939 Hitler intensified pressure on the remainder of the Czech state by encouraging these groups to press their separatist claims. At the same time, pressure was exerted on the Poles to force them to agree to the construction of a major road and railway across the Polish Corridor, and for the return of Danzig to Germany. When the Czech President Hacha visited Berlin in the spring of 1939 the hopelessness of his situation became clear. With Goering gleefully conjuring up the image of Prague being bombed, the ageing Czech leader was left with no choice but to agree to Bohemia and Moravia being placed under Czech protection. German troops entered Prague on 15 March and the next day Hitler incorporated Bohemia and Moravia into the Reich, with the spurious claim that these provinces had actually been part of Germany for a thousand years. With the conquest of Czechoslovakia complete, Hitler then forced Lithuania to return the Memelland on 22 March, reversing a further term of the Versailles treaty.

The cynical destruction of Czechoslovakia had only one saving grace. Finally, there could be no doubt in political circles or in the public mind that Hitler's words were empty and that Germany would not be stopped by a paper agreement. In simple terms, it now became clear that Hitler's intent was to become the dominant power in Europe by the use of force. As attention turned to the future of Poland, Britain guaranteed Polish independence on 31 March and extended the same protection to Greece and Romania on 13 April. Britain had stepped away from her traditional policy of non-involvement in the affairs of Eastern Europe. Conversely, it could be claimed that the failure of the Western powers to offer no more than verbal protests at the treatment of Czechoslovakia simply strengthened Hitler's conviction that these new guarantees from the West were hollow words. Alternatively, it could be assumed that Hitler now knew that Britain would no longer remain on the sidelines and that military action against both Britain and France might have to precede the realization of his long-standing ambitions in the East. Attention now turned to the future of Danzig, the Polish Corridor and Poland itself.

## 11.12  the Nazi–Soviet Pact

A critical turning point in the road to the Second World War came with the announcement in August 1939 that Germany had concluded a non-aggression pact with the Soviet Union. The news that Stalin, the arch-Communist, had signed an agreement with his ideological opposite, Adolf Hitler dealt a shattering blow to the west and cleared the way for Hitler's move against Poland which, in turn precipitated a much wider conflict. It is now clear that overtures received from Germany in the summer suggested that in return for a free hand in Poland, Hitler might be prepared to make significant concessions to Russia in eastern Poland, Bessarabia, the Baltic States and Finland. At the same time the issue of Russia's relations with the western powers were also of paramount importance. During this period of delicate negotiations Britain's attitude towards Russia remained uncertain. Although Chamberlain seemed to desire improved relations with the Soviet Union and became the first British premier to attend a function at the Soviet embassy since the revolution of 1917, there was some evidence to suggest that Britain was anxious to conclude an agreement with Germany that would preclude any agreement with the Soviet Union.

### timeline of key events: 1938–39

*1938*

| | |
|---|---|
| 9 May | Russia promises to help Czechoslovakia in the event of a German invasion if Poland and Romania will allow the passage of Russian troops. This is refused by both nations |
| 11 September | Poland and Romania again refuse to allow the passage of Russian troops to help Czechoslovakia |
| 29 September | Hitler suspends the invasion of Czechoslovakia pending the Munich Conference at which Chamberlain, Daladier, Mussolini and Hitler agree to the transfer of the Sudetenland |

| | to Germany, while guaranteeing the remaining Czech frontiers. The Russians are not invited to take part in the conference |
|---|---|
| December | Western press full of speculation that Hitler intends to attack the Ukraine |

### 1939

| | |
|---|---|
| 11 March | In a major speech to the Soviet Congress Stalin says that 'The Soviet Union is not going to pull the warmongers' chestnuts out of the fire!' This is interpreted as a warning to the Western powers not to try to provoke a German–Soviet conflict. Hitler may have read the same speech as a green light for his planned invasion of the remainder of Czechoslovakia |
| 15 March | German troops occupy rump Czechoslovakia. This secured Germany's rear in the event of war in the west |
| 28 March | Hitler denounces Germany's 1934 non-aggression pact with Poland |
| 18 April | Litvinov, Commissar for Foreign Affairs, proposes a tripartite military alliance between Russia, France and Britain. The offer is not taken up by the Western allies. At the same time similar discussions were taking place between Soviet officials and German secretary of state von Weizsacker |
| 3 May | Litvinov is dismissed by Stalin and replaced by Molotov, Stalin's longest-standing associate. The fact that Litvinov is Jewish is regarded in some circles as significant |
| July | The British press contains detailed reports of talks between top officials at the Department of Overseas Trade with Helmut Wohltat, Head of Goering's four-year plan |
| 12 August | Anglo-French mission arrives in Moscow to begin talks |
| 18 August | Germany signs a commercial agreement with the USSR |
| 22 August | Ribbentrop, the German foreign minister, arrives in Moscow |

**SOURCE**

THE NAZI–SOVIET PACT: EXTRACTS FROM THE SECRET AGREEMENT, 23 AUGUST 1939.

The Government of the German Reich and The Government of the Union of the Soviet Socialist Republics

Directed by the wish to strengthen the cause of peace between Germany and the USSR and proceeding upon the basic provisions of the Treaty of Neutrality concluded between Germany and the USSR in April 1926, have reached the following agreement:

Article 1  The two contracting parties undertake to refrain from any act of violence, any aggressive action, or any attack against one another, whether individually or jointly with other powers.

Article 2    In case any of the contracting parties should become the object of warlike acts on the part of a third power, the other contracting power will not support that third power in any form.

Article 3    The Governments of the two contracting parties will in future remain in contact with each other through continuous consultation in order to inform each other concerning questions affecting their mutual interests.

Article 4    Neither of the two contracting parties will participate in any grouping of powers which is indirectly aimed against the other party . . .

Secret Additional Protocol
On the occasion of the signature of the Non-Aggression Treaty between the German Reich and the Union of the Soviet Socialist Republics, the undersigned plenipotentiaries of the two parties discussed in strictly confidential conversations the question of the delimitation of their respective spheres of interest in Eastern Europe. These conversations led to the following results:

1    In the event of a territorial and political transformation in the territories belonging to the Baltic States (Finland, Estonia, Latvia, Lithuania), the northern frontier of Lithuania shall represent the frontier of the spheres of interest both of Germany and the USSR. In this connection the interest of Lithuania in the Vilna territory is recognised by both parties.

*Source*: J. Noakes and G.  Pridham (ed.), *Nazism 1919–1945: A Documentary Reader. Vol. 3: Foreign Policy, War and Racial Extermination* (1995).

## 11.13  Poland and the free city of Danzig, 1939

In Britain, the public was appalled by Hitler's callous disregard for the promises he had made to Chamberlain at Munich. Amid rumours that German troops were about to march into Poland, Britain finally took a decisive step against Hitler. On 31 March, the British stated that if Poland were the victim of an unprovoked attack, Britain would come to her aid. France quickly gave the Poles a similar guarantee. However, Richard Overy highlights some of the problems that faced the west in taking a stand against Hitler over Danzig. He points out that:

> The League of Nations commissioner . . . Carl Burckhardt, whose task it was to maintain the integrity of the free City was far from committed to its independent survival. Lord Halifax, the British Foreign Secretary from February 1938, thought the status of Danzig and the Corridor a 'most foolish provision of the Treaty of Versailles'. Moreover the city whose independence was to provoke a general European war was, by 1938, a Nazi city. The Nazi Party had taken control of the Danzig parliament in May 1933 . . . Despite League objections the Nazi Party by 1936 had established virtual one-party rule and had imported the repressive apparatus of the parent model . . .
>
> Without firm allies, Poland's chances of persuading other powers to help her safeguard a Nazified Danzig against a predatory Germany seemed remote. Hitler had not chosen his moment idly. Poland was isolated and shunned, Danzig a Nazi outpost abandoned by the League.

Two things transformed the situation: the Polish decision that they would fight rather than abandon the Free City, and the British decision to side with Poland if it came to a fight.[33]

While Hitler eyed Poland he also expanded military preparations in the likelihood of a military showdown with the British and the French. In the autumn of 1938 he demanded a fivefold increase in the air force to establish a capacity for long-range bombers. As the Luftwaffe prepared for a war with Britain new emphasis was also placed on the expansion of the German battle fleet. Hitler knew that these developments might not be complete until the mid-1940s, indicating that he did not expect to go to war with Britain in the summer of 1939.

For a short time Hitler tolerated the option of negotiating with the Poles, offering them territorial gains in the Ukraine in return for their compliance. However, the Polish minister Beck knew that with the Russians watching his every move, room for manoeuvre with the Germans was extremely limited. By the spring of 1939 Hitler's thinking over Poland was becoming clearer, as shown in this extract from his comments to senior army commanders in May 1939:

> Germany was outside the circle of the Great Powers. A balance of power had been established without Germany's participation. It is not Danzig that is at stake. For us it is a matter of expanding our living space in the East and making food supplies secure and also solving the problem of the Baltic States. . . . The problem 'Poland' cannot be dissociated from the showdown with the West. . . There is therefore no question of sparing Poland and we are left with the decision: To attack Poland at the first suitable opportunity. We cannot expect a repetition of Czechia. There will be war. Our task is to isolate Poland. Success in isolating her will be decisive.[34]

In the same speech Hitler made it clear that the success of the enterprise would rest on the extent to which it was possible to isolate Poland. On the eve of the meeting Hitler had concluded the Pact of Steel with Mussolini. Despite the grandiose name given to the agreement, Hitler knew what Italy was ill-prepared for a major war. However, Germany's position was dramatically improved on 23 August by the conclusion of a non-aggression pact with Russia. These developments made Hitler confident that France and Britain would now try to withdraw from their undertakings to Poland, and he went ahead with his plans for invasion at the start of September. However, on 25 August, Britain signed a Treaty of Alliance with Poland and it became clear that France would also stand by her Polish guarantees. Once again, Hitler hesitated at a critical moment in German foreign policy and European history. Yet once more he overcame his doubts and on 1 September German troops marched into Poland. On 3 September Britain and France declared war on Germany. Poland offered brave resistance but this was quickly overcome. In attempting to deal with Hitler the conventional politicians of the Western powers employed discussion, reason, moral force and compromise. Although there was no easy way to deal with Hitler or to solve the problems he presented it is also clear that it took too long to understand that they faced a man whose reasoning was of an utterly different nature.

# the Second World War, 1939–45

## 12.1 introduction

The Second World War was among the most destructive conflicts in human history; more than forty-six million soldiers and civilians perished, many in circumstances of prolonged and horrifying cruelty. During the 2,174 days of war between the German attack on Poland in September 1939 and the surrender of Japan in August 1945, by far the largest number of those killed, whether in battle or behind the lines, were unknown by name or face except to those few who knew or loved them . . .

No one has been able to calculate the number of wounded, certainly amounting to several millions, whose lives were permanently scarred as a result of the war. Physical scars, from the severest disability to disfiguring wounds, and mental scars, accompanied these millions for the rest of their lives. Many died as a direct result of them. Others lived in pain, discomfort, fear or remorse. For those civilians who were fortunate to survive privation, deportation and massacre, similar scars, physical, mental and spiritual, remained – and still remain – to torment them. The greatest unfinished business of the Second World War is human pain.[1]

## 12.2 the destruction of Poland

The German invasion of Poland that presaged the Second World War itself began early in the morning of 1 September 1939, with an Army Group North based in Pomerania and East Prussia and an Army Group South moving from Silesia and Czechoslovakia. Although events had unfolded very differently to the way Hitler had anticipated and Germany was not fully prepared for a major war, the initial military initiative was manifestly with the Germans. On the same day that German troops began an assault which within weeks would bring a crushing victory over the Poles, Hitler addressed the Reichstag in uncompromising terms:

I am not demanding of any German man anything more than what I myself was ready to do voluntarily for four years. There will be no privation in Germany which I myself will not share from the start. From now onwards, even more than before, my whole life belongs to my people. I do not want to be anything other than the first soldier of the German Reich.

I have once more put on the uniform which was once the most holy and precious to me. I shall only take it off after victory or I shall not live to see the end.[2]

It was now clear that Hitler remained hopeful that Britain's threatened intervention would not materialize and that he had called their bluff. He reasoned that Poland's geographical and military position was hopeless and that the British would conclude that they could not realistically offer any genuine assistance. However, the British finally stood firm, on 1 September issuing Hitler with an ultimatum that if Germany had not withdrawn her troops from Poland by 11.00 a.m. a state of war would exist between the two countries. A corresponding ultimatum was issued by the French. When the ultimatum expired Britain formally declared war on Germany on 3 September.

Meanwhile, the Polish army and people witnessed the visitation of the Blitzkrieg, or lightning war, that was to prove so effective for the Germans in the first campaigns of the war. Highly mobile troop movements, motorized infantry and overwhelming air power easily outmanoeuvred the static defensive tactics employed by the Poles. With heavy German armour crashing through brave but flimsy Polish resistance and the German air force, the Luftwaffe, inflicting terrifying damage from the air, the Poles soon gave way. On 17 September the Soviet Union launched an invasion from the East, seizing the territory assigned to it under the terms of the Nazi–Soviet pact. By the end of September 1939 Germany and Russia were in a position to partition Poland. Danzig, Posen and West Prussia were reunited with Germany. Western Poland saw the formation of the *Generalgouvernement* led by Hans Frank. Despite the declaration of war, military assistance from the western powers was not forthcoming. The defensive strategy employed by Britain and France meant that a fleeting opportunity to launch an offensive against Hitler in the West when Germany might have been vulnerable, was lost. On 6 October the resistance of the final Polish units collapsed. In the brief but uneven conflict with Germany, Poland had lost 70,000 troops with more than 130,000 wounded and 700,000 taken prisoner. The Poles also suffered heavy casualties in the fighting with the Soviet Union, while the Germans suffered 11,000 deaths and 30,000 wounded. Yet the suffering of the Polish people and its Jewish community had only just begun. In the words of Laurence Rees:

No country occupied by Germany in the entire war endured as much as Poland. This was the epicentre of Nazi brutality, the place where Nazism achieved its purest and most bestial form. Six million Poles died in the war – around 18 per cent of the population; by comparison, the British lost fewer than 400,000. . . . Sporadic signs showed from the first that this was no ordinary invasion. German SS units displayed terrible and casual brutality as they accompanied the regular army into Poland. . . . The atmosphere in which the Nazis made each decision was one of contempt for the Poles and hatred for the Jews. In Poland during the early years of the war the Nazis initiated a racial policy the like of which had never seen before. Hundreds of thousands of people were uprooted and cruelly cast to the wind. But the Nazis had not finished with Poland yet.[3]

An interesting and challenging interpretation of these events is offered by Karl-Heinz Frieser in his book, *The Blitzkrieg Legend*. As the extract that follows reveals, Frieser does not accept that Hitler successfully masterminded an impressive and well-organized policy:

> Hitler's gambler's policy failed early in September 1939. He thought that he could crush Poland in an isolated campaign, but instead Great Britain and France declared war on him. In that way, he conjured up the spectre of World War I, the two-front war. In 1939, the German Reich, poor in raw materials, was no more able than in 1914 to last through a long, drawn-out conflict with the Western sea powers.

Frieser contends that the initial military success against Poland in 1939 and then France in 1940

> had not at all been planned in advance that way. Instead . . . it sprang from the accidental coincidence of the most varied factors. But Nazi propaganda fashioned the myth that the German victory was due to a concept spelled out long before and garnished it with an as yet relatively unknown catchword blitzkrieg. At the same time, it was suggested that the inventor of these new methods was Adolf Hitler, the 'greatest military genius of all times'. . . . The theory of blitzkrieg strategy has been subjected to increasing doubt in recent years. In this connection, it can be argued that this involves a fiction that was put together by historians only after the fact.
>
> The brilliant blitzkrieg campaign against Poland concealed the fact that the Wehrmacht at this time was also on the brink of disaster. The German forces, it so happens, would not have been able to continue fighting much longer. They had shot their bolt. Only the swift end of this campaign, which actually was completed after eighteen days, saved the Wehrmacht from logistical collapse as far as ammunition was concerned.[4]

## 12.3 the war in Scandinavia

In the spring of 1940 the focal point of the war briefly switched to Scandinavia. Through the winter of 1939–40 Finland was locked in conflict with the

Russian army, which was still coming to terms with the Stalinist purge that had devastated its leadership in 1937. The Western powers wanted to bring support to the Finns, perhaps through the occupation of Norway to free up lines of communication. As British and French forces moved to occupy strategic Norwegian ports, compromising Germany's supplies of iron ore from Sweden, the Germans seized the initiative. German forces occupied Denmark on 9 April and then Norway was attacked. As in Poland, the Germans did not have to wait long for victory. As Norway succumbed, the Allied forces were driven out and the Norwegian royal family and government went into exile in Britain. A puppet regime led by Quisling was installed by the Germans. Germany's victory secured her iron-ore supplies, strengthened her strategic hold in the Baltic and made Britain more vulnerable through the extension of German naval and air bases in this crucial region. Ostensibly a successful mission, the brief campaign in Scandinavia actually saw Hitler tested in war for the first time. Hitler was determined to play an active part as supreme commander and worked closely with Admiral Raeder, the Commander-in-Chief of the navy. When ten German destroyers, half of Raeder's fleet, were sunk and several thousand troops were left stranded, Hitler's nerve broke and he ordered an immediate withdrawal from the port of Narvik. Interestingly, General Jodl did not act upon the order and instead spent three days persuading the edgy Führer to hold on to the port. Hitler was brought round, and by the time the Germans claimed complete control of Norway at the end of April, the Führer's reputation as a devastatingly effective military tactician was only enhanced.

## 12.4 the campaign in Western Europe

With the crisis in Norway over and with security provided in the East by the non-aggression pact with Stalin, Hitler now had a free hand to bring lightning war to the west. On 10 May 1940 German troops attacked the Netherlands, Belgium and France. Six weeks later the world would have to come to terms with the shattering fact that Germany had overwhelmed three countries in such a short space of time.

The aerial destruction of Rotterdam was followed by the total collapse of Dutch resistance after just five days and the capitulation of the Belgians shortly after. German troops swept into France but a tactical pause before Calais allowed the British Expeditionary Force to carry out a large-scale evacuation procedure at Dunkirk, rescuing more than 300,000 British, French and Belgian troops. This prompted Hitler to reverse his orders but it was too late for him to avoid the damaging consequences of this decision later on in the war. Regardless of the halt before Calais, the fact remained that France was prone, and Paris fell into German hands on 14 June. With the majority of French forces trapped in the south, Mussolini pressed Hitler to take humiliating, punitive action against France. However, Hitler believed that Britain would now accept Germany's dominant position in Europe and with this in mind he restrained Mussolini, and took the decision to occupy only the northern half of France and the west coast. France retained her colonies and a French government was permitted at Vichy in unoccupied France. An armistice signed between Germany and France on 22 June reflected these terms and underlined Hitler's desire not to fuel further French resistance. The initial campaign in Western Europe cost Germany 27,000 fatalities and 111,000 wounded. In France, the corresponding figures were 92,000 dead and 200,000 wounded.

## 12.5 the war in the air

In the Reichstag in July 1940 Hitler declared that Britain had to accept the European situation and return Germany's colonies if the war was to come to an end. With Winston Churchill, the new Prime Minister, embodying defiance, there was no chance of Britain coming to terms. Hitler now turned his attention to the invasion of Britain, the so-called 'Operation Sea-Lion'. Given Britain's naval strength, Hitler knew that German air superiority would be critical. Goering was charged with preparing the Luftwaffe for an invasion to commence in September. The initial air strikes targeted the Channel ports and air-force bases. On 7 September Goering switched the efforts of his air force to the bombing of the London docklands. During what came to be known as the Battle of Britain, London and other major industrial centres came under attack. However, the scale of losses among the Luftwaffe prompted Hitler to put Operation Sea-Lion on hold, initially until the spring of 1941, but it was ultimately never to be revived.

## 12.6 the Balkans

The heavy air losses over Britain may have led Hitler to postpone Operation Sea-Lion, but it did nothing to diminish his appetite for fresh conflict in the East. He believed that the defeat of Russia would deter the British and the United States. However, events in the Balkans acted as an obstacle to Hitler's intentions. In October 1940 Mussolini sent Italian troops to invade Greece. This ended in calamity for the Italians. The Greeks forced the Italians out and then British planes inflicted severe damage on the Italian fleet at Taranto. This was an unwelcome development for Hitler, who could not proceed against the Russians until the flank in the Balkans was protected. With troop movements facilitated by the cooperation of Hungary, Romania and Bulgaria, German troops moved towards her third Blitzkrieg campaign, launched in April 1941. Signs of resistance against Germany when a new monarch came to the throne in Yugoslavia prompted Hitler to invade this country as well as Greece. It took eleven days to end Yugoslav resistance and four more to crush the Greeks. In the following month German forces pushed the British out of Crete. Mussolini's errors had been rectified, Hitler's blitzkrieg tactics once again vindicated and the decks cleared for a full-scale attack on Russia.

### Part 1: 1941–42: introduction

At the outset of his book *Russia's War*, eminent historian Richard Overy makes clear the sheer scope of the war between Germany and the Soviet Union: 'The conflict was fought on such a gigantic scale and with such an intensity of feeling that conventional historical discourse seems ill-equipped to convey either very satisfactorily. The human cost, now estimated by some Soviet scholars to be as high as 43–47 million people, can only poorly be conveyed by statistics.'[5]

Although Hitler had been willing, for pragmatic reasons, to conclude a non-aggression pact with Stalin in August 1939, his hatred of everything the Marxist country stood for was immense. Hitler's long-established conviction that he was destined for a historic reckoning with the Russians, the delay in operations against Britain and the depth of Hitler's personal anti-Semitism meant that a conflict on an unimaginable scale was only a matter of time. In a meeting with military and naval chiefs in July 1940 Hitler concluded:

> Decision: Russia's destruction must therefore be made a part of this struggle. Spring '41. The sooner Russia is crushed the better. Attack achieves its purpose only if Russian state can be shattered to its roots with one blow. Holding only part of the country will not do. Standing still during the winter would be perilous. So it is better to wait a little longer, but with the resolute determination to eliminate Russia . . . If we start in May '41 we would have five months to finish the job.[6]

It is interesting to note that a central element in Hitler's personal thinking on the 'battle of annihilation' was the fatally flawed assumption that Russia would be crushed in a rapid campaign in the same manner as Poland and France. The sheer scale of Russia, its massive population and natural resources, its roads in the autumn and spring when the thaws turned the tracks to mud, and its incredibly fierce winter climate all seem to have been given relatively scant consideration by Hitler and the generals he dominated. Despite this, it should be noted that this operation was not merely a personal whim. For at least nine months prior to the invasion, the plan dominated the thinking of the German staff officers.

Despite the emphatic nature of his words of July 1940, Hitler's intentions towards Russia in the autumn of 1940 remain shrouded in mystery. As Noakes and Pridham explain, this

> is one of the most obscure and controversial aspects of his whole career. Many historians argue that his negotiations with the Russians were designed merely to gauge their immediate objectives and to mislead them about his own plans for an invasion. The fact that he specifically ordered those plans to be continued during the negotiations appears to lend weight to the view. On the other hand, it is equally plausible to argue that Hitler was undecided in his strategy at this point. . . . The Army leadership was certainly unclear about what he intended.[7]

It may be a measure of this uncertainty that uneasy discussions between the Germans and the Russians continued into the winter of 1940, including personal meetings between Hitler and the high-ranking Russian, Molotov. Molotov did not try hard to conceal his differences with Hitler, leading the Führer to conclude that Russia would never expect German domination of Europe. In December 1940 Hitler ordered an acceleration of military preparations against the Russians and on the 18th personally issued a military directive for the invasion of Russia to be code-named 'Operation Barbarossa'. Beyond Hitler's ideological desire for *Lebensraum* and the economic pragmatism of seizing the Ukrainian 'breadbasket' lay the conviction that this would be an unprecedented war of annihilation. Hitler's ideological assertion that 'Bolshevism is antisocial criminality', the close involvement of Himmler and Heydrich in the highest echelon of the SS in planning what would happen to Communists and Jews when the invasion took place, and precedents in the brutality visited upon sections of the Polish population reflected this. Within six months the 'war of the century' would begin. The extent to which Hitler had personally underestimated the Russians would soon become clear. The sources that follow indicate why Hitler took one of the most momentous decisions of his career.

## Hitler's decision to invade the Soviet Union

### SOURCE A

PREPARATIONS FOR OPERATION BARBAROSSA: SUMMARY OF HITLER'S APPRAISAL OF GERMANY'S STRATEGIC SITUATION, AT A CONFERENCE WITH MILITARY COMMANDERS, 9 JANUARY 1941.

Stalin, the master of Russia, was a clever man; he would not act openly against Germany, but one must expect that he will increasingly make difficulties in situations which are difficult for Germany. . . . The possibility of a Russian intervention in the war is keeping the English going. They would only give up the race if the last continental hope was destroyed. . . . Russia must be beaten. Then, either the English would give in or Germany would be able to continue the fight against Britain under more favourable circumstances.

Source: J. Noakes and G. Pridham (ed.), *Nazism 1919–1945: A Documentary Reader. Vol. 3: Foreign Policy, War and Racial Extermination*, 1995.

### SOURCE B

EXTRACT FROM GENERAL HALDER'S DIARY, 11 AUGUST, 1941.

The whole situation makes it increasingly plain that we have underestimated the Russian colossus, who consistently prepared for war with that utterly ruthless determination so characteristic of totalitarian states. . . . At the outset of the war we reckoned with about 200 enemy divisions. Now we have already counted 360. . . . And so our troops, sprawled over an immense front line, without any depth, are subjected to the enemy's incessant attacks. Sometimes these are successful, because in these enormous spaces too many gaps have to be left open.

*Source*: as source A.

## SOURCE C

HEINRICH HIMMLER, APRIL 1943.

We have only one task, to stand and pitilessly to lead this race-battle. . . . The reputation for horror and terror which preceded us we want never to allow to diminish. The world may call us what it will.

*Source*: David Cesarini (ed.), *The Final Solution: Origins and Implementation* (1994).

## SOURCE D

LUDWIG VON BECK, COMMANDER-IN-CHIEF OF ARMY GROUP CENTRE, DECEMBER 1941.

Three things have led to the present crisis:

1. The setting in of the autumn mud season. Troop movements and supplies were almost completely paralysed by the mud-covered roads.
2. The failure of the railways . . . the inability of the locomotives and the equipment to withstand the Russian winter.
3. The underestimation of the enemy's resistance and of his reserves of men and material . . .

The Russians have managed in a surprisingly short time to reconstitute divisions which had been smashed.

*Source*: as source A.

## SOURCE E

EXTRACT FROM HITLER'S DIRECTIVE TO ARMY GROUP CENTRE, 20 DECEMBER 1941.

Operation Barbarossa: 22 June 1941.
The fanatical will to defend the ground on which the troops are standing must be injected into them with every possible means, even the toughest. If every unit is equally imbued with it then the enemy's attacks – even if they lead to breaches or breakthroughs at particular points – will ultimately be doomed to fail. However, where this will is not fully present the front will begin to crumble without a prospect of stabilizing it once more in a prepared position . . .

Every piece of territory which has to be abandoned to the enemy must be rendered unusable as far as possible. Every settlement must be burnt down and destroyed without consideration for the population to deprive our opponents of all shelter.

*Source*: as source A.

With reference to each of the sources and your own knowledge, explain why the conflict with the Soviet Union was of such deep and personal significance to Hitler.

The code word 'Dortmund' was released on the morning of 21 June 1941, unleashing the final stages of preparation for the largest invasion force in the entire history of human activity. In excess of 3 million men, 146 army divisions, more than 3,000 tanks and over 2,000 aircraft were mobilized. Recently discovered Russian sources indicate that Germany may have deployed as many as 4,100,000 troops, with a further 900,000 from her Axis allies. Beyond this, it could be claimed that strengths of doctrine, organization and a 'mission-oriented' command system gave the Germans further advantages against the Russians. As the German forces massed in the darkness, Josef Stalin, the dictator at the head of the immense Soviet Union, took to his bed, red-eyed and weary at three o' clock in the morning. As he began his somewhat tortured sleep, the invasion that would mark the start of the most damaging conflict either Russia or Germany had ever seen, was about to begin. When the German troops swept into Russia, Hitler's confident assertion that the conquest would be like kicking down a rotten building initially seemed realistic. Stalin's apparent disengagement with his responsibility for leading the defence of his country, the lasting impact of his military purge of the 1930s that had decimated the army leadership and the rudimentary nature of many of Russia's military fortifications left the country horribly exposed. Russia's failure to disperse or even camouflage her valuable front-line air regiments proved a disastrous mistake, while the rapidity of the German advance meant that 200 out of a total of 340 military supply dumps fell into German hands. The rapid depletion of Russia's tank strength and the fate of the historically important frontier fortress at Brest-Litovsk that bravely held out until 12 July before it succumbed, seemed to provide both logical and symbolic evidence of a looming catastrophe for Russia.

Ominously for the invaders, however, Stalin's speech of 3 July 1941 indicated to the Russian people that the German troops would find that they were occupying a wasteland without 'a single engine, a single railway car, a single pound of grain or a gallon of fuel' in what would not be an 'ordinary war' but rather a 'war of the entire Soviet people'. The rapid assembly of popular militia, draconian martial law measures against 'cowards' or 'panic-mongers', the extension of the working day by three hours and an end to public holidays indicated that the Russian people, faced with the imposition of 'German slavery', were ready to mobilize their resources on an unparalleled scale. The depth of Russian bitterness at the way their country had been assaulted was reflected in the fact that many German soldiers who fell into Russian hands were murdered and mutilated. The elemental skill of the Russian soldiers in hiding in the midst of oncoming German troops in forest, swamp or grassland until they could suddenly strike led the German commanders to place non-smoking men at the front as they could detect the distinctive blend of the smell of sweat and cheap tobacco that indicated the presence of Russian infantrymen among them.

Nevertheless, German troops quickly swept into large parts of the Ukraine and the whole of Western Russia was soon occupied, with the invaded nation suffering heavy losses. As early as 16 July 1941 Hitler was prepared to deliver a 'victory' speech at which he confidently spoke of the future for Russia: 'Occupy it, administer it, exploit it'. Yet even the initial incision from the Russian frontier to the Dvina–Dnepr line took the German forces between 200 and 350 miles into Russia across a breadth of 750 miles. In addition, the European part of the USSR extended to more than 2 million square miles, with the Asiatic section extending a further 6 million square miles.

It is interesting to note that large elements of the German army were still not motorized and that the invasion force took with them more than 600,000 horses. Despite the scale of the country upon which they were imposing unprecedented brutality, the extent of the German advance was remarkable. By the end of September German troops had occupied Kiev, the capital of the Ukraine, and also reached the shores of Lake Lagoda near Leningrad, ready to besiege the city in a struggle that would last for 900 days. In addition, a major German success in the Battle of Viaz'ma-Briansk, a colossal engagement which eliminated the final Red Army concentration on the approaches to Moscow, meant that by the end of 1941 German armies were also close to the Soviet capital.

Ostensibly, it may have seemed that Hitler could have celebrated Christmas 1941 with some satisfaction at the progress of events. In fact, the opposite was true. Despite sustaining heavy losses and conceding immense tracts of land, Russia had not been broken. After an initial period of inertia, Stalin had returned forcibly to the helm, while the German supply lines were becoming significantly over-extended and the Russian weather was about to ensnare the ill-equipped German soldiers in its icy grip. It would soon become clear that Hitler's underestimation of Russia's strength could hardly have been wider of the mark and had ignored the super-industrialization process of the 1930s. Germany had used these assumptions to conclude that the campaign would be over with quickly, that Russia would be unable to put large and effective armies in the field and therefore did not sufficiently explore the implications of what would happen if German troops were still in the field at the onset of the fearsome Russian winter. To make matters worse, December 1941 saw the entry into the war of the United States. Although Hitler does not seem to have appreciated it at the time, it could be argued that these few winter weeks were the time when German victory slipped away.

In fact, the initiative had already been lost in mid-autumn 1941 when Hitler ordered the central army to halt its advance on Moscow so that a significant section of German armour could be switched north to help in the capture of Leningrad and the rest transferred to the south to help conquer the Ukraine. By the time that Hitler issued Directive Number 35 instigating Operation Typhoon ordering the attack on Moscow to resume, it was already too late. Even so, Hitler reached a new level of euphoria at the start of October as his military commanders forecast the imminent destruction of Leningrad and Moscow. At the Berlin Sportpalast Hitler told an enthusiastic audience that he had come from 'the greatest battle in the history of the world' and that the Soviet army was vanquished and 'would never rise again'. The conviction that total victory was imminent led booksellers in Germany to launch advertising displays on guides to Russian grammar. Such was the state of alarm in Moscow that Lenin's embalmed remains were moved hundreds of miles to a former tsarist school at Tyumen. Despite the gravity of the situation Stalin made clear that 'we will not surrender Moscow' and took the decision to remain there in person.

If Stalin's personal resolve symbolized the political leadership of Russia's determination to stand fast, then Georgi Zhukov, the army commander charged with masterminding the defence of Leningrad and then Moscow, represented the military resolve of the Russian people. No single figure played a greater part in the Soviet victory. Through the autumn and winter of 1941 Zhukov defiantly led the Russian people through a period of unimaginable suffering. Pitiful supplies of food, mounting piles of dead bodies at macabre collecting centres, a complete lack of medicines and anaesthetics, a night-time curfew and a city enveloped in snow and ice made the level of deprivation seem insurmountable. However, Zhukov's resolve and the bravery, determination and resourcefulness of the Russian people meant that by the time the thickening ice surrounding the city had become passable, the people of Leningrad were ready to launch a remarkable campaign through the winter of 1941–42 to bring supplies across truck routes into the beleaguered city. At a massive human cost, the siege had been resisted, although it had not yet come to an end. By the time it was over, according to official and probably conservative estimates, more than 600,000 Russian civilians would be dead. German losses on the Eastern Front in the period from June to the end of September 1941 numbered 185,000. It would not be until August 1942 that monthly German losses in the East were greater than those of July, August and September 1941. By the middle of December 1941 the German army claimed to have captured 3.5 million Russians as prisoners of war. In December 1941, after an initial German offensive lasting five-and-half months, a massive Russian counter-offensive launched before Moscow on the 5th demonstrated to Hitler that Stalin's leadership was in place and Russia was far from beaten.

Once again, the scale of the conflict was immense. As 1942 began, with temperatures routinely below −20° Fahrenheit, German soldiers reporting more than 130,000 cases of frostbite, and with their winter clothing clearly in short supply, Stalin lined up nine army groups along the main battle front, demonstrating an extraordinary recovery in Soviet manpower after the serious reverses of the summer and autumn. With Moscow and Leningrad both saved from the German advance, Stalin now wanted to push the enemy back along the front in advance of the spring thaw that would render the roads a muddy, treacherous, impassable morass. Yet despite the psychological damage to the Germans of the loss of momentum, this was not yet necessarily the major turning point classically depicted by some historians. While December and January 1941–42 saw the German lines under immense pressure, the thaws of late March and April saw the Russian momentum ebb away, as the Germans replaced weary commanders with a new cohort of able replacements, and the Russians once again suffered severe losses. A further 440,000 Red Army soldiers fell in this stage of the campaign, set against a German figure of 80,000. One significant element of this stage of the battle for Russia was that, as the Germans were pushed back, the Russians uncovered terrible scenes of the suffering caused by the German army, motivating the soldiers to secure revenge. The poet Surkov wrote: 'The tears of women and children are boiling in my heart. Hitler the murderer and his hordes shall pay for those tears with their wolfish blood. For the avenger's hatred knows no mercy.'[8]

While the Germans held the line they had already been pushed to a dangerous extent and taken heavy losses. Most of all, the anticipated war of annihilation had turned into a war of attrition. The sequence of brilliant victories was at an end, the Blitzkrieg had failed to achieve its objective and Germany was committed to a protracted war for which she was, in almost every respect, ill-prepared. Against this backdrop Hitler accepted General Brauchitsch's resignation and assumed personal command of the army in the field.

It was a measure of Hitler's arrogance that he entered 1942 confident that he could win. In May he ordered a huge offensive on the southern front, with the aim of capturing the Caucasian oilfields and with a new focus on the city of Stalingrad. Stalingrad became an obsession with Hitler, even though he had wanted to avoid the close street-fighting that had been so costly around Moscow and Leningrad. When Hitler's generals reported military setbacks in the Caucasus they noted an expression of 'burning hate' in the dictator's eyes. The recognition that the second attempt to subjugate Russia was also going awry made Hitler search for symbolic compensation in the city that bore the name of his most defiant opponent. More than 400 miles of Russian territory gave way in the face of a brutal assault taking German troops into the Caucasus and to Stalingrad itself. Had Hitler been able to translate this promising position into the final conquest of the Caucasian oilfields and been able to move from there to link with German forces in Egypt, then things might have been different. However, he now discovered that Russian resistance was at its most stubborn when the odds seemed stacked against them. The people of Stalingrad demonstrated a depth of resolve that was almost unfathomable, while exhaustion, heavy losses, dwindling supply lines and harsh conditions hindered the efforts of the German troops, not just in the ruins of the city but also in Caucasia, where they proved too weak to take the oilfields. In Stalingrad the psychological importance of 'the hour of courage' called its inhabitants to new levels of resistance, whereas the letters of German soldiers reveal the depth of their homesickness as they also endured massive deprivation. Within the rubble of their city, soldiers from Red Army garrisons turned warehouses or small factories into redoubts. The smell of burning buildings, the overpowering stench of decaying bodies under the rubble, the thick dust from the bricks of the shattered fortifications, the terrifying use of the flame-thrower to clear out sewers and tunnels, the sickening sight of bloated rats feasting on the dead and the constant screams and crying of wounded men overwhelmed the senses of the soldiers in a city in flames. However, when the generals reported their difficulties to Hitler they met only with seething resentment and temper tantrums. Hitler's mounting irritability and frustration over the lack of progress in the Caucasus and Stalingrad culminated in September 1942 in the dismissal of General Halder, the Chief of the Army General Staff. General Paulus was appointed as chief of the Wehrmacht command staff and charged with bringing the task of raising the battle flag of the Reich over Stalingrad. However, a change in leadership personnel was not enough.

Despite Hitler's insistence to his generals that 'no man will shift us from this spot', a successful Russian counter-offensive in November 1942 launched more than a million men at German soldiers more than 2,000 miles from their own frontier. This offensive relieved the intense pressure on Stalingrad and cut the communication lines of the Sixth German Army. It was with these crushing setbacks in mind that German troops prepared to spend what, for some, was their second winter on unforgiving Russian soil. Not least in the human misery of this campaign was the sheer scale of the fatalities among Soviet prisoners of war. It is estimated that perhaps a third of all of the USSR's military deaths were soldiers who perished in captivity owing to the brutality and neglect of the German POW regime.

## 12.8 Pearl Harbor and the United States' entry into the war

On 7 December 1941 Japan inflicted substantial damage on the American Pacific Fleet when they attacked without warning, prompting an American declaration of war against Japan the next day. Even though these events coincided with the launch of a major Russian counter-offensive on the Eastern Front, Hitler showed a remarkable lack of anxiety about becoming involved in a fresh conflict with another immensely powerful rival. Without hesitation, Germany declared war on the USA and the war convulsing Europe became a global conflict.

Although the terms of the Tripartite Pact of September 1940 did not oblige Germany to come to Japan's assistance, Hitler instinctively supported the Japanese aggression and felt that the attack on the American fleet would only serve to distract the USA from assisting Britain in the ongoing Battle of the Atlantic. Ideologically he condemned the financial interests of Wall Street as the 'Jewish wire-pullers', and bitterly resented the assistance they had provided to the British. He appears to have believed that a declaration of war by Germany against the United States only served to ratify the de facto situation of American economic intervention. He believed that America's lack of military preparedness meant that it would take the United States at least a year to fully mobilize her forces. In the meantime, Hitler's obsession with the war in the east could carry on in its remorseless way. An indication of the nature of Hitler's ill will towards the USA is reflected in the brief extract that follows: 'And now by contrast let me comment on that other world which is represented by that man who, while nations and their soldiers fought in snow and ice, tactfully has a habit of chatting from his fireside, in other words above all the man who bears the main guilt for this war.'[13] Of course, Hitler was not without some strategic ability, but it seems on this occasion his faculties had deserted him. It was a sign of things to come that he seemed incapable of bringing a rational perspective to these events. Put simply, it could surely be argued that Germany's prospects of victory had, at a stroke, been extinguished.

## 12.9 the war in Africa and the significance of the Mediterranean

With Hitler's daily outlook and strategic focus increasingly centred on the cataclysmic struggle in the East, his ability to appreciate the broader elements of the worldwide conflict increasingly came into question. His personal understanding of the immense long-term significance of the US entry into the war in December 1941 seemed somewhat limited. In fact, the sustained application of immense American resources of men and material would mean that the already strained nature of the German war effort, both on the home front and in the heat of battle, would eventually reach breaking point. Meanwhile, events in Africa also slipped through Hitler's grasp. In June 1942 Axis forces under the strategic command of General Rommel forced British troops back into Egypt and placed the key target of Alexandria within the Germans' grasp. This opened up the possibility that German troops in the oilfields of Caucasia could move south to support Rommel's troops in Egypt. Such a configuration could have had devastating consequences for Britain's position in the Middle East and therefore for the war itself in global terms. The fact that this scenario was not realized was due, in part at least, to Hitler's personal fixation with the war in Russia. Operations in Africa were relatively peripheral to Hitler's overall vision and, as a consequence, his strategy failed to provide Rommel with the clear supply lines through the Mediterranean that were pivotal to the success of his mission. With Rommel stalled at El Alamein and lacking crucial supplies of fuel, the initiative passed to the British under the astute leadership of General Montgomery. Rommel was taken aback by Montgomery's surprise attack and his Afrika Corps and their Italian allies were roundly defeated. On 7–8 November 1942 Anglo-American forces moved into Casablanca and Algiers, tilting events inexorably against the Axis forces. Hitler attempted to save the day by sending further troop reserves to Tunisia but British, American and French troops were massed to the East and West, with the Axis forces unable to prevent a catastrophic defeat. At the beginning of May 1943 a quarter of a million German and Italian troops were taken prisoner. Hitler's campaign in the African desert had ended in ignominious failure. The consequences for Hitler and Germany extended far beyond the continent of Africa itself. The entire momentum of the war was now in reverse for Germany.

## 12.10 sources: the impact of the war on the Home Front

Even for a regime accustomed to expending so much of its energy on mobilizing and controlling opinion, the challenge of maintaining morale, curbing dissent, feeding the masses, sustaining some degree of popular support (or at best, compliance) for the war, and meeting the economic demands of a conflict on several immensely challenging fronts placed severe strain on the Nazi state. It could be argued that the turning point from some degree of support to the spectrum of political jokes, grumbling, apathy, despair, war-weariness and even, in some cases, outright opposition, including the painting of anti-war or anti-regime graffiti under the cover of darkness, through to more direct attempts against Hitler's life, correlated directly with Germany's fortunes in the war itself. Therefore negative connotations with the war would have become increasingly widespread towards the end of 1942 and were particularly acute from 1943 to 1945. Once the war came directly to the homes of the German people through the increasingly sustained and venomous Allied bombing campaigns against the German cities from 1940 to 1945, the efforts of the regime to sustain morale may have sounded increasingly more hollow. The fact that Goebbels was never high in the nation's affections may have made the messages offered by the tiny propagandist even less convincing. The extracts that follow show the range of emotions that the German people experienced on the Home Front.

## SOURCE A

MORALE.

The mood of the German people on the outbreak of war has been summed up by two German historians, one of whom had personally witnessed it, as 'reluctant loyalty'. The great foreign policy successes of the preceding years – the Rhineland, the Anschluss with Austria, Munich, Prague etc. – had been extremely popular. But the most popular thing about them had been that they had been achieved without war. Only a few fanatical Nazis and naïve Hitler Youth members actually wanted a major war.14

Source: J. Noakes (ed.), *Nazism 1919–1945: A Documentary Reader.*
*Vol. 4: The German Home Front in World War II* (1998).

## SOURCE B

TOTAL WAR.

Extract from Goebbels's 'total war' speech of 18 February 1943, at the Berlin Sports Palace.

The English allege that the German people are no longer in a mood to shoulder the ever-increasing war work demanded by the Government. [Shouts of 'Shame!'] I ask you: Are you and the German people determined, if the Führer orders it, to work ten, twelve and, if necessary fourteen and sixteen hours a day and to give your utmost for victory? [Loud shouts of 'Yes!' and lengthy applause]. . . . The English allege that the German people are resisting the total war measures of the Government. [Cries of 'Never!'] They don't want total war, they want to surrender, say the English [Loud shouts of 'No! Shame!'] I ask you: Do you want total war? [Loud cries of 'Yes!' Loud applause] Do you want it, if necessary more total and more radical than we can even imagine it today? [Loud cries of 'Yes!' Applause]. . . .

I have asked you; you have given me your answers. You are part of the nation, so your voices have demonstrated the attitude of Germany. You have told our enemies what they must know to prevent them from indulging in spurious fantasies. . . . If ever we have faithfully and irrevocably believed in victory, then at this moment of national reflection and inner renewal we can see it within our our grasp – we need only seize it. We must simply develop the determination to subordinate everything to its requirements. That is what is needed now! And so from now onwards the motto is: now let the nation arise let the storm break!

*Source*: as source A.

## SOURCE C

Extracts from a letter from Josef Goebbels to Hitler, 18 July 1943.

At this critical phase of the war, when we are having to face the attacks of our enemies on all fronts, I feel obliged to inform you once again about my ideas on the total utilization of our national energies in order to ensure the victory of our arms. You know, my Führer, that I am not influenced by any scepticism or timidity. Throughout the war, even during its most critical phases, I have never doubted our final victory even for a moment. I am too much a man of faith to have ever harboured any doubts about you or your historic work. Moreover, the political and military circumstances of this war are such that at every new juncture it offers us new chances of success. Furthermore, do I still need to emphasize that I cannot and will not contemplate that I or the nation could survive in the event of our failure to win the day? I have stood by you for twenty years and I believe that I have been a stronger support for you in difficult than in easier times . . .

After Stalingrad I proclaimed total war in the Sports Palace; but its effect was only superficial. At the same time, the front and our blitzed cities got to know it. What is preventing us from extending it now to the whole nation, to the Party, Wehrmacht, the state, and the whole of public and private life? . . . Such measures could produce an unimaginable improvement in the morale of the whole nation . . .

Our people await great decisions. The daily reception of the current news from the front can have a debilitating effect in the long run if nothing decisive is done about the crisis. So the moment to act has arrived. In war one can never be too concerned about one's strength and never possess too much strength. Let us throw everything that we call our own onto the scales of decision, then we shall be certain of victory. If you, my Führer, give the command then your people will not only follow your orders but also obey them. But do give them orders. You will see what friends and comrades in arms, but also what a nation you have.

*Source*: as source A.

EXTRACT FROM A CIRCULAR ISSUED BY MARTIN BORMANN, 1 MARCH 1943.

The Führer has instructed me to make the following comment.
The measures for the conduct of total war, which have been ordered by the
Führer and which are decisive for the further development of the war, will
only be able to be successfully implemented with the aid of the strength of the
movement. Every leading party comrade must be conscious of his responsibility.
The personal example of each individual Party leader is of decisive importance
for the strengthening of such a commitment to the struggle. The whole nation
will be given fresh heart. . . . From now onwards, we have no more time for teas,
for receptions and banquets. . . . Moreover, the nation has no sympathy for
peacetime pleasures or for lengthy alcoholic sessions indulged in by individual
leaders.

*Source*: as source A.

SOURCE E

EXTRACT FROM A SECURITY SERVICE (SD) REPORT, 8 JULY 1943.

There are reports from almost all parts of the Reich according to which a not
insignificant number of young people have an attitude towards admission to
the party which leaves much to be desired. . . . Most boys and girls have not
the slightest interest in becoming a member of the NSDAP. All attempts by the
relevant authorities to get them involved have been in vain.

*Source*: as source A.

SOURCE F

CRIME.

German crime statistics during the Second World War are deeply problematic
and even more unreliable than usual. There were the problems of continually
moving geographical boundaries; the different spheres of jurisdiction – civil,
military and SS/police; and varying degrees of enforcement of particular
offences, often dictated by political criteria. . . . Furthermore, the range of acts
which were defined as 'criminal' changed all the time . . . in spite of these and
other problems, the . . . statistics give some indication of trends such as the
increase in female and juvenile crime.

*Source*: as source A.

SOURCE G

INSTRUCTIONS ISSUED BY REINHARD HEYDRICH, 20 SEPTEMBER 1939.

A distinction must be drawn between those (cases) which can be dealt with
in the ordinary way and those which must be assigned for special treatment.
The latter case covers those for whom, in view of their reprehensibleness , the
threat that they pose, or through their propaganda effect, it is appropriate that

they should be eliminated through ruthless action (namely through execution) irrespective of the persons involved. Such cases are, for example, sabotage attempts, the encouragement of members of the army to mutiny or of large numbers of people to rebel or to undermine their morale, hoarding on a large scale, Communist or Marxist activities etc.

*Source*: as source A.

## SOURCE H

THE WARTIME ECONOMY

The most striking feature of the history of the German war economy is the contrast between its early phase, 1939–41, marked by a poor productive performance in which output per worker in the arms industry actually fell by 24 per cent and Germany was outperformed by Britain in the production of most types of weapon, and the period 1942–44, when German production grew by leaps and bounds despite the growing problems created by the air war.

*Source*: as source A.

## SOURCE I

THE ROLE OF WOMEN

Women bore the brunt of the war on the home front. Not only did they – literally in many cases – keep the home fires burning, but they also kept the wheels of industry and transport turning; they sustained the health and wealth and welfare services, even more vital in war than in peace-time; they helped maintain the morale of the fighting men at the front and, by providing home comforts both physical and emotional, they sustained the male workers who remained in Germany.

The war enormously increased the burdens on women, particularly on married women with children. Rationing and shortages of food, clothing, household goods and fuel necessitated time-consuming queuing and caused women constant worry about how to feed and clothe their families and keep them warm during a series of particularly harsh winters. Continual air raid warnings and increasingly frequent and serious air raids robbed them of sleep and kept them in a permanent state of anxiety. Many were forced to abandon bomb-damaged homes and seek refuge with other family members or to be evacuated to distant parts of the country. . . . There was the nagging concern about the well-being of husbands, sons and brothers at the front, whose absence imposed on them additional responsibilities.

*Source*: as source A.

## the bombing of German cities

## SOURCE K

In early February 1945, there were about 800,000 people living in Dresden, perhaps a million. About 640,000 of them were regular residents; the rest were refugees. The two groups sacrificed a total of forty thousand people on February 13 and 14, 1945. Next to Hamburg, this marked the highest human losses of a German city during the air war. . . . The 'thunderclap' was to come to a city so remote and insignificant for the war effort that it had been ignored for four and a half years. . . . The master bomber and the marker leader made sure that no gaps remained that the fire could not close up. It was a matter of the exact angle taken by each plane within the fan. . . . It covered three-quarters of the Old Town. Owing to the substantial weight of the airplane fuel, only 877 tons of bombs could be loaded. . . . Harris therefore ordered a double attack. . . . The double attack did not merely double the devastation, it multiplied it because it struck just as the people in the city thought the worst was over. . . . As expected, there was no longer ground visibility when the second attack fleet arrived at 1:16 a.m. The firestorm shot a mile-high cloud of smoke into the air. The Old Market was nevertheless the designated point target in the middle of the fan. This corresponded to the purpose of the double blow; it delivered a knock-out punch. The first attack chased the people into shelters and the second attack hit those leaving their protection with feelings of relief. The protective effect of cellars was exhausted after two hours. After that, under a blazing city district, the basements no longer preserved life. . . . From January 1945 until the capitulation, the bombing killed 1,023 people daily, a total of 130,000.

*Source*: Jorg Friedrich, *The Fire: The Bombing of Germany 1940–1945* (2006).

## QUESTION

With reference to all of the sources and your own knowledge, examine the impact of the Second World War on the German people between 1939 and 1945.

## 12.11 the role of Italy

Mussolini's willingness to stand aloof from the process of Anschluss with Austria in March 1938 was of immense significance to Hitler. Seldom can Hitler have heaped such lavish praise on a fellow statesman as he did upon Mussolini in a telephone call at the time of the conquest of Austria from Prince Philip of Hesse, who told Hitler: 'I have just come back from the Palazzo Venezia. The Duce accepted the whole thing in a very friendly manner. He sends you his regards.' Hitler replied: 'Tell Mussolini I will never forget him for this . . . I shall be ready to go with him, through thick and thin, no matter what happens.'[9]

At the Munich Conference in September 1938 Mussolini reiterated his backing for Hitler but expressed his concerns over the possibility of a general war and his support for the Munich settlement. This process of cooperation culminated with the conclusion of the 'Pact of Steel', a formal military alliance with Italy signed in May 1939 just months before the outbreak of war. While Italian support was psychologically essential to Hitler at key moments, it is possible to evoke parallels between Germany's uneven military partnership with Austria-Hungary in the First World War and the problems that befell the alliance during the Second World War. In both cases, the military capacity and effectiveness of Germany's key ally could be called into question. As MacGregor Knox puts it:

> The leaders of Fascist Italy and Nazi Germany claimed a common origin and destiny for their two regimes. Yet Fascist Italy's last war collapsed within six months of its beginning in June 1940; Greeks and British inflicted staggering defeats in Albania, the Mediterranean, and North Africa. The Fascist regime itself then dissolved mutely in July 1943 in the bloodless royal and military coup d'état provoked by the Anglo-American landings in Sicily. . . . By contrast the frenetic outward thrusts of Hitler's dictatorship between 1938 and 1942 subjugated Europe from the North Cape to the Pyrenees and from Finisterre to the Don steppes. Then Germany bitterly resisted over three years of concentric ground and air attacks by three world powers, and only disintegrated as Hitler's suicide released the German people from their allegiance.[10]

The shortcomings in the Italian military effort, as summarized by Knox, were highlighted by Italy's disastrous campaign in Greece in October 1940. Acting unilaterally, the invasion proved a disaster for the Italians only reversed when Germany launched a lightning campaign against Yugoslavia and Greece (see 12.6, the Balkans) A further disastrous reverse in the North Africa campaign in May 1943 (see 12.9, the War in Africa) saw huge numbers of German and Italian troops fall into enemy hands. The endgame began when Anglo-American troops landed in Sicily in July 1943. Mussolini was deposed but for a time, the country he had led into war continued the struggle until the Italians signed an armistice in September 1943. Hitler responded in dramatic fashion, taking control of strategic points in Italy, disabling the Italian army and freeing Mussolini. Briefly, Hitler controlled Italy but when Allied forces moved into Southern Italy a further point of stress was placed on the German war effort. A war of attrition in Italy meant that the Allies only gradually forced the Germans back into Northern Italy, where they remained until almost the bitter end. The Germans fought bravely and effectively in Italy, using many hardened troops from the Eastern Front, but the fact remained that Germany was now close to breaking point. With the Russians in the driving seat in the East and an Anglo-American landing planned in the West, the existence of a third military front presented an insurmountable problem. It was in this context that attention now switched to the beaches of Normandy.

## 12.12   the Normandy landings

Although German forces had appeared to stem the breach with their staunch resistance in Italy, dramatic developments in France pointed the way towards the final stages of the conflict. On 6 June 1944 Allied forces under the strategic command of Eisenhower launched a major offensive on the beaches of Normandy. The nature of the fissures between Hitler and some of his key military leaders was reflected in Hitler's scathing criticism of his generals for the latest setbacks. When the gifted tactician Rommel suggested that armistice negotiations should begin, he was stripped of his command. The Allies' beach offensive could not be stemmed, with control of the skies a notable factor in their favour. By the beginning of August the First American Army was making rapid progress and the Germans fell back to the Seine. On 25 August General de Gaulle entered Paris and only weeks later the Belgian capital was also liberated. The military disasters for Hitler were now legion. In the Balkans, Romania looked for an armistice and in September 1944, Bulgaria surrendered. German forces also began to withdraw from Greece and Yugoslavia.

Just as all seemed to be in disarray, there seemed to be temporary respite. Hitler's tendency to grasp at any development that seemed positive as a potential turning point was evident in the autumn and winter of 1944. Initially, the Allied forces in the West had intended to press their advantage into Germany itself but poor weather, supply difficulties and the resilience of the German troops meant that the offensive came to a halt in the early autumn. As a new line of resistance stabilized, stretching from the Vosges though the southern Netherlands to the sea, Hitler began to believe that the Allies might be vulnerable to a new offensive which could in turn, prompt them to seek peace terms before turning together against the Russians. Just before Christmas 1944, Hitler launched a final attempt to regain the initiative, with his last 28 divisions thrown against the Americans in the Ardennes. However, a brief success was quickly followed by a comprehensive reverse, forcing Hitler to withdraw German forces from the Ardennes front in January 1945. More than 100,000 German troops had been killed in this final offensive. Hitler was no longer in any position to launch a further initiative and in March, British and American troops crossed the Rhine and moved into the Ruhr, Lower Saxony and south Germany. As if this was not bleak enough, the war with Russia was now in an exclusively downward spiral.

## 12.13   the war with the Soviet Union, 1943–45

### defeat at Stalingrad

As the German army headed into the winter of 1942–43, its southern front was in disarray. With dead soldiers piled up in twisted, frozen piles, fast-moving Soviet armoured columns causing panic, and some German troops beginning to hand themselves in to the enemy, the situation on the Eastern Front deteriorated still further in January 1943 when General Paulus's Sixth Army at Stalingrad was completely encircled by three Russian army groups. Once again Hitler's tendency to directly intervene from his remote East Prussian lair had damaging consequences. Paulus believed that the only way out of the crisis was for him to try to lead a break through the Russian positions before it was too late. Hitler refused Paulus permission to make his move and the German troops were completely trapped. For several weeks his men endured the most extreme conditions and when Paulus surrendered at the end of the month, 147,000 German soldiers were dead and almost 100,000 taken prisoner. Hitler would never regain the initiative in the East. Clearly, Stalingrad marked a military, psychological and strategic turning point in the conflict. Yet it is also evident that there remained substantial enough capacity on the German side to ensure that the struggle would still entail a huge additional degree of sacrifice on both sides.

Richard Overy makes the following observation:

> The eventual victory of Soviet arms in 1943 and 1944 has usually been portrayed as a result of the Soviet Union's overwhelming resources, of what one German general later described as 'the gigantic Russian superiority of men and material. More commonly German defeat has been interpreted as a result of German errors – Hitler's poor strategic grasp, sloppy intelligence, logistical overstretch and so on. Neither interpretation does justice to the historical reality. In the decisive battles from Stalingrad to the autumn of 1943 the numerical imbalance was much less marked than it was to become in the final stages of German defeat. German forces were not overwhelmed by sheer numbers . . . the operational experience and technological assets at the disposal of German forces in 1943 rendered their fighting power more remarkable than it had been in 1940. Soviet victory came as the result of a profound transformation of the way the Red Army made war.[11]

## the Battle of Kursk, 1943

Following a pause in military operations in the spring of 1943 the momentous struggle resumed with the German launch of Operation Citadel, an initiative that culminated in the largest-scale tank battle in human conflict, the Battle of Kursk.

table **12.1 comparison of forces deployed at the Battle of Kursk**

|  | men | tanks and SPGs | guns and mortars |
|---|---|---|---|
| Russia | 1,340,000 | 3,440 | 2,800 |
| Germany | 900,000 | 2,730 | 10,000 |

*Source*: Ewan Mawdsley, *Thunder in the East* (2005).

The Battle of Kursk, with its immense scale, was an iconic moment of the Second World War, and is often seen as a major turning point. Operation CITADEL was a German operation aimed at surrounding and then eliminating the large Soviet salient created during the February 1943 Soviet offensive. This was predominantly agricultural land, but centred on the Russian city of Kursk, whose population in 1939 exceeded 100,000. Utilizing unprecedented resources, Operation CITADEL finally began, after repeated delays, on 5 July, but within a week the German attack ground to a halt. The German panzers were halted by the Red Army's field defences and then hit by massed Soviet armoured counter-attacks. The pivotal engagement was fought west of the village of Prokhorovka on 11–12 July where the Second SS Panzer Corps faced the Soviet Fifth Guards Tank Army and two independent mobile corps. Hitler ordered the SS Corps to withdraw, and on 13 July he called a halt to the whole offensive with only a negligible amount of territory captured. The German delays in starting the operation reflected the setbacks the Wehrmacht had suffered in defeats at Stalingrad and in North Africa and gave the Russians valuable time to arrange their field defences and to assemble powerful forces.

Ewan Mawdsley offers this analysis:

> The giant Battle of Kursk was a sensational event, but I would argue that both the nature of the battle and its impact on the war are generally misunderstood. Kursk appeals to military historians, if simply because of the concentration of new tanks and notorious SS divisions. It was certainly a German defeat ... but the central event, the big tank battle in the south of the bulge, and especially at Prokhorovka, was less devastating for the Wehrmacht than is often suggested. Soviet personnel losses (killed, died of wounds, and missing) in the Battle of Kursk proper (5–23 July 1943) were 70,000, with much the greater part (54,000) suffered in the southern side of the bulge. Some 1,600 Soviet tanks were lost in the fighting, and 460 aircraft. These losses were considerably higher than those of the Germans. Zetterling and Frankson, using German archival sources, came up with a figure of 57,000 German casualties for the offensive period of the battle which would suggest about 15,000 fatalities. Another recent estimate of German personnel losses by Overmans gave a figure for the whole Eastern Front in July 1943 of 71,000 deaths, and of 59,000 in August. ... More important than the initial Soviet defence of the Kursk bulge was the Red Army summer offensive which followed it. The German concentration areas north and south of Kursk were now themselves the target of massive Red Army reserves.[12]

It is certain that Germany's defeat at Kursk sealed the fate of the German operation in Russia.

## the tide turns against Germany

Gradually, and in the face of sustained heavy losses on both sides, the Russians would push the Germans back out of Russia and from Poland back towards German territory itself. After the Battle of Stalingrad in the autumn and winter of 1942–43, Hitler and the Germans experienced nothing but disaster, yet the nature of Nazi ideology meant that years of suffering were preferred to the prospect of any kind of negotiation, peace talks or surrender. In the final months of the war, from July 1944 to May 1945, more Germans were killed than in the previous four years combined, with approximately 50,000 German soldiers and civilians killed per month. Hitler's character made surrender impossible.

With the tide turned irreversibly in the East, Hitler also had to contend with setbacks and crisis points in a host of other areas. The global nature of the conflict saw reverses across Africa, Italy, the Middle East, on the Home Front, in the Balkans, on the beaches of Normandy and in the Ardennes. Yet all the time it was probably the Russians that concerned Hitler most. It may be that the savagery of the Holocaust was intensified in a manner that corresponded with the military reverses Hitler suffered against the Russians.

The pressure of the calamitous military events could not but impact upon the structure of Hitler's government and on Hitler's personal political leadership. The wartime period and Hitler's increased personal isolation corresponded with the increasing influence of his trusted political aide, Martin Bormann. Between January and August 1943 a new 'Committee of Three', comprising Lammers, Keitel and Bormann – referred to sarcastically by Goering as 'the Three Kings' – was established and met 11 times. Against the backdrop of military disaster, the traditionally bitter rivalries in the Nazi hierarchy were more pronounced than ever. Motivated by jealousy and self-interest, Goering and Goebbels in particular used their influence to undermine the committee in an attempt to reduce Bormann's influence on Hitler. However, Goering's inability to protect the German cities and people from the Allied bombing had fatally damaged his standing with Hitler. The new 'Committee of Three' was unable to surmount the administrative chaos in the Third Reich, as illustrated by the bizarre issue they considered: whether to ban horse-racing during the period of total war. Even on trivial matters Hitler was consulted, but once again the old habit of indecision returned and the decision on horse-racing was endlessly discussed.

Meanwhile, it was the Russians who would come crashing towards Berlin itself, bringing the war and Hitler's nihilistic and destructive campaign to a bitter end. In January 1945 the Red Army pushed almost 200 divisions into a general offensive that detached East Prussia and brought the Russians ever closer to Berlin.

Meanwhile, as Russian troops swept through the German positions, Hitler had left the Wolf's Lair in East Prussia on 20 November 1944 and had returned to Berlin for the last time. He now lived in the Reich Chancellery, joined by Eva Braun, who had travelled from Obersalzberg to be with him, along with Goebbels and Bormann. By January 1945 the Reich Chancellery buildings themselves were under heavy attack and Hitler increasingly had to make use of the substantial underground bunker that had been constructed there. By now, the trembling caused by the onset of his Parkinson's disease had become increasingly pronounced. Stooped and shuffling, he now looked like an old man. Increasingly detached from the military reality and indulging in the fantasy that some kind of miraculous recovery could still be forthcoming, he was now trapped in Berlin where the Russians arrived in April 1945. News that Goering wanted to assume full powers to act in Germany's interests was followed by radio reports that Himmler had tried to discuss peace terms with the Allies. With these acts of treachery, as he saw them, Hitler now decided to bring his life to an end. On 29 April he married Eva Braun and dictated his final will and political testament in which he condemned the Jews and blamed his own generals for his military defeat. The next day, he committed suicide with Eva Braun. Admiral Dönitz, Hitler's successor, announced Hitler's death to the German people on 1 May. On 7 May Admiral von Friedeburg and General Jodl signed an instrument of unconditional surrender of all German forces and a few days later, Dönitz was arrested to await trial with the other war criminals. The provisional government Dönitz had tried to establish was officially dissolved on 23 May and the Third Reich, dreamt of by Hitler as an institution that would last for a thousand years, came to an end after twelve.

## 12.14 downfall: chronology of Hitler's final years as a wartime leader, 1943–45

### 1943

| | |
|---|---|
| January | Hitler's New Year Proclamation is issued at the 'Wolf's Lair' |
| 13 January | Hitler gives personal approval to special measures for the 'total mobilization' of German men and women |
| 30 January | On the tenth anniversary of the Nazi seizure of power, Hitler remains at the Wolf's Lair but orders Goebbels to read the Führer proclamation over the radio. His focus is on the Sixth Army. He is desperate that their surrender does not coincide with this key date in the Nazi calendar |
| 15 February, 18 February | Goebbels delivers his 'total war' speech at Düsseldorf and in the Sports Palace in Berlin |
| 19 February – 13 March | Hitler moves to Werwolf, near Vinnitsa, for a month |
| 24 February | Hitler issues Special Order Number 7, giving military commanders powers to execute any ill-disciplined soldiers on the spot |
| 10 March | Hitler briefly inspects the HQ of Army Group South near Zaporozhie |
| 13 March | Hitler issues the first operational orders for 'CITADEL' in the Kursk region. On the same day, when he makes a stopover at Smolensk at the HQ of Army Group Centre, an explosive device planted by military conspirators under the command of Field Marshal von Kluge fails to explode |
| 20 March | Hitler follows doctor's orders to leave the Wolf's Lair for a long break |
| 21 March | Hitler delivers his Heroes Memorial Day speech at Berlin's old arsenal. He survives a further abortive bomb plot planned by Colonel Rudolf von Gersdorff |

| | |
|---|---|
| 12 April | Martin Bormann is confirmed in his position as Secretary to the Führer |
| 4 May | Hitler declares the postponement of 'CITADEL'. The final decision to go ahead is taken on 16 June – it will become the large-scale German offensive on the Eastern Front |
| 20 July | Hitler flies back to Rastenburg |
| 25 July | Goebbels complains in his diary that the Führer has still not visited a single German city damaged by Allied bombing. This coincides with a massive attack against Hamburg, leaving 40,000 civilians dead. Privately, Goebbels calls it 'a catastrophe, the extent of which simply staggers the imagination' |
| 2 September | Hitler issues orders for the 'Concentration of War Economy' and invests Albert Speer with new powers as Minister of Armaments and War Production |
| 8 September | Hitler flies to the HQ of Army Group South at Zaporozhie – his last ever visit to an army group HQ on the Eastern Front |
| 4 October | Himmler addresses senior SS officers at Posen on the 'Final Solution' |
| 5 October | Hitler discusses with Goering the 'failure' to protect the German cities from Allied bombing |
| 7 October | At the Wolf's Lair Hitler tells assorted party functionaries that 'the bridges behind us are burned down; there is only one path left pointing ahead . . . till the final victory' |

*1944*

| | |
|---|---|
| 1 January | In his New Year Proclamation Hitler states: 'The year 1944 will make severe and heavy demands on all Germans. During the course of the year, this momentous war will approach its climax.' He promises to rebuild all damaged German cities |
| 30 January | On the eleventh anniversary of his seizure of power Hitler uses a radio speech to say 'One thing is absolutely certain – in this struggle there can only be one victor, and this will be either Germany or Soviet Russia! Germany's victory means the preservation of Europe, the victory of Soviet Russia its destruction!' |
| 24 February | Hitler leaves the Wolf's Lair for Berchtesgaden so that the bunkers of his HQ can be reinforced against air raids |
| 9 March | A further attempt on Hitler's life fails when the military assailant is not able to gain access to the conference room at the Berghof |
| 5 May | Himmler speaks to army generals on the 'Final Solution' and makes it clear that he was following explicit orders from the Führer |
| 26 May | In a secret speech to generals at Obersalzberg, Hitler |

| | justifies the Final Solution and blames the 'entire bestiality' of the war on the Jews |
|---|---|
| 31 May | Bormann tells the Gauleiters about special instructions for the party in the event of the invasion of the Reich |
| 16 July | Hitler leaves his house at the Berghof for the last time, returning to East Prussia |
| 20 July | Hitler narrowly survives the bomb plot at the Wolf's Lair. |
| 31 July | Hitler says that he can no longer fly because of the eardrum damage sustained in the bomb plot, and cannot speak in front of a large audience because he could suffer a vertigo attack and collapse |
| 1 August | Start of the Warsaw uprising |
| 7–8 August | Roland Freisler opens the first sessions of the Peoples' Court to try the first conspirators in the July Plot |
| 16 September | Hitler issues special orders demanding 'fanatical determination' from 'every able-bodied man' |
| end of September–October | Hitler complains to his personal physician of 'acute stomach cramps' that last for a week |
| 12 November | Himmler stands in for Hitler at the normal showpiece oration of 8 November in Munich |
| 20 November | Hitler leaves the Wolf's Lair for the last time, arriving in Berlin the following day. He moves into the Reich Chancellery, where he will be joined by Eva Braun |
| 22 November | Hitler has a small polyp removed from his vocal cords at a clinic in Berlin |
| 10 December | A special train takes Hitler to his new HQ at Adlerhorst to direct the Ardennes offensive |
| 26 December | Bormann notes the extent of Hitler's physical deterioration |

## 1945

| | |
|---|---|
| 1 January | In his New Year Proclamation Hitler casts blame on the failings of his allies |
| 16 January | Hitler returns by special train to Berlin. He will now be confined to that building and its underground bunker. The physical trembling has now extended to the entire left side of his body |
| 19 January | Martin Bormann and Eva Braun join Hitler at the Chancellery |
| 27 January | Soviet troops liberate Auschwitz-Birkenau |
| 6 February | Bormann records Hitler's comments about the military situation |
| 13 February | General Guderian, Army Chief of Staff has a two-hour encounter with Hitler in which the Führer completely loses control, screaming and shouting at the General |

| | |
|---|---|
| 11 March | On Heroes' Memorial Day, Hitler visits for the last time the battle front, now pushed back to the River Oder |
| 19 March | Hitler personally issues the 'Scorched Earth Order', ordering destruction on a vast scale |
| 20 March | Hitler's final public appearance in the Reich Chancellery Garden when he reviews a small group of Hitler Youth. A 12-year-old is rewarded with an Iron Cross. This is the last film that exists of Hitler |
| 2 April | Bormann takes notes of Hitler's last recorded monologue |
| 20 April | The entire Nazi hierarchy gather together for the last time for Hitler's 56th birthday. |
| 23 April | Hitler expresses his fury over Goering's telegram request to take over the leadership from Hitler. Hitler accuses him of treachery and strips him of all posts |
| 27 April | Hitler says that he must obey the orders of fate |
| 28 April | Hitler responds furiously to news that Himmler has secretly opened negotiations with the Western powers |
| 29 April | Bormann and Goebbels act as witnesses as Hitler marries Eva Braun. Hitler dictates his political testament |
| 30 April | At 3.30 p.m., Hitler and Eva Braun commit suicide. Both swallow potassium cyanide capsules and Hitler also shoots himself in the mouth with a pistol. Bormann sends a telegram to Grand Admiral Dönitz, informing him that Hitler has named him as successor |

*Source*: Milan Hauner, *Hitler: A Chronology of his Life and Time* (2005).

## 12.15 sources: analysis of Hitler as a wartime leader, 1943–45

**SOURCE A**

Until the visible signs of dissolution set in during the final months of his rule, his power remained intact – unbroken in the sense that his orders were carried out and not disobeyed, and . . . that he continued to function as the legitimating instance of all forms of authority in the Third Reich. On the other hand, in the face of mounting adversity Hitler had lost the power to determine the course and character of events. The initiative had been permanently relinquished. . . . From 1943 onwards he was in many ways a sick man. . . . Hitler was under acute nervous strain in late 1942 and early 1943. . . . Hitler usually ate alone and left his own quarters as little as possible. He slept badly. . . . His mood was one of deep depression . . .

Hitler's detachment from reality broke new bounds in the last war years. His self-imposed isolation in his remote headquarters in East Prussia . . . intensely magnified his tendency to exclude unpalatable reality in favour of an illusory world in which 'will' always triumphed. He no longer visited the front, paying his last visit to any army field headquarters in September 1943:

the war was conducted entirely from the map-room of the Führer bunker. His trips to Germany became ever rarer as, without successes to proclaim, he cut himself off from the German public. He did not visit a single bombed city . . . Speer's impression was of a man who was in the process of burning out . . . directing Germany's fortunes from a headquarters part way between monastery and concentration camp. . . . Hitler's authority remained paramount and incontestable. . . . Hitler had in effect for long been a 'part-time Reich Chancellor'. Goebbels complained on a number of occasions in early 1943 of a 'lack of leadership in domestic and foreign policy', of a 'complete lack of direction in German domestic policy.'

*Source*: Ian Kershaw, *Hitler: Profiles in Power* (1991).

## SOURCE B

No long-range strategic planning was undertaken at the Führer's headquarters after the end of 1942 for it was known that the conclusions would only displease him . . . His suspicion of the general staff reached paranoid proportions; from September 1942 stenographers took down the proceedings verbatim at the daily war conferences so convinced was the Führer that his generals were deliberately disobeying his orders . . . he interfered more than before in the minutiae of military operations; he regularly deployed troops at battalion level, even single tanks on occasions, a practice which robbed local commanders of all initiative at crucial stages of the battle. Overwhelmed by the sheer volume of work he had taken upon himself, Hitler was physically and mentally exhausted, and fluctuated uneasily between snap decisions and the old inability to make up his mind . . .

In Speer's eloquent words, 'he had reached the last station in his flight from reality' . . . Only on 22 April was Hitler ready at last to admit openly that the end was near . . . treason, lies, corruption and cowardice surrounded him on all sides; everyone had deserted him . . . he invited the Goebbels family to join him in the bunker and immolate themselves on the funeral pyre with him.

*Source*: William Carr, *Hitler: A Study in Personality and Politics* (1978).

## SOURCE C

EXTRACT FROM GOEBBELS'S DIARY.

It is tragic that the Führer has so cut himself off from life and is leading an excessively unhealthy life. He no longer gets out in the fresh air, no longer has any relaxation; he sits in his bunker, acts, and broods. . . . The solitude in the Führer's headquarters and the whole method of work there naturally have a depressing effect on the Führer.

*Source*: Joachim C. Fest, *Hitler* (1974).

## SOURCE D

From the beginning of the Russian campaign on, Hitler led a retired life. His headquarters, which also housed the High Command of the armed forces, was . . . located in the extensive woods beyond Rastenburg in East Prussia. A system of walls, barbed wire, and mines protected the grouping of bunkers and buildings.

The prevailing atmosphere was peculiarly gloomy and monotonous. . . . During the early months of the war Hitler had taken occasional trips to the front, and visited battlefields, headquarters, or military hospital. But after the first failures he began to shun reality and withdraw into the abstract world of map tables and military conferences. From that time on, his experience of the war was almost exclusively as lines and figures in public landscapes. He faced the public less and less often. . . . There is some evidence that from the end of 1942 on, the entire stabilization system of his nerves gave way. He concealed this only by a tremendous act of desperate self-discipline. . . . Hitler's weakness in leadership emerged most sharply in the course of 1943, when he had as yet developed no strategic conception of the further course of the war. He was uncertain, reluctant to make decisions, vacillating; and Goebbels spoke unequivocally of a 'Leader crisis'. . . . In annihilation, on the other hand, the regime displayed the greatest effectiveness.'

*Source*: as source D.

## SOURCE E

20 JULY 1944: THE BOMB PLOT.

The Führer's wartime command centre – the Wolf's Lair – had been breached. Its isolated position in a forest clearing near the East Prussian town of Rastenburg was no defence because the assassins were more than familiar with the surroundings. The massive security which surrounded the Führer could not contend with the fact that the man who had decided to take Hitler's life had his own security pass. In any case the face of the handsome, highly-decorated general was well known to the guards. As a result, Claus von Stauffenberg was able to enter the innermost security zone, known as the Führer Restricted Area, without arousing suspicion.

The war briefing had already begun and Stauffenberg was late. He would rush into the Führer's Headquarters offering apologies for his delay. The case which he clutched contained two pounds of high explosive. He was unable to get as close to Hitler as he would have liked but Stauffenberg did not have much time. After placing his case on the far side of the table he withdrew, muttering quietly as he left, as if he had something urgent to deal with. Within minutes of leaving the building the blast went off. The wooden barracks were completely destroyed. The wreckage was lifted high into the air. Stauffenberg looked back at the shattered barracks and concluded that Hitler was dead. In the confusion he was able to leave the base and take a flight to Berlin. By the time he arrived there it had emerged that Hitler had suffered burns and minor injuries but he had not been seriously wounded.

The July Plot had failed and Stauffenberg and his supporters were doomed. Stauffenberg was arrested within hours and was executed on the night of 20–21 July. The most well-known episode in the German resistance to Hitler had come close to success but was unable to dislodge Hitler. The attention which the July Plot has received has tended to obscure the fact that there were no less than fifteen attempts to kill Hitler.

*Source*: John Traynor, *20th Century Dictatorships: Hitler and Stalin* (1999).

The chaos and extreme violence of the last stages of the Second World War was the consequence and culmination of Nazi war: war which had been inspired by a crude Darwinian and racist vision of humanity, which was characterised by a refusal to calculate rationally the likely outcome of actions, which led to the collapse of normative constraints on civilised behaviour, which opened the vistas for committing mass murder on a hitherto unimaginable scale, and which had turned the continent of Europe into a gigantic prison and a sea of blood. If there was a distillation of Nazism, it lay in the senseless destruction of human life during the final months of the war. In the end, Nazism offered no vision of a 'post-war'; planning for what might come after a German defeat was completely outside the frame of Nazism. In the end, all Nazism had to offer was war and destruction, war without end or an end through war.

*Source*: Richard Bessel, *Nazism and War* (2004).

I should now like to offer an alternative interpretation. . . . It assumes that Hitler had early realized that final victory was out of reach. According to General Jodl's testimony immediately after the war, the first indications of such a pessimistic situation assessment came as early as November 1941. During the months that followed, hope and despair alternated before it became clear to Hitler in the late summer of 1942 that the Blitzkrieg strategy had definitely failed. From that time on. . . . Germany had no 'grand strategy'. . . . Hitler himself unintentionally admitted as much when he let slip: 'I have been muddling through from month to month'! The very last comprehensive strategic memorandum of the whole war, submitted by the Wehrmacht High Command and expressing Hitler's own ideas, is dated 10 December 1942 . . .

We must first consider the strong interdependence between war and genocide. On the one hand, war was the indispensable cover under which the 'final solution' was carried out. This means that the 'War against European Jewry', regarded by Hitler as his real historical mission, could be brought to a 'successful' conclusion only as long as the military war continued.

If military victory in the traditional sense could no longer be attained, moral victory could . . .

For (Hitler) the choreography of collective self-annihilation was not senseless bloodshed, but a prerequisite for Germany's resurrection. It was, so to speak, the second-best solution. If short-term military victory was out of reach, long-term historical victory could still be achieved.

*Source*: Bernd Wegner, *The Ideology of Self-Destruction: Hitler and the Choreography of Defeat* (2004).

## ESSAY QUESTION

To what extent was Germany's defeat in the Second World War caused by Hitler's personal leadership of the military campaign?

the Holocaust

## 13.1 chronological overview: 1939–1942

**1939**

30 January     On the sixth anniversary of his coming to power, Hitler delivers a venomous speech to the Reichstag predicting the future annihilation of the Jewish race.

14–15 March     German troops occupy Czechoslovakia

1 September     Germany invades Poland. Special SS units accompany the regular troops. They display great brutality towards the Polish Jews, but killings are generally confined to the leaders of the Jewish community

6 October     Conquest of Poland complete

12–17 October     Jews deported from Austria and Czechoslovakia to Poland

18 November     Through his military adjutant, Hitler dismisses concerns amongst sections of the Army leadership about the violence of the anti-Jewish policy as 'childish'

23 November–December     Polish Jews obliged to wear the yellow Star of David Officials planning Poland's future discuss the destruction of Jewish 'sub-humanity' living in the ghettos.

**1940**

     Early in the year it is decided to place the Jews of Lodz in a ghetto in the northern part of the city. In April the ghetto is sealed, trapping 164,000 Jews inside.

3 July     Discussion takes place of the 'Madagascar plan' – to place the Jews on an island off the coast of Africa. Some historians interpret this as a sign that the decision to launch the final solution has still not been arrived at.

**1941**

17–30 March     In a military conference Hitler tells his generals that the campaign in Russia will be a war of annihilation

22 June     Germany invades the Soviet Union

| 23 June | The Einsatzgruppen (mobile SS units 'Action Squads) advance into Russia |
|---|---|
| 2 July | Heydrich instructs the *Einsatzgruppen* to 'execute Jews in the service of the Party or the State'. In the first instance it appears that women and children were generally excluded from executions |
| 31 July | Goering signs authorization to Heydrich (see source I, p. 321). This document is seen by some historians as of vital importance in the launching of the final solution |
| August | Himmler visits the East to witness the killings, but reports that he is worried about the 'burden' this places on German soldiers |
| mid-August | Sudden commencement of execution of Jewish children in Russia |
| 1 September | German Jews obliged to wear the yellow Star of David. In the same month, 33,371 Jews are murdered by the *Einsatzgruppen* at Babi Yar, on the outskirts of Kiev in the Ukraine |
| 14 October | Order passed to move Jews from Reich territory to the eastern ghettos |
| 15 October–11 November | 20 trains leave the Third Reich, carrying Jews to Lodz |
| 29 November | High-ranking civil servants and bureaucrats are invited to a conference at Wannsee on 9 December, later postponed to 20 January 1942 |
| December | first use of 'gas vans' for mass execution of Jews at Chelmno in Poland. By the end of the year it had been decided that the camp at Auschwitz could not cope with the volume of prisoners being sent there and so plans for Auschwitz II–Birkenau was built. It became the largest Nazi extermination camp. It is estimated that eventually one million Jews were gassed there |

*1942*

| 20 January | Wannsee Conference in Berlin. Detailed discussion of the bureaucratic and organizational details of the Final Solution led by Heydrich |
|---|---|
| July | Mass executions begin at Treblinka in Poland. 800,000 Jews are killed there by August 1943, under the administration of just 50 Germans and 150 Ukrainians |
| winter | Polish Catholics form the Zegota, a group aiming to provide safe areas for Jewish children |

## 13.2 interpretations of the Holocaust

In 1951 Leon Poliakov became one of the first historians to face the difficult task of detailing the timing of the Final Solution. Based on documents from the Nuremberg trials, he concluded that the initial plan was 'shrouded in darkness',[1] but that it was likely that three or four key figures had been pivotal in the decision-making process. Poliakov also noted that as the policy of Jewish emigration appeared to have been at the centre of German planning until 1939 it seemed unlikely that important decisions had been taken before this time. Two years later Gerald Reitlinger claimed that it was likely that 'an actual Führer order'[2] was issued in the spring of 1941 with March as a likely date. In 1961 a major investigation by Raul Hilberg – *The Destruction of the European Jews* – moved away from a specific date towards 'the emergence of an idea'[3]. Nevertheless, he placed considerable importance on a document issued by Goering to Heydrich on 31 July 1941.

Lucy Dawidowicz's study, *The War Against the Jews*,[4] was published in 1975 against a background which was moving towards the emerging notion of Hitler's Reich as a less autocratic regime than had traditionally been depicted. While some historians began to see policy towards the Jews as something which was improvised and not always coherent, Dawidowicz took a very different stance. In a book that came to represent the 'intentionalist' school of thought, she argued that Hitler had as his goal the extermination of the Jews from the end of the First World War onwards. Where others depicted improvisation, Dawidowicz saw planning. She focused on the period between December 1940 and March 1941 as the time when 'the decision for the practical implementation of the plan to kill the Jews was reached'. The extent to which sharp differences of interpretation had begun to emerge was reflected in the work of Martin Broszat, published in 1977. He argued that 'no comprehensive order for the extermination existed and that the "programme" for the extermination of the Jews developed through individual actions and gradually attained its institutional and factual character by the spring of 1942 after the construction of the extermination camps in Poland'.[5] Broszat saw the initial waves of mass killings including the use of poison gas as essentially local and ad hoc initiatives designed, for example, to resolve issues of overcrowding in the Polish ghettoes. These liquidation initiatives were not necessarily instigated by Hitler or from Berlin but were subsequently approved and consolidated into a comprehensive 'programme'.

Work of similar importance by Christopher Browning[6] now followed. Browning claimed that no initiative could have gone forward without Hitler's approval and that the impression of improvisation highlighted by some experts masked the fact that at the very least, approval for the preparation of an extermination plan was given in the summer of 1941. Ad hoc arrangements may have been present in an interim period but they were merely taking place while more substantial murder sites were in preparation. Browning contended that evidence of a plan taking shape in the period between October and December can be clearly discerned, citing in particular the culmination of the process of forced emigration throughout Europe, construction work on the death camps and the first gassings of Polish Jews at Chelmno at the start of December.

Meanwhile the direction of interpretation initiated by Broszat seemed to be taken further through the work of Hans Mommsen in 1983. Mommsen saw Hitler as fundamentally prone to indecision and procrastination. His conclusion was that 'Hitler gave no formal order to carry out the Final Solution of the "European Jewish question"'.[7] Mommsen saw Hitler as 'out of the loop' of policy making until a very late stage and depicted Himmler as more influential in the development of Jewish policy. Even as late as January 1942 and the Wannsee Conference mass killing was still only regarded as one possibility rather than as a final policy. The Holocaust was depicted as an improvisation rather than a programme and Hitler's role was shifted from the centre. Clearly this interpretation prompted a heated response. In particular the reduction of Hitler's role was forcefully rejected by historians such as Saul Friedlander. Further controversy came in 1988 with the publication by Princeton historian Arno Mayer of *Why Did the Heavens Not Darken?*[8]

He played down the role of the Einsatzgruppen, claiming that they tended to incite attacks against the Jews by the local populace. It was only when the Russian campaign ran into difficulty that the German forces took action against the Jews in a retaliatory and vindictive manner. Essentially the impact on the Jews was seen as a collateral consequence of the war itself.

A further key text came with the work of Omer Bartov on 'the barbarisation of warfare'. As the following extract shows, Bartov believes that the invasion of the Soviet Union and the savagery that accompanied it amounted to a further incremental step in what the Nazis were capable of, and allowed a 'radicalization' of what Hitler and his cohort believed was now possible.

**SOURCE A**

We still need to probe the manner in which a whole body of cultural images and ideas came to be transformed into what we call . . . 'Nazi ideology' . . . when we speak of . . . redemptive anti-Semitism, scientific assertions of 'life unworthy of life' . . . we must concede that these were not ideas that sprang from one mind, not even one ideology or one generation. It was their deep-rooted cultural origins that made them familiar and attractive to Germans in the Third Reich, when they became elements of national policy. It was under the impact of such notions that German soldiers could both participate in mass crimes and believe that they were taking part in a great and glorious struggle to create a better world. . . . The barbarisation of warfare on the Eastern Front was the consequence of a number of interrelated factors, such as the brutality of the fighting itself, the harsh living conditions at the front, the susceptibility of the junior officers and probably of many of the soldiers to Nazi ideology, and the constant political indoctrination of the troops. . . . The collaboration of the army with the Nazis and its role as the instrument which enabled Hitler to implement his policies, were most evident during the war against Russia. It should therefore not surprise us that the army's criminal activities in the East remained taboo among the more traditional German historians for many years after the fall of the Third Reich. . . . During the Second World War some 5 700 000 Russian soldiers fell into German hands, of whom about 3 300 000 died in captivity. . . . Christian Streit has argued convincingly that this terrible tragedy was both the result of the ideological concepts of the Nazi regime . . . and a consequence of Hitler's fear that the economic burden of caring for millions of prisoners would bring about unrest among the German population.

Source: Omer Bartov, *The Eastern Front, 1941–45* (2001).

## Daniel Goldhagen, *Hitler's Willing Executioners*

In 1996, Harvard academic Daniel Jonah Goldhagen provoked further intense debate with his work *Hitler's Willing Executioners*, which offered a controversial explanation as to why it was the Germans rather than any other nation who turned anti-Semitic prejudice into mass murder. For an academic text by a junior professor of political science at Harvard University, this book received exceptionally intense media attention and provoked a storm of criticism in Germany. Goldhagen's claim is that Germans killed millions of Jews not because they were forced to, nor because of blind obedience, or for career advancement but fundamentally because they enjoyed doing it, and they enjoyed doing it because they shared a deeply pervasive, long-standing cultural anti-Semitism.

**SOURCE B**

The perpetrators . . . were overwhelmingly and most importantly Germans . . . this was above all a German enterprise; the decisions, plans, organizational resources, and the majority of its executors were German . . . no Germans, no Holocaust. . . . They were Germans acting in the name of Germany and its highly popular leader, Adolf Hitler. . . . Their chief common denominator was that they were all Germans pursuing German national political goals – in this case the genocidal killing of Jews.

The Holocaust was the defining aspect of Nazism. . . . It was also the defining feature of German society during its Nazi period . . . the program's first parts, namely the systematic exclusion of Jews from German economic and social life, were carried out in the open, under approving eyes, and with the complicity of virtually all sectors of German society, from the legal, medical, and teaching professions, to the churches, both Catholic and Protestant, to the gamut of economic, social, and cultural groups and associations. Hundreds of thousands of Germans contributed to the genocide and the still larger system of subjugation that was the vast concentration camp system. Despite the regime's half-hearted attempts to keep the genocide beyond the view of most Germans, millions knew of the mass slaughters. Hitler announced many times, emphatically, that the war would end in the extermination of the Jews.

Germans' anti-Semitic beliefs about Jews were the central causal agent of the Holocaust. They were the central causal agent not only of Hitler's decision to annihilate European Jewry but also of the perpetrators' willingness to kill and to brutalize Jews.

Source: Daniel J. Goldhagen, *Hitler's Willing Executioners: Ordinary Germans and the Holocaust* (1996).

In *Re-reading German History: 1800–1996*, Richard Evans offers this sustained critique of Goldhagen's work:

> In fact, around the turn of the century, at least two other major European powers witnessed prolonged outbreaks of anti-Semitism far in excess of anything seen in modern Germany up to that time. In France . . . in Tsarist Russia. . . . There was only one pogrom in Germany in the Imperial period . . . in 1881. In comparison with Russia or even France around the turn of the century, Germany was not a bad place for Jews to live. . . . Remarkably in view of his general thesis, Goldhagen devotes no more than a single page to the Nazi seizure of power. If his overall argument is correct, then we would expect this to be largely due to the popularity of the Nazi's anti-Semitic message. But even he is aware of the fact that modern research has overwhelmingly demonstrated that anti-Semitism was not an important factor in generating votes for the Nazis in the elections of 1930–1933 when they became a mass party. . . . Goldhagen persists in asserting that in 1933 the vast majority of Germans subscribed to the Nazi view of the Jews – virulent, racist and murderous. . . . In a curious way, what Goldhagen is doing is endorsing the view relentlessly propagated by Hitler and Goebbels that the German people were deeply anti-Semitic from the outset.[9]

## 13.3 Hitler's speech of 30 January 1939: impending war and the radicalization of anti-Semitism

While the events of Reichkristallnacht were disturbing enough, a grim sign that even worse was to come came with Hitler's speech to the Reichstag of 30 January 1939. Hitler stated that if 'international Jewish finance' led the world into war the outcome would not be 'the bolshevization of the earth and the victory of Jewry' but the 'annihilation of the Jewish race in Europe.'[10] In the section which follows we will examine the various interpretations which have been made of this speech, before moving on to consider the Holocaust which was to follow.

Each year on 30 January the Reichstag was convened in ceremonial fashion to commemorate Adolf Hitler's rise to power. At 8.15 p.m. Hitler began a speech which was to last for almost three hours. In the first part of the speech he spoke of the history of the Nazi movement before moving on to international issues. The section shown here came towards the end and is worth examining in detail:

> I believe that this [Jewish] problem will be solved – and the sooner the better. Europe cannot find peace before the Jewish question is out of the way. . . . The world has enough space for settlement, but one must once and for all put an end to the idea that the Jewish people have been chosen by the good Lord to exploit a certain percentage of the body and the productive work of other nations. Jewry will have to adapt itself to productive work like any other nation or it will sooner or later succumb to a crisis of unimaginable dimensions.

It was at this stage in the speech before a packed and emotionally charged Reichstag that Hitler's tone became even more extreme.

> One thing I should like to say on this day which may be memorable for others as well as for us Germans. In the course of my life I have very often been a prophet, and have usually been ridiculed for it. During the time of my struggle for power it was in the first instance only the Jewish race that received my prophecies with laughter when I said that I would one day take over the leadership of the State, and with it that of the whole nation, and that I would then among other things settle the Jewish problem. Their laughter was uproarious, but I think that for some time now they have been laughing on the other side of their face. Today I will once more be a prophet: if the international Jewish financiers in and outside Europe should succeed in plunging the nations once more into a world war, then the result will not be the Bolshevizing of the earth, and thus the victory of Jewry, but the annihilation of the Jewish race in Europe![11]

## interpretations of the speech by historians

### SOURCE A

There is no evidence that Hitler had any idea at this stage how or when he would carry out this threat. Indeed, some historians have seen it as pure rhetoric designed to intimidate those engaged in anti-German activities abroad by using the Jews as hostages. Nevertheless, there does seem to have been a widespread view among the Nazi leadership that war would bring about an intensification of Nazi persecution.

Source: J. Noakes and G. Pridham (ed.), *Nazism 1919–1945: A Documentary Reader. Vol. 3: Foreign Policy, War and Racial Extermination* (1995).

### SOURCE B

Hitler's threats of extermination, accompanied by the argument that his past record proved that his prophecies were not to be made light of, may have been aimed in general terms at weakening anti-Nazi reactions at a time when he was preparing for his most risky military-diplomatic gamble. More precisely the leader of Germany may have expected that these murderous threats would impress the Jews active in European and American public life sufficiently to reduce what he considered to be their warmongering propaganda. . . . It would be a mistake, however, to consider Hitler's January 30 speech merely in its short-term tactical context. The wider vistas may have been part calculated pressure, part uncontrolled fury, but they may well have reflected a process consistent with his other projects regarding the Jews, such as their transfer to some remote African territory. This was, in fact, tantamount to a search for radical solutions, a scanning of extreme possibilities. Perceived in such a framework, the prophecy about extermination becomes one possibility among others, neither more nor less real than the others. And – like the hostage idea – the possibility of annihilation was in the air.

Source: Saul Friedlander, *Nazi Germany and the Jews: The Years of Persecution 1933–1939* (1997).

It is also worth noting that the tone of Hitler's speech was echoed in an article published in Das Schwarze Korps on November 24, 1938 which stated: 'This stage of development [of the situation of the Jews] will impose on us the vital necessity to exterminate this Jewish sub-humanity, as we exterminate all criminals in our ordered county: by the fire and the sword! The outcome will be the final catastrophe for Jewry in Germany, its total annihilation.'[12]

## 13.4  the invasion of Poland and its consequences

A clear indication that the invasion of Poland in September 1939 would have horrendous consequences for the Jewish population is contained in the surviving shorthand notes that summarized a meeting between Hitler and army leaders on 22 August 1939. The notes referred to: 'The destruction of Poland. The Goal is the elimination of the living forces, not reaching a particular line. Close one's heart to sympathy. Brutal approach.'[13] The German invasion of Poland brought with it the opportunity to intensify the physical persecution of the Jews. The initiative here stemmed from the activities of special security police task forces known as the *Einsatzgruppen*, five highly mobile units working in groups of between 600 and 1,000 men. The brutality of their actions led to concerns being raised by the Wehrmacht but on 21 September Heydrich intervened by issuing the following instructions to the leaders of the Einsatzgruppen:

> With reference to the meeting which took place today in Berlin. I would like to emphasize once again that the overall measures envisaged (i.e. the final goal) must be kept strictly secret.
>
> A distinction must be made between.
> 1  The final goal (which will require a lengthy period) and
> 2  The stages towards the achievement of this final goal (which can be carried out on a short-term basis).
>
> The measures envisaged require the most thorough preparation both in the technical and in the economic sense'. . . . The first preliminary measure for achieving the final goal is the concentration of the Jews from the countryside to the larger cities. It must be speedily implemented. . . . You should ensure that only those cities are designated which are either railway junctions or at least lie on a railway line. . . . To achieve these goals I expect the absolute commitment of all forces of the Security Police and the Security Service.[14]

Between September 1939 to 1940 the Polish Jews were faced with a wide range of repressive measures. By December 1939 all those between the ages of 14 and 60 were faced with compulsory labour, were not allowed to change their address without permission and were subject to a curfew between 9 p.m. and 5 a.m. All Jews over the age of 10 had to display a band on their right arm bearing the Star of David. Meanwhile the Jews were being concentrated into ghettos, the first of which opened in Lodz, Poland's second largest city, in April 1940. A secret document of December 1939 made clear that 'the creation of the ghetto is . . . only a provisional measure'. The largest of the ghettos was created in Warsaw. Under the direction of a Resettlement Department which combed other sections of the capital city and forcibly removed the Jews, the total Jewish population in the ghetto was estimated to be between 470,000 and 590,000 people. A document drawn up by the Resettlement Department showed that

> In the Jewish residential district there are around 27,000 apartments with an average of 2½ rooms each. This produces an occupation density of 15.1 persons per apartment and 6–7 persons per room . . . the district is separated off from the rest of the city by the utilization of existing walls and by walling up streets, windows, doors and gaps between building. The walls are three metres high and raised a further metre by barbed wire placed on top. They are also guarded by motorized and mounted police patrols.[15]

Conditions within the ghettos were exceptionally harsh. The official food allocation gave Germans 2,310 calories a day, Poles 634 per day and Jews just 300 calories per day. The vast majority of apartments had no heating at all. In addition to the lack of food and heating materials, the most primitive hygiene conditions led to widespread outbreaks of typhus, dysentery, tuberculosis and pneumonia. By the summer of 1941 as many as 5,550 people were dying per month as a result of illness and deprivation. The Nazis merely used these outbreaks of disease to illustrate their propaganda claims that the Jews had brought these outbreaks upon themselves because of their own poor standards.

## 13.5  the Madagascar plan

Despite the outbreak of war in September 1939 the process of encouraging Jewish migration from the Reich territory was still maintained. However, the defeat of France in June 1940 created the possibility of an alternative solution to the Jewish question. As early as the winter of 1938 the French Foreign Minister had mentioned to Ribbentrop the possibility of moving Jews to the colonial island of Madagascar in the Indian Ocean. This was mentioned in the German press in 1939 and then discussed in more detail by the German Foreign Ministry's Department for Internal German Affairs in July 1940. Historians believe that the SS and even Hitler himself gave this plan serious and even enthusiastic consideration. However, the invasion of the Soviet Union in June 1941 utterly transformed the political and military horizon, placing the future of the Jewish population in the East in a more perilous situation than ever before and effectively rendering the Madagascar plan obsolete.

## 13.6  the invasion of the Soviet Union and the *Einsatzgruppen*

The invasion of the Soviet Union in June 1941 marked a fiercely ideological campaign against 'Jewish Bolshevism' and Nazi policy against the Jews now moved towards the systematic extermination of Russian Jews. Longerich makes it clear that 'In the course of the preparations for the racist war of extermination against the Soviet Union, it was Hitler who converted Nazi ideological thought into concrete instructions.'[16] On 3 March 1941 General Jodl received these instructions from Hitler: 'The forthcoming campaign is more than just an armed struggle; it will also lead to the conflict of two world views. In order to end this war, given the vastness of the territory, it will not suffice merely do defeat the enemy army . . . the Jewish-Bolshevik intelligentsia, hitherto the oppressor of the people, must be eliminated.' After a meeting on 30 March 1941 General Halder recorded Hitler's comments in his diary:

> Devastating assessment of Bolshevism: it is the equivalent of social delinquency. Communism is a tremendous danger for the future. . . . It is a war of extermination. If we do not regard it as such, we may defeat the enemy, but in thirty years' time we will again be confronted by the communist enemy. We are not fighting a war in order to conserve the enemy. . . . The struggle will be very different from that in the west. In the east toughness now means mildness in the future. The leaders must make the sacrifice of overcoming their scruples.[17]

Longerich states that, 'By March 1941 at the very latest, the Nazi leadership was clear about the true destination planned for the Jews who, long-term were to be expelled from 'the whole of Europe': they were to be deported to the newly-conquered Eastern territories after the war against the Soviet Union for which Hitler had concretely begun preparations as early as the last months of 1940.'[18]

Historians are in doubt as to the importance of the Einsatzgruppen in creating a climate in which extreme treatment of the Jews became a matter of clinical routine. Although these highly mobile killing squads were relatively small numerically, their ruthless efficiency meant that they were responsible for the murder of literally thousands of Jews, Communists and others when they moved into Russia in June 1941. Research has shown that the leaders of these action squads were highly educated, often to doctorate level. The extract that follows gives an indication of the role played by the Einsatzgruppen in perpetrating the Holocaust:

> What made it objectively possible to turn a nightmare into sober fact – and this was a fact of the utmost importance – was the existence of a highly organised police apparatus controlled by another fanatical racist and a man thoroughly loyal to the Führer. Himmler's Einsatzgruppen had already proved their mettle and were, by sheer coincidence, beginning in the autumn of 1941 to experiment with gas, a silent and swift method of execution making it technically feasible to dispose of millions rather than thousands of victims.[19]

Longerich confirms that the invasion of the Soviet Union in June 1941 had taken events to a new level of barbarism. He refers to comments made by Hitler at a conference in July 1941 in which he said 'The vast area must naturally be pacified as quickly as possible; this will best be achieved by shooting everyone who even looks oddly.'[20] Longerich's conclusion from this is that:

With the initiation of the mass murder of the Soviet civilian population in the summer of 1941, a stage had been reached by which these statements and similar ones by Hitler could no longer be understood as general threats of violence. The 'eliminatory' language of the dictator must be seen in the context of the mass murder that was now underway and that was being carried out by special units specially set up 'by special order of the Führer'. When Hitler now spoke of the 'extermination' (Vernichtung) of people, his subordinates must have understood it as it was intended: as direct or indirect instructions for the radicalisation of the mass murder already begun.[21]

## 13.7 the Wannsee Conference, 1942

On 29 November 1941 SS-Obergruppenführer Reinhard Heydrich issued invitations to a number of key figures in the SS and secretaries of state in strategic ministries. Initially planned for 9 December, the meeting was eventually postponed until 20 January 1942. Recently the historian Christian Gerlach has claimed that the original guest list was at first restricted to those charged specifically with the fate of German Jews and only later attained a European dimension. Gerlach contends that this extended remit adds support to the view that Hitler had not committed himself to genocide on a European scale until December 1941. In addition, Gerlach draws attention to a meeting of 12 December 1941 at which Hitler, according to Goebbels, let it be known that he had 'decided to sweep the floor clean. He had prophesied to the Jews that if they ever caused a world war again, they would suffer extermination. This was not just mere phrasemaking. The world war is upon us; the extermination of the Jews is the necessary consequence. This question should be regarded without any sentimentality.[22]

The venue for the rearranged meeting was a well-appointed villa in the beautiful setting of Lake Wannsee, an affluent suburb of Berlin. On a wintry Tuesday morning some fifteen senior officials came together for a meeting whose formalities would last for only 90 minutes or so. Seldom can the tranquillity of a setting have so completely belied the purpose of a meeting. On the agenda was the physical annihilation of the entire Jewish race in Europe. The most significant passage of Heydrich's address at the conference was as follows: 'After appropriate prior approval by the Führer, emigration as a possible solution has been superseded by a policy of evacuating of the Jews to the East. These actions [the deportations that had already been begun] are to be regarded merely as practical experience here is already being gathered that will be of extreme importance with respect to the impending final solution of the Jewish question.'[23]

## present at the Wannsee Conference, 20 January 1942

Reinhard Heydrich
Dr Alfred Meyer
Dr George Liebbrandt
Dr Wilhelm Stuckart
Erich Neumann
Dr Roland Friesler [Justice Ministry]
State Secretary Dr Josef Buhler [General Government]
Martin Luther
Dr Gerhard Klopfer
Dr Wilhelm Kritzinger
Otto Hoffman
SS Gruppenführer Heinrich Müller [RSHA]
SS Obersturmbannführer Adolf Eichmann [RSHA] (Who prepared the minutes of the meeting)
SS Oberführer Karl Schoengarth
SS Sturmbannführer Dr Otto Lange [Commander of the Security Police and SD in Latvia]

The following extracts indicate some recent interpretations by historians of the importance of the Wannsee Conference.

### SOURCE A

The significance of the Wannsee Conference was overrated for may years and has since been downgraded to little more than a platform for Heydrich to display his new powers.

Source: David Cesarani, *The Final Solution: Origins and Implementation* (1994).

### SOURCE B

It was hardly a conference. A group of bureaucrats at the level of secretaries of state were asked by Heydrich, who had an equivalent status as head of the security apparatus of the SS, to coordinate the execution of a Hitler order to murder all the Jews in territories within German reach that had evolved in the previous year. We have some oral testimony of what actually transpired there, but the protocol we have is doctored; it contains a censored version of what was said and does not deal with much that was said there. There is an aura of unreality about all that. It is a slanted version of past history, and, I think, of the plans for the future. Little of what was said there was executed in detail: Jews were not 'combed', as Heydrich put it, from western to eastern Europe, but were murdered in Poland from late 1941 on, and then in the summer of 1942 transports began to be sent from western Europe to the death camps. . . . The purpose of the exercise was to make clear to the representatives present that the Führer had empowered the SS to take over the Final Solution of the Jewish question, that Heydrich was the man responsible and to make sure they all collaborated when asked to do so. The transport people were not invited – their collaboration had apparently been assured already. Nor was the army there – perhaps because they might have caused problems. They would have to toe the line, in the name of the Führer. . . . The others were friendly, understanding, and dealt, as Heydrich surely must hoped, with details. No wonder he drank to the success of the meeting after it was over.

Source: Yehuda Bauer, *The Final Solution: Origins and Implementation*, ed. David Cesarani (1994).

## SOURCE C

Some of the old arguments have become redundant. The intentionalist-functionalist controversy has, I believe, ended. Hitler emerges as the radicalizing factor, and Eichmann's protocol mentions that explicitly. Some will emphasize the role of Heydrich, others that of Himmler. . . . In the eyes of too many of our contemporaries, Wannsee was the place where the Final Solution was decided upon. We of course know better. Wannsee was but a stage in the unfolding of the process of mass murder. The significance that people read into Wannsee is quite different from that accorded to it, presumably, by the conference participants. And yet, a post factum significance can be read into the meeting which goes beyond the factual description and historical analysis: we know of few cases where high representatives of a modern government bureaucracy met to discuss the implementation of a plan of total mass murder. The post factum significance appears to be that given a murderous ruling elite, and the identification of large parts of the middle class and intelligentsia with the regime as such – not necessarily with the ideological underpinning of the murder itself – the machine of the state and the ruling party will coalesce to execute total mass murder.

Source: as source B.

## SOURCE D

Wannsee itself was not the moment of decision. Nobody at Wannsee, not even Heydrich, was senior enough to decide on such matters . . . if the right arguments could be passed up to Hitler, agreements secured at the Wannsee conference could be undone. Conversely, where Hitler's approval was assured, Himmler would undoubtedly have proceeded even if Heydrich had not secured the active and passive assents he obtained at Wannsee. The Wannsee Protocol was rather a signpost indicating that genocide had become official policy. Yet Heydrich undoubtedly took the assent he had engineered at Wannsee very seriously. The signals he and Eichmann gave out after the event showed it had immeasurably strengthened their confidence. Even in May, visiting security officials in France for the last time before his assassination, Heydrich's account of the planning for the Final Solution emphasized the agreements reached on 20 January. Speaking to one another with great politeness, sipping their cognac, the Staatsekretare really had cleared the way for genocide.

Source: Mark Roseman, *The Villa, The Lake, The Meeting: Wannsee and the Final Solution* (2002).

The Wannsee Conference of 20 January 1942 served Heydrich's intention to present the mass murders in the various occupied areas as part of a general plan – ordered by Hitler and directed by the RHSA – for the 'solution to the European Jewish Question'. This presentation was to take place in the presence of a number of high-ranking functionaries of the Party and the SS, as well as leading ministerial officials, which allowed Heydrich to ensure that they, and especially the ministerial bureaucracy would share both knowledge of and responsibility for this policy. . . . First and foremost, therefore, Heydrich was making it clear that the new 'possible solution' had been explicitly authorised by Hitler.

Source: Peter Longerich, *The Unwritten Order: Hitler's Role in the Final Solution* (2001).

## ESSAY QUESTION

Examine the significance of the Wannsee Conference in the development of the Holocaust.

## 13.8 the roles of Heydrich and Himmler in the planning and organization of the Holocaust

### Reinhard Heydrich

Born in Halle, the son of classically trained musicians and a talented violinist himself, Reinhard Heydrich was a gifted, charismatic, ruthless and opportunistic figure. Utterly devoid of compassion, cold, efficient and driven by his own personal ambition, he was enlisted by Himmler when he established the Security Service and probably became more widely feared than any other leading figure in the Nazi regime. He presented Himmler with a grandiose vision of the SS and its Security Service at the heart of a highly organized new system of policing and control. He became the driving force in the radicalization of Jewish policy in November 1938 when he filled in during Himmler's absence. In 1940 he announced that the Führer had entrusted him with the planning of a territorial solution to the Jewish question, and the Madagascar plan emerged. In September 1941 Hitler personally appointed him deputy Protector for the occupied Czech territories. Heydrich embraced this post with relish and ruled the Czech people with an iron fist. When Germany invaded Russia in 1941 special regulations allowed the Einsatzgruppen of the SS and SD to operate with virtual impunity under the authority of Reinhard Heydrich. In addition, the 'Guidelines for the Conduct of the Troops in Russia' sanctioned complete ruthlessness against 'Bolshevik agitators, guerrilla, saboteurs and Jews' and demanded the total elimination of all types of resistance. In January 1942 Heydrich developed his role in the leadership of the Holocaust even further when he convened the Wannsee conference, where details of the bureaucratic, technical and organizational issues concerning the Holocaust were examined in detail.

This mission, code-named 'Operation Anthropoid', had been carefully planned by the British Special Operations Group. It could hardly have been more dangerous. On a winter's night in December 1941 a British plane was to drop two Czech activists, Jan Kubis and Josif Gabcik, behind enemy lines into Czechoslovakia, a country which, since March 1939, had been held in the iron grip of Nazi occupation. With the support of a tiny number of local activists the men would then prepare and carry out the execution of Reinhard Heydrich. In September 1941 Heydrich had been appointed Deputy Reich Protector of Bohemia and Moravia. Immediately he imposed brutal 'security measures' on the Czech people. Indeed, it was precisely because Heydrich had instilled such terror into the Czech people that he believed he was safe. He was unaware that as he imposed his reign of terror on the Czechs, British secret agents were training the Czech activists to carry out his execution. The British agents planning his execution knew that Heydrich was openly contemptuous of the tight security measures, which surrounded his colleagues. He deliberately followed the same route to his office each day as if to assert his confidence that no one would dare to act against him. Despite warnings about his lax security from Himmler and even Hitler, British intelligence knew that Heydrich was regularly driven through Prague in an open-topped car, without protective armour plating. Heydrich was normally accompanied solely by his chauffeur.

What is less clear is whether the consequences of such an action against one of the most senior figures in Hitler's government had been fully appreciated. How would the Nazis respond to the murder of Himmler's deputy? Surely Himmler and Hitler would not allow such a high-profile assassination to go unpunished? Did Operation Anthropoid needlessly endanger the lives of literally thousands of ordinary Czech citizens who, had this action not taken place, might have lived out the rest of the Nazi occupation in relative safety?

On the morning of 27 May 1941 the dark green, open-topped, unarmoured Mercedes began its routine journey. Heydrich's chauffeur had picked up the deputy leader of the SS at the normal time. Later that day, Heydrich was due to fly to Berlin for a high-level meeting with Hitler himself. The car slowed down as it approached a sharp bend on the road to Heydrich's headquarters at the Hradcany Palace in Prague. The assassins were waiting. An agent lifted his arm in a prearranged signal. A second man stepped out and squeezed the trigger of his machine-gun. The machine-gun jammed but a third agent threw a small bomb at the car. It exploded under one of the rear wheels. The force of the explosion drove fragments of metal, seat cover and clothing into Heydrich's open wound. Even so, Heydrich managed to stumble from the car and fire at his attackers before he collapsed. Initially, Heydrich's doctors believed his life was not in serious danger and were optimistic that he would recover.

However, it soon became clear that fragments of steel, car seat and uniform had become lodged in Heydrich's spleen. The wound became infected and led to the onset of blood poisoning. Himmler authorized his own private doctors to rush to Prague to save Heydrich. It was too late. Although a medical report of 3 June gave some grounds for optimism, the onset of blood poisoning proved devastating. Within 24 hours, Heydrich was dead. He died on 4 June 1942. In Berlin a massive funeral was arranged for 9 June. In the presence of Heydrich's wife and children Hitler praised the 'iron heart' of his former colleague. Himmler swore the massed ranks of the SS to pitilessly avenge Heydrich's death.

Meanwhile it was already becoming clear that the German authorities were prepared to take extreme measures in the wake of Heydrich's death. No community felt the heavy hand of German reprisals more severely than the small village of Lidice, six miles north-west of Prague. On 10 June, the day after Heydrich's funeral, every single one of the 199 men in the village were rounded up and shot. All of the children and their mothers were taken to camps at Ravensbruck, Auschwitz and Mauthausen. In the village of Lezaky 33 adults were shot and 14 children taken to concentration camps. Meanwhile a thousand Jews were taken from Prague to camps in the east. In his biography of Himmler, historian Peter Padfield states:

> Lidice was a comparatively minor, though the most notorious, part of the reprisal measures in the Protectorate: over 13,000 people were arrested and nearly 700 executed or gunned down when eventually the assassins were betrayed for the reward, and surrounded. And in Mauthausen concentration camp nearly 3,000 Czechs were killed. The Jews also suffered, as they had feared: between 10 and 12 June some 3000 from Theresienstadt were entrained for 'resettlement' at an extermination camp.[24]

## Reinhard Heydrich

| 1904 | |
|---|---|
| 7 May | Born in Halle, near Leipzig. |
| 1922 | |
| March | Became a cadet in the German navy |
| 1926 | |
| | Became second lieutenant |
| 1931 | |
| | Forced to resign his naval commission after a sex scandal In the same year, at the age of 27, joined the Nazi Party. Came to Himmler's attention and given the chance to create an intelligence-gathering service known as the SD Promoted through the SS in 1931, 1932 and 1933 until he reached the post of SS Brigadier General before the age of 30. By 1934 Heydrich became Himmler's deputy. |
| 1939 | |
| | Became Head of the Reich Main Security Office. Following the invasion of the Soviet Union organized the extermination of Jews in occupied areas of Eastern Europe. Chaired the infamous Wannsee conference held near Berlin in |

January 1942. This meeting was vital in terms of organizing the Final Solution

1941
September     Appointed acting vice-Reich Protector in Bohemia-Moravia (former Czechoslovakia). Immediately introduced stringent security measures to oppress the Czech people.

1942
May     Shot while driving through Prague. Died in June 1942 as a result of injuries sustained.

## Heinrich Himmler

Heinrich Himmler became the leader of the fledgling SS in 1929. This unit originally acted as Hitler's private bodyguard and 'Protection Squad' (Schutzstaffel, hence the abbreviation 'SS') and became answerable solely to Hitler. Himmler rapidly expanded the membership of the SS but by 1934 he was thinking of the SS in more ambitious terms than just a special force of loyal troops at Hitler's disposal. He conceived the ambition of turning the SS into the core elite of the new Nazi racial order. In deliberate contrast to the brown-shirted street thugs who thronged the SA, Himmler intended his SS to be strictly hierarchical, racially pure, unquestioningly obedient, incorporating what he regarded as the strongest elements in the German race. The older generation of SS men were systematically replaced by a younger, better educated generation of officers. The SS wore military-style uniforms with not just the original silver death's-head badge of the organization but also a runic version of the letters 'SS', shaped like a double bolt of lightning. Himmler shared Heydrich's cold and ruthless nature and the fiercely ideological commitment required in those who served in the highest echelons of the Nazi hierarchy. These characteristics saw him emerge as not just the leader of the SS but also the head of the police state and concentration camp system founded on his initial power base in Munich, where he set up a model concentration camp at Dachau.

### Heinrich Himmler

1934
April     Goering appointed the SS leader Inspector of the Secret State Police (*Gestapo*) in Prussia. Goring replaced Diels with Himmler at the head of the Gestapo. Goering and Frick were forced to recognize that they were unable to control the Gestapo, whatever formal powers they might claim to possess over it. Then a decree issued by Hitler on 17 June made Himmler Chief of the German Police. In this capacity Himmler put Heydrich in charge of the Gestapo and the Criminal Police, as well as the SS Security Service.

June     SS murdered the SA leadership

1936
June     Himmler (Reichsführer SS; 'Chief of the German Police) set up the 'order police' under Karl Daleuge and the Security Service (SD) under Reinhard Heydrich

Richard Breitman provides an excellent comparison of the relative importance of the roles played by Himmler and Heydrich:

> In my view Hitler, Himmler and Heydrich all played major, if somewhat different, roles in developing the plans for the Final Solution. . . . I regard Hitler as the originator of the idea of the Final Solution and as the single most important influence. . . . I would simply add that outside foreign policy and military affairs, Hitler was not a man to control all the details, a tendency all the more likely in this case because there were political grounds for him to maintain some apparent distance from the vast crimes. Hitler gave the commission for genocide, but he needed people who would do his bidding without insisting on formal laws or written authorization, without showing or giving in to moral qualms or doubts, without shirking from the task of persuading or compelling large organizations to participate or cooperate. He had a number of people who possessed those qualifications, but the most important ones were Heydrich and Himmler. . . . And when Himmler finally initiated implementation of the Final Solution outside the Soviet territories, he appears to have referred to it as Heydrich's plan. The designation of the extermination programme for Polish Jews, Aktion Reinhard, was an apparently posthumous honour given to Heydrich. This by no means exhaustive list of Heydrich's accomplishments raises a question: what was left for Himmler to do.
>
> Most of his contemporaries underestimated Himmler, and it would not be difficult for historians to lose him in the umbra of Hitler and Heydrich. Yet Himmler not only hired Heydrich in the first place, but trained him ideologically. . . . Although there were undoubtedly some personal strains between Himmler and Heydrich produced partly by Himmler's management technique, partly by Heydrich's ambition, and partly by close contact between two very different personalities, I have found no evidence of political or policy disagreements between the two.[25]

## 13.9 sources: the role of Himmler in the Nazi State

**SOURCE A**

Himmler had his first key success in his efforts to control the entire police and bring about its amalgamation with the S.S. true, he did not get his own Police Ministry, but he was empowered by a decree of Hitler's of 17 June 1936, to 'unify the control of police duties in the Reich' and was given the title 'Reich S.S. Leader and Chief of German Police within the Reich Ministry of the Interior.' Like the law on the Gestapo, this hotly disputed definition of Himmler's official role contained two conflicting elements. This title, which was achieved against Frick's opposition, signified over and above the personal union the institutional joining of the S.S. leadership to the control of the police. The addition of the words 'within the Reich Ministry of the Interior' and the further stipulation contained in the decree that the Chief of German Police was personally and directly subordinate to the Reich and Prussian Minister of the Interior', was by contrast a concession to the Reich Minister of the Interior, who wanted to preserve the connection between the police and the internal administration. Another sign of compromise was the fact that, as Chief of German Police, Himmler did not get ministerial rank but was merely given the position of State Secretary, and he was only authorized to attend meetings of the Reich cabinet 'in so far as matters within his sphere of authority are concerned'. Supplementary decrees made it clear that his subordination to Frick was more or less purely nominal. It was above all because Himmler was directly responsible to the Führer in his capacity as Reich S.S. leader (his subordination to the Chief of Staff of the S.A. was formally ended after 30 June 1934) that he could easily escape from the simultaneous responsibility to the Reich Minister of the Interior, or even indeed reverse this relationship.

*Source*: Martin Broszat, *The Hitler State* (1981).

## SOURCE B

REINHARD HEYDRICH, SPEAKING AT THE GERMAN POLICE CONVENTION, 1941.

The secret police, the criminal police and the security forces are shrouded in the whispered secrets of the political crime novel.

*Source*: David F. Crew, *Nazism and German Society, 1933–1945* (1941).

## SOURCE C

The absolute conviction, the hard will, the ordered analysis followed by unequivocal decrees, the painstaking hours of work that Himmler put in and demanded from his subordinates inspired respect. But Himmler also exerted charm; there are too many accounts of his seemingly genuine concern for his people and their families to doubt this. Without these qualities, it is difficult to imagine how he could have built up and retained his tight grip on all the instruments of national-racial and political control, the S.S., S.D., police and concentration camps.

*Source*: Peter Padfield, *Himmler: Reichsführer SS* (1990).

## SOURCE D

EXTRACT FROM HIMMLER'S SPEECH TO THE SS AT POZNÁN, 4 OCTOBER 1943.

I want to tell you about a very grave matter in all frankness. We can talk about it quite openly here, but we must never talk about it publicly . . .

I mean the evacuation of the Jews, the extermination of the Jewish people. It is one of those things one says lightly – 'The Jewish people are being liquidated,' party comrades exclaim; naturally, it's in our programme, the isolation of the Jews, extermination, okay, we'll do it.' And then they come, all the 80 million Germans, and every one of them has a decent Jew. Of course, the others may all be swines, but this particular one is an A-1 Jew. All those who talk like this have not seen it, have not gone through it. Most of you will know what it means to see 100 corpses piled up, or 500, or 1,000. To have gone through this and – except for instances of human weakness – to have remained decent, that has made us tough. This is an unwritten, never to be written, glorious page of our history.'

*Source*: J. Noakes and G. Pridham (ed.), *Nazism 1919–1945: A Documentary Reader. Vol. 3: Foreign Policy, War and Racial Extermination* (1995).

## SOURCE E

Himmler called in Rudolf Hoess to turn Auschwitz into an extermination camp. Himmler's much-touted weakness at the scene of mass shootings seems to have had a direct bearing on his decision to rely on gas chambers in extermination camps. . . . Auschwitz (meant as a generic term) was the creation of bureaucrats, a term that fits Himmler far better than Heydrich, the man with the heart of iron. Himmler therefore was the architect of genocide because he devised or selected the preferred, even essential means by which it was carried out: the extermination factory, where death came or was supposed to come deceptively, smoothly and efficiently.

*Source*: Richard Breitman, *The Final Solution: Origins and Implementation*, ed. David Cesarani (1994).

## SOURCE F

'It is hard to conceive of a serious attempt to physically eliminate the Jewish people across the continent without Auschwitz-Birkenau, Chelmno, Maidanek, Belzec, Sobibor and Treblinka. Here, Himmler's stamp is far stronger, especially in the planning stages. Of course, Hitler had raised the idea of gassing Jews in Mein Kampf, Himmler did not have to show great originality, but only loyalty, faith and persistence to pursue its feasibility on a vast scale.'

*Source*: as source E.

## ESSAY QUESTION

Using the sources and your own knowledge, explain how the importance of Heydrich and Himmler in the implementation and execution of Nazi policies developed between the period 1933–45.

## 13.10 Auschwitz-Birkenau

Initially conceived not as a place for mass murder but as a response to an over-crowding problem in Upper Silesia, the camp that came more than any other to symbolize the enormous inhumanity of the Holocaust was originally a former Austrian barracks near the small Polish town of Oswiecim (Auschwitz) and was selected for development because of its relative isolation and its convenient position on the railway network. After initial surveys and expressions of unease because of the rudimentary nature of the site and the basic conditions there, Himmler finally gave orders to Rudolf Hoess for the construction of a concentration camp at Auschwitz in April 1940. The first, small-scale gassing of Russian prisoners of war probably took place in September 1941. As transports of Jews began to rapidly increase from 1942, new construction work took place at Birkenau, three kilometres away from the main camp. From the summer of 1942 the process of transports of Jews arriving at a railway platform and being 'selected' for life or death by an SS doctor began to take shape. The escalating scale of the process was accompanied by proportionate developments not just in the facilities to gas people but also with the construction of crematoria to dispose of the bodies. By mid-1944 the industrial killing process had been honed to the extent that a railway line now brought people directly into the Birkenau camp, and it was in the summer of this year that the rate of murders at the camp reached its peak. In a statement made in a post-war hearing, Hoess gave figures for the numbers of Jews murdered at Auschwitz that are generally regarded as fairly accurate. Although the camp was liberated by the Soviet Union in January 1945, the suffering of those who were imprisoned there but survived could not come to an end at that point. The memory of Auschwitz was irremovable.

**SOURCE A**

Unlike the history of anti-Semitism, Auschwitz has one certain beginning (the first Polish prisoners arrived on 14 June 1940) and unlike the history of genocide, it has one definite end (the camp was liberated on 27 January 1945). In between these two dates Auschwitz had a complex and surprising history that in many ways mirrored the intricacies of Nazi racial and ethnic policy. It was never conceived as a camp to kill Jews, it was never solely concerned with the 'Final Solution' – though that came to dominate the place – and it was always physically changing, often in response to the constant shifts in fortunes of the German war effort elsewhere. Auschwitz, through its destructive dynamism, was the physical embodiment of the fundamental values of the Nazi state.

*Source*: Laurence Rees: *Auschwitz: The Nazis and the Final Solution* (2005).

**SOURCE B**

FROM THE POST-WAR DESCRIPTION OF AUSCHWITZ BY SS MEMBER, PERY BROAD.

A long train made up of closed goods wagons is standing at a side platform of the marshalling yard. The sliding doors are sealed with barbed wire. The squad of troops has taken up position around the train and the ramp. . . . The SS men of the inmate control section ensure that the prisoners leave the train. There is chaos and confusion on the ramp. . . . To start with the men and women are separated. There are heart-breaking scenes. Married couples separate. Mothers wave good-bye to their sons for the last time. The two columns stand in ranks of five several metres apart from one another on the ramp. Anyone who is overcome with grief and tries to rush over to embrace his or her loved one once more and give them words of comfort is hurled back by a blow from one of the SS men. Now the SS doctor begins to select those fit for work from those who, in his opinion, are unfit for work.

*Source*: J. Noakes and G. Pridham (ed.), *Nazism 1919–1945: A Documentary Reader. Vol. 3: Foreign Policy, War and Racial Extermination* (1995).

FROM THE RECOLLECTIONS OF A FRENCH DOCTOR, ANDRÉ LETTICH.

More than five hundred metres further on were two barracks: the men stood on one side, the women on the other. They were addressed in a very polite and friendly way: 'You have been on a journey. You are dirty. You will take a bath. Get undressed quickly.' Towels and soap were handed out, and then suddenly the brutes woke up and showed their true faces; this horde of people, these men and women were driven outside with hard blows and forced both summer and winter to go the few hundred metres to the 'Shower Room'. Above the entry door was the word 'Shower'. One could even see shower heads on the ceiling which were cemented in but never had water flowing through them. . . . The doors were shut and, ten minutes later, the temperature was high enough to facilitate the condensation of the hydrogen cyanide . . . this was the so-called 'Zyklon B', . . . Then SS . . . threw the gas in through a little vent. One could hear fearful screams, but a few moments later there was complete silence.'

*Source*: as source B.

EXTRACT FROM THE DIARY OF DR JOHANN KREMER, PROFESSOR OF MEDICINE AT THE UNIVERSITY OF MÜNSTER, WHO WAS STATIONED AT AUSCHWITZ AS A DOCTOR FROM AUGUST TO NOVEMBER 1942.

2. IX. 1942. This morning at three o'clock I attended a special action for the first time. Dante's hell seemed like a comedy in comparison. Not for nothing is Auschwitz called an extermination camp . . .
6–7. IX. 1942 Sunday, an excellent lunch: tomato soup, half a chicken with potatoes and red cabbage, petits fours, a marvellous vanilla ice cream. . . . Left at eight in the evening for a special action, for the fourth time . . .
12. X. 1942. Inoculation for typhus. Following this, feverish in the evening; still went to a special action that night (1,600 Dutch). Terrible scenes near the last bunker. The tenth special action.

*Source*: as source B.

Interest from I.G. Farben transformed Auschwitz from a minor camp within the SS system into potentially one of its most important components. Symptomatic of this change in the camp's status was Himmler's decision to make his first visit to the camp on 1 March 1941. . . . The prospect of war against the Soviet Union clearly released the most radical ideas imaginable in the minds of leading Nazis . . . during the summer of 1941, the war on the Eastern front – the war without rules – came to Auschwitz . . .

The new evidence does not support the once prevalent view that there was some conclusive decision taken by Hitler in the spring or summer of 1941 to order the destruction of all the Jews of Europe, of which the 31 July authorization is an important part. The more likely scenario is that as all the leading Nazis focused their attention on the war against the Soviet Union, the decision to kill the women and children in the East was seen as the practical way of solving an immediate and specific problem.'

*Source*: Laurence Rees: *Auschwitz: The Nazis and the Final Solution* (2005).

## 13.11 sources: the interpretations of historians: Hitler's personal role in the Holocaust

**SOURCE A**

The effect of years of research has been that historians have moved away from a picture of Hitler and his closest accomplices stricken with racial mania, making deep-laid plans to translate their fantasies into reality and then implementing these plans with demonic thoroughness, while keeping the fact from public knowledge throughout. Today we know how complex and contradictory were the processes that led to the gradual and growing radicalisation of Nazi racial policies and extermination methods.

*Source*: Detlev J. K. Peukert, *The Genesis of the Final Solution* (1994).

**SOURCE B**

By underscoring that Hitler and his ideology had a decisive impact on the course of the regime, I do not mean in any way to imply that Auschwitz was a pre-ordained result of Hitler's accession to power. the anti-Jewish policies of the thirties must be understood in their context, and even Hitler's murderous rage and his scanning of the political horizon for the most extreme options do not suggest the existence of any plans for total extermination in the years prior to the German invasion of the Soviet Union.

*Source*: Saul Friedlander, *Nazi Germany and the Jews: The Years of Persecution 1933–1939* (1997).

**SOURCE C**

The images of the gas chambers would forever shape and define Nazism. But one should not read History backwards . . . The journey to the gas chambers was not a simple one. Stages along the route included the anti-Semitism engendered in the wake of the World War One defeat; the desire to exclude Jews from German life and the Nazis' belief that Jews were both a dangerous and inferior race: the invasion of Poland, which brought 3 million Polish Jews under Nazi control; and finally the decision to kill Communists and Jews in the wake of Operation Barbarossa. No blueprint for the holocaust existed before 1941: the Nazi regime was too chaotic for that. Above all, it was the invasion of Russia that caused a radical change in the Nazis approach to the Jews.

*Source*: Laurence Rees, *The Nazis: A Warning From History* (1997).

In mid-March of 1942, some 75 to 80 per cent of all victims of the Holocaust were still alive, while some 20 to 25 per cent had already perished. A mere eleven months later, in mid-February 1943 the situation was exactly the reverse. Some 75 to 80 per cent of all Holocaust victims were already dead, and a mere 20 to 25 per cent still clung to a precarious existence. At the core of the holocaust was an intense eleven-month wave of mass murder. The centre of gravity of this mass murder was Poland, where in March 1942, despite two and a half years of terrible hardship, deprivation, and persecution, every major Jewish community was still intact; eleven months later, only remnants of Polish Jewry survived in a few rump ghettos and labour camps.

*Source*: Christopher R. Browning, *One Day in Jozefow: Initiation to Mass Murder* (1994).

Hitler was the inspiration behind the 'Final Solution', even where the direct initiatives came from others. Goebbels called him the 'unswerving protagonist and advocate of a radical solution. The 'order' or 'wish' of the Führer was invariably invoked at every level in setting in motion and carrying out the murder of the Jews. Crucial decisions required Hitler's approval. Himmler claimed Hitler's authority for the order around mid August 1941 to extend the killing in the Soviet Union to Jewish women and children. At the prompting of Goebbels and Heydrich, Hitler consented in August 1941 to the introduction of the 'Yellow Star' to be worn by German Jews – something which, for tactical reasons, he had hitherto rejected. There is no doubt that Hitler himself in mid-September took the decision to deport the German Jews to the east, sealing their fate. No written directive from Hitler ordering the 'Final Solution' has survived. Almost certainly none was ever given. But there can be no serious doubt that Hitler gave the verbal orders to kill the Jews of Europe – even if such orders amounted to no more than a simple blanket empowering of Himmler and Heydrich.

*Source*: Ian Kershaw, *Hitler: Profiles in Power* (1991).

Hitler's responsibility for the murder of the European Jews can be seen directly as well as indirectly: on the basis of the way in which the apparatus of power was structured one can assume with complete certainty that an operation like the murder of millions of people in all areas of Europe, an operation therefore with such wide ramifications and necessitating such huge resources in terms of personnel and materials, was only possible with the consent of the man at the top, the man in whom all the various threads came together.

However, Hitler's responsibility for the Holocaust is also subject to documentary proof. Initially this includes his attitudes to certain key groups amongst the servants of his regime – his repeated speeches to generals, for example, and other significant instructions for the preparation of the racist campaign of destruction against the Soviet Union in spring 1941, his statements concerning the 'new order' of the occupied Soviet area on 16 July 1941, or his speech to the Reichs and Gauleiter on 12 December 1941.

*Source*: Peter Longerich, *The Unwritten Order: Hitler's Role in the Final Solution* (2001).

## SOURCE G

The simple answer, which has not always been voiced as openly as it might have been, is that our need for precise answers is greater than the ability of the documentation to supply them. Most historians continue to assume that, however twisted the road may have been to reach this point, in such a Hitler-centred system Hitler must still at some point have taken the ultimate decision. His role in redefining the character of warfare and introducing numerous pacification and social engineering had been crucial. But how closely did he now direct the killing of Jews? Was his approval given or merely presumed? Did the transition from mass killings or genocide indeed involve a clear decision, or was the kind of programme outlined at Wannsee more of a retrospective codification of a process already under way.

Even more than in peacetime, Hitler carefully concealed his involvement in the Jewish question. The paucity of official records is not compensated by the existence of private ones. Hitler kept no diary and sent no letters expressing views on the Jewish question. A number of those close to him recorded his views, but often the notes of Hitler's subordinates are ambiguous too. . . . In any case, we have virtually no record of probably the most important channel of communication on the Jewish question, Hitler's conversations with Himmler. The occasional entries in Himmler's appointments diary regarding Hitler and the Jewish question are abbreviated and cryptic.

*Source*: Mark Roseman, *The Villa, The Lake, The Meeting: Wannsee and the Final Solution* (2002).

## SOURCE H

The exact point at which the decision was taken to murder the whole of European Jewry is shrouded in obscurity and still a matter of dispute amongst historians. Some have argued that Hitler did not decide on the 'final' solution until late October–November 1941 when it dawned on him that the Russian campaign was running into difficulties. . . . Yet precisely at this point when doubts were beginning to assail him, Hitler ordered the acceleration of the deportation of the Jews which had greatly slowed in pace since the first half of 1941 when preparations for the attack on Russia had prior claim on available transport. In October the first mass deportations from German cities to Lodz commenced. Had the entire Jewish population of Europe – three million Polish Jews and two million from other lands – been crowded into the ghettoes the Nazis would have been unable to contain the situation. To relieve the pressure on overcrowded and typhus-ridden accommodation some local SS commanders had already begun to execute Jews by shooting as soon as they arrived from the west. When Himmler discussed these executions with Hitler it seems likely that the latter ordered the extension of this 'final' solution to encompass the whole of European Jewry, the visceral reaction of a fanatical racist determined to be rid of the Jews . . .

However, other historians maintain that Hitler decided on mass extermination not in the autumn but in the summer of 1941. The Russian campaign was the decisive factor. Already in March Hitler declared that this would be a racial war of annihilation different in kind from the campaign in the west; for example, political commissars were to be shot on capture. Five Einsatzgruppen followed the German armies into Russia in June with specific instructions to murder 'the Jewish-Bolshevik ruling class'.

*Source*: William Carr, *Hitler: A Study in Personality and Politics* (1978).

## SOURCE I

If the historian wants to know when the Nazi leadership decided that the mass murder of Russian Jewry was no longer a future task but rather a goal to be achieved immediately, he must ascertain when the decision was taken to commit the necessary manpower. On 16 July Hitler spoke with Goering . . . in a way that showed his clear conviction that victory was at hand . . . Himmler did not attend this meeting but was in close proximity to Hitler from 15 to 20 July. What Hitler confided to him personally, we do not know, but we do know what he did in the following weeks. . . . Within a week of Hitler's 16 July 'victory speech' Himmler had increased the number of SS men operating behind the advanced German Army by 11,000 men. . . . In Burrin's view Hitler's mood was one of steady degeneration from mid-July confidence of early victory to a grim awareness by mid-September that the blitzkrieg against Russia had failed, the US was about to enter the war, and Germany was doomed to a prolonged struggle on all fronts. This, for Burrin, was precisely the 'condition' under which Hitler had long 'intended' to kill all the European Jews. In my view, Hitler's mood did not steadily degenerate. Rather it fluctuated. Furthermore, one can once again chart a striking coincidence between the peaks of German military success and Hitler's key decisions.

When Hitler gave his 'victory' speech in mid-July and instigated the systematic mass murder of Soviet Jewry, he also in my opinion conveyed to Himmler and Heydrich his desire for a 'feasibility study' for the mass murder of European Jewry. This is what lay behind Heydrich's subsequent visit with Goering on 31 July to have the latter sign his authorization to draw up and submit a plan for a 'total solution' of the Jewish question.

*Source*: Christopher R. Browning, 'Hitler and the Euphoria of Victory: The Path to the Final Solution', in D. Cesarini (ed.), *The Final Solution: Origins and Implementation* (1994).

## ESSAY QUESTIONS

1 Examine the reasons why Auschwitz has such a significant position in the history of the Holocaust.
2 Using all of the sources and your own knowledge, explain the extent to which the decision to carry out the 'Final Solution' was the personal responsibility of Adolf Hitler.

## 14.1 the destruction of Germany

While Hitler and his closest acolytes made their nihilistic farewells in the smouldering ruins of a once-proud capital city, the country they left behind faced complete ruination. More than three million German soldiers had been killed in action, with one million taken as prisoners of war in Russia, many never to be seen again. Many of those who survived carried with them serious wounds, injuries and disfigurements that would remain for the rest of their lives. Few can have emerged without some degree of psychological damage. Many had to face the fact that they had committed wartime atrocities either against the Jews or against the civilian populations in the occupied countries, most obviously Russia and Poland. The savage allied bombing raids accounted for the lives of half a million civilians. Those who remained physically intact were left a country whose great cities, so diligently and energetically constructed were now reduced to ashes. While Hitler bore no semblance of remorse or compassion for what had been inflicted on the German people, ordinary people were left to contend with the most brutal of circumstances. A teenage girl wrote a post-war account of her experiences in moving from East Prussia to the west in part of a general migration in the spring of 1945 in which it is calculated that a further million German people lost their lives:

> The ice was brittle and in places we had to wade through water 25cm deep. We kept testing the surface in front of us with sticks. Numerous bomb craters forced us to make detours. Often one slipped and thought one had had it. Our clothes, which were soaked through, only allowed us to move clumsily. But fear of death made us forget the shivering which shook our bodies.
>
> I saw women performing superhuman feats. As leaders of the treks they instinctively found the safest paths for their wagons. Household goods were strewn all over the ice; wounded people crept up to us with pleading gestures, hobbling on sticks; others were carried on small sledges by their comrades. . . .

On the next day we walked in the direction of Danzig. On the way we saw gruesome scenes. Mothers in a fit of madness threw their children into the sea. People hanged themselves; others fell upon dead horses, cutting out bits of flesh and roasting them on open fires. Women gave birth in the wagons. Everyone thought only of himself – no one could help the sick and the weak.[1]

This was the Germany Hitler left behind. As the *Guardian* reported: 'Millions of Germans are on the move. Groups trek hundreds of miles and lose half their numbers through disease and exhaustion. Children have arrived in Berlin looking like the emaciated creatures of Belsen.'[2] In the words of historian Daniel Yergin: 'Most of Berlin was a city of rubble, bombed-out buildings, and broken sewers, wandering women, children and old men – a city of the dead.'[3]

Hitler's people now faced a long and anguished period in which on all sides, politicians and civilians struggled to come to terms with his legacy. Key elements of this process took place at Yalta in February 1945 and Potsdam in July 1945.

## 14.2 the Yalta Conference

The strain of war had taken its toll not just on the civilians caught up in its ruinous privations, but on the physical well-being of those who had led their countries during the momentous events of the wartime years. Exhaustion was written all over the face of the American President, Franklin D. Roosevelt, when he completed the tiring journey from the United States to Saki airport on the Crimean peninsula. With only months to live, he had summoned up the last vestiges of his energy to meet with Russian dictator Josef Stalin and his other wartime partner, Prime Minister Winston Churchill of Great Britain. These three towering figures now witnessed at first hand what Germany had done to the Soviet Union. It must surely have been a deeply moving and astonishing sight. As they convened in the grandeur of a former tsarist palace they knew that the latest Russian offensive had drawn the Red Army to the distant outskirts of Berlin. Meanwhile the forces of the United States and Britain were massed on the German borders with Belgium, Luxembourg and France, poised for an offensive that would take them into Germany and then across the Rhine. While military success was now imminent, the political future of Europe in general and Germany in particular was fraught with difficulty. In the words of Churchill, 'the whole shape and structure of post-war Europe clamoured for review.' Michael Dockrill summarizes where the members of the Grand Alliance stood over the future of Germany.

> A casual remark by Roosevelt that he doubted that the American people would allow American troops in occupation of Germany for more than two years after the war, and the obvious lack of any carefully thought out American proposal for the future of Germany, may have convinced Stalin that the United States was not greatly concerned about the fate

of Central and Eastern Europe. The three powers merely accepted the agreements their officials had reached in 1944 on the military zones the three allies would occupy in Germany after her surrender – although on Churchill's insistence, France was also given a small zone. A four power military council for Germany was set up in Berlin, which was also to be divided into four Allied military sectors. The future of Germany was left for determination by a future peace conference.

Neither did Stalin appear to have any definite policy about Germany, except to insist that the Russians should extract as much compensation as possible from the German economy for the damage the Nazis had inflicted on the Soviet Union. At Yalta the Soviets put forward figures of from $10 to $20 billion. . . . The conference postponed a decision on this issue by setting up a Reparations Commission to determine how much Germany would pay and in what form she should pay it – although the Soviet claim was accepted as the basis for discussion.[4]

While the Yalta Conference undoubtedly marked the high point of allied unity and contained some genuinely amicable moments between the three leaders, the illusion of co-operation was short-lived. Poland's fate fell squarely into the hands of the Russians and the principle that Germany would be divided had been accepted. By the time a new configuration of leaders came together in the Berlin suburb of Potsdam, the atmosphere had changed and the chill of the Cold War became evident.

## 14.3  the Nuremberg trials

The sheer scale of the Second World War and the depth of the atrocities it contained meant that arrangements for a judicial reckoning of events were complex and difficult. The process of denazification commenced with the cooperation of all four of the major powers to arrange the most important war-crimes trial of the century to take place at Nuremberg from 1945 to 1946. Nuremberg was carefully selected to stage the trials, as to many observers it seemed to be a spiritual home of Nazism. It was here that Leni Riefenstahl had made her celebrated film, *Triumph of the Will*, portraying the annual party rally and its homage to Hitler in epic terms. Although several leading figures including Hitler, Goebbels and Himmler had committed suicide, there were important Nazis, such as Goering and Hess, and Generals Keitel and Jodl, who remained to face trial. Ultimately 22 individuals went into the dock. Three were acquitted, twelve were sentenced to death, and the remainder faced prison terms of varying length. Although Goering took his own life in his prison cell, the remaining executions were carried out on 1 October 1946.

## 14.4  the Potsdam Conference

Key decisions had to be ratified concerning the future of Germany. Issues raised at Yalta and discussed subsequently were to be agreed at Potsdam. Germany was to be divided into four zones, with Britain, France and America occupying areas in the west, and a Russian zone in the east, where Soviet soldiers had been stationed since the spring of 1945. The Russian zone contained the strategically and psychologically important city of Berlin. The Allies decided that this city would remain as the capital but would also be divided into four zones. Authority would be granted to an Allied Control Council, comprising the four commanders-in-chief who would convene in Berlin. Germany would undergo an immediate process of demilitarization and denazification. Unlike the First World War, reparations would be paid in kind rather than in money.

When the leaders of the Grand Alliance parted company at Yalta in February 1945 they cannot have envisaged how quickly events would unfold. Ironically, after all they had done to resist Hitler, the Alliance was unable to see the day of triumph with all of its members still together. On 12 April the American President suffered a massive brain haemorrhage and died. He was replaced by Vice-President Harry Truman, a man who would develop a more abrasive approach towards Stalin than Roosevelt had traditionally employed. Within weeks, Russian and American soldiers came together for the first time on the banks of the River Elbe. At the end of April the object of the alliance, Adolf Hitler, committed suicide in the Berlin bunker. It was agreed that the new President would meet with Stalin and Churchill for the first time in July 1945 in the suburb of Potsdam, just outside the shattered remnants of Berlin. It soon became clear that the unity of Yalta had been replaced with a tougher edge, particularly from Truman, who commented privately that 'force is the only thing the Russians understand'. When the United States successfully tested the atomic bomb for the first time in history, the President's hand was significantly strengthened. As Churchill noted of the President on the day that Truman learned that the atomic bomb was far more destructive than had been expected, 'He was a changed man. He told the Russians just where they got on and off and generally bossed the whole meeting.'[5]

Meanwhile, a dramatic and unexpected election reverse saw Prime Minister Winston Churchill replaced by the Labour leader Clement Attlee. With these personnel changes in place, the new leaders soon found dealing with Stalin to be a challenging and frustrating experience. As Truman observed on the way home from the conference: 'On a number of occasions I felt like blowing the roof off the place. . . . Stalin was an S.O.B. but I guess he thinks I'm one too.'[6]

Michael Dockrill provides a useful summary of the outcome of the Potsdam Conference and highlights the issue of reparations.

> The Potsdam Conference of the Three Great Powers (17 July–1 August 1945) did not produce any major constructive agreements but it did conceal temporarily the growing divergence between East and West. A reparations agreement was reached designed to reduce Soviet claims to German industrial capital in the three western zones. Each occupying power was allowed to extract reparations freely from its own zone, while the Soviet Union was authorised to take 10 per cent from the Western zones and a further 15 per cent provided that this was matched by supplies of food

and raw materials from the Soviet zone. The Soviets again promised free elections in Poland. The United States finally accepted the Oder–Western Neisse line as Poland's future Western frontier. Substantive issues such as the long-term future of German and peace treaties with Germany's former European allies (eventually signed in 1946) were referred to future meetings of the foreign ministries of the great powers.[7]

## 14.5 the reparations issue and the development of Bizonia

The sharp variations in the way the powers conducted themselves over reparations heightened the sense of mistrust and suspicion that contributed so much to the development of the Cold War. As the Russians stripped their zone of industrial capital the American delegates at Potsdam noted how this was fuelling anti-Russian sentiment. Joseph E. Davies observed that

> the hostility to Russia is bitter and surprisingly open – considering that we are here to compose and secure peace. There is constant repetition of the whispered suggestions of how ruthless the Russian Army had been in looting and shipping back vast quantities of everything from cattle to plumbing fixtures . . . the atmosphere is poisoned with it. The French are carrying everything, including the kitchen stove, out of their territory. Our own soldiers and even some members of this delegation are 'liberating' things from this area. But the criticisms are levelled only at the Soviets.[8]

The understandably feverish and rapacious nature of the Russian army was bound to have a highly damaging impact on German living standards and in the longer term, for the prospects of German economic recovery. A proposal to centralize offices bringing all zones together as one economic unit was forcibly rejected by the Russians and the French. In addition, disputes afflicted the Level of Industry Agreement approved by the four powers in March 1946. Whereas in principle the objective was to curtail any prospect of the German economy developing new potential for the conduct of war, it became clear that the Russians wanted to set low figures for German industrial output so that they could take the surplus capacity in reparations. Russia's desperate economic plight meant that Germany was being plundered for reparations and the defeated country now seemed caught up in the bitterness of the rapidly escalating Cold War. Effectively, the terms of the Potsdam agreement were being interpreted differently by each of the powers to suit their own needs. In May 1946 the British and Americans called a halt to any further dismantling of industrial plant not already destined for Russia and in September they merged their two zones into what was termed Bizonia. This may have been an understandable response in economic terms and it certainly would boost the recovery of the German economy in the American and British zones, but the fissures that characterized the prone nation were becoming increasingly evident.

### developments in the Russian zone

Just as the issue of the economy and reparations had threatened to divide the powers, the process of a return to political activity in the post-Nazi era was also a complex and troubled affair. In the Russian zone, four parties were created in the summer of 1945:

- the Communists (KPD)
- the Socialists (SPD)
- the Christian Democrats (CDU)
- the Liberals (LDPD)

Although ostensibly the Russians appeared to be ideologically inclusive in this arrangement, in practice, the guiding hand of the Kremlin was soon discernible. At the end of April a group of German Communists under the leadership of Walter Ulbricht came back from their period in exile in Russia to be offered key positions in the nascent administration. As 1945 came to a close the Russians came to the decision to merge the two parties of the left, the KPD and the SPD. This plan was strongly opposed by the charismatic figure of Kurt Schumacher, a Socialist leader in the British Zone who was an outspoken critic of the Communists. He urged the Berlin SPD to hold a referendum on the Russian plan but this was forbidden in East Berlin, which was under Russian control. Although the majority voted against the merger the outcome was that the SPD was banned in the Russian zone and the new Socialist Unity Party (SED) was created. In the Land elections in October the SED obtained 47.5 per cent of the popular vote and took effective control of the Landtage in the five Länder in the eastern zone. However, such levels of support were not forthcoming in Berlin where the western powers allowed the SPD to take part. Less than 30 per cent voted for the SED, while 43.6 per cent offered support to the SPD. This antagonized the Russians even further and in subsequent elections in the Russian zone, electors were given a single list of candidates in a 'united anti-fascist front' to approve or reject. Within the SED, the Stalinists soon had the upper hand and their policy of enforced land reform, dividing up large estates to the benefit of the poorer rural population, proved extremely popular with smaller farmers.

### developments in the western zones

Despite an anti-Stalinist sentiment in the west, the KPD managed to obtain 5.7 per cent of the vote and 15 seats in the Bundestag in the federal elections of 1949. This was above the minimum threshold of the support allowed in the constitution, but in the elections of 1953, when support fell to just over half a million votes, the party could no longer be represented in the Bundestag. Even table **14.1**  German federal governments since 1949

| legislative period | cabinets/chancellors | coalition partners |
|---|---|---|
| 1949–53 | 1 Adenauer | CDU, CSU, FDP,DP |
| 1953–57 | 2 Adenauer | CDU,CSU, FDP, DP, GB/BHE |
| 1957–61 | 3 Adenauer | CDU,CSU, DP |
| 1961–65 | 4 Adenauer (until 1962) 5 Adenauer (1962–63) 1 Erhard (from 1963) | CDU, CSU,F DP |
| 1965–69 | 2 Erhard (from 1966) 2 Kiesinger (from 1966) | CDU, CSU, FDP CDU, CSU, SPD |
| 1969–72 | 1 Brandt | SPD, FDP |
| 1972–76 | 2 Brandt (until 1974) 1 Schmidt (from 1974) | SPD, FDP |
| 1976–80 | 2 Schmidt | SPD, FDP |
| 1980–83 | 3 Schmidt (until 1982) 1 Kohl (from 1982) | SPD, FDP CDU, CSU, FDP |
| 1983–87 | 2 Kohl | CDU, CSU, FDP |
| 1987–90 | 3 Kohl | CDU, CSU, FDP |
| 1990–94 | 4 Kohl | CDU, CSU, FDP |
| 1994–98 | 5 Kohl | CDU, CSU, FDP |
| 1998–2002 | 1 Schröder | SPD, Greens |
| 2002–06 | 2 Schröder | SPD, Greens |
| 2006– | 1 Merkel | |

when the party returned to political life in 1968, it remained marginal. This pattern continued throughout the 1970s and 1980s.

This contrasted with the buoyant fortunes of the largest party in the western zone, the Christian Democrats (CDU) and its Bavarian wing the Christian Social Union (CSU). In the federal elections of 1949 the CDU obtained 31 per cent of the vote and 139 seats in the Bundestag. Both Catholics and Protestants came together in the post-Hitler epoch. By 1949 the party's centre of gravity had shifted from its initial anti-capitalist stance towards the right and its espousal of the 'social market economy' advocated by the dynamic Economic Director of Bizonia, Ludwig Erhard. Under the astute leadership of Konrad Adenauer, a highly gifted politician, the CDU held office for 20 years, bolstered by a very substantial degree of Catholic support.

The second largest party was the SPD which, in the elections of 1949, fared only marginally less well than the CDU. The SPD gained 29.2 per cent of the popular vote and 131 seats in the Bundestag. Despite this support it took until 1966 for the SPD to exercise power at the federal level, when it formed a coalition, initially with the CDU and then with the Free Democratic Party (FDP).

The FDP carried on the traditions of the former Democratic Party, campaigning against Marxism but also against the religious element of the CSU with its support for confessional schools. Its support came from the professional sector and from white-collar workers. Even at its height in 1961, the FDP polled less than 13 per cent of the vote, although this afforded 67 seats in the Bundestag, reflecting the fact that the party has exerted more influence than its level of support might suggest. The fortunes of the FDP were threatened by the emergence of the Greens in the 1983 election, when the FDP's support fell to 6.8 per cent, whereas the Greens, appealing to the same social class, attracted 5.4 per cent. However, when the Greens fell below the 5 per cent threshold in 1991, the FDP returned to what seemed to be its natural level at around 11 per cent.

## 14.7 the Truman Doctrine and the Marshall Plan

Richard Dockrill provides this helpful definition of the Cold War:

> the Cold War has been defined as a state of extreme tension between the superpowers, stopping short of all-out war but characterised by mutual hostility and involvement in covert warfare and war by proxy as a means of upholding the interests of one against the other. The Cold War remained 'cold' because the development of nuclear weapons had made resort to war a suicidal enterprise: both sides would be totally destroyed by such an eventuality.[9]

No politician defined the Cold war in such evocative terms as Winston Churchill, speaking at Fulton, Missouri in the United States, on 5 March 1946:

> A shadow has fallen upon the scenes so lately lighted by the allied victory. Nobody knows what Soviet Russia and its Communist international organisation intends to do in the immediate future, or what are the limits, if any, to their expansive tendencies . . .
>
> From Stettin, in the Baltic, to Trieste, in the Adriatic, an iron curtain has descended across the continent. Behind that line lie all the capitals of the ancient states of Central and Eastern Europe – Warsaw, Berlin, Prague, Vienna, Budapest, Belgrade, Bucharest and Sofia. All these famous cities, and the populations around them, lie in the Soviet sphere, and all are subject to a very high and increasing measure of control from Moscow.[10]
>
> The gloomy tone of Churchill's 'iron curtain' address reflected the fact that in Germany the western and eastern zones were on divergent tracks. With the issues of reparations and the treatment of Germany as an economic unit, continuing to divide the powers, the Cold War took a turn for the worse when President Truman responded to the prospect of a communist-supported uprising in Greece, with his announcement of the 'Truman Doctrine' and his offer of direct assistance to Greece and Turkey.

President Harry S. Truman, 12 March 1947.

At the present moment in world history nearly every nation must choose between alternative ways of life. The choice too often is not a free one. One way of life is based upon the will of the majority and is distinguished by free institutions, representative government, free elections, guarantees of individual liberty, freedom of speech and religion and freedom of oppression. The second way of life is based upon the will of a minority forcibly imposed upon the majority. It relies upon terror and suppression of personal freedoms. I believe that it must be the policy of the United States to support free peoples who are resisting attempted subjugation by armed minorities or outside pressures.

*Source*: John Traynor and Eric Wilmot, *Britain in the 20th Century World* (1994).

Although the United States had emerged from the Second World War as undoubtedly the most powerful economy on earth, its sustained economic well-being was inextricably linked with the economic fortunes of Europe. In April 1947 Secretary of State George C. Marshall returned from a meeting in Moscow with Stalin, overwhelmed by a sense of the Soviet leader's complete indifference to the suffering faced by the people of Europe. Marshall felt that Stalin wanted to see Europe descend into chaos. In a speech in London in May Churchill described Europe as 'a rubble-heap, a charnel house, a breeding ground of pestilence and hate'.[11] Truman knew that this might be the preconditions for further communist expansion. In a major speech delivered at Harvard University in June 1947, Marshall called for a systematic US effort to promote the economic revival of Europe. This became known as the Marshall Plan.

US Secretary of State George C. Marshall, speaking at Harvard University on 5 June 1947.

It is logical that the United States should do whatever it is able to do to assist in the return of normal economic health in the world, without which there can be no political stability and no assured peace. Our policy is directed not against any country or doctrine but against hunger, poverty, desperation, and chaos. Its purpose should be the revival of a working economy in the world so as to permit the emergence of political and social conditions in which free institutions can exist.

*Source*: as source A.

Marshall and his advisers feared that unless generous American aid to Europe was provided soon, the deterioration in the economic life of Western Europe would lead to a severe slump which would have dire effects on the American economy. An economic crisis of such magnitude might encourage the peoples of Western Europe to turn to communism and the Soviet Union for their salvation . . .

In a speech at Harvard University on 5 June 1947 Marshall called for a determined United States effort to promote the economic revival of Europe and thus ensure the continued prosperity of the American economy. . . . An additional invitation was extended to the Soviet Union and the Central and East European states, although the State Department hoped that it would be refused. In view of the growing hostility towards the Soviet Union it was not likely that Congress would have approved the vast sums that the shattered Soviet economy required, or indeed would have passed the programme at all if it had been linked to massive aid to the Soviet Union.

*Source*: Michael Dockrill, *The Cold War 1945–1963* (1988).

Between 1948 and 1952 the United States injected $13 billion into European recovery through the Marshall Plan. Although substantial aid was also offered to Russia and Eastern Europe, the offer was rejected as 'American imperialism' and the rift between East and West grew ever wider.

**QUESTION**

Examine the impact of the Truman Doctrine and the Marshall Plan on the devlopment of post-war Germany.

## 14.8 the constitution and the Basic Law

The merger of the British and American zones was consolidated a year later when the French also joined, creating a single western zone. In response, the Russians tightened their grip extending still further their hold over the military, economic and political life of East Germany and the rest of Eastern Europe. In March 1948 Britain, France and the Benelux countries signed the Treaty of Brussels, a mutual defence pact. This resolved the signatories to take mutual action in the event of outside aggression. Such steps reflected British anxiety that the USA might not sustain its defensive commitment to Europe indefinitely.

In London a month later, and with the support of the United States, it was announced that the German people should now be given political institutions, and a council meeting in Bonn led by Adenauer produced the constitutional principles and provisions of the Basic Law in May 1949. The Federal Republic of Germany (GFR) came into being on September 21 1949.

### key elements of the Basic Law

1 The principle of the Rule of Law. Basic rights to be safeguarded by a Federal Constitutional Court
2 Democratic rights guaranteed to all citizens. The Bundestag or Federal Parliament to be elected every four years by universal suffrage. Half the members to be directly elected, the other half via party lists. Parties polling fewer than 5 per cent of the vote are not to be represented in the Bundestag

3 Power divided between the federal government and the *Länder*. The *Länder* to control administration, cultural issues and education in their own territories through their own Landtage. The government to submit all bills to the Bundesrat or Federal Council. Federal Governments obliged to modify their proposals to achieve consent form the Bundesrat. The President to be a ceremonial figure, elected indirectly by a federal assembly of members from the Bundestag and the *Länder* governments. Only one term of office and not the supreme commander of the armed forces. The Minister of Defence to be the supreme commander of the armed forces. The president cannot declare a state of emergency or dissolve the Bundestag or dismiss chancellors. The chancellor is the key political officer and can only be removed by a no-confidence motion that stipulates a named successor

4 A commitment to the creation of a social welfare state

Meanwhile the fears that the United States might withdraw from Europe were reduced by the creation of the North Atlantic Treaty Organisation (NATO) in April 1949. The Brussels Pact signatories were now joined by a further group of European nations, Canada and, most importantly, the United States. This represented a formal recognition by the latter of the threat posed by the Soviet Union to world peace. The critical clause of the NATO agreement was article 5, which established the principle of collective self-defence. Yet just as the formation of the GFR was closely followed by the GDR, so too was the defensive alliance of NATO, followed by its Eastern European equivalent, the Warsaw Pact. These developments reduced the likelihood of any move towards the reunification of Germany. Even though the Cold War atmosphere briefly improved during the mid-1950s, the four powers each recognized by the end of the decade that reunification would not take place in the near future.

## 14.9 the Berlin blockade, 1948–49

Since 1945 the city of Berlin had been in a unique position, with the three western sectors located deep inside the Soviet zone of Germany, and more than 100 miles from West Germany. All contact between the outside world and the western zones of Berlin relied on the maintenance of the key road and rail links from West Germany to the western zones of Berlin. In April 1948, the Soviet Union halted the passage of western military supplies to West Berlin. Mounting interference with traffic into Berlin culminated with the startling announcement on 23 June that the 'Soviet administration is compelled to halt all traffic to and from Berlin from tomorrow at 0600 hrs because of technical difficulties.' All land and water routes to the western sectors of Berlin were cut off. With limited food supplies to the people of West Berlin, the Soviets had clearly calculated that the only way in which the West could prevent the people of West Berlin from starving would be to allow West Berlin to become part of the Soviet Union. The West would lose their only remaining foothold in Eastern Europe and the division of the area would be complete.

Despite the pressure this unprecedented situation imposed on the West, the complete withdrawal from Berlin was never seriously contemplated. It was felt that the loss of Berlin could precede the loss of West Germany itself. It was decided to supply West Berlin from the air, through three narrow air corridors. The blockade lasted from June 1948 to May 1949. The first Allied flight, on 26 June 1948, delivered 80 tonnes of milk, flour and medicine. At the height of the Berlin airlift, planes were landing in West Berlin every three minutes around the clock. To discourage a military response from the Russians, the United States deployed a number of B-29 heavy bombers. Stalin was not prepared to risk American military action and the blockade was lifted in May 1949, handing a symbolic and psychological victory to the West.

## 14.10 the creation of the GDR and the economic contrast with the West

### the GDR and Walter Ulbricht

The creation of the West German state in September 1949 prompted an immediate response in the East. In May 1949 a draft constitution was approved by an elected People's Congress and the German Democratic Republic (GDR) came into being on 11 October 1949. The first president was Wilhelm Pieck, with Otto Grotewohl as minister-president. Walter Ulbricht, a fervent communist, returned to Germany in 1945, serving as deputy minister-president in 1949, first secretary of the SED's Politburo from 1953 to 1971 and as chairman of the council of state upon the death of President Pieck in 1960. The new constitution handed legislative power to an elected *Volkskammer*, or Parliament, with the *Landerkammer* representing the five *Lander* into which the Soviet zone was divided. Although Russia exerted significant control over the new government, the rights of freedom of speech, assembly, religion and the right to strike were all technically upheld by the constitution. It was not until the uprising in Berlin of 1953 that Russia gave some limited degree of autonomy to the GDR. Despite the promises offered by the constitution, the realities of daily life in the GDR became a rather grim affair. Ulbricht, autocratic and dedicated to the principles and needs of the Soviet Union, led the country towards what he called the 'building of socialism'. Like Russia in the 1930s the emphasis here was on heavy industry rather than the well-being of the individual citizen. In another parallel with Stalin's Russia, the forced collectivization of agriculture placed the countryside under exceptional strain. Several groups, including organized religion, farmers and the middle class, suffered directly at the hands of the government. The grey, inflexible and unrewarding environment generated by the government prompted a steady flow of refugees to the more enticing West. In the summer of 1953 a major uprising in key towns and cities led to dozens of deaths and thousands of injuries. The Russians were disturbed by events and suspended their policy of endlessly stripping the area for reparations.

Although Ulbricht now seemed to have a mandate for change, emphasized perhaps by the death of Stalin in March 1953, he quickly reverted to his socialist ways with an emphasis once again on heavy industry. An instinctive autocrat, he purged the SED of dissidents and stepped up the pace with his collectivization process. As a direct consequence of the hardship this caused the GDR entered the 1960s facing a serious economic crisis and a deteriorating shortage of manpower because of the steady stream of skilled workers moving to the West. Nevertheless, Ulbricht demonstrated a certainty of touch when it came to hanging on to office regardless of changes in external or internal circumstances. For example, when he continued to support his Russian masters during the Hungarian uprising of 1956 his loyalty was appreciated by the Kremlin. In 1961, when the economy of the GDR reached crisis point, with the issue of a shortage of skilled workers becoming ever more acute, the Russians supported Ulbricht in the construction of the Berlin Wall.

Despite the manpower difficulties that prompted the construction of the Wall, it is now established that not all aspects of the East German economy underperformed. William Carr offers this insight into the performance of the GDR under Ulbricht in the 1960s:

> Decentralization of decision-making, the use of pricing policy and the reintroduction of the profit motive improved efficiency and brought about a significant improvement in living standards. Though shortages of consumer goods and poor service standards remain characteristic of East European economies, nevertheless between 1965 and 1970 the percentage of GDR workers owning refrigerators rose from 25.9 to 36.4, washing machines from 27.5 to 53.5 and television sets from 48.5 to 69.1. Improved material conditions were underpinned by an extensive welfare system and by considerable efforts to improve educational facilities. To reflect these changes a new constitution was introduced in 1968 which described the GDR as a 'socialist state of the German nation.[12]

As Pol O'Dochartaigh explains, this degree of improvement had significant social consequences: 'Living standards did increase, and there is strong evidence from West German opinion researchers that young East Germans increasingly came to identify with the GDR, favouring diplomatic recognition of their state, while also maintaining a sense of German nationality.[13]

Despite these positive aspects of the GDR's economy, as Ulbricht entered the 1970s his authority quickly ebbed away. New domestic economic difficulties, a downturn in economic production, and on the international stage, a deteriorating personal relationship with Russian premier, Leonid Brezhnev, combined to force the ageing Ulbricht from the stage he had dominated for so long. In 1971, authority passed from Ulbricht to his protégé Erich Honecker. Honecker was a dull, unimaginative bureaucrat, happy to act within the rigid constraints imposed by his masters in the Kremlin. Despite his limitations, a further period of progress now followed so that the GDR became the second-ranking economy in the Eastern bloc, after the Soviet Union. The earlier process of educational reform paid dividends when thousands of university graduates with degrees in technical subjects and sciences helped to correct the long-standing skill shortage, leading to an annual increase in national income in the 1970s of almost 5 per cent.

Despite this growth, the contrast with the economic well-being of the citizens of the GFR remained pronounced. The process of dynamic economic growth in the post-war period was down to the inspirational leadership of Ludwig Erhard. The former Economics Director for Bizonia presided over an economic miracle which saw Germany rise from the rubble of 1945 to become a prosperous, successful and innovative industrial nation. Rationing, controls and taxation, so important in the East, were either reduced or abandoned altogether under Erhard's programme. International events such as the war in Korea in the early 1950s fuelled a demand for the type of industrial production at which the Germans excelled. Substantial American investment was also of crucial importance. These elements coalesced to create a period of remarkable economic growth during which the GNP trebled. By 1961 less than a quarter of a million people were registered as unemployed. Above all, perhaps it was the diligence and ingenuity of the German people that enabled their country to become one of the most successful economies in Europe by the start of the 1960s. Economic growth was accompanied by the creation of a robust social welfare system and by the Equalisation of Burdens Law (1952), which passed millions of Deutschmarks from those who had been relatively unscathed by the war to those who had lost most. This spectacular period in German history was led by Chancellor Adenauer, who had been elected to office in 1949 at the age of 73.

This perspective is offered by Pol O'Dochartaigh:

> Konrad Adenauer was the towering figure in West German political life until the early 1960s. Born in 1876 in the Catholic Rhineland, he had been the mayor of Cologne from 1917 to 1933 and President of the Prussian State Council from 1924 to 1933, when the Nazis removed him from both posts. . . . He quickly rose to prominence within the CDU and was the obvious choice for Chancellor after the 1949 election.
>
> If Erhard may be seen as the father of the economic miracle, then Adenauer was without doubt the father of Western integration. The reasons for this are unclear. Time and again in Adenauer's biography he appears first and foremost to be not a German nationalist but a Rhinelander with a pro-Western orientation typical of that region. . . . He identified clearly with what he saw as West European values such as Catholic conservatism and liberal democracy. He himself regarded his decision to opt for a pro-Western policy as the most important decision he made in 1949. . . . Adenauer created what many have termed a 'chancellor democracy' in 1950s West Germany. His style was almost presidential, and he combined the roles of Chancellor and Foreign Minister in the early years, thus retaining ultimate control of both national and foreign policy while leaving the economics to Erhard. . . . Adenauer and the CDU made West Germany

in the 1950s their own. They brought economic prosperity, material wealth, political stability and relative security to a population that wished to move on and put the recent past behind it. . . . Adenauer also secured for the Federal Republic a respected place in the international community, thanks to a policy of co-operation with neighbours and of reparations towards Israel.'[14]

Combative, authoritarian and willing to employ questionable tactics against his opponents, Adenauer nevertheless provided stability and strength. As one observer noted, 'he met the great imperative of his moment in German history – the restoration of national self-respect without the record of intransigence'. William Carr states that he:

> Contributed more than any other German political leader to the reestablishment of his half of Germany to a position of equality among the western nations by tenacious political tactics, relentless anti-Communism and wholehearted commitment to the west. Above all a realist cast in the mould of Bismarck and Stresemann, Adenauer supposed that the temporary division of Germany was likely to be of long duration and that West Germany's only hope of recovery lay in full co-operation with the western powers. He was helped enormously by the American and British desire to see the GFR tied firmly to the west . . . and by European initiatives such as the Coal and Steel Community and the European Economic Community.'[15]

Adenauer's only major reverse, until the circumstances of his resignation in October 1963 at the age of 87, came over the delicate issue of German rearmament. Adenauer supported a French proposal that German forces be part of an integrated European Defence Community (EDC), even though this went against the wishes of many Germans who feared a return to the militarism of the past. To Adenauer's disappointment the proposal was rejected by the French assembly in August 1954. Meanwhile Russia, with the shadow of Stalin passing into history, restored sovereignty to the GDR and withdrew the Soviet High Commission. This was followed by the establishment in 1955 of a new defensive alliance of the East European States known as the Warsaw Pact.

## 14.11 Berlin

The brief improvement in superpower relations in the mid-1950s was short-lived and, as relations deteriorated towards the end of the decade, it was Germany and in particular the city of Berlin that found itself at the centre of the renewed international rivalry. The new leader of the Soviet Union, Nikita Khrushchev, was a brash, volatile risk-taker. His demand of November 1958 that the western powers sign a peace treaty with the two Germanies signified that he was about to raise the stakes, most of all in Berlin itself. Khrushchev was never short of self-confidence, but the news in 1957 that Russia had successfully tested an intercontinental ballistic missile made him even more assertive. As far as Berlin was concerned Khrushchev repeated his demand that a peace treaty with the GFR and the GDR was now long overdue. Khrushchev claimed that the West was in breach of the Potsdam agreement and that they were using West Berlin as a centre for spying and espionage. It followed, he reasoned, that West Berlin should become a demilitarized city with access in the hands of the GDR. In June 1961 Khrushchev came face to face with the young American President John F. Kennedy at a summit in Vienna. Khrushchev was not impressed with the youthful, and in his mind, naïve President. The Russian premier was in an aggressive mood, setting December as a deadline for his demands over Berlin. The atmosphere at the meeting was exceptionally tense and Kennedy came away from Vienna determined to increase military developments and calling Berlin 'the great testing place of western courage' which must be defended 'at all costs'.[16] On a visit to Berlin in June 1963 Kennedy proclaimed:

> Two thousand years ago the proudest boast in the world was 'Civis Romanus sum'. Today, in the world of freedom, the proudest boast is 'Ich bin ein Berliner'. There are many people in the world who do not understand what is the great issue between the free world and Communism. Let them come to Berlin, and there are some who say in Europe and elsewhere that we can work with the Communists. Let them come to Berlin.[17]

Meanwhile the steady flow of skilled workers and professionals from East to West showed no signs of abating. It is estimated that between January 1949 and June 1961, approximately 2.6 million refugees fled from East to West Germany. And in the period from July to August 1961 it is believed that 45,000 people left the East behind. This was a source of huge embarrassment and economic distress for the Russians. Their solution to the problem astounded the people of Berlin and raised the tension of the Cold War to new heights. On 13 August 1961 the authorities in the GDR began to construct a wall to completely separate East and West Berlin. It was claimed that the Wall was a defensive measure against Western spies, but it is more likely that the GDR was desperate to end the humiliating spectacle of people voting with their feet, in their thousands, to escape the dreariness of the Ulbricht regime. The East Germans had learnt by the mistakes of the Berlin blockade and there was no attempt this time to interfere with Western access routes to Berlin. Kennedy decided to seek a negotiated solution and Khrushchev withdrew his deadline demands, but the latter had succeeded in physically dividing the German nation.

## 14.12 the post-Adenauer era

By the start of the 1960s there were clear signs that Adenauer's long period in office was drawing to a close. Within the CDU/CSU there were increasing signs of dissent. During a dispute in 1960 Adenauer spoke of becoming the new President but retaining control over foreign policy. Although he was forced to back away from this proposal, he indicated that he would never step down as leader of the party. During the crisis over Berlin in 1961 the contrast between the rather fractious old man of German politics and the dynamically defiant mayor of Berlin, Willy Brandt, seemed very pronounced. A fall in votes for the CDU/CSU in the elections of 1961 and the government's heavy-handed treatment of the staff of the well-respected *Spiegel* magazine after a dispute with the Ministry of Defence, all indicated that Adenauer had had his day. After lengthy negotiations with the FDP it was agreed that he would step down in 1963. He resigned at the age of 87 in October 1963. William Carr offers this verdict:

> A controversial figure over whose foreign policy historians will probably argue as hotly as they have done over Stresemann's. Adenauer left the imprint of his personality on the GFR. And, despite the negative features of 'chancellor democracy', it is greatly to his credit that he reconciled the older generation to a pluralist democracy which after over forty years is remarkably stable. It has been said of him that he was the first German statesman who succeeded in overcoming the 'unconscious tendency of his fellow countrymen to believe that statesmen could only be taken seriously when they wore a uniform.[18]

With the old man gone, the father of the economic miracle, Ludwig Erhard, was the natural successor as Chancellor, but the succession period turned out to be more problematic than he might have expected. Despite an encouraging performance in the elections of 1965, there was evidence that the long-standing economic success was coming to a conclusion. A rise in unemployment, an increase in inflation and a decline in economic growth indicated problems in store. Meanwhile, balancing his instinctive commitment to the United States with a positive relationship with the French under the outspokenly anti-American Charles de Gaulle proved extremely difficult. Domestically, the emergence of the extreme right-wing neo-Nazi party, the National Democratic Party (NDP), added to a general sense of lost direction. Support for Erhard within his own party quickly drained away and he was replaced by Kurt Kiesinger, who served as Chancellor from 1966 to 1969 in a Grand Coalition of the CDU/CSU and the SPD, bringing members of the latter party into the cabinet for the first time since the last years of the Weimar Republic. The new government responded well to the economic challenge and by 1969 unemployment had fallen to 200,000, with an encouraging reduction in price increases. These economic issues were overshadowed by the political issues of the day. The continued activity of the far right, a burgeoning student protest movement, indignation over America's war in Vietnam and demands for reform of the outdated university system culminated in levels of street violence not seen since the final desperate days of Weimar. The student protests were at their most intense in the spring of 1968 but did not have a lasting impact into the next decade.

After serving three years as Chancellor, Kiesinger was succeeded by the former mayor of Berlin, Willy Brandt, who was Chancellor from 1969 to 1974. When he presented his programme to the Bundestag in October 1969 he called for radical reform in criminal law, the penal system and education, where in particular he advocated 'the removal of outmoded hierarchical structures' at university level. His ambition in foreign policy was to reach an accommodation with the DDR and to improve relations with the East. He received support from Karl Schiller, who presided over a 'super ministry' combining trade, industry and finance. His stated economic goal was 'stabilization without stagnation', but Schiller's arrogant political style left him isolated and ineffective at cabinet level. When he resigned in a dispute with colleagues over exchange rate policies, he was succeeded by the ambitious and exceptionally able Helmut Schmidt, who had taken a step further towards becoming Chancellor.

Brandt was an able and dynamic leader but it was his fate to serve during the period when the nation faced some of the most difficult and unforeseen problems of the entire post-war period. Brandt was half-way through his period of office when the violence of the student movement was overshadowed by two different forms of terror which scarred the German consciousness in the 1970s. First, the extremism of the terrorists known as the Baader-Meinhof gang, with their murders of prominent Germans, bank heists and bomb outrages, appalled the German public. In 1969 Andreas Baader and Gudrun Ensslin formed the Red Army Faction. Although Baader was arrested, he escaped thanks to the efforts of the left-wing journalist Ulrike Meinhof. The emerging group fled to Syria a year later, where they received training in terrorism from members of the Palestine Liberation Organization (PLO). A series of terrorist attacks followed in 1972, including one on the American army HQ in Germany and the Springer building in Hamburg. Baader was rearrested in June 1972 and was followed into custody by Meinhof. In 1977 it was announced that Andreas Baader and two of his closest associates had committed suicide in their prison cells in Starnheim. Critics of the government on the left claimed that they had been murdered.

The worrying corollary of this period of terrorist activity was the government's response with anti-terrorist measures, passed by the Bundestag in 1972, which seemed to herald a drift towards an increasingly authoritarian state. The chance to uplift the public mood seemed to present itself with the staging of the Olympic Games in Munich in September 1972. However, when a Palestinian terrorist group called 'Black September' breached the security of the Olympic village and took members of the Israeli team hostage the whole event was thrown into disarray.

When German Special Forces tried to free the hostages, all of the athletes were killed. It was a terrible day for the Olympic movement and for the German nation. The instability in the Middle East that so violently impinged on the Olympics was also reflected in the Yom Kippur War of 1973. This new conflagration between the Arabs and the Jews had a devastating impact on oil supplies to the West. Oil prices increased threefold overnight. Unemployment spiralled from 300,000 in 1973 to 600,000 a year later and to 1.1 million by 1975. The rise of overseas competition and a further oil crisis in 1979 meant that the days of spectacular economic performance became a thing of the past. Despite these challenging economic circumstances, Brandt and his successor, Helmut Schmidt (1974–82), showed a commitment to modernity and reform that at least moved the nation on from the rather limiting constraints of the Adenauer period. This was symbolized by the move into a futuristic chancellery building constructed during the Brandt period. Once again, Germany's reputation as a country synonymous with technological prowess seemed to be restored. University reform, modernization of marriage and family law and an extension of the social welfare system were just some of the progressive measures passed by an active Bundesrat. Nevertheless, the Schmidt era also witnessed further, substantial problems as Germany moved into the 1980s with a serious economic crisis looming. Unemployment had soared from 400,000 to 1,370,000 within a year, while inflation reached a damaging 7 per cent. Turkish guest-workers and asylum seekers became the victims of a worrying rise in incidents of right-wing violence.

In 1982 the political constellation changed once more. The SPD/FDP coalition that had served both Brandt (SPD) and Schmidt (SPD) came to an end over a budget dispute. The vote of 1 October left Schmidt as head of a minority government. As the FDP became more right-wing, it backed a constructive no-confidence motion initiated by the CDU/CSU culminating in the appointment of Helmut Kohl of the CDU who replaced Schmidt as chancellor in 1982, in a CDU/CSU–FDP coalition.

These developments brought to the helm a man who would dominate German politics in the 'Kohl era' from 1982 to 1998. This reflected the stability that has characterized both the German party system, the behaviour of the electorate and the broader stability of the Federal Republic. This has seen the two-party dominance of the CDU/CSU and the SPD, with their periodic alteration in office and the corresponding failure of the extremist parties to gain representation at the federal level. Even the highly disruptive events of German unification have not led to the degree of electoral diversification and splintering that might have been imagined.

When Kohl became Chancellor at the age of 52, he was the first chancellor from the post-war generation, the first, as he succinctly put it, to benefit from the 'favor of a later birth'. Kohl was born in Ludwigshafen am Rhein on 3 April 1930. His older brother served as a teenage soldier and was killed in the Second World War, but although Helmut was inducted for military service he was not involved in any combat. He completed a doctorate in history and political science at the University of Heidelberg in 1958. Deeply aware of Adenauer's legacy, he was also a provincial, this time from the Palatinate, his fondness for that region's local delicacies reflected in his imposing frame. Kohl was willing to evoke national themes, engender a sense of pride in the recent past and construct expensive new museums dealing emphatically with difficult themes in German history. Kohl's obsession with the deployment of his personal authority was to lead to a catastrophic conclusion to what had been a stable and distinguished career. In the elections of March 1983, the CDU/CSU achieved an increase of 4.3 points compared to their performance in 1980, with a total vote of 48.8 per cent. The SPD had lost its figurehead, Helmut Schmidt, owing to a combination of personal ill-health and a lack of support from the party caucus. His replacement, the respected but somewhat lacklustre former mayor of Berlin, Hans-Jochen Vogel, presided over a drop of 4.7 points compared to 1980.

Meanwhile anxiety over nuclear issues, a fierce debate over the stationing in Germany of NATO mid-range missiles and a growing level of awareness of environmental issues led to the emergence of the Green Party, with 5.4 per cent of the vote and 27 seats in the Bundestag. The country had backed a chancellor with conservative tendencies who wanted to enhance a sense of patriotism, move on from the shadow of Hitler, promote reconciliation with France and encourage a fuller understanding of Germany's contemporary history.

However, the new parliament immediately became entangled in a serious scandal concerning payments to politicians from the Flick industrial empire. Kohl survived a lengthy, complex and damaging trial only because of the willingness of three leading witnesses to commit perjury. Even against this backdrop, millions of marks in illegal payments to Kohl were being hidden away in secret accounts in Switzerland and Liechtenstein.

Meanwhile the Greens grew in popularity, boosted by the widespread sense of anxiety created by nuclear disasters such as those at Three Mile Island in Pennsylvania, USA and at Chernobyl in the Soviet Union; accusations of political sleaze were commonplace and attitudes towards the militarism of the past remained steadfast. Despite the occasional political scandal, such as Kohl's display of insensitivity with the controversial visit of President Ronald Reagan to Bitburg military cemetery in 1985 when it was established that this was also the resting place of some soldiers who had served in the SS, the FRG remained on course as the most potent economic unit in Europe. Further controversy came a year later with the publication in the highly respected *Frankfurter Allgemeine Zietung* of an article by Ernst Nolte in which he suggested a causal link between the Russian Gulags and Auschwitz, and claimed that while Nazi war crimes received endless attention the Stalinist murders were virtually ignored. Nolte went so far as to suggest that Hitler had merely reacted to communist crimes and therefore the burden of guilt could be lifted from Germany's shoulders. The article caused a sensation and received a robust reply, most notably from the philosopher, Jürgen Habermas, who accused Nolte of removing all moral issues from Germany's historical past and of depicting the horrors of Auschwitz-Birkenau as a 'mere technical innovation'. The increasingly personalized and fractious debate culminated in the *Historikerstreit*, in which the majority of the historical profession coalesced against Nolte and his neoconservative supporters. Meanwhile, while the historians bitterly debated, the accession to power of Mikhail Gorbachev in the Soviet Union in May 1985 was set to transform the European scene in a way that no one can have imagined. Gorbachev's radical reforms would also cast a large shadow over the unapologetically intransigent East German leader, Erich Honecker, who had been in power in the DDR since 1971 and who in 1987, following Kohl's third federal election victory, had become the first East German serving head of state to visit West Germany.

## 14.13 the reunification of Germany, 1989–90

In the same sense that the discussion of German unification at the start of this book began with a charismatic individual, Otto von Bismarck, it could be argued that the examination of the process of reunification of 1989–90 should logically begin with consideration of the impact of Mikhail Gorbachev.

Gorbachev joined the Politburo of the Soviet Union in 1980 at the age of 49, serving under Brezhnev and Andropov and as number two under Chernenko. On an official visit to London in 1984 he made an outstanding impression, appearing open, confident, intelligent and dynamic. When Chernenko died the following year Gorbachev was unanimously elected as party leader. Only 54, he was much younger than the men who had immediately preceded him. His insight into the real nature of Russian society was intense and his open contact with the ordinary people of the Soviet Union convinced him that his own country was teetering on the brink of economic chaos. Profound economic problems and chronic difficulties in many aspects of the nation's infrastructure were combined with huge levels of spending on the military and on nuclear weapons. Although the arms race with the United States could not be won, its escalating cost was bringing the Soviet Union to its knees. With this in mind, Gorbachev launched his programme of restructuring (*perestroika*) and openness (*glasnost*). Over the next two years, Gorbachev took steps that would not have been dreamt of by his lethargic predecessors. The dissident scientist, Andrei Sakharov, was released from exile and open reference was made by the leader to the 'victims of Stalin'. A major speech by Gorbachev in 1988 condemned the country's 'ossified system of government'. Gorbachev had dramatically raised expectations of reform and the promise of an improvement in living standards but the depth of the economic difficulties faced by the Soviet Union were so immense that these economic needs could not quickly be satisfied. With no visible improvements in the standard of living, but with the traditional shackles of Soviet repression lifted, the policy of openness was put to the test amid nationalist uprisings, strikes, sporadic demonstrations, and in some circles, outspoken criticism. Even amid this challenging climate, Gorbachev did not hold back. In the words of the *Independent* newspaper in June 1988: 'What Mikhail Gorbachev set out in the enormous vastness of the Kremlin's Palace of Congress yesterday was nothing less than a vision of a new socialism for a new millennium, in which not a shred of the evil authoritarianism of Stalin, nor of the slothful incompetence of Brezhnev remains.'[19]

On the international stage, Gorbachev's vision was equally bold. In a speech to the General Assembly of the United Nations on 7 December 1988 he announced:

> The use or threat of force can no longer and must no longer be an instrument of foreign policy. This applies above all, to nuclear arms. . . .

All of us, and primarily the stronger of us, must exercise self-restraint and totally rule out any outward-orientated use of force. . . . We are witness to the emergence of a new historic reality, a turning away from the principle of super-armament to the principle of reasonable defence sufficiency.[20]

Such profound announcements inevitably had a dramatic effect on Russia's neighbours. It was now the moment for the reforming words of Gorbachev to be put to the test by the spontaneous actions of the ordinary people of the Eastern bloc. In the past, any sign of popular reform had been crushed by the heavy hand of the Kremlin. In 1989, it became clear that things had changed for good. Crucially, for example, the Russians simply stood by when the progressive regime in Hungary, the country where 'the fuse was finally ignited', commenced discussions in February 1989 on the introduction of a multi-party system and began to take down its normally fortified border with Austria in the early summer. Equally startling was the official recognition given to the rapidly developing Solidarity movement in Poland which secured 99 of the 100 seats in the Senate and all of the seats in parliament that were freely contested.

The dramatic effect of this sequence of events was soon transmitted to East Germany, where a degree of satisfaction that the country was second only to the Soviet Union in its economic capacity and had outperformed its eastern bloc neighbours, and the visible pride of the DDR in the ostensibly glittering display internationally of their performance-enhanced, skilfully doped athletes, could not mask the gulf between the East and the West. Under Honecker's dull leadership style since 1971, the disenfranchised citizens of the DDR had not experienced any questioning of the limitations of a police state. The heavy hand of the security police combined with the economic assurances of a job, wage and price controls and provision of social services, plus the relentless propaganda message from the leaders of the DDR, meant that political change always seemed unlikely.

However, the fact that developments in Hungary went unchecked was not lost on the people of East Germany, who had seen the DDR remain apparently impervious to reforms and where, in February 1989, a man was shot attempting to cross the Berlin Wall. During the summer of 1989 thousands of East Germans on holiday in Hungary took advantage of the new political climate to flee to the West. Despite these developments, the brutal repression by the police and the Stasi (secret police) of political protest seemed as fierce as ever. Even so, with 25,000 new refugees having left in the summer, the spectre of an acute labour shortage once again threatened the very essence of the GDR.

As the summer holidays came to a close, and with West German embassies in Budapest, Warsaw and Prague inundated with potential East German refugees, attention now switched to the city of Leipzig. At what became known as the 'Monday demonstrations' crowds initially of just over a thousand gathered only to be broken up by the secret police, the feared and hated Stasi. The most significant opposition group within the DDR, the New Forum, gained much of its support from the fact that it was not a political party and did not bring ideological dogma to the increasingly volatile situation. With an increasing emphasis on human rights and democracy the reformers came up against the forcible methods of the Stasi, who denounced the 'slanderous insults' of the hard-core protesters.

By 2 October the Monday night crowd in Leipzig had reached around 25,000. Events were gathering pace just as the GDR leader Honecker prepared to hold a celebration of the fortieth anniversary of the GDR at the Palace of the Republic in Berlin. The guest of honour, Gorbachev himself, bluntly told his more conservative hosts that they were in danger of being left behind by the great events that were unfolding around them and with such rapidity. By the end of October, the crowds gathering in Leipzig, no longer threatened by the secret police, were immense and were matched by other huge demonstrations across the country, in Halle, Dresden, Magdeburg and most of all, in the capital itself. Late in the day, Honecker attempted some minor, cosmetic changes but he was ousted in an October coup, on the 18th, when on grounds of 'ill health' he was stripped of his offices as secretary-general, and secretary of the Central Committee, to be replaced by Egon Krenz. Krenz used his first address to promise that the SED would resolve all outstanding problems, that he supported Gorbachev's policy of perestroika and that restrictions on travel to 'socialist brother-states' would be ended or modified. Immediately 10,000 people took advantage of new arrangements to travel to West Germany via Czechoslovakia but this was not accompanied by any public confidence that Krenz had genuinely embraced the reform movement. His earlier expression of outspoken support for the Chinese authorities when they had put brutally put down the reform movement and his willingness for the police to confront demonstrators remained at the forefront of the public mood. A crowd of 300,000 in Leipzig on 30 October, followed by a live broadcast of a huge demonstration in East Berlin, brought the SED regime to its knees. On 7 November the government resigned, followed a day later by all members of the Politburo. It was only at this point that the dire economic circumstances of the entire East German state were laid bare, with party diehards now coming to the bitter understanding that they had been deluded by a carefully sustained propaganda image of a healthy economy.

Meanwhile Mary Fulbook provides this analysis of the role played in the West by Chancellor Kohl:

> Kohl narrowly evaded a rather poor historical write-up. His chancellorship
> had been characterised by navigation around a series of scandals . . . yet
> Kohl was saved from an unfavourable historical verdict by having the
> German question thrust upon him, and by seizing the opportunity with
> considerable astuteness and strength.[21]

Fulbrook praises Kohl's 'energetic intervention' but states that 'The most important factor which led to the unification of the two Germanies was economic: the GDR simply was not viable as a separate state once it was open to the competition of the capitalist West, while the latter was placed under intolerable strain by the influx of migrants from the East.'[22] When events reached their climax in Berlin in November 1989, Kohl was visiting Poland, a sign that even the political leaders at the highest level had not anticipated what would happen next. When a Politburo official stated, in a rather low-key way, that new travel regulations would allow almost all GDR citizens to apply for receive travel visas for visiting the West 'immediately', thousands of people began to gather demanding access to West Berlin. As the excitement gathered, the border guards simply opened the checkpoints and thousands of East Germans began to flood into West Berlin. Amid scenes of unparalleled joy and jubilation, strangers hugged, danced and sang, scaled the Wall and even began hacking off pieces of it with hammers to claim souvenirs of the hated barrier. The next day Kohl, Genscher and Willy Brandt, the man who had been mayor of Berlin when the Wall was built, joined the crowds. Brandt observed 'that which belongs together is now coming together' but opposition groups in the DDR were still strongly opposed to the idea of reunification. Perhaps the most striking counter-argument to reunification was made by the well-known Green politician, Joschka Fischer, who argued that the German nation-state, having caused two world wars and constructed the gas chambers, should never be revived.

Pol O'Dochartaigh summarizes the final unfolding of events:

> The most concrete symbol of the division of Germany, the Berlin Wall, was gone. By the end of November, fifty new crossings had been opened, both in Berlin and along the East–West German border. On 22 December 1989 the Brandenburg Gate was symbolically reopened by Chancellor Kohl and the new GDR Prime Minister, Hans Modrow. Meanwhile, in November Chancellor Kohl published a ten point plan for overcoming any remaining barriers to the completion of German unity. Detailed negotiations on a Treaty of Unification began in July 1990, culminating in the extension of the Federal Republic to incorporate the territory of the former GDR. The GDR ceased to exist and its land and people became part of an extended Federal Republic. The Unification Treaty was passed in the Bundestag and Volkskammer on September 20 1990, with the date for unification set at 3 October 1990. Having watched the initial events with some disquiet, Helmut Kohl had eventually demonstrated skill and enthusiasm in pursuing the unification agenda and as a result he was elected as the first Chancellor of the new, united Germany, in the election of December 1990.'[23]

Kohl secured a landslide victory over the opposition candidate and Prime Minister of Saarland, Oskar Lafontaine. The story appeared to have come full circle, but the journey was not yet complete and further difficulties lay ahead.

# Germany in the post-unification era

## foreign affairs

Germany's place in the wider world in the post-war era has generally been significantly constrained. Under the old Federal Republic a great deal of emphasis was placed on maintaining American support for its security needs and for securing a wide degree of international support for its claims to legitimacy above those of the old German Democratic Republic (GDR). Since the 1980s, Germany's highly successful economy, its emphatic support for the European Community and NATO, has made Germany a significant global power. On the other hand, the fact that Germany is a non-permanent member of the UN security council, constitutional limitations on the role played by German troops (amended by Kohl's approval of 'out of area' deployment), the singular lack of appetite among its people for military intervention in foreign disputes, and its emphasis on its role as a trading nation, all mitigate against a high degree of direct impact on the international stage.

The events of 11 September saw Chancellor Schröder initially promise President Bush emphatic support. In November 2001 the Chancellor personally led an initiative to deploy German troops in Afghanistan. However, in the election campaign of 2002 Schröder made plain his strong opposition to direct German intervention in the Iraq crisis, even with the backing of a UN mandate. This marked a significant step away from Germany's traditional stance of what has been termed 'reflexive multilateralism'. Two interpretations are possible here. On the one hand it could be claimed that this showed Germany's sense of self-confidence and willingness to follow its own path, with a degree of independence from the United States. An alternative would stress the resulting lack of German influence in the United Nations and as a member of NATO. A further element in Germany distancing itself from the United States can be seen in the gulf between the two administrations in their attitudes towards climate change. President Bush's dismissal of the Kyoto Agreement and the perception of the United States as slow to acknowledge global warming have caused some dismay in German environmentalist and Green circles. On the other hand, Germany's significant role in promoting political changes, such as the break-up of Yugoslavia and its outspoken criticism of the right-wing Austrian Freedom Party when it entered the government in 2000, have pointed to a degree of active involvement in foreign affairs that has caused some discomfort amongst those who argue that Germany should play an essentially passive role internationally.

## the economy, politics and the post-unification search for 'inner unity'

While to outside observers the unification of Germany may have appeared complete on 3 October 1990 when the GDR passed into history and the new Germany was reconstituted into five states or Länder, merged with the Federal Republic, the search for what many Germans refer to as 'inner unity' remains incomplete. The euphoria of the iconic events of 1989–90 raised expectations on both sides of what lay ahead. In many respects, the buoyant self-confidence that characterized the German people as they entered the twentieth century was less obviously present a hundred years later. On so many occasions in the German past, the economy could be characterized as dynamic, powerful, innovative and highly successful, buttressed by German values of order and stability and the notion of the state as a guarantor of social cohesion. Even in the difficult aftermath of the Second World War, the widely acclaimed 'economic miracle' of the Federal Republic made the German model appear highly attractive to outside observers. Not least, the prodigious performance of the economy in the field of exports brought benefits to the wider European community. However, the recent picture is more worrying. The immense cost of unification, combined with global economic changes, have made it difficult for the German economy to sustain its success. In the period since 1991 more than a trillion dollars have been transferred from West Germany, which is four times more populous than the East, to the former GDR. In addition, the end of the Deutschmark, as it gave way to the Euro on 1 January 2002, against the instincts of many Germans, has taken away a powerful symbol of economic strength and stability. Germany's willingness to support the European Union (EU), most notably perhaps, through Chancellor Kohl's work on the Maastricht Treaty, has promoted a close sense of cohesion between the economic and political institutions of the German state and the European model. With the future of Germany and the EU so closely intertwined it was possible for the influential political weekly, *Der Speigel*, to envisage, in September 2002, 'a crisis so elemental that it could endanger the whole future of the country'.[1] With unemployment standing at more than 4 million at the end of 2002, an oversized and inefficient welfare state with its roots in the Bismarck era, healthcare expenditure rising by almost 50 per cent in the last ten years of the twentieth century, escalating state debt, widespread concerns about the poor performance of the education system with German students faring badly in international comparisons with other European nations, the nation seemed on many counts to have lost its traditional sense of self-confidence and purpose.

In addition, in a broader sense, the country also faced the problems faced by so many of the other industrial economies. Climate change, the future of energy supplies, crime and the related issue of drug abuse, terrorism and the implications of European integration are all issues clamouring for the attention of the current generation of Germany's leaders.

To be sure, investment in the East has been substantial. Approximately 3 million East German pensioners now receive substantial benefits in their retirement. Since 1991, almost 10 million telephone lines have been provided, 12,000 kilometres of new roads, 5,000 kilometres of new railway lines, and no less than 5 million apartments equipped to Western levels of comfort. Further massive investment of DM20 billion has targeted environmental issues, such as factory emissions, sewage treatment and recycling. Despite this expenditure, from the perspective of the East Germans, the prosperity they felt they were 'promised' has not yet materialized and the new political freedoms have not been completely able to outweigh the sense of economic disadvantage and the sometimes patronizing attitudes of the West. Surveys have repeatedly shown that an increasing number of Easterners consider themselves to be 'second-class citizens' compared to their Western counterparts. Further difficulties have included the issues faced in the privatization of uncompetitive industries and the resulting mass redundancies, bitter debates over property rights, the loss of housing subsidies, and the nature of anguished debates over 'de-Stasification'. A troubled economic climate, combined with a further influx of economic migrants and asylum seekers, has created a breeding ground for increased activity by the neo-Nazi far right and for racist incidents.

Experts have pointed out that the development of a high level of support and approval for a new political entity – as was the case with the Federal Republic – can take at least twenty years to accrue. An interesting battle for the hearts and minds of these people can be said to have been fought between the old East German educational and propaganda systems on the one hand and the Eastern exposure to the West German radio and television stations that delivered overt and subliminal messages about the values of Western democracy. Some analysts, such as Frederick Weil (1993), have contended that the pervasive influence of the western media meant that some East Germans were 'born virtually democratic'.[2] Alternatively, it could be argued that evidence such as residual and substantial support for the former, ruling Communist Party and the disproportionate degree of support in the east for violent and xenophobic right-wing extremists points towards a degree of political 'regression' in the East that may take a while to overcome. Attitudinal surveys among the East German population have shown a lack of personal satisfaction and a sense of doubt as to whether the democratic system can deliver the economic security and equality they crave. Their willingness to sacrifice political freedom and desire for government intervention in reducing income differentials, controlling wages and salaries, guaranteeing full employment and limiting prices marks a significant contrast with attitudes of those in the West. In short, the degree of dissatisfaction in the East may in some respects have exacerbated a sense of the gulf between the economic and social circumstances of the region compared to the West, leading the East Germans to feel that they have been annexed rather than unified.

Against this background, by the mid-1990s Chancellor Kohl appeared to be more popular among East German voters than among those in the West. In 1994 Kohl became the first chancellor since Adenauer to win four straight elections, although his majority had fallen from 134 seats to only 10. Kohl was beginning to pay the price for the slow pace and high cost of economic and social unification, combined with the difficulties of economic recession and voter alienation in the West over the higher tax burden needed to foot the bill for unification. Nevertheless, in 1997 Kohl became the longest-serving German chancellor since the towering figure of Otto von Bismarck.

In the landmark elections of 1998, after a record 16 years in power, the long-term success of the Christian Democrat movement, with its consistent ability to exert a broad social appeal, came to a shuddering end when the German electorate denied Helmut Kohl a fifth term as chancellor. Martin Kitchen offers this useful analysis of the reasons behind the electoral change:

> By 1998, when the country once again went to the polls, the electorate no longer had any confidence in Helmut Kohl, whose promises had all been broken and who no longer provided a convincing vision of the future. The national debt had increased by 65 percent during his chancellorship, unemployment had risen by 60 percent and economic growth had ground to a halt. He was no longer the statesman who had achieved national unity, he was the politician responsible for Germany's decline. National unity had been achieved, and the country thereby weakened. The SPD had a convincing chancellor candidate in Gerhard Schröder, who had won a resounding victory in the state elections in Lower Saxony, and who, like US President Bill Clinton and Britain's Tony Blair, fought the campaign on behalf of what he chose to call the 'new middle'. This was where the swing votes lay, and there were much more such votes than at any time since the 1950s. Pollsters predicted a victory for the Social Democrats, but were surprised that it was so decisive. With 35.1 percent of the vote, Kohl's CDU/CSU had its worst showing since 1949. . . . These elections were a turning point in the history of the republic. This was the first time that a chancellor had been turned out of office as the result of a general election. The Greens entered government for the first time. The SPD was, for only the second time, the strongest party, and therefore selected the president of the Bundestag.[3]

Kohl's legacy was not just the election debacle of 1998. His inability to be straightforward about the source of huge donations to the CDU led to him and his party to be found guilty of not publishing the donations in the party's accounts. In turn, Kohl's successor as party leader after the election, Wolfgang Schauble, had to step down in April 2000 after admitting that he had also benefited from secret donations to the party. This left the CDU with the challenge of finding a substantial and credible long-term successor to Kohl. In the first instance, Angela Merkel, seen as competent and shrewd and also with the added dimension of being from the East, had not yet established herself amongst the party faithful as having sufficient gravitas and drive to genuinely challenge Schröder at the forthcoming election. In January 2002 Merkel stepped aside to accommodate Edmund Stoiber, the Minister-President of Bavaria and leader of the CSU, while Merkel retained the position of leader of the CDU.

Gerhard Schröder came to power in 1998 at the head, for the first time in the country's history, of an SPD Red–Green coalition government, led by a Social Democrat. Schröder was born in April 1944 in Mossenberg-Wohren. With a degree in law from Göttingen University, he was elected to the Bundestag in 1980 and won important regional elections in Lower Saxony in 1994 and 1998.

His triumph over Kohl in 1998 meant that for the first time in its history, the Federal Republic witnessed a total rather than partial change of government, with none of the three former coalition partners – the CDU, the CSU and the FDP – represented in the new government. Although Schröder made it plain during the 1998 election campaign that he did not intend to overturn all of the key policy decisions of his predecessor, Helmut Kohl, many of his supporters expected a greater sense of new direction than was the case. Incremental policy change characterised the approach of the new Chancellor.

At the same time, analysts have argued that Schröder's period in office also saw a marked increase in the concentration of executive power in the hands of the Chancellor. The sudden resignation of Oskar Lafontaine as Minister of Finance and chairman of the SPD in March 1999 took away a powerful figure form the scene, removing Schröder's only real challenger. In addition, Schröder's public criticism of the Green Minister of the Environment, Jürgen Trittin, heightened Schröder's image as the undisputed leader of his government. Additionally, Schröder worked hard to develop a positive relationship with the media in the wake of Kohl's acrimonious relationship with certain members of the press. During the 1998 campaign, the media highlighted his expensive clothing and he became known as the 'lifestyle chancellor'. Despite this honeymoon period, by mid-1999 Schröder responded to criticism that his emphasis was on style rather than substance by reducing his appearance on light-hearted television game and chat shows. During the ongoing scandal over Kohl and political funding Schröder worked hard to convey a sense of personal gravitas, indicating to the media that he had a serious job to get on with. Progressive measures on immigration and on homosexual relationships placed the Chancellor on more positive ground than when he was coping with ongoing economic difficulties. Schröder was closely associated by voters with the Agenda 2010 reform program, which included cuts in the system of social welfare and reformed regulations on employment law. However, the profound changes needed in the health sector, the pension system and energy policy remained problematic.

Germany's politicians entered the 2002 election campaign with the sense that the country faced a stark alternative between long-deferred economic reform and a depressing spiral of economic decline. Yet in a sense, even the political class, charged with overcoming these myriad problems, represented in themselves some of the issues facing the German state. For example, more than 50 per cent of the composition of the 1998–2002 parliament came from the sectors of public servants, party and interest group officials and education professionals. The inherent 'conservatism' of this bloc may have created a systemic climate of risk aversion, rendering the radical solutions that the country needs less likely. For example, in the election year of 2002, unemployment in the East stood at 18 per cent, virtually double the level in the rest of the country. The overall immigration balance for 2001 saw almost 200,000 people leave the East for the West, with an emphasis on younger, better-educated groups seeking their future elsewhere.

By the narrowest of margins, 306 seats in the reduced 603-seat parliament and a majority of just 9, the SPD–Green coalition was able to cling on to office in the elections of September 2002. This victory, largely brought about by an improved performance by the Greens, seemed to vindicate Chancellor Schröder's tactic of relying on the Greens as the SPD's preferred coalition partner. The re-election of the Red–Green coalition which had seemed unlikely only weeks before the elections seemed to demonstrate that in the modern era of German politics, coalitions and stability are not necessarily a contradiction in terms. The elections were fought against a backdrop of high unemployment and a declining economic performance that made it seem likely that the CDU/CSU and FDP, led by Stoiber, would take the reins of government. However, in the summer of 2002 the force of nature intervened when catastrophic flooding afflicted the East in particular. Schröder's demonstration of concern and willingness to open the governmental purse strings for flood relief swayed wavering voters. Then Schröder and Fischer's steadfast opposition to the impending war against Saddam Hussein in Iraq struck a chord with the majority in German public opinion. In May 2005, after the SPD suffered a reverse to the Christian Democrats (CDU) in North Rhine-Westphalia, Schröder decided to call federal elections as soon as possible. The elections took place in September 2005, leaving the incumbent's SPD–Green coalition and the CDU/CSU FDP alliance, led by Angela Merkel, short of a majority in parliament, but with the CDU/CSU ahead by one percentage point. Although Merkel's party had begun the campaign with a significant lead over Schröder's coalition, her personal popularity was felt to be lagging behind the charismatic incumbent, particularly after she made some embarrassing errors over income tax during a televised debate. Under these circumstances both Schröder and Merkel initially claimed victory and the chancellorship. After a period of negotiation it was announced on 10 October that the key parties had agreed to form a grand coalition, with Schröder ceding the chancellorship to Merkel, but the SPD holding the majority of government posts and therefore effective control over the direction of government policy. Meanwhile, Schröder announced that he would not take a seat in the new cabinet and would leave politics once Merkel took office. Merkel, born in Hamburg in July 1954, therefore became the first female Chancellor of Germany and the first former citizen of the GDR to lead the reunited country. Her Chancellorship marks a fittingly symbolic note on which to finish. The future of Germany promises to be a fascinating journey.

*notes*

## notes to chapter 1

1   Katherine Anne Lerman, *Bismarck: Profiles in Power* (Longman, 2004), p. 266.
2   Geoff Eley, 'Bismarckian Germany' in *Modern Germany Reconsidered, 1870–1945*, ed. Gordon Martell ( Routledge, 1992), pp. 1–32, p. 6.
3   Arden Bucholz, *Moltke and the German Wars, 1864–1871* ( Palgrave, 2001), p. 78.
4   Gordon A Craig, *Germany 1866–1945* (Oxford University Press, 1981), pp. 1–2.
5   Lothar Gall, *Bismarck, The White Revolutionary, Vol. 1* (Routledge, 1994).
6   David Blackbourn, *History of Germany 1780–1918* (Blackwell, 2003), p. 195.
7   Bucholz, *Moltke and the German Wars*, p. 139.
8   Ibid., p. 81.
9   William Carr, *A History of Germany 1815–1900* (Edward Arnold, 1991).
10  David Blackbourn, *History of Germany 1780–1918* (Blackwell, 2003), p. 192.
11  A. J. P. Taylor, quoted in Eric Wilmot, *The Great Powers 1814–1914* (Nelson, 1992), p. 257.
12  John Breuilly, *The Formation of the First German Nation State* (Macmillan, 1996), p. 78.
13  Dennis Showalter, *The Wars of German Unification* (Oxford University Press, 2004), p. 153.
14  Bucholz, *Moltke and the German Wars*, p. 131.
15  W. H. Russell quoted in W. G. Shreeves, *Nationmaking in Nineteenth Century Europe* (Nelson, 1984), p. 129.
16  Richard J. Evans, *Rereading German History 1800–1996* (Routledge, 1997), p. 6.
17  Craig, *Germany 1866–1945*, p. 3.
18  Ibid., p. 4.
19  Gall, *Bismarck*, p. 301.
20  Carr, *History of Germany*, p. 135.
21  Hans-Ulrich Wehler, *The German Empire 1871–1918* (Berg, 1989), p. 25.
22  Ibid.
23  Craig, *Germany 1866–1945*, p. 27.
24  Evans, *Rereading German History 1800–1996*, p. 6.
25  Gall, *Bismarck*, p. 377.

## notes to chapter 2

1   Roger Chickering, *Imperial Germany and the Great War, 1914–1918* (Cambridge University Press, 1998), p. 1.
2   Richard J. Evans, *Rereading German History 1800–1996* (Routledge, 1997), p. 7.
3   William Carr, *A History of Germany 1815–1990* (Edward Arnold, 1991), p. 69.
4   David Blackbourn, *History of Germany 1780–1918: The Long Nineteenth Century* (Blackwell, 1997) p. 191.
5   Eric Wilmot, *The Great Powers: 1814–1914* (Thomas Nelson, 1992), p. 251.
6   Hagen Schulze, *Germany, A New History* (Harvard University Press, 1998).
7   Heinz Gollwitzer, quoted in Hans-Ulrich Wehler, *The German Empire 1871–1918* (Berg, 1985), p. 59.
8   Ibid.
9   Ludwig Bamberger, quoted in ibid.
10  Lerman, *Bismarck*, p. 161.
11  Ibid.
12  Mary Fulbrook, *A Concise History of Germany* (Cambridge University Press, 1990), p. 134.
13  Carr, *History of Germany 1815–1990*, p. 123.
14  Evans, *Rereading German History*, p. 46.
15  Blackbourn, *History of Germany 1780–1918*, p. 191.
16  Feuchtwanger, *Bismarck*, p. 204.
17  Lothar Gall, *Bismarck: The White Revolutionary, Vol 1: 1815–1871* (Routledge, 1990), p. 95.
18  Gordon Craig, *Germany 1866–1945* (Oxford University Press, 1981), p. 129.
19  Annika Mombauer and Wilhelm Deist, *The Kaiser: New Research on Wilhelm II's Role in Imperial Germany* (Cambridge University Press, 2003), p. 104.
20  James Retallack, in Gordon Martel, *Modern Germany Reconsidered 1870–1945* (Routledge, 1992), p. 41.

## notes to chapter 3

1   Paul Kennedy, *The Rise and Fall of the Great Powers* (Unwin Hyman, 1998), p. 221.
2   T. Kemp, quoted in John Traynor, *Europe 1890–1990* (Macmillan, 1991), p. 46.
3   James Joll, *The Origins of the First World War* (Longman, 1984), p. 25.
4   Lothar Gall, *Bismarck: The White Revolutionary Vol. 1 1815–1871* (Routledge, 1994), p. 47.
5   Otto Pflanze, *Bismarck and the Development of Germany: The Period of Unification 1815–1871* (Princeton, 1963).
6   Gordon Craig, *Germany 1866–1945* (Oxford University Press, 1981), p. 230.
7   Edgar Feuchtwanger: *Bismarck* (Routledge, 2002), p. 240.

## notes to chapter 4

1   James Retallack, 'Wilhelmine Germany', in *Modern Germany Reconsidered 1870–1945*, ed. Gordon Martell (Routledge, 1992), pp. 33–53, p. 43.
2   Ibid., p. 42.
3   Christopher Clark, *Kaiser Wilhelm II* (Longman, 2000) p. 97.
4   Isabel V. Hull, 'Military culture, Wilhelm II, and the end of the monarchy in the First World War' in Annika Mombauer and Wilhelm Deist (eds), *The Kaiser: New*

Research on Wilhelm II's Role in Imperial Germany. (Cambridge University Press, 2003), pp. 235–58, p. 74

5    Retallack, 'Wilhelmine Germany', p. 41.
6    David Blackbourn, *History of Germany 1780–1918* (Blackwell, 2003), p. 265.
7    John Rohl, *Kaiser Wilhelm II New Interpretations* (Cambridge University Press, 1982), pp. 24–9.
8    Isabel V. Hull, *The Entourage of Kaiser Wilhelm II 1888–1918* (Cambridge University Press, 1982), p. 208.
9    John Rohl, *The Kaiser and his Court: Wilhelm II and the Government of Germany* (Cambridge University Press, 1996), p. 23.
10   Michael Balfour, *The Kaiser and his Times,* (Penguin, 1972), p. 17.
11   Hans-Ulrich Wehler, *The German Empire 1871–1918* (Berg, 1985), pp. 62–4.
12   Rohl, *Kaiser Wilhelm II*, Introduction.
13   Katherine Lerman 'The Kaiser's Elite? Wilhelm II and the Berlin Administration, 1890–1914', in Mombauer and Deist, *The Kaiser*, pp. 63–90, p. 77.
14   Lerman, 'The Kaiser's Elite?', p. 72.
15   Gordon A. Craig, *Germany 1866–1945* (Oxford University Press, 1981), p. 287.
16   Lerman, 'The Kaiser's Elite?', p. 72.
17   Craig, *Germany 1866–1945*, p. 287.
18   Roger Chickering, *Imperial Germany and the Great War, 1914–1918.* (Cambridge University Press, 1998), p. 9.
19   Ibid., Introduction.

## notes to chapter 5

1    H. W. Koch, *The Origins of the First World War: Great Power Rivalry and German War Aims* (Macmillan, 1972), p. 288.
2    Ibid., p. 289.
3    William Carr, *A History of Germany 1815–1900* (Edward Arnold, 1991), p. 193.
4    John Traynor, *Europe 1890–1990* (Macmillan, 1991), p. 48.
5    Isabel V. Hull, *The entourage of Kaiser Wilhelm II: 1888–1918* (Cambridge University Press, 1982), p. 236.
6    Niall Ferguson, *The Pity of War* (Penguin, 1999), p. 150.
7    Carr, *A History of Germany 1815–1900* (Edward Arnold, 1991), p. 198.
8    Traynor, *Europe 1890–1990*, p. 20.
9    Ibid.
10   Ibid., p. 21.
11   Fritz Fischer, quoted in Koch, *The Origins of the First World War*, p. 79.
12   Traynor, *Europe 1890–1990*, p. 22
13   Ibid., p. 49.
14   Ibid., p. 23.
15   Ibid., p. 33.
16   Ibid.
17   Ibid., p. 34.
18   Ibid., p. 36.
19   Ibid.
20   Ibid.
21   Ibid.
22   Ibid.
23   Ibid.

24 Ibid., p. 37.
25 Ibid.

## notes to chapter 6

1   William Carr, *A History of Germany 1815–1900* (Edward Arnold, 1991), p. 217.
2   Paul Kennedy, *The War Plans of the Great Powers 1880–1914* (Allen & Unwin, 1985), p. 3.
3   Jay Winter and Blaine Baggett, *1914–18 The Great War and the Shaping of the 20th Century* (BBC, 1996), p. 107.
4   James Joll, *The Origins of the First World War* (Longman, 1984), p. 171.
5   Carr, *History of Germany*, p. 21.
6   Richard Bessel, *Germany after the First World War* (Oxford University Press, 1993), p. 2.
7   Roger Chickering, *Imperial Germany and the Great War, 1914–1918* (Cambridge University Press, 1998), p. 14.
8   Ibid.
9   Winter and Baggett, *1914–18*, p. 52.
10  Bessel, *Germany after the First World War*, p. 3.
11  Ibid.
12  Winter and Baggett, *1914–18*, p. 57.
13  Ibid., p. 80.
14  Kennedy, *War Plans of the Great Powers*, p. 201.
15  Ibid.
16  Joll, *Origins of the First World War*, p. 82.
17  Gordon A Craig, *Germany 1866–1945* (Oxford University Press, 1981), p. 279.
18  Kennedy, *War Plans of the Great Powers*, p. 204.
19  Ibid.
20  Robert M. Citino, *The German Way of War* (University Press of Kansas, 2005), p. 199.
21  Carr, *History of Germany*, p. 212.
22  John Horne and Alan Kamer, *German Atrocities 1914: A History of Denial* (Yale University Press, 2001), p. 23.
23  Niall Ferguson, *The Pity of War* (Penguin, 1999) p. 237.
24  Ibid., p. 288.
25  Chickering, *Imperial Germany and the Great War*, p. 143.
26  Bessel, *Germany after the First World War*, p. 48
27  Ibid., p. 33.
28  Richard Pipes, *The Russian Revolution 1899–1919* (Fontana, 1992), p. 219.
29  Fritz Fischer, *Germany's Aims in the First World War* (Norton, 1967), p. 6.
30  Adam Ulam, *Lenin and the Bolsheviks* (Fontana, 1966), p. 3–7.
31  Ibid.
32  Bessel, *Germany after the First World War*, p. 47.
33  Ibid., preface.

## notes to chapter 7

1   Conan Fischer, '"A Very German Revolution"? The Post-1918 Settlement Re-Evaluated', *German Historical Institute of London Bulletin*, 28:2 (2006), pp. 6–32.
2   Ibid., p. 12.

3    John Traynor, *Europe 1890–1990* (Macmillan, 1991), p. 102.
4    J. A. Thompson, 'Woodrow Wilson and World War I – a Reappraisal', *Journal of American Studies* (1985), pp. 325–37.
5    Traynor, *Europe 1890–1990*, p. 45.
6    Ibid.
7    Sally Marks, *The Illusion of Peace: International Relations in Europe 1918–33* (Macmillan, 1976), p. 17.
8    Traynor, *Europe 1890–1990*, p. 107.
9    A. Lentin, *Guilt at Versailles* (Methuen, 1985), p. 75.
10   Joachim C. Fest, *Hitler* (Weidenfeld and Nicolson, 1974), pp. 67–86.
11   Ibid., p. 117.
12   Kershaw, *Hitler*.
13   Lentin, *Guilt at Versailles* (Methuen, 1985).
14   Marks, *The Illusion of Peace*.
15   Henig, *Versailles and After (1919–1933)* (Methuen, 1984).
16   Marks, *The Illusion of Peace*.
17   Ibid.
18   Jonathan Wright: 'Stressmann and Weimar', *History Today* 39:10 (1989), pp. 35–41.
19   William Carr, *A History of Germany 1815–1900* (Edward Arnold, 1991).
20   Marks, *The Illusion of Peace*.
21   Ibid.
22   Carr, *History of Germany*.

## notes to chapter 8

1    Laurence Rees, *The Nazis: A Warning from History* (BBC, 1997), p. 38.
2    Alan Bullock, *Hitler: A Study in Tyranny* (Odhams Press, 1954), p. 137.
3    Thomas Childers, *The Nazi Voter* (University of North Carolina Press, 1983).

## notes to chapter 9

1    Richard Bessell, *Nazism and War* (Weidenfeld & Nicolson, 2004), pp. 63–4.
2    Ian Kershaw, *Hitler Vol. 1, 1889–1936* (Penguin, 1998), p. 427.
3    John Traynor, *Europe 1890–1990* (Macmillan, 1991), p. 254.
4    Ibid., p. 255.
5    Richard J. Evans, *The Third Reich in Power* (Allen Lane, 2005), p. 11–14.
6    Ian Kershaw, *Hitler: Vol I* (Penguin, 1998), p. 466–8.
7    Evans, *The Third Reich in Power*, p. 33.
8    J. Noakes and G. Pridham (eds), *Nazism 1919–1945: A Documentary Reader. Vol. 2: State, Economy and Society 1933–39* (University of Exeter Press, 1995) p. 594.
9    Evans, *The Third Reich in Power*, p. 120.
10   Ibid., pp. 125–7.
11   Bessell, *Nazism and War*, p. 3.
12   Ibid., p. 4.
13   Ibid., p. 50.
14   Adam Tooze, *The Wages of Destruction: The Making and Breaking of the Nazi Economy* (Allen Lane, 2006), p. 204.
15   Noakes and Pridham, *Nazism 1919–1945: Vol. 2*, p. 574
16   Tooze, *The Wages of Destruction*, p. 157.

17  Ibid., pp. 163–4.
18  Evans, *The Third Reich in Power*, p. 73.
19  Ibid., pp. 232–3.
20  J. Noakes and G. Pridham (eds), *Nazism 1919–1945: A Documentary Reader. Vol. 3: Foreign Policy, War and Racial Extermination* (University of Exeter Press, 1988), p. 1002.
21  Ibid., p. 1021.
22  Peter Longerich, *The Unwritten Order: Hitler's Role in the Final Solution* (Tempus, 2001), p. 49.
23  Kershaw, *Hitler: Vol. I*, pp. 5–9.
24  ibid., p. xiii.
25  Klaus-Michael Mallmann and Gerhard Paul, 'Omniscient, Omnipotent, Omnipresent? Gestapo, Society and Resistance', in David F. Crew, *Nazism and German Society 1933–1945* (Routledge, 1994), pp. 166–96, p. 166.

## notes to chapter 10

1   John Traynor, *20th Century Dictatorships: Hitler and Stalin* (Nelson, 1999), p. 29.
2   Saul Friedlander, *Nazi Germany and the Jews: The Years of Persecution 1933–39* (Weidenfeld & Nicolson, 1997), p. 331.
3   Ian Kershaw, *Hitler Vol 1, 1889–1936* (Penguin, 1998), p. 152.
4   Ibid., p. 434.
5   Friedlander, *Nazi Germany and the Jews*, p. 4.
6   Joachim C. Fest, *Hitler* (Weidenfeld & Nicolson, 1974), p. 419.
7   Ian Kershaw, *Hitler: Vol. II 1936–1945* (Penguin, 2000), p. 529.
8   Martin Gilbert, *The Holocaust: The Jewish Tragedy* ( Collins, 1986), p. 38.
9   William Carr, *Hitler: A Study in Personality and Politics* (Edward Arnold, 1978), p. 41.
10  Friedlander, *Nazi Germany and the Jews*, p. 3.
11  Ibid.
12  Ibid.
13  Avraham Barkai, '*Volksgemeinschaft,* "Aryanization" and the Holocaust', in David Cesarani (ed.), *The Final Solution: Origins and Implementation* (Routledge, 1994), pp. 33–50, p. 33.
14  Friedlander, *Nazi Germany and the Jews*, p. 3.
15  Eric Johnson, *Nazi Terror, the Gestapo, Jews and Ordinary Americans* (Basic Books, 2000), p. 107.
16  Victor Klemperer, quoted in Kershaw, *Hitler Vol. II*, p. 8.
17  Deborah E Lipstadt, quoted in Johnson, *Nazi Terror*, p. 107.
18  Kershaw, *Hitler Vol. II*, p. 127.
19  Ibid., p. 130.
20  Johnson, *Nazi Terror*, p. 109
21  Friedlander, *Nazi Germany and the Jews*, p. 247.
22  Klaus-Michael Mallmann and Gerhard Paul, 'Omniscient, Omnipotent, Omnipresent? Gestapo, Society and Resistance', in David F. Crew, *Nazism and German Society 1933–1945* (Routledge, 1994), pp. 166–96, p. 166.
23  Gilbert, *The Holocaust*, p. 70.
24  Friedlander, *Nazi Germany and the Jews*, p. 281.
25  Kershaw, *Hitler: Vol II*, p. 130.
26  Ibid., p. 1061.

27  Laurence Rees, *The Nazis: A Warning from History* (BBC, 1997), p. 77.
28  Kershaw, *Hitler: Vol II*, p. 149.
29  Ibid.
30  Carr, *Hitler*, p. 72.
31  Daniel Jonah Goldhagen, *Hitler's Willing Executioners: Ordinary Germans and the Holocaust* (Abacus, 1997), pp. 140–1.

## notes to chapter 11

1   Ian Kershaw, *Hitler, Profiles in Power* (Longman, 1991), p. 7.
2   Ibid., pp. 17–21.
3   John Traynor, *Europe 1890–1990* (Macmillan, 1991), p. 283.
4   Ibid.
5   Ibid., p. 284.
6   Ibid.
7   J. Noakes and G. Pridham, *Nazism 1919–1945: A Documentary Reader. Vol. 3: Foreign Policy, War and Racial Extermination* (University of Exeter Press, 1988), p. 671.
8   Ibid., p. 629.
9   Adam Tooze, *The Wages of Destruction: The Making and Breaking of the Nazi Economy* (Allen Lane, 2006), p. xxv.
10  Bessell, *Nazism and War*, p. 50.
11  Ibid., pp. 50–1.
12  Noakes and Pridham, *Nazism 1919–1945: Vol. 3*, p. 669.
13  Traynor, *Europe 1890–1990*, p. 133.
14  Ibid., pp. 290–1.
15  Bessell, *Nazism and War*, p. 48.
16  Zachary Shore, *What Hitler Knew: The Battle for Information in Nazi Foreign Policy* (Oxford University Press, 2003), pp. 48–67.
17  Tooze, *The Wages of Destruction*, p. 203.
18  Traynor, *Europe 1890–1990*, p. 293.
19  Bessell, *Nazism and War*, p. 61.
20  Alan Bullock, *Hitler: A Study in Tyranny* (Odhams Press, 1954), p. 384–5.
21  Ibid., p. 386.
22  R. A. C. Parker, *Chamberlain and Appeasement: British Policy and the Coming of the Second World War* (Macmillan, 1993), p. 177.
23  Ibid., p. 1.
24  Ibid., p. 93.
25  Ibid., p. 324.
26  William R. Rock, *British Appeasement in the 1930's* (Edward Arnold, 1977), p. 11.
27  ibid., p. 13.
38  Donald Cameron Watt, *How War Came: The Immediate Origins of the Second World War 1938–39* (Heinemann, 1989) pp. 28–9.
29  Noakes and Pridham, *Nazism 1919–1945: Vol. 3*, p. 724.
30  Public Record Office, London.
31  Keith Robbins, *Appeasement* (Basil Blackwell, 1988), p. 74.
32  Noakes and Pridham, *Nazism 1919–1945: Vol. 3*, p. 724.
33  Richard Overy, *The Road to War* (Macmillan, 1989), p. 10.
34  Noakes and Pridham, *Nazism 1919–1945: Vol. 3*, p. 736–8.

## notes to chapter 12

1 Martin Gilbert, *The Second World War* (Guild Publishing, 1989), pp. 1, 747.
2 J. Noakes and G. Pridham, *Nazism 1919–1945: Vol. 3: Foreign Policy, War and Racial Extermination* (University of Exeter Press, 1988), p. 755.
3 Laurence Rees, *The Nazis: A Warning from History* (BBC, 1997), pp. 125, 127, 163.
4 Karl-Heinz Frieser, *The Blitzkrieg Legend: The 1940 Campaign in the West* (Naval Institute Press, 2005) pp. 9–11.
5 Richard Overy, *Russia's War* (Allen Lane, 1997), p. xvi.
6 Noakes and Pridham, *Nazism 1919-1945: Vol. 3*, p. 791.
7 Ibid., p. 799.
8 Overy, *Russia's War*, p. 124.
9 J. Noakes and G. Pridham, *Nazism 1919–45: A Documentary Reader. Vol. 4: The German Home Front in World War II* (University of Exeter Press, 1988), p. 705.
10 MacGregor Knox, 'Expansionist zeal, fighting power, and staying power in the Italian and German dictatorships', in *Fascist Italy and Nazi Germany: Comparisons and Contrasts*, ed. Richard Bessel (Cambridge University Press, 1996), pp. 113–33.
11 Overy, *Russia's War*, p. 187.
12 Ewan Maudsley, *Thunder in the East: The Nazi–Soviet War 1941–1945* (Hodder Arnold, 2005), p. 267.

## notes to chapter 13

1 David Cesarani, *The Final Solution: Origins and Implementation* (Routledge, 1994), p. 4–11.
2 Ibid.
3 Ibid.
4 Ibid.
5 Ibid.
6 Ibid.
7 Ibid.
8 Ibid.
9 Richard J. Evans, *Rereading German History 1800–1996* (Routledge, 1997), p. 150.
10 Peter Longerich, *The Unwritten Order: Hitler's Role in the Final Solution* (Tempus, 2001), p. 95.
11 J. Noakes and G. Pridham (ed.), *Nazism 1919–1945: A Documentary Reader. Vol. 3: Foreign Policy, War and Racial Extermination* (University of Exeter Press, 1988), p. 1049.
12 Saul Friedlander, *Nazi Germany and the Jews: The Years of Persecution 1933–39* (Weidenfeld & Nicolson, 1997), p. 4.
13 Noakes and Pridham, *Nazism 1919–1945: Vol. 3*, ch. 37.
14 Ibid., p. 1051.
15 Ibid., p. 1066.
16 Peter Longerich, *The Unwritten Order- Hitler's Role in the Final Solution* (Tempus, 2001), p. 63.
17 Noakes and Pridham, *Nazism 1919–1945: Vol. 3*, p. 1087.
18 Longerich, *The Unwritten Order*, p. 60.
19 William Carr, *Hitler: A Study in Personality and Politics* (Edward Arnold, 1978), p. 76.

20  Longerich, *The Unwritten Order*, p. 69.
21  Ibid.
22  Mark Roseman, *The Villa, The Lake, The Meeting, Wannsee and the Final Solution* (Allen Lane, 2002), p. 61.
23  Longerich, *The Unwritten Order*, p. 95.
24  Peter Padfield, *Himmler Reichsfuhrer SS*. (Weidenfeld Military, 2001), p. 387–8.
25  Richard Breitman, 'Himmler, the Architect of Genocide', in Cesarani, *The Final Solution*, p. 74.

## notes to chapter 14

1   J. Noakes and G. Pridham (ed.), *Nazism 1919–1945: A Documentary Reader. Vol. 3: Foreign Policy, War and Racial Extermination* (University of Exeter Press, 1988), p. 664–5
2   *Guardian*, quoted in John Traynor and Eric Wilmot, *Britain in the 20th Century World* (Nelson, 1994), p. 106.
3   Daniel Yergin, *Shattered Peace: The Origins of the Cold War and the National Security State* (Houghton Mifflin, 1978), p. 112.
4   Michael Dockrill, *The Cold War 1945–1963* (Macmillan, 1988), p. 19.
5   Yergin, *Shattered Peace*, p. 115.
6   Ibid., p. 119.
7   Dockrill, *The Cold War*, p. 27.
8   John Lewis Gaddis, *The United States and the Origins of the Cold War 1941–47* (Columbia University Press, 1972), p. 243.
9   Dockrill, *Cold War*, p. 1.
10  John Traynor, *Europe 1890–1990* (Macmillan, 1991), p. 331.
11  Winston Churchill.
12  William Carr, *A History of Germany 1815–1900* (Edward Arnold, 1991), p. 388.
13  Pol O'Dochartaigh, *Germany since 1945* (Palgrave, 2004), p. 87.
14  Ibid., pp. 68–71.
15  Carr, *History of Germany*, p. 375–6.
16  Ibid., p. 380.
17  Traynor and Wilmot, *Britain in the 20th Century World*, p. 154.
18  Carr, *History of Germany*, p. 382.
19  *Independent*, 29 June 1988.
20  Mikhail Gorbachev, speech to the General Assembly of the UN, 7 December 1988.
21  Mary Fulbrook, *Interpretations of the Two Germanies, 1945–1990* (Macmillan, 2000), p. 82.
22  Ibid., p. 83.
23  O'Dochartaigh, *Germany since 1945*, p. 189.

## notes to postscript

1   Stephen Padgett, William Paterson and Gordon Smith, *Developments in German Politics* (Palgrave 2003), p. 1.
2   Ibid., p. 271.
3   Martin Kitchen, *A History of Modern Germany 1800–2000* (Blackwell, 2006), p. 407.

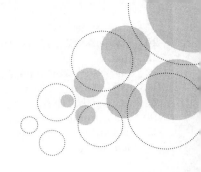

index